HOOLIGANS, HARLOTS, AND HANGMEN

THE UNIVERSITY OF
WINCHESTER

Martial Rose Library
Tel: 01962 827306

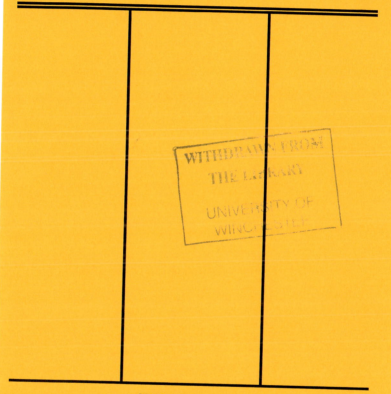

SEVEN DAY LOAN ITEM

To be returned on or before the day marked above, subject to recall.

HOOLIGANS, HARLOTS, AND HANGMEN

Crime and Punishment in Victorian Britain

DAVID TAYLOR

A Criminal History of Britain
Barry Godfrey, Series Editor

PRAEGER

AN IMPRINT OF ABC-CLIO, LLC
Santa Barbara, California • Denver, Colorado • Oxford, England

Copyright 2010 by David Taylor

Library of Congress Cataloging-in-Publication Data
Taylor, David.
  Hooligans, harlots, and hangmen : crime and punishment in Victorian Britain / David Taylor.
      p. cm. — (The criminal history of Britain series)
  Includes bibliographical references and index.
  ISBN 978-0-313-38355-7 (print : alk. paper) — ISBN 978-0-313-38356-4 (ebook)
1. Crime—Great Britain—History—19th century. 2. Punishment—Great Britain—History—19th century. I. Title.
  HV6943.T39 2010
  364.94109'034—dc22   2009046236

ISBN: 978-0-313-38355-7
EISBN: 978-0-313-38356-4

14 13 12 11 10   1 2 3 4 5

This book is also available on the World Wide Web as an eBook.
Visit www.abc-clio.com for details.

Praeger
An Imprint of ABC-CLIO, LLC

ABC-CLIO, LLC
130 Cremona Drive, P.O. Box 1911
Santa Barbara, California 93116-1911

This book is printed on acid-free paper ∞

Manufactured in the United States of America

To Rosey, Keelan, Poppy, Jessica, and Jamal

If men could learn from history, what lessons it might teach us! But passion and party blind our eyes, and the light which experience gives is a lantern on the stern, which shines only on the waves behind us!

Samuel Taylor Coleridge, *Table Talk*, 1835

The one duty we owe to history is to rewrite it.

Oscar Wilde, "The Critic as Artist," *Intentions*, 1891

CONTENTS

PART IV: PUNISHMENT

ILLUSTRATIONS

SERIES FOREWORD

The books in *A Criminal History of Britain* series—together comprising the history of crime, policing, and punishment from the Middle Ages to the 21st century—make some demands upon us as readers. We are required to address complex and sometimes uncomfortable issues from the history of British society. The authors pose questions about attitudes and events in our past that have shaped, and continue to shape, our relationships with those we believe transgress accepted norms within society—lawbreakers, deviants, outlaws, and criminals. But how was "crime" socially constructed and legally defined, and how did those conceptions develop through the ages? How was authority expressed within society; by whom; and with what results? How did the aim to maintain order in society in the 18th century—to control the dangerous revolutionary mobs that threatened to overturn the ruling classes—then transform into an aim to improve effective policing? How did notions about "the criminal other" change over time—from the lazy and disobedient apprentices of the 17th century, to the violent criminals who lurked in the growing 19th-century cities as members of the shadowy and dangerous "criminal classes," to the "joy-riders," cannabis users, youth gangs, and binge-drinkers who became the folk-devils of the 20th century? How did our attitudes toward transgressors change, and what part did the rise of scientific criminology play in this process? Why did forms of punishment for offenders shift from punishing the body, or banishment in one form or other, to forms of incarceration designed to inhibit liberty and bring about a change in the character of individual criminals: to bring about their reformation rather than their containment? What are the legacies of these changes in today's criminal justice system?

Finding the answers to these questions has provided a challenge to the authors, and they have all produced lively and accessible books that comprehensively explore the key elements of crime in their period. As expected of experienced researchers and acknowledged experts in their fields, the books comment on contemporary and modern debates, with detailed footnotes and references, so that readers can go on to immerse themselves in scholarly works if they so wish. All of the volumes contain quotes from historical documents, case studies of particular episodes in history, and a range of contemporary illustrations that bring color to the text. An important aspect of the whole series is that connections are made between the books. Each volume discusses the institutions of order, the groups that were identified as a problem to mainstream respectable society, and the steps taken to control and to punish criminals—and this approach has unified the series into a complete history of crime in Britain.

In this first volume, for example, David Taylor's examination of crime in the Victorian period discusses some of the debates and themes that were current in the Middle Ages, demonstrates how the worries and fears of the Victorians produced particular criminal justice solutions, and thereby provides the foundation for a discussion of crime in the modern period (where many of those fears and anxieties about change, "foreigners," and urban living then produced their own solutions to the problems of law and order).

The seven decades under discussion in this volume probably represent the most dynamic and fast-moving years that Britain has ever experienced. In the 1830s most people in Britain lived in the countryside. By the time Queen Victoria died in 1901, the majority of the population lived in towns and cities. The population had boomed over the same period, and so had the economy—producing new forms of industrial output and a proletariat with new leisure and social pursuits. The British Empire became vast, stretching across the world and establishing expectations and norms of behavior that tried to distinguish the civilized from the uncivilized. Meanwhile, at home, the poor lived in cramped lodging houses and workhouses and on the streets. They appeared to some to be a breed apart—with their own forms of speech (criminal argot or slang), entertainment, and ways of earning a living. The rougher areas of towns fascinated and scared respectable dwellers in equal measure, and Victorian social explorers penetrated the dark hearts of the major cities to bring back information on the unrespectable and criminal poor. This information helped to feed society's appetite for tales of degradation and vice amongst the atavistic and the immoral. David Taylor skillfully weaves together these contemporary narratives and illustrations with modern understandings of the place of class, gender, and race in defining and categorizing those labeled as deviant in Victorian society. His book comprehensively describes the impact of new forms of policing on the lives of ordinary men and women, as well as the impact they had on thieves, pickpockets, and scallywags that fell into the hands of the New Police. These uniformed public servants are perhaps the most recognizable and iconic of 19th-century institutions. The "Peelers" had an immediate effect, but Taylor rightly explores other forms of authority and order, notably the development of a magistrates' court system that could then bring to justice the masses of petty offenders (therefore massively inflating the number of offenses brought to prosecution from the 1870s onwards). In those courts, particular groups in society were over-represented. Taylor profiles the criminal groups that caught the public imagination—drunken violent uncivilized Irishmen; the degraded criminal classes lurking in the heart of the cities; street prostitutes, drug takers, and roughs; and the juvenile delinquent. Despite popular conceptions, most criminals appeared before local magistrates, rather than the Old Bailey judges—although, as Taylor describes, many notorious criminals did appear there and suffered dreadful punishments for their crimes. He examines all of the forms of punishment that were developed in this period, the start of mass incarceration, and the emergence of the prison as the natural disposal for offenders—replacing the stocks, the scaffolds, and the ships that transported felons to America, then Australia. Lastly, Taylor asks three extremely important questions—questions that still perplex us today: What was the point of the system in this period? How successful was it in achieving its aims? What lasting impact do the changes made to crime and its control have on British society in the 21st century? Society cannot afford to leave such questions unanswered.

—Barry Godfrey
Director of the Research Institute for Law,
Politics and Justice, Keele University

PREFACE

There is a fascination about crime and punishment that draws people from all walks of life. Crime present has a fascination rooted, in part at least, in fear; crime past has a fascination rooted in curiosity. Today's street mugger has an ominous presence; his Victorian counterpart, the garrotter, has more of the exotic. It might be argued that the fascination with crime past is a form of self-indulgence. We can scare ourselves with stories of highwaymen and hooligans, knowing that they do not pose a real and present threat; much as children scare themselves with stories of giants and ghosts that they know to be fictitious. But in a more profound sense, exploring crime past (rather like reading Grimm's fairy tales) enables us to confront some of the darker aspects of human nature in a relatively safe environment. Safe in the knowledge that we are no more likely to meet Jack the Ripper than Jack the Giant-killer, we can consider not only the criminals of the past and what motivated them, but we can also reflect on the extent to which we share such characteristics.

There are also similarities in attitude toward punishments today and punishments in time past. The urgency that surrounded the debates about public executions in the mid-19th century, for example, has disappeared with time, and we can reflect on the progress we have made since the streets of London and other towns and cities were periodically brought to a halt as crowds assembled to watch some poor unfortunate be dispatched for a relatively petty crime. But past and present are intimately linked. The debates of the 1860s on capital punishment raise questions that are still pertinent today. The death penalty may have been abolished in Britain, but the questions constantly recur: Should it be reinstated for certain criminals? Should murderers, drug dealers, or child molesters be executed rather than imprisoned? And if imprisoned, what form should prison take? As I write, Jack Straw, the advocate of Titan prisons, in yet another restatement of New Labor policy, is stressing the need to put "punishment and reform" at the heart of the criminal justice system, while reassuring people that this does not represent a return to harsh Victorian notions of crime and punishment.[1] It would be reassuring to think that Straw has looked at the Victorians' attempts (for there was never a single Victorian experience) at implementing a system of punishment and reform, for it would have brought home to him the enormous gulf between rhetoric and reality and the repeated failures to establish effective regimes, either in Victorian Titan prisons, such as Pentonville, or in smaller, local prisons. In many respects, the Victorians were pioneers in the use of prison and had little choice but to learn from experience that prisons were, for the most part and at best, expensive failures that did little to satisfy those worried by the threat of crime and less to deter or reform criminals. Ignoring (or unaware of) the historical realities, Straw asks us to invest yet more money into an approach that has a track record, going back over a century and a half, of persistent failure, notwithstanding repeated expressions of high hopes and good intentions.

It would be naïve to suggest that there are simple lessons from the past to be learned from the study of history, but an awareness of the past does provide insights and perspectives that can inform and enrich contemporary debate. The following chapters are intended to provide a brief but critical introduction to how the Victorians and Edwardians sought to understand and confront the problems of criminal behavior. There is much that is positive, for example, the reduction in the use of capital punishment and a growing awareness of the complex mix of factors that account for criminal behavior. Also, there is much that is negative—such as the failure to devise an effective, alternative system of punishment and reform based on the prison—but the purpose of the book is not to judge our forefathers or award them points for their efforts but to better understand how they sought to grapple with a problem (or, more accurately, a nexus of problems) that they did not fully understand and with limited resources. With the benefit of hindsight, it is easy to point up and mock the follies of the past—the simplistic explanations of criminal behavior, the excessive fears of crime, the overoptimistic hopes of reformers, and so forth—but such an approach is unproductive. A better, more sympathetic awareness of the Victorians does not minimize their failures but makes them more understandable. This makes for better history, but it also makes for more useful history, in the sense that it encourages a degree of humility and honest skepticism when considering the problems of today. Many of the issues that confront society in the early 21st century were familiar to the Edwardians 100 years ago and the early Victorians 150 years ago. Violent gangs of young men and women are nothing new, nor are alleged professional criminals. Each generation likes to believe that it faces new and unprecedented threats. To some extent this is true: the problems associated with illegal drugs are on a scale that would shock a Victorian time traveler, though she or he might be amazed at the self-inflicted damage that has resulted from our narrow and counterproductive preoccupation with the criminalization of certain drugs. But many of the problems of today are but variations on well-worn themes. In times past, intelligent, well-intentioned men and women, constrained (as are we) by the intellectual and material limitations of the time, struggled with these problems. Understanding better the successes and failures of the past can play an important part in achieving success and minimizing failure in the present.

In the writing of this book, I am indebted to many people. I owe much to fellow academics in institutions across the world on whose detailed research I have drawn and also to my colleagues and students at the University of Huddersfield who have provided a critical but encouraging environment in which to work. Above all, I owe a debt to my family for their contribution. My children (and in some cases their friends), despite very busy lives, have given up time to read and comment on various drafts. Not constrained by the blinkers of the academic historian, their perceptive comments have greatly improved this book. Finally, and not for the first time, my greatest debt is to my wife, Thelma. Not only has she read and commented on every draft of every chapter—in itself a cruel and unnatural punishment, some would think—she has provided constant support and encouragement throughout the writing of this book. Finally, it is to the grandchildren that this book is dedicated in the hope that they may find both interest and insight in the study of the past.

INTRODUCTION

Crime and Its Context

The web of our life is of a mingled yarn, good and ill together, our
virtues would be proud if our faults whipped them not; and our crimes
would despair if they were not cherished by our own virtues.
> —William Shakespeare, *All's Well That Ends Well*
> (Act 4, Scene 3)

Only crime and the criminal . . . confront us with the perplexity of
radical evil . . .
> —Hannah Arendt, *On Revolution*, 1963
> (chapter 2, part 5)

The Victorians and Edwardians prided themselves on their civilization,
the progress they were making, and the example (as they saw it) they
gave to the world. For the British, law and liberties were intimately related.
Time and again they quoted Locke's dictum that "where there is no law, there
is no freedom." But at the same time they worried about the problems that
seemed to threaten their civilization–and crime and the criminal were among
the greatest of these problems. Furthermore, the threats to stability and order
appeared to be clearly located among the dangerous classes that inhabited the
slums and back streets of the sprawling towns and cities that were multiplying
across the length and breadth of the country. The working classes needed to
be disciplined, and the law, and particularly its newly formed agents in blue,
the new police, had a critical role to play in this disciplinary venture. There is
much truth in the observation that "the history of crime . . . is largely the history of how better-off people disciplined their inferiors."[1] As a consequence,
crime (almost irrespective of its cost to the nation as a whole, rather than to
the individual victim of crime)[2] was seen as a key indicator of the health of
the nation and the criminal seen as the embodiment of wider problems associated with a rapidly modernizing and increasingly urbanized society, and in the
latter years, with an imperial power that was losing its standing in the world.

The "modern" criminal justice system that was to survive until the late 20th century, if not beyond, emerged in the second quarter of the 19th century. The emergence of the adversarial criminal trial, the creation of professional police forces, and the replacement of the scaffold by the prison as the dominant site (and sight) of punishment did not take place overnight, but when Victoria came to the throne these key elements of the modern criminal justice system were in place. Not all were fully developed and remnants of the old persisted, but something distinctively new had been created. Important changes took place in the following years with periods of pessimism, especially in the last third of the 19th century, followed by years of optimism, notably from the late 1890s to the outbreak of war in 1914, but these changes were refinements of a system rather than a fundamental reformulation of principle and practice.[3]

The criminal justice system, as it evolved, was influenced by a range of broader socioeconomic and intellectual trends. Urbanization, perhaps more than industrialization, was a relentless force that impacted on more and more of the population of the British Isles. The growth of high-density towns and cities necessitated a new set of rules and regulations for urban living. Public space in particular had to be regulated and not simply to ensure that bourgeois values were imposed upon the working classes. At the same time, Britain was becoming a less religious, more secular, more rationalist society. This impacted directly on explanations of criminal behavior and the best ways of tackling it. The criminal justice system was also shaped by other moral influences, notably notions of respectability, themselves evolving over time, and redefinitions of masculinity and femininity. More specific and more mundane influences were also at work. Considerations of practical politics and economics cannot be denied. Change—law reform, police reform, and so forth—had to be negotiated. There was no Whiggish progress from a barbaric old system to a modern new; there was no guarantee of success. Finally, the evolution of the criminal justice system owed much to sheer pragmatism. There was a strong element of learning by doing. Police forces were something new—the army at best provided a partial and not wholly appropriate model to draw from; large prisons and long sentences were also daringly new—no one knew how best to run such institutions in which the inmates were involuntary. It is no surprise, on reflection, that the Victorian and Edwardian criminal justice system was less than perfect.

The term *criminal justice system* is convenient shorthand for a series of institutions and organizations that had emerged at different times, for different reasons, and that did not necessarily mesh comfortably. Furthermore, and exacerbated by the absence of a formal penal code, there were different, indeed competing, perspectives on the criminal justice system as a whole as well as on specific component parts. Many Victorians and Edwardians believed in an idealized judicial system firmly centered on due process. The rhetoric of "equality before the law," of "innocent until proven guilty," of "the right to a fair trial," the (ill-defined) concept of "reasonable doubt," and the oft-repeated assertion that it was "better ten guilty men go free, than one man be wrongly convicted" was crucial not simply to perceptions of the criminal justice system but also to perceptions of what it meant to be British.[4]

However, this "due process" model, not unproblematic in itself, coexisted somewhat uncomfortably with alternative perspectives. One such alternative emphasized the importance of protecting society from the threat of the criminal and stressed the role of the police in arresting wrong-doers and the prisons in punishing the guilty. It was an easy step to foreground the victim and condemn the "rights" of criminals that stood in the way of true justice. Another perspective emphasized the need for speedy and efficient justice. Trial by jury was both costly and (relatively) time-consuming compared with summary justice dispensed in magistrates' courts. Similarly, the constraints imposed by finite resources—finances for trials and manpower in the police and prison services—impinged on the ideas and practices of due process. Less obviously, an awareness of criminals as victims of circumstance and a desire to achieve rehabilitation ran contrary not just to crime control and punishment models, but also, where certain offenders were diverted away from the criminal justice system into alternative institutions with alternative procedures, with due process notions of equal treatment before the law for all offenders.

Yet more complex are the questions that surround the making and enforcement of the law. The rhetoric of "equality before the law" sits uncomfortably with the fact that the laws were made by a minority and imposed on a majority who had little or no say in the matter. Further, many laws appeared to be (and were) class biased. Working-class leisure activities, not least street gambling, were made illegal; working-class street prostitutes were targeted; respectable middle-class people were given the benefit of the doubt in courts in a way that was not extended to the working classes, especially if "rough" and/or Irish. The law (and its implementation) was gendered. Women did not enjoy the same range of rights as men; their evidence was more likely to be "laughed out of court"; crimes of violence against them less likely to be brought to a successful prosecution, particularly in the early years of Victoria's reign. But the law was also increasingly used to discipline working-class men. Between 1861 and 1901, the chances of a man falling foul of the law worsened from 1 in 29 to 1 in 24, whereas for women the corresponding figures were 1 in 120 and 1 in 123. The underlying realities were more grim. Poorer, younger working-class men in urban Britain were significantly more likely to have a criminal record.[5]

And yet, while there are clear examples of class, gender, and ethnic bias in the making and enforcement of the law, it would be naïve and misleading to see the Victorian and Edwardian criminal justice system as a means of preserving the rights of the propertied or upholding patriarchy or even maintaining the dominance of the English. The passing of laws and their enforcement, in particular, were complex processes. There was no consensus of opinion among the propertied classes; nor among the working classes. Extra-parliamentary pressure groups, politicians, judges and magistrates, police chiefs, and ordinary policemen did not share a common agenda; nor did the great masses of the policed have a single (and negative) view of the law and its enforcement agents. Nonetheless, for many working-class men and women there was an uncomfortable tension between the criminal justice system considered in the abstract (something necessary, even beneficial) and their experience of it (something discriminatory, even brutal and corrupt). As a consequence, there was anger, particularly about specific pieces of legislation, about the way in which certain laws were enforced and the way in which courts chose to punish the guilty, and yet neither the law nor the courts or the police lost the overall confidence of the country at large. In part this was because of the pragmatism with which the law was enforced, which tempered some of its worst shortcomings, but in no small measure it was due to the fact that the courts and the police could be and were used to protect and improve the condition of working-class men and women, though references to the law in terms of "multiple-use right" can give a misleading impression of equal access to and use of the law. The fact remains that the Edwardian working classes, more so than their early Victorian forebears, were more closely regulated and more likely to be prosecuted than any generation until the dramatic advent of the surveillance society in late 20th and early 21st-century Britain.

The following chapters provide an overview of the criminal justice system in Victorian and Edwardian Britain. Although there were important similarities between the problems facing law enforcement agencies and the strategies that they adopted to solve them, it is essential to recognize that there was not a common legal system that encompassed England, Scotland, and Wales.[6] England and Wales operated under a common law tradition, deriving from judges' decisions in specific cases, whereas Scottish law owed more to Roman law with its system of rights and obligations and its emphasis on "first principles" as opposed to precedent. The Act of Union (1707) recognized the existence of Scottish law as it stood but made clear that it would be subject to change by the new parliament. And through the 18th and 19th centuries English influences, especially the doctrine of judicial precedent, increased. Unlike in England, institutional writings such as Baron Hume's *Commentaries on the Law of Scotland respecting Crimes,* first published in 1797, played a more important role in the development of the Scottish legal system. There were also more important specific differences. For example, the principle of diminished personal responsibility was established in Scotland in 1867 but was unknown in Victorian and Edwardian England and Wales.

There were other important differences. The High Court of Justiciary, established in 1672, was the supreme criminal court in Scotland and dealt with the most serious cases, including murder, rape, and treason. Sheriffs' courts, presided over by full-time and legally qualified judges, played a central role in other serious criminal (and civil) cases. As in England and Wales, the trial was adversarial, but the 15-man jury had the choice of three verdicts: guilty, not proven, and not guilty. Minor offenses were dealt with by burgh courts, which survived until 1975. Unlike England and Wales, Scotland had a public prosecution system. The Lord Advocate, the senior of the two Scottish Law Officers, was responsible for the system of prosecution and also the investigation of deaths. Crimes tried on indictment ran in the name of the Lord Advocate.[7] Unlike England and Wales, prosecutions by an individual were relatively rare. In Scotland the key figures were the procurators fiscal, who acted as public prosecutors and to whom the police were responsible for investigating crimes.[8]

History is about interpretation, and interpretation requires selection of themes and evidence. This book is necessarily selective, reflecting, in part, the balance of research and knowledge but more the author's interests and views (or blinkered vision, as others might see it). Despite a conscious attempt to look at Britain, there is probably too much about England and too much about London, but hopefully, these very shortcomings will provoke readers to read more widely and to explore further and to redress the imbalances in this account. One last point needs to be made. History is a dialogue between the past and the present. While recognizing that Victorian Britain was a very different country (one might say divided from the present by a common language) and acknowledging the need to understand the Victorians in their own terms, it is important (and impossible not) to view them from a perspective of the early 21st century. The issues of the 19th century are remarkably similar to the issues of today. Looking at the difficulties our predecessors had in dealing with complex and novel problems may bring a sense of humility and realism, and maybe even some insight, as we struggle with our problems today.

PART I

CRIME AND CRIMINALS

CHAPTER ONE

CRIME IN VICTORIAN BRITAIN

Miracle or Mirage?

Thomas Plint, writing in 1851, unashamedly refused to apologize "for an attempt to determine whether or not Crime is on the increase," not least because it would provide "a test of the moral condition of the people" and cast light on the widespread concern that "ignorance and immorality are greatly on the increase."[1] Plint was not alone in reflecting and responding to anxieties about the moral health of the nation. Crime was seen by many Victorians as "a symptom of disorder in the body politic" that was both fascinating and frightening.[2] Though fascinated and frightened by crime, the Victorians retained a remarkable faith in their ability to measure and analyze crime (and, indeed, other social issues) and thus to find solutions to problems that, in their various and changing forms, threatened their much-prized civilization. The government was responsible for collecting and commenting annually on criminal statistics, while a variety of local statistical societies and individual investigators produced detailed studies into various aspects of the nation's criminal behavior. Such statistics, often imperfect, more often poorly understood and, at times, deliberately misrepresented, played an important part in the contemporary debate on crime and punishment. Although opinions on the state of crime varied, sometimes spectacularly so, a powerful and positive official view emerged. In his introduction to the *Judicial Statistics for 1893*, the distinguished civil servant C. E. Troup declared that "the decrease in crime . . . is real and substantial."[3] Similarly, readers of the *Judicial Statistics for Scotland for 1899* were reassured that "[t]he answer to the question 'Is serious crime decreasing?' . . . is clearly in the affirmative."[4] In contrast to other industrializing and urbanizing societies, then and since, where modernization and crime grew apace, the late Victorians appeared to have bucked the trend, but was this more mirage than miracle?

The preoccupation with crime statistics, in the sense of both collecting and analyzing numerical information, was a distinctive feature of Victorian society, but its origins dated back to the turn of the 19th century and the widespread and highly vocal concerns with the failure of the so-called Bloody Code (comprising over 200 offenses carrying the death penalty) to prevent a seemingly inexorable rise in criminal behavior at a time when the nation itself was at war with revolutionary France. Finally, in 1810 parliament decided that key statistics should be collected and published to help inform the ongoing debate about the effectiveness of the death penalty. Clerks of court or circuit were instructed to make annual returns, related to a list of some 50 offenses (back-dated to 1805), of the number of people in each county of England and Wales who had been committed for trial for indictable offenses, discharged on "no true bill," acquitted, and convicted. The list was somewhat arbitrary but included the major "serious offenses," such as murder, manslaughter, and rape, along with robbery, housebreaking, and various forms of larceny, as well as riot. These were the crimes that aroused the greatest fears and captured the most attention, but they represented only the tip of the iceberg of crime. Minor crimes tried summarily fell beneath official view.

The official collection of crime statistics was a rough-and-ready process that was modified over time. A number of significant changes took place that created major discontinuities in the official statistics, thereby making long-term comparisons highly problematic. In 1833 the original list of serious crimes was increased from roughly 50 to 75, and a new six-fold classification, which remained largely constant thereafter, was introduced by the Criminal Registrar, Samuel Redgrave.[5] The addition of new offenses, for example, simple assaults and assaults on police officers under the general heading of offenses against the person, clearly gave an artificial inflation to the recorded crime figures, but it remained the case that the official recording of crime only began at the trial stage. Redgrave was responsible for a further and more far-reaching reorganization of the official statistics following the passing of the County and Borough Police Act of 1856. In addition to court and prison returns, the new statistics included the number of people tried summarily by offense and also the number of indictable offenses known to the police. From 1859 the Criminal Registrar provided a commentary and review as part of the annual report. Existing information was refined. Data on juvenile offenders sent to industrial and reformatory schools was tabulated separately and information on the birthplace and occupation of prisoners was also included. Finally, a further reorganization in 1893 saw returns standardized on the calendar year and figures given as ratios per 100,000 of the population for ease of comparison, but the underlying structure of the official criminal statistics remained largely unchanged.

The annual *Judicial Statistics*, for Scotland as well as for England and Wales, are impressive documents in which the criminal behavior of the country is categorized and counted: table after table details the offenses that have come to be known by the authorities. For contemporary commentators (not to mention later historians) here was a wealth of information that charted in increasing detail the criminal activities of the criminal classes of Victoria's realm—or so it might seem—but it would take bravery bordering on folly to assume that the official figures provided an accurate measure of the real incidence of criminal activities in society at large. The first problem lies with the notion of crime itself. It might be thought that the concept of a crime is unproblematic: surely, murder, rape, and theft are all unequivocally, intrinsically, and consistently illegal actions? But what of incest, which was made a criminal offense only in 1908? Or of homosexual behavior between men, criminalized as "gross indecency" as a result of Labouchère's infamous amendment to the 1885 Criminal Law Amendment Act? The official statistics show a sharp increase in the incidence of sexual crimes in the decade or so before the Great War, but it stretches credibility to suggest that this was a measure of changes in real-world behavior.[6] Crimes were not absolutes; they were created by changes in the law. The criminalization of a range of leisure activities and work-place practices illustrates the point well. In addition, seemingly unambiguous crimes, particularly those involving violence to the person, were more problematic on closer inspection. On paper there was a range of defined nonfatal offenses against the person—assault, aggravated assault, battery, assault occasioning actual bodily harm, wounding, causing grievous bodily harm—but in practice the distinctions were far from clear and much depended upon the police in determining the offense to be prosecuted. Likewise, it is clear that there were ambiguities (if not downright deceptions) surrounding infanticide and even murder. Coroners court decisions, such as accidental death or death by misadventure or even suicide (let alone an open verdict), in an unknowable number of cases, hid more sinister actions.[7]

A further complication was the dramatic expansion of summary justice in Victorian Britain. The most important pieces of legislation were the Juvenile Offenders Acts of 1847 and 1850, which extended summary justice to simple larcenies committed by those under 14 and 16 years of age, respectively, and the 1855 Criminal Justice Act and the 1879 Summary Jurisdiction Act, both of which were motivated by a desire to deal more expeditiously with crimes that were no longer viewed so seriously. The former allowed for summary trial in larceny cases under the value of 5 shillings (25p/40 cents) with the agreement of the accused, and for larceny cases over the value of 5 shillings where the accused pleaded guilty. This led to a significant increase in the work of magistrates as some three-fifths of larceny cases at quarter sessions involved property valued at less than 5 shillings. The latter extended the principle to all children under the age of 12, except for cases of murder and manslaughter; to all juveniles under the age of 16, if they consented, for larceny, embezzlement, and receiving stolen goods; and to all adults pleading guilty or consenting to being tried summarily for similar offenses to the value of £2 ($3) Subsequent Acts of 1899 and

1914 built on this breakthrough.[8] This extension of summary jurisdiction, and particularly the acts of 1855 and 1879, had a profound effect on the official statistics, which makes long-term analyses problematic. In 1857 it was estimated that justices in petty sessions dealt with 20 times the number of cases dealt with in all other courts.[9] By the late 19th and early 20th centuries the predominance of summary justice was overwhelming. Of all those dealt with by the courts, 98 percent were tried summarily (91 percent for nonindictable offenses and 7 percent for indictable), while the remaining 2 percent were dealt with at quarter session or assize.

The statistics relating to summary justice were inflated not just by the downgrading of indictable offenses but also by the creation of a range of new regulatory offenses, for example, under legislation relating to compulsory education and vaccination.[10] In the late 1870s just over 100 people per 100,000 inhabitants were prosecuted for Education Act offenses; by the early 1890s this figure had risen to just under 300. Indeed, by the end of the century more people were being tried for such offenses than were being summarily tried for assault.[11]

Yet more problematic was the continuing role in the criminal justice system of discretion on the part of prosecutors, which involved both their willingness and ability to take formal action. It has long been recognized that only a relatively small percentage of crimes actually came to court in the 18th century. The centrality of the victim as prosecutor meant that the individual had important decisions to make at various stages in the prosecution process. Was the crime sufficiently serious to instigate formal account? Were there more acceptable (and cheaper) informal alternatives? Was it practical to give up time and money to pursue a case?[12] To complicate matters there appear to have been important changes in attitudes toward the courts in the early 19th century as people became more willing to prosecute. At the same time parliament passed legislation that facilitated the process of prosecutions. As early as 1828 a Select Committee recognized that a rise in recorded crime did not necessarily mean that crime itself was increasing.[13] Taking the first half of the 19th century as a whole, the consequence of these attitudinal and legislative changes was significant variations in the gap between the totality of crime and recorded crime (the so-called dark area of unknown and unrecorded crime) over the period.

It has also been assumed that by the mid-19th century discretionary justice was largely a thing of the past, which in turn meant that the recorded crime rate provided a more accurate indication of the totality of crime than before. This assumption has been seriously challenged in recent research. Scrutiny of the official statistics reveals some remarkable facts. While the population doubled, urbanization and industrialization proceeded apace, and police numbers trebled, the number of indictable offenses known to the police in 1906 (91,665) was less than the corresponding figure (91,671) in 1857.[14] Assault prosecutions dropped dramatically to a point where the figures for individual towns become unbelievable. In 1900 there were only 13 common assaults prosecuted in Crewe and a mere 8 in Durham. In early 20th-century Middlesbrough, not known as an oasis of tranquility, there were barely 10 cases per year in total of murder, attempted murder, manslaughter, and wounding known to the police.[15]

In its starkest form, it has been argued that there has been a conscious rationing of crime since the 1850s. At a time when the police were taking a more central role in bringing prosecutions, the fact that they were underfunded, as well as under pressure to keep crime figures down, meant that the police "exercised the *de facto* role of gatekeepers to criminal justice."[16] In particular, expensive murder cases were subject to close scrutiny. "Safe bets" were prosecuted while other cases were effectively covered up.[17] The argument is overstated, but as a number of local studies have shown, the police filtered out the number of people they dealt with formally, not simply for financial reasons.[18] In part, it reflected a judgment on how best to maintain a *modus vivendi* with the wider community, in part, unwillingness to accord the same degree of importance to certain offenses, particularly interpersonal violence, as the victims.[19]

The continuing use of discretion was not confined to serious crime. Recourse to the courts remained one of a number of options open to would-be prosecutors. In the mid- and late 19th century, ordinary men and women, employers, and the police exercised their discretion in matters legal in the same way as their Georgian predecessors.[20] The evidence of the London police courts, for example, shows a growing number of working-class prosecutors, but this did not mean that informal sanctions had been largely abandoned. Stranger theft was more likely to lead to prosecution—the options for informal action were necessarily limited—but a failure to apologize or to return stolen goods could lead to formal action, even though victim and perpetrator were well-known to each other. In other cases, the law was used to administer a shock as alleged perpetrators were arrested but the case not prosecuted in court. Even more complex were the motives behind assault prosecutions. The prosecutions for "clothes line quarrels," to be found in Middlesbrough as much as Marylebone, or the equally ubiquitous "Irish rows," were often a reflection of long-standing and complex grievances within working-class society that were obscured by middle-class reporting, which reduced such events to semicomic incidents of uncivilized behavior among those less fortunate than the readership of the local press.

Employers similarly adopted a selective approach to the law. Faced with a widespread problem of theft, in part exacerbated—indeed created—by the criminalization of customary "perks of the trade," employers walked a fine line between economically foolish toleration of petty stealing and counterproductive firm action.[21] For large employers, such as the London dock companies, it was easier to carry the burden of theft, and more importantly, there was greater scope for the use of dismissal, which was equally effective as a deterrent and significantly cheaper. That said, in times of good trade and a tight labor market, dismissal lost some of its threat, and it is no coincidence that it was in these times, years such as 1862 and 1871, that prosecutions increased. And even then there was no serious intent to eradicate workplace theft but rather to set limits and to make examples of those whose actions overstepped reasonable bounds of illegality. Similar responses took place in other parts of the country, but there was no simple or uniform pattern. Employers in the Black Country, especially after the 1855 Criminal Justice Act, made greater use of the courts than the large iron and steel companies in and around Middlesbrough.[22] In some parts of the country there were long-established procedures to deal with workplace theft. In the West Riding of Yorkshire the so-called Worsted Committee dated back to the 1777 Worsted Acts, which laid down penalties for the embezzlement, buying, and selling of woolen and worsted goods and was reinforced by six subsequent pieces of legislation, which also covered the breaking of contracts.[23] On the surface this might represent a clear determination to use the full force of the law to stamp out workplace theft. In fact, as in other parts of the country, only a small proportion of offenders were actually prosecuted. Unofficial sanctions were used, particularly against women and children. Interestingly, the number of prosecutions fell between the 1840s and 1880s, which may well represent a greater use of informal measures, not least because the percentage of female employees increased. This is not to minimize the importance of the law in industrial relations in the West Riding but to highlight, once again, the discretionary way in which the law was used.

Smaller employers were in a more difficult position. Although less able to withstand losses from theft than many larger employers, they were constrained by the time and money involved in bringing a prosecution. In some cases dishonest employees were kept on to pay off the cost of their thefts. Dismissal was still an option, but recourse to law appears to have been a reluctantly taken course of action, often after years of tolerance of dishonesty.

It was the police, however, that came to play a major, indeed dominant, role in the bringing of prosecutions in the second half of the 19th century. But, as with other potential prosecutors, they exercised discretion, choosing from a range of options of which arrest and prosecution was the one that left a clear record. The extent to which the police simply gave verbal warnings, or used a night in the cells followed by release without charge, let alone inflicted rough justice with a fist or a rolled cape, is unknowable, but that such practices took place is beyond dispute. Numerous factors, varying over time, influenced the decision whether or not to prosecute. There were resource constraints—finances and manpower were finite. The need to retain the acquiescence, if not outright support, of working-class society was another obvious and continuing constraint, but other pressures were more variable. The police might find themselves under pressure to reduce the incidence of drunk and disorderly behavior or prostitution on the streets of London and elsewhere, and as a consequence, the recorded crime rate rose; but an injudicious arrest, such as that of Elizabeth Cass in 1887 or Eva d'Angely in 1906, (discussed more fully in chapter 5) could set in motion a reaction against police excesses, which then resulted in a fall in recorded crime.[24] In sum, police action was (and had to be) selective. The variable pressures of public opinion, the declared priorities of the Home Office or the local Watch Committee, police perceptions and priorities, plus considerations of practical policing created a complex and ever-changing network of influences that determined the number of people that were arrested and prosecuted. There is one final point of detail to be made. Magistrates also played their part in dispensing discretionary justice, which further impacted the official crime statistics.[25]

Much remains unknown and unknowable, but of two things we can be certain. First, a significant degree of law-breaking behavior was condoned or overlooked by the police, as well as by employers and other private prosecutors; second, the volume of such officially unrecognized criminal behavior varied from year to year and from town to town. Crime, as measured by the official statistics, in a very real sense was a construction that emerged from "a complex interaction of public attitudes and perceptions, law-enforcement strategies and popular behaviour."[26]

It is undoubtedly the case that, as it became easier and cheaper to use the courts, particularly with the expansion of summary justice in the second half of the 19th century, there was greater use of the criminal justice system, but this should be seen as a redrawing of the line between informal and formal sanctions that had for generations been a feature of British justice. Equally, there was a greater degree of continuity in terms of discretionary prosecution behavior, which reinforces the need to be skeptical of and cautious in the interpretation of the official crime figures.

Having considered the various factors that influenced the official crime rate, it is time to offer an interpretation of the figures. It is tempting to follow Taylor (H), Tobias, and Sindall, all of whom see the official statistics as almost valueless.[27] Tobias's preference for literary sources is highly problematic, but, while conceding this point, Rob Sindall has reiterated trenchantly the skeptics' case, quoting with approval the Recorder of Birmingham's observation in 1868 that "crime in Sheffield, Leeds and Birmingham was taken to have a very different meaning from what it had in the minds of those who made the returns for Liverpool and Manchester."[28] There is much force in Sindall's argument. Criminal statistics are important as an indicator of what people believed was happening. However, to see them as no more than this is to lose much of the value that can be derived from them if used sensitively and in conjunction with other evidence.

The skeptical argument centers on two key observations. First, the crime figures do not measure the totality of criminal activity, that is, there is a dark area of unrecorded and unknown crime. Second, the relationship between real and recorded crime is likely to vary over time because of a variety of factors affecting attitudes toward the law and its administration. Both points are clearly correct, but it does not necessarily follow that this renders useless the crime figures. Such is the nature of crime, in almost any society, that the totality of crime is both immense and unknowable. Even if it were possible to count every infraction of the law, however petty, this would not automatically generate useful knowledge. The crucial consideration is not so much the overall total of criminal behavior, and its changing composition, but the nature and level of what is deemed to be unacceptable crime and the effectiveness with which it is dealt. All societies tolerate certain levels of crime and a degree of inefficiency on the part of their law-enforcement agencies. The historian's interest lies in the way in which levels of toleration toward crimes (including the creation of new criminal activities) have changed over time and how society has dealt with this changing problem. This is not to deny the imperfections of the data. Clearly, there are real problems relating to the classification and recording of criminal behavior that result in a degree of inaccurate and misleading information, but it is not clear that these subjectivities are sufficiently widespread or damaging to invalidate the use of the material as a measure of society's willingness and ability to deal with what it deems as unacceptable criminal behavior. Furthermore, by examining those factors that might change the willingness and ability to prosecute (i.e., broad factors such as changes in values that bring new definitions of "acceptable" behavior, changes in attitude toward the legal system as a means of seeking redress, or narrower considerations such as changes in the cost of prosecution) the historian is able to comment on likely changes in the underlying incidence of "real" crime.[29] However, only by appreciating how the crime figures were generated can one hope to arrive at a sensible interpretation of them.[30]

The recorded crime figures for the first half of the 19th century, which largely coincides with the classic Industrial Revolution, appear to show a dramatic growth in recorded serious crime.[31] The numbers committed for trial at quarter sessions and assizes, the overwhelming majority of which were tried for offenses against property, rose dramatically from around 4,500 a year in the early 19th century to just over 20,000 in the early 1830s. The number of trials in the early years of Victoria's reign averaged 16,500 and rose at a more modest rate to 30,000 a year by the early 1840s. The number of those convicted increased at a greater rate. Averaging about 2,700 in the early 19th century, the figure had risen to 14,500 in the early 1830s and topped 20,000 by the early 1840s. Even allowing for the doubling of population that took place at the same time, this was still a substantial increase and one that alarmed many contemporaries. Urbanization and industrialization seemed to have created the conditions for a spectacular increase in criminal behavior—a view echoed by some later historians, including such influential figures as Harold Perkin, who had no doubt of the reality of a "vast increase in crime and prostitution" in the first half of the 19th century.[32]

However, the crime statistics cannot be seen simply as a direct measure of changes in offending behavior. Rather, the figures tell us more about the willingness and ability to prosecute. The upward trend in recorded crime was well under way before reforms in the criminal law and the advent of the new police, which suggests that attitudinal changes were of paramount importance. However, other factors played their part. The establishment of the new police is likely to have had an upward effect on the numbers apprehended, and the reduction in the number of capital offenses may well have increased the willingness to take legal action. Establishing the precise link is altogether more difficult. Indeed, national figures, aggregating all serious crimes from all parts of the country, will necessarily obscure the impact of changes that, by their nature, affected either a specific area (as with the piecemeal development of the new police) or a specific crime (as with the reduction of capital offenses). The most rapid increase in the recorded crime rate came in the early 19th century, during the years of war and its immediate, disruptive aftermath. In contrast, the early Victorian years witnessed a more modest annual increase in recorded crime. Thus, it is likely that there was no significant long-term increase in serious crime rates, particularly in Victorian Britain, but rather a diminution of the "dark gap" between actual and recorded crime.

This is not to say that were no real increases, especially in the short run. The sharp rise in the number of committals after the end of the Napoleonic Wars reflects, in part, a real increase. The demobilization of a relatively large number of men, drawn from those sectors of society that produced the highest number of criminals, and an overstocked and dislocated job market created considerable suffering. Not for the first time, there was a sharp increase in the number of cases brought to trial.[33] But even in these circumstances it is likely that postwar concerns about the threats to stability amplified the real increase in crime. Similarly, it is not entirely coincidental that some of the sharpest downturns in economic activity were accompanied by a sharp increase in the number of committals in the early 1840s and especially the peak years of 1842 and 1848. If one looks specifically at crimes against property there is a clear and inverse correlation between fluctuations in economic activity and the number of crimes against property. However, crimes of violence increased in times of relative prosperity. The reasons for this are not immediately clear, but the prevalence of drink-related assaults may provide one important explanation. The likelihood of drink-related incidents was increased as more alcohol was purchased in relatively good times.

From the 1860s to World War I there was a steady decline in the recorded serious crime rates. The rate for all indictable offenses shows a long-term decline, with a slight blip in the early 1880s, from its peak in the early 1860s until the second half of the 1890s when the decline is in excess of 40 percent. Thereafter, there is a slight upturn, but even in the Edwardian years the rate is still one-third lower than it had been in the mid-Victorian years.

Unsurprisingly, given their preponderance in the overall total, the pattern for larceny offenses is almost identical to the general pattern. The figures for assaults and burglaries follow different patterns. The long-term trend for the assault rate is clearly downward. At its trough, in 1906 through 1910, it is 35 percent below the level of the early 1860s. However, the greatest falls took place in the late 1860s and early 1870s and again in the first decade of the 20th century. The figures for the 1870s and 1880s are somewhat sticky. Moreover, there was an increase in the immediate prewar years that leaves the assault rate at a level 25 percent below its peak. The burglary figures are even more distinctive. Having dropped to a level 35 percent below the early 1860s peak within a decade, the figures stay at roughly the same level until the turn of the century when they start to rise, slightly exceeding the mid-Victorian peak by the eve of the Great War.

Here then was the Victorian miracle, but in the light of the criticisms of Taylor (H), Godfrey, and Davis, was it more a mirage? Certainly it would be naïve to conclude that these figures reflect the true level of crime (though even the most optimistic interpretations of the figures have never suggested that) or even the true scale of change, but it is overstating the case to suggest that there was no improvement at all. If the level of real crime did not change over the course of the 19th century, then there would have had to have been a significant reduction in the willingness or ability of the various groups of prosecutors to take formal action after 1850 or 1870 to explain the changes in the official crime statistics. The police were undoubtedly constrained financially, and no doubt some potentially high-cost cases (almost exclusively murder) were not pursued because of the likelihood of not achieving a successful prosecution. Similarly, the police, as they came to dominate prosecutions after 1880, were more skeptical about prosecuting because they were less inclined to ascribe the same degree of seriousness to certain crimes as the victims. Putting together all these factors scales down the extent of the changes that had taken place but does not invalidate the contention that a real improvement had taken place.

The situation is complicated by the extension of summary justice, especially in 1855 and 1879. The first act resulted in approximately 75 percent of offenses against property without violence being tried summarily, but this figure had risen to almost 90 percent by the end of the 19th century, largely as the result of the second act. By redefining certain forms of larceny as summary offenses, the changes in the law had the effect of reducing the serious crime figures. In addition, the relative speed and cheapness with which cases were dispatched in petty sessions and police courts brought an increase (of around 10%) in the number of cases brought to trial immediately after the 1879 act. The figures for offenses against property without violence show a steady fall after the early 1880s. This is consistent with the gradual improvements in working-class living standards that were a feature of the last third of the 19th century.

The figures relating to crimes of violence are more varied and more problematic. The rate for murder and manslaughter stood at around 1.6 per 100,000 of population in the late 1850s and early 1860s. Thereafter it declined steadily, and by the eve of the Great War the figure had fallen to 0.8 per 100,000. It is unlikely that this was simply the result of misclassifying murders at coroners' courts. A less dramatic decline took place in the incidence of felonious and malicious wounding from a rate of 4.8 per 100,000 in the peak years of the early 1870s to 3.3 in the prewar years. The pattern of decline is stepped rather than gradual. After a drop from the high levels of the 1860s and 1870s, rates stagnated at about 4.2 per 100,000 for the next two decades before dropping slightly again in the early 20th century. However, there may have been an artificially deflationary effect stemming from a downgrading of the seriousness of certain wounding offenses to assaults. Notwithstanding the problems of underrecording, notably in cases of domestic violence, these figures reflect genuine changes in interpersonal behavior.

The other figures for assaults are less clear cut. The decline in the rate for all assaults (that is, common assault, aggravated assault, and assault on the police) is dramatic. From a peak in the 1860s of around 420 per 100,000 of population, it had plummeted to around 120 by the prewar years. As one might expect, the figures are dominated by cases of common assault, which were nonindictable. The figures may exaggerate the actual change in the level of violence in society during these years. The Criminal Registrar noted in the 1890s that there was a growing disinclination to prosecute trivial cases of assault. In contrast to the tenser and socially divided years of the mid-19th century, the latter decades saw a more relaxed, more confident attitude, which led to a greater tolerance of acts of petty violence. Responses to late 19th-century football hooligans illustrate the point well. The growth of football as an organized spectator sport brought with it, or revitalized, parochial rivalries in a manner that appalled those who had seen in an amateur participatory sport a means of civilizing the masses. Adolescent gangs of supporters came into conflict in a variety of predictable places—around football grounds and at railway stations. Serious assaults sometimes occurred, and in extreme cases there were fatalities. Legal action was taken at times, but there is little evidence of any widespread moral panic. Indeed, local press coverage suggests that such acts of violence were to be expected, and not to be worried over, when large groups of working-class men were gathered together.[34] The figures relating to assaults on the police also give an exaggerated impression. Outright hostility toward the police may well have declined in the last third of the 19th century as they were recognized to be a permanent feature. This was probably reinforced by the deterrent effect of the provision under the 1869 Habitual Criminal Act, which stipulated a penalty of a maximum £20 ($30) fine or six months' imprisonment for assaulting a police officer. However, it is also likely that the police themselves were no longer so keen to prosecute for minor cases of assault.

In stark contrast to the declines recorded elsewhere are the figures relating to sexual assaults. The rate of sexual assaults known to the police in England and Wales increased from 2.5 per 100,000, or less, in the third quarter of the 19th century to almost 5.0 by the second decade of the 20th century, with a dramatic and sustained increase dating from the period 1886–1890. However, these figures are almost entirely the result of significant changes in attitude, which were translated into important pieces of legislation. As was recognized by contemporary observers, the 1885 Criminal Law Amendment Act created a range of new sexual offenses, and this, coupled with the determination that existed to prosecute in such cases, greatly inflated the official statistics. The Act, which was primarily intended to provide a means of suppressing brothels, also raised the age of consent for girls to 16 and, in the notorious Labouchère amendment, criminalized male homosexual behavior both in public and private. Subsequent legislation, notably the 1898 Vagrancy Act and the 1912 Criminal Law Amendment Act, further strengthened the sanctions against prostitution and homosexuality. The 1908 Children Act provided for the summary trial of indecent assaults on children under the age of 16, while the Prevention of Incest Act of the same year made incest by men, previously an ecclesiastical offense, a criminal offense punishable by imprisonment for a period of between three and seven years.[35] The rise in sexual offenses coming before the criminal courts is important to note, but it does not invalidate the overall argument that there was a real decline in violence during these years. Attitudes toward male violence were changing, and this was reflected in the volume of critical material condemning assaults on women and children. There was greater awareness and less tolerance of such behavior. Attitudes and actions were changing, and many contemporary observers certainly felt that their world was a safer place and that violence had declined since the mid-19th century.

Assaults figured large among summary offenses, so too did drunkenness and vagrancy offenses, but as many people were prosecuted for offenses against police regulations and local bye-laws. This reflects a growing desire to regulate public spaces and to enforce standards of respectable behavior, but there were other ways in which a regulatory state developed in Victorian Britain. The need to control the rapidly growing urban traffic was reflected in the number of prosecutions for offenses against carriage and cab regulations (around 6,000 at its 1890s peak) and for obstructing highways. The decade after 1895 saw a 50 percent increase in the number of cyclists prosecuted, and a sign of things to come, the immediate prewar years saw a sharp increase in the number of motorists falling foul of the law.[36] The determination of central and local government to improve various aspects of life is reflected in the prosecutions for breaches of the elementary education acts (an average of around 80,000 people per year in the 1880s and 1890s) and the vaccination acts (around 2,500 people per annum in the 1880s but falling thereafter), not to mention prosecutions for the sale of unfit or underweight food and breaches of the sanitary laws.[37] Private organizations also used the law to protect the weak and less fortunate. Prosecutions for cruelty to animals rose from an annual of around 9,000 in the 1880s to some 14,000–15,000 in the early years of the 20th century. At the same time there were about 3,500 prosecutions for cruelty to children. The growing importance of the regulatory state cannot be denied, but as ever, the statistics need to be considered skeptically. It is easy to overlook the extent to which (often unexplained) changes in relatively obscure pieces of legislation could impact overall totals. As the Criminal Registrar noted in his report for 1900, an important element in the fall in summary crime compared with 1899 was "the great diminution in the number of cases under the Dog-Muzzling Orders."[38]

In broad terms, and notwithstanding the very real problems associated with the official crime statistics, a number of conclusions can be drawn. Some are obvious, but important, nonetheless. The growth of summary justice, predating the Victorian period, continued inexorably. Images of trials at the Assizes might have dominated the popular imagination, but such an experience was not common at the start of Victoria's reign and had become quite rare at its end. The growth of summary justice was also linked to the emergence of the regulatory state, which extended its influence into ever more aspects of day-to-day life and thus increased the likelihood (especially for young working-class men) of falling foul of the law. Other conclusions, though less clear cut, are more important. For reasons given previously, the official statistics gave an exaggerated view of the Victorian crime miracle, but if the reality was less spectacular (as it undoubtedly was), it was not unimportant. Edwardian Britain, for the most part, was safer, both in terms of threats to the person and to property, than early Victorian Britain. The fact that serious crime did not increase in the long term (and even the harshest critics have not suggested this was the case) is remarkable—and the product of a fortuitous combination of social, cultural, and economic circumstances; that serious crime probably fell is even more remarkable. Finally, and of no little significance in itself, the late Victorians and Edwardians, for all their concerns about hooligans, habitual drunkards, and professional criminals, believed they lived in a society that was safer and more civilized than any that had gone before. In an age when the fear of crime (however ill-founded) casts a shadow over so many ordinary people's lives, this also was no mean achievement.

CHAPTER TWO

CRIMES OF VIOLENCE

Parliamentary reports and statistical enquiries were undoubtedly important in shaping governmental attitudes toward criminality, but this was
not how the vast majority of Victoria's subjects came to know crime or criminals. For some, a minority it must be stressed, knowledge came through firsthand experience as a victim of crime, or as a family member or close friend of
a victim. For another small minority their knowledge was also their experience as perpetrators, though all too often the insight that such people had
has been totally overlooked. For the majority, a knowledge and understanding of crime came either through press reporting of real crime in newspapers,
journals, and the like or via the representations of crime in the myriad forms
of popular culture that characterized the 19th century. Such was the rate of
change that early Victorians would have struggled to recognize the cultural
world of their grandchildren. New technologies transformed the production of the written word and spawned a popular press and a popular culture
that saturated everyday life, and a staple of that popular culture was crime.
The dry figures of the judicial statistics were given life in numerous ways.
A few people attended courts to hear for themselves, others relied on
gossip; some read the accounts of crime and edited court reports to be found
in every newspaper in the land; yet others owed their knowledge to cultural
representations of crime in novels, plays, and melodramas.

Crime, however, was not simply something to be reported (or mis-
reported), it was also something that was constructed culturally. The
meaning of crime, in general, and of specific crimes, particularly crimes
against the person, was not constant. Around the turn of the 19th century, probably as a result of concerns with both socioeconomic change
(the early "Industrial Revolution") and sociopolitical developments
(the French Revolution and the spread of radical ideas), crime took on
a wider significance as an indicator of the well-being (or otherwise) of
society.[1] The rise in recorded crime reflected (or so it seemed) a more profound malaise. Through a process of displacement, wider anxieties were
heaped upon the shoulders of the criminal. In the early 19th century, including the opening decade or so of Victoria's reign, there was a greater
concern with the threat to property, but increasingly, and particularly in the

more tranquil years following the "Hungry Forties," concern with threats to the person came to the forefront.[2] Bill Sikes, the archetypal sinister criminal created by Charles Dickens in *Oliver Twist*, typified the threatening burglar of early Victorian years, while the habitual criminal, a drunkard and petty thief, was seen as the embodiment of racial degeneracy that underpinned declining imperial power and loss of economic dominance in the late Victorian period.

Attitudes and values were not constant throughout Victorian society at any point in time. Working-class views of "perks" of the job clashed with employers' notions of industrial theft; evangelical determination to curb (if not eradicate) sinful activities such as drinking and gambling ran contrary to the beliefs of entrepreneurs of leisure; definitions of unacceptable violence varied within and between classes; and so on. Furthermore, over time attitudes changed, new values replaced old, and as they did the significance attached to crimes changed. Behavior that was once deemed acceptable was now criticized and punished. A masculinity in which the physical chastisement of wives, children, and servants was acceptable in early Victorian Britain had been replaced, in part at least, by a new masculinity that condemned wife-beating and cruelty to children and that also sought to control male violence in other activities, such as leisure pursuits—notably boxing and football. Concerns, such as garroting, that created alarm in one decade were seen to be overstated, moral panics, in another. Violent crimes never disappeared and were always unpleasant but, like crime in general, were seen as a worrying but "more-or-less normal part of social life" by the turn of the 20th century.[3]

MURDER AND OTHER INTERPERSONAL CRIMES

Murder has always exercised a peculiar attraction, and the Victorians were no exception. Their concern with violence and fascination with murder coexisted, somewhat perversely, with a long-term decline in violent crime and a historically low level of homicide. Nonetheless, the fact remained that there was a large and growing audience for murder and large numbers of people willing to satisfy that demand. Serious newspapers such as *The Times*, respectable middle-class weeklies such as *The London Illustrated News*, and earnest working-class publications such as *The Northern Star* catered for this market as much as the more prurient popular press such as *Police News*. The reality was that most murders were rather sad and sordid domestic affairs. The causes of the vast majority could be ascribed to "poverty and sordid conditions; to incidents in miserable lives; domestic quarrels and brawls; drinking, fighting, blows; a long course of brutality and continued absence of restraint. Nearly half of them were murders on the part of men of wives, mistresses and sweethearts."[4]

But popular perception was dominated by the sensational: the horrific multiple murders of Jack the Ripper, the poisonings of William Palmer or Florence Maybrick, the child murder at Road Hill House, or the serial killings of the "brides in the bath" murderer, George Joseph Smith. Other murders attracted disproportionate attention because of some distinctiveness on the part of the participants, such as the husband and wife murder team of Mr. and Mrs. Manning or the Swiss-born servant Courvoisier, the murderer of Lord William Russell; others because of the location of their crime, such as Franz Müller, the first railway murderer; and others still because of the means by which they were brought to justice, such as Müller, again, the first murderer apprehended via the use of the Atlantic cable, or Dr. Crippen, the first murderer caught via the use of wireless telegram, sent on the order of Captain Kendall of the SS *Montrose*. Closer examination of such cases reveals a more complex picture. These murders raised wider issues and touched on deep-seated anxieties thus giving them greater resonance and contemporary cultural significance.[5]

Nowhere is this more clearly seen than in the infamous Whitechapel murders of 1888. The fact that the murders were particularly gruesome, involving as they did sexual mutilation, and that no murderer was ever brought to trial, was sufficient to attract considerable attention, but there were other issues that contributed to the unprecedented coverage of the mysterious Jack the Ripper and his dreadful acts. The geography was worrying. Here, in the heart of the richest city in the greatest empire the world had ever known, was the recently discovered East End of London tainted by working-class poverty, squalor, and immorality. This was a dark, labyrinthine world, a warren of lanes and byways with sinister sounding local names—Blood Alley and Do As You Please Street—in which even the much-vaunted Metropolitan police feared to venture. The existence of this "Darkest England" heightened middle-class fears that urban degeneration would bring moral collapse and social upheaval.

Class fears about the threat of "outcast London" were compounded by gender fears and fantasies. At a time when traditional gender values were being threatened by a middle-class male retreat from marriage and a challenge from the "new woman," here was further evidence of the corruption of femininity and the family ideal. Somewhat paradoxically, given the sorry state of the Ripper's victims, there was also something disconcerting about these women and their defiant rejection of conventional morality.

There was a brutal morality tale being played out in Whitechapel. Working-class prostitutes who had sold their femininity were being punished for their sins, but at the same time, there was a violence that underlined more general fears about unacceptable working-class male attitudes and actions. To compound matters, very recent scientific work, associated particularly with Dr. Richard Krafft-Ebing, had introduced the notions of lust murder and sexual sadism into contemporary debate. The coincidence of a West End

HE SAW A BODY ON THE PAVEMENT.

Victim of Jack the Ripper, Whitechapel, 1888. P.C. Neil found the body of Mary Ann Nicol in Buck Row, Whitechapel, August 31, 1888. (Courtesy Mary Evans Picture Library)

production of Stevenson's immensely popular *The Strange Case of Dr. Jekyll and Mr. Hyde* underlined the ever-present threat of the barbarity innate in man and allowed people like W. T. Stead, the editor of the *Pall Mall Gazette*, to speculate about a "savage of civilization" lurking in the slums. Speculation about Jack the Ripper revealed a further set of anxieties that centered on race. Whitechapel was seen as someplace *other*. Entering the Jewish district in 1896, Henry Walker found himself "in a foreign land. The street we enter might be a street in Warsaw or Cracow. We have taken leave of everything English and entered an alien world . . . In the heart of London, it is yet like a foreign town, with its . . . own segregated peoples, religions, customs."[6] This influx of Jewish refugees, fleeing pogroms in Russia in the 1880s, had created tensions in the labor and housing markets. The highly publicized Lipski murder trial of 1887 created a link between Jewish immigrants and serious crime in the popular mind, and it was no surprise that rumors abounded that the culprit was (and could only be) a Jew.[7]

The extensive coverage of the Ripper murders throws interesting light on the anxieties of late Victorian Britain and the role of the press in shaping perceptions of the crimes and their location, the victims, and the possible perpetrator; but it can also distort. Unsolved murders of prostitutes were not limited to the Ripper's victims—in 1889 the murder of four London prostitutes went unsolved. Nor was the Ripper the only mass murderer in late 19th-century London—four prostitutes were poisoned during the winter of 1891 by tonics given them by Dr. Thomas Cream. And nor was London unique in this sad and sorry regard—prostitutes were beaten and murdered across the length and breadth of Victorian Britain.

Murders committed by women, despite being significantly less common than the murder of women by men, received considerable publicity, though this is not surprising given the dominant gender assumptions of the time, which emphasized the nurturing nature and subordinate role of women.[8] Maria Manning was not the first woman to be hanged in Victoria's reign—17 preceded her to the gallows—but her fate attracted more attention than most, not least because her execution was attended by Charles Dickens.[9] The crime was mundane—a bungled murder motivated by greed—but, behaving passionately in court and strikingly dressed in black satin, the revelations of her sexually promiscuous behavior and the dominant role she played in her marriage with Frederick and in the murder of Patrick O'Connor challenged early Victorian notions of femininity. The fact that she was a foreigner (Swiss) added further piquancy to the case and enabled the problem she posed to be resolved by stressing her *otherness*. "Thank God she wasn't an English woman," one relieved correspondent wrote to *The Times*.[10] More threatening were those women who committed petty treason by murdering their husbands. The seriousness of this threat to the patriarchal order was compounded by the deceitful way in which the majority of such murders were carried out. The poisoning panic of the late 1840s and early 1850s marks the highpoint of such concerns.

Changing perceptions of female murderers lessened fears of petty treason, but alleged female killers still attracted considerable attention that was both complex and contradictory. The murder of Jess McPherson in Glasgow in 1862 was particularly brutal. She had been attacked with an axe, and some 40 wounds had been inflicted on her body. Jessie McLachlan, a servant girl, was brought to trial. Her pretrial statements to the Procurator Fiscal had been muddled, if not dishonest, and she consistently denied knowledge of the death of Jess McPherson yet asserted that her master, "Old Fleming," was the murderer. In fact, Old Fleming was the chief witness against her. The case went badly, and a verdict of guilty was returned by the jury after only 15 minutes consideration. With the judge about to pass sentence, black cap to hand, McLachlan's agent read a statement to court that contradicted much of her earlier evidence but accused Old Fleming not only of murdering the old woman but also of attempting to "use liberties with her" when drunk. The death penalty was pronounced, but such was the scale of public anger in the light of the confession—a petition was signed by 50,000 Glaswegians—that the execution was postponed, an official enquiry held, and Jessie McLachlan reprieved.[11]

Perhaps the most high-profile case was that of the American Florence Maybrick in 1899. The case had touches of the exotic: a rich, attractive young
woman married to a successful businessman several years her elder; the use of
arsenic by both partners—she as a cosmetic, he as a sexual stimulant; and the
open confession of adultery by the accused. This admission provided the core
of the prosecution case. Sir James Fitzjames Stephen was unequivocal that a
woman who had carried on "an adulterous intrigue with another man" had "a
very strong motive why she should get rid of her husband."[12] Despite doubt as
to the actual cause of death, and in contrast to other similarly accused women,
such as Adelaide Bartlett and Madeleine Smith, Florence Maybrick was found
guilty. The verdict gave rise to a massive press debate and large-scale petition-
ing that resulted in a reprieve. The attention focused on the case cannot be
explained simply in terms of concern about a possible miscarriage of justice,
though there was undoubtedly some doubt as to the actual cause of death. It
attracted attention because it focused on wider gendered concerns relating to
the role of men and women, the state of marriage and contemporary morals.[13]

Florence Maybrick on Trial at Liverpool, 1889. (Courtesy *Illustrated London News
Ltd*/Mary Evans Picture Library)

The suspicious death of a child also aroused considerable attention. Infanticide was often treated sympathetically, as were some cases of child murder, though this was not the case where children had been farmed out into the care of others.[14] Many cases passed largely unnoticed, but others received widespread coverage. One such was the murder in 1860 of Saville Kent at Road Hill House in the village of Road in Wiltshire.[15] The child had had his throat cut and was then dumped in the outside lavatory for the servants of the house. That the head was almost severed from the body was shocking enough, but disposing of his body in a cesspit was worse. The shock and concern was further heightened by the very location of the crime. The sanctity of a respectable Englishman's home had been cruelly violated. An innocent child had had his life cut short in brutal fashion in the very environ that should offer him protection. The *Bath Chronicle* noted that

> [n]o assassination within our recollection caused so singular, and so painful a sensation . . . [because of] the strange character of the deed, and the helpless innocence of the victim . . . The mothers of England, thinking of their own little ones sleeping in peace and purity, shudder at the tale of a child, as gentle and innocent as their own, being dragged in the still morning from its slumbers and cruelly sacrificed . . . [It is a] deed that sends a shudder through every English home, [and which] acquires a social importance which justifies any amount of attention to the subject.[16]

But who was responsible for this appalling crime? There was no evidence to suggest an outsider was responsible; the guilty person was a member of the household. Suspicion was centered initially on the servants, most particularly the nursemaid, Elizabeth Gough, but increasingly, as time passed and no progress was made in solving the mystery, attention switched to members of the family, particularly Saville's stepsister, Constance, and the child's father, factory inspector Samuel Kent. What passions and perversions had taken place in the Kent family? How thin was the veneer of bourgeois civilization in Victorian Britain? The case was subject to close scrutiny. Minute details of the house were made public as were worrying details of the Kent family life. Constance was the daughter of Samuel Kent's first marriage. Her mother had gone insane before she died, and her father married, with almost indecent haste, the governess who became the mother of the unfortunate Saville. References were made to mistreatment by and jealousy of the stepmother. Constance was portrayed as a strange and unpredictable girl, once running away with her brother William and fascinated by the case of Madeleine Smith, who had brazenly asserted her innocence and had not been found guilty of a murder that many believed she had committed. It was speculated that Constance had witnessed a sexual liaison between her father and the then governess, which fueled her jealousy. Samuel Kent, not a popular man locally, appeared in poor light as revelations of his private life were made. The madness of his first wife (and alleged madness of his second) pointed to syphilis, an incurable disease that appeared to threaten the civilian (as well as military) population. Since the Crimean War the country was all too well aware of the shocking extent of venereal diseases, syphilis in particular, that could sweep through the civilian population, aided by hypocritical men who contracted the disease only to infect innocent wives and children. Worse, it was suggested by some that he was responsible for the death of his son because of what he had seen between his father and his governess. As was the case with the later Ripper murders, the Road Hill House murder tapped into wider fears.

The extensive coverage of the Kent case is a measure not simply of commercial acumen but of the deeper concerns that such cases aroused. Inevitably the case lost its appeal, but there was a final twist to the tale. In April 1865 Constance Kent confessed to the murder of Saville, for which she was sentenced to death, though the sentence was commuted to penal servitude for life. Her story was far from plausible, but it was the manner of her confession—to the Puseyite Rev. Arthur Douglas Wagner—that aroused controversy; this time between high and low church factions in the Anglican Church. Once again, a "simple" murder chimed with wider social concerns and controversy.[17]

Murder was an untypical crime and the high-profile cases untypical examples. The reality of most Victorian murder was sordid and depressingly predictable. William Lace kicked his wife to death in 1872—he was drunk at the time; John Daly, a Belfast coal carrier, kicked to death Margaret Whiteley in 1876—both were drunk; Thomas Daley, a laborer from Kent, beat his wife to death with a poker in 1898—he was drunk; Charles Scott slit the throat of his girlfriend, Eliza O'Shea, in 1899—they had quarreled after drinking; John Cronin of Longford murdered his father after a quarrel just before Christmas 1885; William Arrowsmith, a Shropshire laborer, brutally killed his uncle in 1888 and stole coppers from him; Thomas Richard smothered his sister in law and stole a pony, her wedding ring, and some cash in 1894; Bernard Kelly, an innkeeper in County Cavan, murdered his father in 1899 after several quarrels; Edward Gough, of Sunnyside, Durham, stabbed to death a fellow pitman after a drunken dispute in the local pub in July 1874; John Golding quarreled with his long-time friend Daniel Lord in Edge Hill in August 1877—he lost his temper, attacked Lord with a poker, and killed him; James William Richardson, a Barnsley laborer, argued with William Berridge, the foreman of the brickyard at which he worked, then stormed out of work, only to return and shoot Berridge in May 1882; Peter Stafford shot Patrick Crawley, the culmination of a longstanding quarrel—they were in a public house at the time. Such crimes did not go unreported, but they did not receive the attention given to some cases. In part this was because they were too ordinary, with nothing exotic or shocking to raise them above the run-of-the-mill murders that took place every year; in part it was because these cases did not touch on wider anxieties; but it was also because such mundane murders actually raised profound questions about the economic and social organization of Victorian Britain, which the majority did not wish to confront. The poverty, squalor, and drunkenness that provided the backdrop to these crimes challenged the comfortable notions of civilization, prosperity, and opportunity that were such a central part of the bourgeois Victorian self-image. There was an important element of self-censorship as many Victorian commentators hid behind explanations of crime that emphasized individual moral failures, the lack of education and religious training, and the innate beastliness lurking within man.

Violence manifested itself in a variety of other ways and, for the most part, did not result in death. While there was a long-term move away from the culture of violence that characterized Regency England, acts of violence remained far from uncommon, and concerns about barbarism were very close to the surface of Victorian society. Masculinity was redefined in a number of important ways during Victoria's reign, but the importance of physical strength and courage was such that, particularly among unskilled working-class men, the ability to defend oneself and gain respect when

"A MERE TRIFLE."

First Liverpool Rough. "I SOY, BILL, WHAT'LL THEE GIT FOR THIS 'ERE?"
Second Liverpool Rough (who has beaten his Wife within an inch of her life). "FOIN O' TEN BOB MAYBE, SAME AS 'AD FOR WALLOPING THAT JACKASS, THOUGH AH'VE GIVED IT TO 'ER SMARTER-LOIKE!"

Domestic Violence, 1875. Concerns with the brutality of working-class men ran alongside worries that the law was too lenient in cases of domestic violence. (Courtesy Mary Evans Picture Library)

appropriate never disappeared. As a consequence, fighting, often but not exclusively with fists and feet, was a common feature in town and country-side, albeit probably less so at the end of Victoria's reign than at the beginning. Men (not always young and not always when drunk) fought with each other, women (in practice not always the angel of the hearth) attacked each other in "clothes line quarrels," and men attacked women and children (sometimes women attacked men); the English fought the Scots and Irish, the Irish fought amongst themselves (the men of Connaught against the men of Munster), and all, men, women, English, Scots, and Irish, tangled with the police. Violence was associated more with certain towns, such as Cardiff, Liverpool, or Middlesbrough; or certain districts, such as the Gorbals in Glasgow, China in Merthyr, Whitechapel and Hoxton in London; and even certain streets, such as Castlegate, Huddersfield, Campbell Bunk, Islington, or Wilmer Gardens, Hoxton, otherwise unambiguously known as Kill Copper Row. There were known violent families in every town (a disproportionate number of whom were said to be Irish) as well as individual hard men. Many contemporary commentators described and explained violence in class and ethnic terms.

The civilized English gentleman did not resort to violence, unlike the unruly laborer or the troublesome foreigner. As attitudes changed and the limits of acceptable violence were redefined, the problem was seen to reside within the residuum—the roughs who were separated from the respectable working class, let alone the middle classes—or to have been imported by aliens, knife-wielding Italians or Greeks and revolver-touting Russian Jews. There was some reassurance to be found in such simplifications. The realities were more complex. To take but one example, wife beating was not confined to the "roughs" in the kicking districts of Lancashire, where metal-tipped clogs were used to mete out justice. On the contrary, seemingly respectable ex-army officers had a reputation for severe discipline that brought them to the attention of the National Society for the Prevention of Cruelty to Children, but "parents of the most respectable and conformist families were the staunchest upholders of 'discipline," in Edwardian Salford at least.[18]

Fights took place for a variety of reasons. Some were simply an expression of frustration and anger or of a desire for excitement; some were acts of defiance against authorities, not least the police, that imposed an alien code of behavior on the working classes; some were little more than drunken outbursts; some were sectarian; yet more were a means of resolving a grievance between individuals (including quarrels over the affections of young women); but many were also a means of gaining respect and/or maintaining the reputation of the neighborhood. Particularly worrying was the gang violence that was to be found in the large towns and cities of Britain. "Scuttlers" in and around Manchester were a considerable cause for concern in the 1870s and 1880s as were "cornermen" and gangs such as the High Rip in Liverpool; while hooliganism was a blight in London a decade later. Press coverage exaggerated the scale of the problem and also gave an oversimplified account of events. Contrary to popular belief, gangs were not confined to the poorest districts, nor was every young man a gang member; further, membership was not exclusively male, and despite the frightening size of certain scuttles or hooligan fights, gang conflict was essentially inward looking. For the most part, gang members inflicted damage upon each other, not on other members of the public. Furthermore, their actions (however mystifying and frightening to outside observers) were not simply random and mindless.[19] There was a clear contrast between the law and popular conceptions of right and wrong. What was seen as unacceptable violence on the part of respectable members of society was both acceptable and expected in rougher sections of the community. As a consequence, many crimes of violence went unreported simply because those involved (and this could include the police) felt that it was inappropriate to use the law even though technically a crime had been committed. This gives added importance to those actions that were prosecuted because they throw light on the boundaries of acceptable violence determined by local communities as much as by the courts.

This was particularly true of domestic violence. There was a widely held belief in a husband's right to chastise his wife. Furthermore, many women accepted the "right" of their husbands to chastise them and accepted that a degree of rough usage was an unavoidable part particularly of working-class marriage. This, combined with the economic and legal weaknesses of most women, meant that many incidents of assault were never brought to court, though a number were dealt with by mediation before coming to formal trial. Failure to provide a meal on time or to show proper respect for the head of the household could lead to beatings, which in many cases were seen as justified by the women themselves, but (and it is important to see matters in the context of their times) there were limits. Local communities often decided when the boundary of acceptable chastisement had been overstepped.[20] In some instances this involved intervention in an actual assault; in other cases wife-beaters were publicly condemned in the traditional manner known as rough music. Villagers and townsfolk paraded through their community, carrying an effigy of the offender, banging pots and pans, blowing horns, and generally creating a din that reached a crescendo outside the house in which the guilty man lived. Wife-beaters might also be ostracized by their neighbors and in extreme cases driven out of the community.[21] A correspondent to *The Times* wrote that "on any brutality being committed by a man towards a woman the villagers assemble together" to protest. The problem was determining what constituted brutality. Looking back from the early 21st century, it is easy to be shocked by the violence that was accepted in years gone by. Equally, what was unacceptable to a philosopher such as John Stuart Mill or Harriet Taylor Mill was seen in a different light by many working-class men and women of their time.

However, attitudes changed, particularly in the second half of the century. In their different ways, people like Mill and Taylor Mill or Frances Power Cobbe drew attention to the scandal of wife torture.[22] The spread of working-class respectability also led to a reappraisal of acceptable behavior within marriage. More problematic is assessing the extent of improvement in the late Victorian period. The passing of the Aggravated Assaults on Women and Children Act in 1853, the Matrimonial Causes Act of 1878, and the Wife Beaters' Act of 1882 changed the situation in theory, but translating this into effective action was not easy. Relatively little was done in practical terms to improve the position of women. Indeed, recourse to law, particularly if the punishment was four hours in the pillory or a whipping, could be counterproductive. More disturbingly for would-be reformers, there was something of a male backlash around the turn of the century. Concern for weak and emasculated husbands led Philip Gibbs to opine that "a touch of brutality now and then" was needed.[23] In a stunning attempt at role reversal, Dr. Crippen was presented as the victim of a slatternly wife whose neglect of her house and husband was such as to provide extenuating circumstances. The jury was unimpressed and Crippen duly hanged for murder.

The Crippen case threw light on less salubrious aspects of Edwardian suburban life, but all too often, domestic violence was seen as an overwhelmingly working-class problem with certain northern districts achieving particular notoriety. Such barbarous behavior had a wider political significance and was seen as proof positive, by some at least, of the unfitness of the ordinary working man and the folly of contemplating the extension of the franchise to such a person. In condemning this behavior and seeking to criminalize it, parliament showed itself to be more concerned with redefining acceptable masculine behavior than with extending protection for women. The legal fiction of marital unity was a powerful force that led to the rejection of anything that suggested spousal equality.[24] Further, sexual harassment, in a wide variety of forms, was a major problem, particularly for working-class women, and yet few cases ever reached the courts.[25] Wife beating remained a grossly underreported crime—and doubts must be raised about the figures that appear to show it declined in the latter years of Victoria's reign—but there can be no doubt about the violence inflicted on certain women. Often on the slightest provocation, a less than subservient look or word, let alone a meal not ready on time, men kicked and punched their wives and partners. Black eyes, bruised limbs, and broken bones bore witness to the suffering endured by many women, not all of whom came from the working classes. Unlike the more ritualized public fights between men, where there was agreement on what constituted a fair fight, domestic conflicts were more volatile, though not necessarily unplanned, and less self-regulated.

Rape and other forms of sexual violence were also underreported. Those cases that did come to court revealed a brutality and indifference toward women that was scarcely disguised by the constraints upon women giving evidence and the conventions of reporting. Women were raped by men they knew. Sarah Johnson was going out with Henry Goodlock, who persuaded her to go to Stepney Fair in the early summer of 1845 and, after giving her some alcohol, raped her in a nearby field.[26] Others were raped by strangers. Being in the company of her boyfriend was no defense for Ann Curtis. The pair was attacked by a gang of four or five men, one of whom held her down while another raped her.[27] Gang rapes were particularly frightening. Five men attacked Jane Shore on Hackney Marshes in 1871 but, to make matters worse, "the neighbourhood . . . looked on as if it was no concern of theirs to interfere and to endeavour to rescue the woman."[28] Similarly shocking was the outrage at Cliviger, near Burnley in 1874. Two young colliers, coming upon an intoxicated woman, raped her in front of their friends who saw nothing wrong in what was happening. The unfortunate women was left in a field where she died of exposure.[29] Most rapes, however, were solitary assaults. Servants or would be servants were particularly vulnerable. Ellen Singleton was forced to drink beer and spirits before being assaulted by her master.[30] Fanny Chapman believed James Oven wished to engage her as a servant when she went to his house in Rayleigh, Essex, in 1885. He used chloroform (or some other narcotic) to render her insensible before raping her.[31]

Assaults could take place in almost any location. Sarah Batty was raped early in the morning by a stranger who had come to her assistance (or so it seemed) when he offered to ferry her across the Trent to meet her husband.[32] Edith Stannard was on a footpath, walking through a wood in Martlesham, when she was attacked; Eliza Cummins was on her way to work in Bishopwearmouth when she was raped, while Mary Thomas was walking on a road by the farm near Llandarff that she worked with her husband when a 19-year-old youth sexually assaulted her.[33] Women on their own were clearly at risk, even more so if in "inappropriate" places, such as public houses. Martha Appleby, a middle-aged married woman, had stopped for a drink in a public house in Northampton. She was followed out by several men, knocked unconscious, and dragged to Dallington moor where two men held her down while the third raped her.[34] Mary Hopkins was the victim of an atrocious rape perpetrated by three men who had seized and blindfolded her as she went into the yard of a public house in Notting Hill, London. The judge's condemnation was notable, even though she appeared so little "an object of sympathy" as she was a woman who "was in the habit of spending her husband's earnings on drink and neglecting her children."[35] Nor was age a safeguard. Young children were assaulted and so too were old women. Having walked 32 miles from Blanchard to Washington, County Durham, to visit her son, 64-year-old Maria Page, described as a feeble old woman, stopped at a pub for some refreshment at 10 P.M. Despite specifically asking for a room in which there were no men, she was shown into a room in which several pitmen were drinking. Three followed her out and in the course of a brutal rape inflicted serious facial damage, including several broken teeth.[36] Sadly, the sorry list of ill-treated women could easily be extended—and these represent only those cases that were brought to court and reported in any detail.

Changing attitudes and the limitations of the criminal statistics make it difficult to arrive at firm conclusions, but generally speaking, life was less violent on the eve of World War I than it had been when Victoria came to the throne. The extent (and even rate) of change was exaggerated by the official figures, but it would be perverse not to accept that there had been a decline in violence in many walks of life. Street brawls were less common; leisure activities, such as football and boxing, had been sanitized and subjected to defined rules; and public meetings were less violent (or less often violent) than they had been. In a more general sense, there was less visible violence in everyday life: animals were no longer baited in public, and criminals were no longer hanged before the eyes of ordinary men, women, and children. However, violence had not disappeared, and fears of the threat to civilized and ordered society remained to a greater degree than many historians have recognized. There were armed burglaries in the early 1880s, rampaging crowds of unemployed in central London later in the same decade; protection rackets in Sheffield, Glasgow, and London in the early 20th century; three policemen were killed and two more wounded in a single incident in Houndsditch in 1910; violent protests scarred the immediate prewar years—additional police and troops had to be sent to Liverpool, and a warship was moored in the Mersey during the transport strike of 1911; while suffragette outrages and images of policemen wrestling with protesting women, from respectable families to make matters worse, shocked many Edwardians. The impact on public opinion is difficult to chart, but the response of *The Times* to the Tottenham Outrage of 1909 is illuminating. The streets of this relatively prosperous and respectable north London suburb witnessed a shoot-out in which a 10-year-old boy and a policeman were killed. A further 3 constables were wounded as were 14 passersby in what was described as more "of a fray in a type of Western mining camp."[37] The sense of otherness was strengthened by the revelation that the two criminals, who had "armed themselves with revolvers . . . determined to shoot any number of innocent persons to get away with their booty," were aliens, members of a Russian revolutionary party. "This type of crime," *The Times* pontificated, "is fortunately not indigenous." So far so reassuring for its readers, but the editorial continued in tones that betrayed a certain anxiety about the state of Edwardian society that went beyond the threat posed by two anarchists. "This affair may serve to remind us of the savagery that underlies the fine surface of civilization, and of the thinness of the crust that divides us from the elemental fires." To underline the message it concluded. "There are many sentimentalists going about just now assuring people that society no longer depends on force, but merely upon persuasion . . . This outbreak of savagery may help some superficial persons to comprehend how preposterous is that contention."[38] Such were the fears that still lurked close to the surface of Edwardian society.

CHAPTER THREE

GARROTERS, BANK ROBBERS, AND POACHERS

The Victorians and Edwardians read much about crimes of violence, but (like their early 21st-century counterparts) the majority were rarely victims of, or even witnesses to, such crimes. They were more likely to be victims of a crime against property that did not involve violence. Such crimes accounted for roughly four out of five indictable committals.[1] There were some regional variations, notable in Wales where, contrary to the popular (and prejudicial) rhyme, Taffy was less of a thief.[2] However, despite being significantly less common, crimes against property involving violence bulked largely in press reportage and popular perception.

At a time when the highwayman was being romanticized as the cultured and courteous "gentleman of the road" in the writings of the likes of William Ainsworth, the violent robbers of Victoria's reign were seen as descendant of the despised footpad of Georgian Britain.[3] The garroters of the 1850s and 1860s generated a moral panic in the media.[4] Press coverage of a "New System of Robbery" gradually built up from early 1851, with accounts of garrote attacks in a variety of provincial centers, including Manchester, Birmingham, and Leeds, and reached a crescendo in 1856 with attention increasingly focused on London.[5]

The number of people charged with robbery and attempted robbery increased sharply, but it is unlikely that this reflected a real increase in violent street robbery. Rather, the growing public concern led to a greater number of cases being sent to the higher courts. However, the very fact of increased committals for these offenses gave further substance to the fears. The 1850s panic finally blew itself out, but not without long-term effect. The debate on penal servitude and the legislation of 1853 and 1857 were shaped by public perceptions of the threat posed by "ticket-of-leave" men, that is, convicts released on license before the end of their sentences.[6] A further panic broke out, as if afresh, in 1862, precipitated by a murderous attack on Hugh Pilkington, the M.P. for Blackburn, who was robbed at night of his watch and £10, while walking from the House of Commons to the Reform Club. Public concern, already sensitized by the ongoing debate

Le *Rough* au travail.

Street Mugging in London, 1867. Garroting panics were a feature of the 1850s and 1860s. (Courtesy Mary Evans Picture Library)

on the treatment of criminals, was further heightened by the press coverage of this and similar attacks. With little hard evidence to support the assertion, elements of the press could claim that "highway robbery is becoming an institution in London, and roads like the Bayswater Road are as unsafe as Naples."[7] Fears led to more arrests by the police and more prosecutions while the courts also took a tougher line. Once again, a crime wave was created by a popular panic, and parliament reacted by passing an exceptional measure, the Security Against Violence Act, which reintroduced flogging for robbery with violence. The panics of 1856 and 1862 were initially centered on London, but increasing frequent references to garroting attacks can be found in the provincial press, although the concern with provincial juvenile gangs, notably the Scuttlers in Manchester and Salford in the 1870s and the 'cornermen' and the High Rip Gang in Liverpool in the 1870s and 1880s, did not develop into full-scale panics. Similarly, the absence of a more general sense of insecurity and fear may explain why the attack in 1874, near Marble Arch, upon a high court judge, Chief Baron Kelly, did not precipitate a moral panic. Concern with gangs never disappeared, but reporting was less intemperate.[8]

These violent incidents need to be kept in perspective. In 1850 robbery accounted for only half a percent of all crimes tried at the Old Bailey, and the figure was to fall further.[9] The streets of late Victorian London were undoubtedly safer but not danger free. Llewellyn Price was robbed of a watch, chain, and locket while walking along Pentonville Road at night in 1880.[10] William Palmer, a ship's agent, was robbed of a gold watch and chain (valued at £60) in broad daylight in Royal Mint Street in 1886. Arthur Morley, described as "well dressed [and] clean shaven," was found guilty of stealing a watch and chain, a scarf pin, some money, and a fur coat from the man he attacked and robbed on Pimlico Embankment in early 1897.[11] Although such attacks were less common by the end of the century, they were frightening for the victim and created a sense of unease in the wider community that did not sit comfortably with the general discourse of declining crime rates.

Nor should London's reputation blind the historian to what was happening elsewhere. In the Black Country between 1835 and 1860 there were just fewer than 500 cases of robbery. Typically the offense took place at night when the victim was returning home, often after having spent some time drinking in a local public house. John Roahan, for example, was attacked by three men in Caribee Island, the Irish quarter of Wolverhampton. Knocked down by one, held down by another, his pockets were searched by the third who stole his purse containing 5 shillings and 6 pence (27.5 p or 44 cents). James Beddow was robbed in similar fashion when leaving a public house in Walsall after he had been paid. Although his assailants had been in the same pub, they were not known to him; John Clough, however, was attacked and robbed by two men whom he knew well.[12] The pages of the provincial press bear witness to continuing violent robberies. Certain parts of towns and cities—"over the border" in Middlesbrough, Castlegate in Huddersfield—were dangerous, especially at night. Men were particularly vulnerable when drinking in or leaving a public house. One unfortunate sailor in "a low part of the town" of Middlesbrough was inveigled into a public house by a young woman only to be attacked and robbed by two men.[13] Edward Jones was attacked and robbed of his watch and chain while walking along a canal path after leaving the *Patriot Inn* in Merthyr.[14] Their fates were by no means exceptional, but attacks could take place at other, less obviously dangerous, times of the day. James Burns was kicked, punched, and robbed of a knife and three halfpence by two men in Leeds in broad daylight.[15] And it was not only men who were victims. Catherine Hancock was attacked and robbed while crossing a field on her way home from work in Staffordshire. She lost a shawl, mackintosh, and umbrella.[16] In a similar incident in Cardiff, the unfortunate Mrs. Williams had her umbrella and kerchief stolen.[17] Nor was robbery simply a large town phenomenon. A Shrewsbury coal agent, whilst at work, was robbed of £12 by two men, while the street attack on an Ipswich clerk, who was robbed of £2, shocked the respectable readers of the *Ipswich Journal*.[18] The tranquility of rural life could also be disrupted. For example, on 17 January 1866, Arthur Battley was attacked and robbed of a watch, various items of jewelry, and money as he walked from the village of Fornham All Saints to Bury St. Edmunds.[19]

Yet more serious were the crimes of breaking and entering and burglary. Although intrinsically the same offence, that is, breaking into a property and stealing, burglary was made a distinct and more serious offense in law by virtue of the action taking place during the hours of darkness, which brought the additional element of fear. Actual crimes varied widely in their scale and nature. Particularly in London, certain burglaries and housebreakings were committed by organized gangs and involved substantial sums of money, but most crimes were less spectacular. When the Reverend Father Johnson of Skipton was burgled in December 1866, he lost two sovereigns, five or six shillings, and small quantities of sugar and tea, while Robert Holt of Fishponds, Gloucestershire, lost five sheets, some towels, and miscellaneous items of clothing when his cottage was burgled, also in December 1866.[20] Some crimes involved considerable violence and conformed to the popular image. Thus, for example, Samuel Thompson, a Black Country publican, was burgled in 1836 by three men armed with iron-tipped bludgeons who assaulted his two sons. This was exceptional. More were relatively small-scale affairs and said more about harsh economic conditions than innate depravity. In 1842 the house of Mr. and Mrs. Reynolds was broken into in the early morning and some beef, pork, bread, and cheese stolen. It was the eagle-eyed Mrs. Reynolds who was able to identify the teeth marks on the stolen piece of beef and marrow bone, thus bringing the culprit to book![21]

An analysis of housebreaking cases tried at Quarter Session in the North Riding of Yorkshire during the same period confirms this picture of relatively mundane crime, though the money or goods involved were significant to both victim and perpetrator. The largest theft of property involved two men's shirts, one woman's chemise, four children's shifts, and five nightcaps, but more common were sums of around £1. At a time when an agricultural laborer could be paid 10 shillings (50 p or 80 cents) a week, or less, £1 ($1.60) was a considerable sum of money. Some took both money and goods. James Lee and William Leighton, transported for 15 years in 1844, took money to the value of 19 shillings (95 p or $1.44), two pairs of stockings, two handkerchiefs, and a piece of bread from a house in North Kilvington. The majority of housebreaking charges involved the theft of relatively small but not insignificant quantities of goods. Robert Scott, for example, was charged with the theft of a white loaf of bread, an apple pie, and two geese. Nor does the situation appear to have changed significantly in the latter part of the century. Burglary cases tried at the York Assizes, for example, reveal a catalog of stolen watches, teaspoons, small pieces of jewelry, and relatively small sums of money or quantities of goods. Typical was Thomas Wade, who stole a purse and the sum of £1–5-0 (£1.25 or $2), or Patrick Marron, who stole an overcoat, a cloak, and a pair of boots.

Unsurprisingly, housebreaking cases followed a similar pattern. On occasions, the items stolen could be quite considerable in number, if not value. Two hawkers, Christopher Brown and Andrew Quinn, broke into the house of William Ryder in Ellington and took over 20 items of clothing. The relatively wealthy were obvious targets. William Thompson, a laborer, broke into the house of Blanchard Ringrose at Thirkleby and helped himself to two loaves of bread, a pound of bacon, a pound of sugar, and a quarter pound of coffee. Servants, with their knowledge of the geography and possessions of a house, appear frequently in the records. Bessy Eccles, a servant, pleaded guilty in 1874 to the theft of six silver teaspoons, a pair of silver sugar tongs, a petticoat, a worsted scarf, and a handkerchief from Jesse Eccles of Ampleforth. But not all victims were in this position. John Brooks, a sawyer, broke into a house in Middlesbrough, stealing shoes and clothing from two Irish laborers who lodged in the house. Working men and women were the most common victims of theft, but in many instances the crimes were not brought to court.

As Victoria's reign lengthened there was an upsurge of interest in allegedly daring bank robberies committed by ingenious thieves, who, it was claimed, operated in gangs across the country. In 1887 four men, suspected to be members of an "expert gang from England" stole £886 from a branch of the British Linen Company's bank in Glasgow.[22] A Manchester bank robbery the following year saw a gang of three men taking £3,000 ($4,770) from a cab in which money from the Manchester and County bank had just been placed.[23] The Didsbury branch of the same bank was robbed by a disturbed, revolver-touting man who subsequently committed suicide.[24] Even more daring was the raid on the North Eastern bank in Sunderland in 1897. A total of approximately £6,000 ($9,540), including £3,500 ($5,565) in gold, was taken in a night-time raid in which both the outer door of the bank and that of the strong room had been opened with duplicate keys. The perpetrators were eventually arrested in Soho after a large-scale fight involving 100 policemen. The case was originally described as a "cleverly executed plot . . . unique for its ingenious daring," but as details emerged certain weaknesses in bank security became obvious. Impressions of the outer door keys were obtained when a bank clerk—the manager's son, no less—left the keys unattended in the pocket of his jacket, which he had taken off to play billiards with one of the gang. Worse, the chief cashier, having been induced to take a Turkish bath with another gang member, left the keys of the bullion room similarly unattended.[25]

Other audacious bank raids similarly appear more a triumph for incompetence. Bank-counter robberies occurred in various parts of the country. A bundle of £10 notes to the value of £800 ($1,272) was snatched from the Union Bank of London when a "very experienced cashier [was distracted] only for a moment."[26] At the bank of William Deacon & Co., a 70-year-old clerk had a wallet, containing notes and securities valued at £30,000 ($47,700), snatched by an "expert thief." The description of what happened would have done justice to the Keystone Cops. "Not more than a few seconds could have elapsed when the old gentleman discovered his loss and raised a desperate hue and cry . . . a few [more] seconds were lost by the messenger becoming involved in the hurry of pursuit with several well-dressed men who stood in the doorway of the bank . . . Luckily the cashier had some of the notes in his hand, or the robbery would have been more serious."[27]

Other crimes were semitragic, not least the baffling theft of almost £70,000 ($111,300) from Parr's bank in Bartholomew Lane, London in 1899. £36,000 ($57,240) was in the form of £1,000 notes and a further £11,000 ($17,490) in £500 notes. The bank manager, Mr. Disney—a name with no obvious connotations at the time—maintained a discreet silence while the police declared themselves baffled. Then £40,000 ($63,600) was returned, followed a little later by another £20,000 ($31,800). The *Daily News* reported an alleged American gang at work but also noted that, providing one did not wear a hat, robbing Parr's was "no more difficult than to slip behind a grocer's counter and steal a tin of sardines."[28] Finally, a relatively junior employee of the bank, Charles Edward Goss, was charged and confessed to the crime, though denying criminal intent. It had become, in the words of the prosecution, an "ordinary case of bank robbery," except for the sum of money involved.[29]

Goss's trial for the Parr's bank robbery draws attention to a number of crimes committed by employees at various levels. William Fowler, another junior clerk, was arrested in Plymouth as he sought to flee to Australia with money he had taken from the Aberdeen Town and County Bank in 1882.[30] The more senior George Warden was sentenced to 12 years' penal servitude for stealing securities valued at £150,000 ($238,500) from the River Plate Bank in the following year. His accomplice in crime was the seemingly respectable stockbroker John Watters who was found guilty of receiving.[31] This case provided an insight into one of the darkest areas of unrecorded crime—white-collar crime. A strong case could be made for the proposition that the most serious and fastest growing area of crime in the 19th century was that of "white collar" offenses, ranging from breaches of the factory acts or food adulteration acts to often spectacular cases of embezzlement and fraud. The shortcomings of the historical record are most striking when one considers the latter.[32] Very large sums were involved, and the subsequent suffering could extend widely. The burden of the £1,000,000 ($1,590,000) collapse of the Liberator Building Society in 1892 fell on the thousands of small investors in the company. Some 2,600 individuals were reduced to "total or semi-destitution." Over half the victims were widows and spinsters, many over 60 years of age. Financial crimes were not unique to the 19th century, but the dramatic growth of industry (and indeed of local and national government), the transformation of finance, the underdeveloped nature of accounting and auditing, and the inadequate protection offered by the law meant that the opportunities for such activities increased dramatically but with no corresponding increase in legal protection. As a consequence, large sums of money were illegally expropriated and thousands of often ordinary men and women suffered financial ruin, but only a few of the financial criminals ever appeared before the courts. The railway boom of the mid-19th century led to numerous scandals. George Hudson of York, "the railway king" was spectacularly involved in one such case, though the precise scale of his criminal activities is difficult to establish. In another case, Leopold Redpath, registrar of the Great Northern Railway, defrauded the company of some £240,000 ($381,600) over a period of 10 years. Banking frauds could also involve large sums of money. In 1849 the manager of the Rochdale saving bank, George Haworth, was found to have embezzled £71,000 ($112,890) in the previous 10 years, while in 1855 the manager and chief cashier of the Shropshire Banking Company were found to have embezzled some £200,000 ($318,000) over a 13-year period. The keeping of fictitious ledgers and books and fraudulent borrowing were major problems revealed in the banking crises of 1857 and 1866. Proof was not always easy to find. For example, the prosecution for fraud of the directors of the bank of Overend, Gurney and Company, which collapsed on May 11, 1866, failed. The law "put few obstacles in the path of white-collar criminals [and] the depressing history of fraud and chicanery detailed before parliamentary committees in 1867, 1875 and 1878 had little influence on resulting legislation."[33]

The growth of local government also opened up possibilities for financial crime as shown by the rather melodramatic tale of the seemingly respectable borough accountant of Middlesbrough in the 1860s.[34] After several successful years' employment, Thomas Cameron Close was accused of embezzling £2,500 ($3,975) from the town council. Close managed to sell his house before fleeing to Australia. Doggedly pursued by a member of the local constabulary, he was arrested in Melbourne and brought back to Middlesbrough before being tried at Leeds assizes where he was sentenced to five years' penal servitude; but not all cases led to successful prosecutions.[35]

The failure of historians to highlight white-collar crime is quite staggering. Individual losses could lead to ruin, even suicide, while in a broader sense, the loss to the nation's economy was considerable, not least given the vulnerability of new industries and new technologies to fraudulent promotions. William Pullinger, bank clerk and embezzler, was found guilty in 1860 of illegally obtaining some £260,000 ($413,400). In the same year, Henry

Mayhew estimated the total value of goods stolen by thieves in London to be a mere £71,000. Literary evidence is not always an accurate guide, but in this instance, Victorian novelists were far more perceptive than many later historians in portraying crooked financiers as the villains of the day.[36]

As the number of bank robberies increased, the number of other high-profile crimes against property decreased. Arson and machine-breaking had aroused considerable fear in the years immediately prior to Victoria's accession when criminality appeared to be linked to political protest. The destruction that could be wrought by even a small fire could be considerable. Fire-fighting resources were scarce, and in the countryside, in particular, it was difficult to get to the scene of a fire with the speed necessary to prevent widespread damage. During the early 19th century, arson became associated predominantly with the countryside and with eastern England in particular. The greatest numbers of fires were recorded in the years 1843–46 and 1849–51.[37] Although there was a diminution during the 1850s and 1860s the problem never entirely disappeared and, as in 1868, could still assume large proportions. Nor were Norfolk and Suffolk exceptional in this respect. Lincolnshire, Cambridgeshire, and Kent faced similar problems as did, to a lesser extent, counties such as Bedfordshire and Essex. Not all fires were arson attacks. Sparks from a machine or an accidentally dropped lucifer match could start a conflagration. However, as the insurance companies well knew, a significant number of the fires were started deliberately. Pyromaniacs, insurance company fraudsters, and embittered individuals pursuing private vendettas all played their part. But there was more to it than this. The frightening element for the propertied classes of rural England was the selectivity with which individuals were targeted—farmers known to pay low wages or to treat laborers badly, or poor-law officials—and the open animosity that was directed at the victims by laborers and their families who witnessed the conflagrations. What was worse, there appeared to be a wider degree of support from the community for the arsonist. The relationship is a complex one. Arson, by destroying crops and equipment as well as buildings, could destroy jobs. The arsonist was not a universally liked guerrilla fighter acting on behalf of the community in which he lived. That said, there were incidents that demonstrate varying degrees of support. Refusal to help in the attempt to put out the fire, assaults on firemen, and the cutting of hoses were very explicit actions. So too was the rejoicing and frolicking that accompanied fires in some areas.

Arson was a cheap, quick, easy, and effective weapon of vengeance and intimidation and, as such, aroused fears out of proportion to the actual incidence of the crime. Closely related and equally worrying for many 19th-century observers was the crime of animal maiming. If arson was seen as second only to murder, then animal maiming, which carried overtones of symbolic murder, also ranked highly in the catalog of detestable offenses, though not all were crimes of protest.[38] There were also fewer cases brought to court. The number of animal maiming incidents in Norfolk and Suffolk was little more than one-tenth of the number of fires in these counties between 1815 and 1870. Only in three years, 1828, 1834, and 1849, did the number of incidents reach double figures, and while the level of attacks remained roughly constant from the 1820s to the 1840s, there was a clear decline after 1850. Nonetheless, this crime, less public than arson and involving a greater degree of intimacy between criminal and victim, still shocked. The killing of sheep and the display of the head and skin before the door of the owner's farmhouse was a macabre indication of feelings. More explicit was the note left by Edmund Botwright to his employer Mr. Watling after he, Botwright, had strangled two of the farmer's bullocks.

> You bluddy farmer could not live it was not for the poore, tis them that keep you bluddy raskells alive, but their will be a slauter made amongst you verry soone. I should verry well like to hang you the same as I hanged your beastes. You bluddy rogue I will lite up a little fire for you this first opertunity.[39]

Botwright, who among other things was unhappy with the new equipment that Watling had introduced, was as good as his word; two days later one barn, three stables, and four animals were burnt. He himself was brought to court and tried in 1844. In cases such as these, few and far between as they were, social relations had reached their nadir.

Despite the attention given to crimes such as these, it was nonviolent crime against property that dominated the work of the courts. Until the early 19th century all forms of larceny, except petty larceny, which involved goods under the value of 12 d. (5 p or 8 cents), were capital offenses. Pickpocketing ceased to be a capital offense in 1808. In 1827 the distinction between grand larceny and petty larceny was abolished and a new offence of simple larceny was created, which could be punished by imprisonment or transportation. In 1832 the last two capital larcenies—larceny in a dwelling house of goods valued at more than £5 ($7.95) and larceny of horses, sheep, and cattle—disappeared from the statute book.[40] A variety of local studies clearly show that the many larceny cases were concerned with relatively humdrum, everyday items of comparatively little value. The short-term fluctuations in the recorded crime figures for nonviolent crimes against property show a correlation between economic activity and the incidence of theft. In many, though not all, cases where the stolen goods comprised small quantities of food, fuel, or clothing, or even money, there was a close link between necessity and criminality.

Detailed local case studies reveal a problem of theft in both urban and rural centers. Farms were more likely to be robbed in the countryside and shops in the towns, but the stolen property commonly took the form of food (including small animals), clothing, household utensils and money, or other valuables.[41] Grain and flour, potatoes, turnips, cabbages, and other vegetables were stolen from field and garden, often on a very small scale. Richard Hewlett, an Oxfordshire laborer, was fined for stealing vegetables but explained to the court in March 1863 that "he'd not been in work since last November, and had 6 children."[42] Hay and firewood were also commonly stolen items, while poaching was a perennial problem that persisted well into the 19th century. In urban areas the pattern was necessarily different. It was still possible to steal poultry and small domesticated animals as they grazed on open land or in urban farms, but it was more common to steal food from shops or market stalls. Butchers and bakers were the most common victims of opportunist thefts. The theft of wood for fires was also to be found, but in many towns there was the additional opportunity of "black gleaning," that is, the taking of coal from railway companies and factories. The theft of relatively small quantities of food, or of firewood and coal, again suggests a close link between crime and poverty. Many of those brought to court came from the poorly and irregularly paid ranks of the unskilled for whom life was both hard and precarious. There were cases of extreme hardship, and particularly in the severe winter of 1841–1842, several Black Country prisoners claimed hunger in mitigation. However, many thefts were carried out by people in employment who did not simply steal to assuage immediate hunger and who did not plead want in their defense.[43]

The theft of clothing was almost as common as the theft of food, accounting for between 20 and 30 percent of all stolen items. Clothes were stolen from employers, fellow lodgers, and from the washing lines of neighbors as well as from pawn shops, clothes shops, and stalls. Such thefts were easy to carry out, and the items stolen were easy to dispose of in a pub or pawn shop. Some thefts were more acquisitive than necessitous. The Black Country police knew where to go to apprehend suspects, and the courts gave severe punishments in certain cases. Both facts suggest the existence of known multiple offenders.

Theft from the person was largely opportunistic and unplanned and sometimes related to poverty. The most common situation involved men drinking in a public house. As one fell into a drunken stupor, another rifled his pockets or took unattended money. But other cases were more calculated. Stall-holders haggling with would-be customers had to be careful that their attentions were not so distracted as to overlook the accomplice stealing the petty cash. Men buying sexual favors, or simply allowing themselves to be bought drinks by women, ran the risk of being robbed and with no guarantee of a sympathetic hearing should they overcome their embarrassment and bring the case to court. And finally, there were the professional pickpockets, operating in a variety of ways, who quite clearly sought to make a living from theft.

More contentious were some forms of poaching and the taking of firewood, coal, raw materials and manufactured goods, and of tools. There was a clash of values, particularly acute during the Industrial Revolution, that gave rise to a popular perception that rightful perks were being denied and that customary rights were being criminalized. Nowhere is the social construction of crime more easily seen than in this contested area of occupational or industrial larceny.[44] The rapid expansion of outwork, which involved the putting out of expensive materials and the recruitment of new workers, increased the risks faced by entrepreneurs; but there were two other important and interrelated elements involved. The first was the growing emphasis upon individual property rights; the second, the move to a wholly monetarized wage. As employers in a growing range of industries moved away from the mixed wage, there was a decline in the practice of payment in kind. Perks, which had been an essential part of the mixed wage, were now being withdrawn. The employer now saw himself as the sole owner of all the property and felt he had the right to prosecute an employee who took that property; but one man's industrial larceny was another man's legitimate perk. This conflict can be traced back into the 18th century—the 1777 Worsted Act being the most obvious example—but as industrialization proceeded apace the number of prosecutions increased, though there were variations between industries as well as regions.

In the Black Country in the early years of Victoria's reign almost 30 percent of committals for larceny fell into this category of industrial theft. Men were prosecuted for taking iron and selling it to dealers or other workshop masters, while women, more than men, fell foul of the law for taking coal. Jeremiah Cocklin was prosecuted for stealing a sledge hammer; Benjamin Scriven for stealing iron for chain-making, which he sold to another workshop owner; Mary Ann Whatmore for taking of coal. The number of such prosecutions increased with time. In the late 1830s some 17 percent of all theft prosecutions were for industrial larceny, but by the late 1850s the figure was 36 percent. The link with industrialization seems obvious, but this pattern was not repeated in all industrializing districts. In Middlesbrough between 1835 and 1855 only 13 percent of thefts were industrial larcenies. The Ironmasters, who dominated the local economy and played an important role in the political life of the town, showed little desire to make large-scale use of the law. Bolckow & Vaughan, the largest employer in the town, paid for their own constable at the works to prevent theft but rarely prosecuted. Informal sanctions, such as dismissal and blacklisting, were effective, especially in a local economy dominated by relatively few manufacturers.[45]

The question of customary rights occurs most frequently with regard to coal-stealing, where the right of "black gleaning" was claimed. With its clear allusion to agricultural gleaning, this was a commonly mounted defense and one that seems to have had some impact as the Chairman of the Staffordshire Quarter Sessions felt it necessary to remind the Grand Jury, on more than one occasion, that "however small the value, the party was equally guilty of stealing." The authorities and local employers were aware of the strength of popular feeling and sought to dispel the belief that the taking of coal was not a criminal offense, but they were forced to come to terms with the strength of local feeling. Some colliery owners, recognizing this fact, either allowed traditional perks to be retained or offered their employees cheap, concessionary coal.

The commercialization of agriculture led to attacks on customary activities such as gleaning. A late 18th-century ruling had made it clear that there was no common law right to glean in harvest fields, but gleaning itself was not declared illegal—prosecutions had to be for trespass—and the decision did not necessarily override local custom.[46] Wood-gathering had also been the subject of parliamentary action. An Act of 1776 sought to clarify the situation regarding the right to collect snap-wood and laid down stiff penalties for those found guilty. In many parts of southern England, notably Hampshire and Wiltshire, a bitter battle raged that generated more prosecutions than for any other offense. However, the Game Laws attracted the most attention. The old Game Laws had been strengthened by legislation passed in the late 18th and early 19th centuries and were intended as much to preserve aristocratic privileges from the grasp of aspiring members of the bourgeoisie as to prosecute working-class poachers. Poaching offenses rose dramatically. In Bedfordshire they accounted for less than 4 percent of prison commitments in the first decade of the 19th century, but by the 1840s the figure had risen to 36 percent. Game Law convictions were four times greater than the national average in counties such as Bedfordshire and Buckinghamshire. The patchiness of the figures raises problems. While the very low prosecution figures in Cornwall, Cumberland, and Westmoreland might be explained in terms of nondetection, it is less easy to explain why there was so little recorded poaching in Cambridgeshire, or why the level in Norfolk was some 50 percent of that in Suffolk. The picture is further compounded by the complex motives involved. Undoubtedly there were poachers who stole for the pot. Rural poverty was a major problem in many southern and eastern counties of England, but not all poachers were responding to economic privation, let alone fighting a class war against aristocratic privilege. Many of the poachers of Bedfordshire or Hertfordshire were involved in the illegal but lucrative trade in game with the poulterers and hoteliers of London. Poaching was as much an entrepreneurial enterprise in many southern counties as sheep rustling was around the northern industrial towns.[47] Nonetheless, there were many ordinary men and women who believed that they had a God-given right to game. Joseph Arch told a parliamentary committee in 1872 that he believed hares and rabbits "were the fair property of anybody."[48] Magistrates recognized the strength of popular feeling that "all the wild things under heaven were free for all."[49] Unlike arson and animal maiming, which went into decline in the latter part of Victoria's reign, poaching remained a highly contentious area. Indeed, the 1862 Night Poaching Act exacerbated a difficult situation and effectively refueled the poaching war.[50] Such was the animosity that as gamekeepers and poachers fought—often with fatal consequences—public opinion became polarized, and even the commercial poaching gangs, whose motives were indisputible commercial, could present themselves and be seen as victims of unjust laws and tyrannical landowners.

Crimes against property dominated the work of the courts of Victoria's Britain, but over the course of her long reign, property became less insecure. Improving living standards, new values, and more efficient policing all had a part to play, but it is easy to exaggerate the extent of change, particularly in the eyes of the Victorians. The official statistics do not provide an accurate measure of change, but insofar as they provide a useful approximation of change, it is clear that there was still a considerable problem that appeared more threatening in a supposedly more civilized society. The persistence of hostility in the countryside and the widespread popular rejection of the law were shocking to many respectable Victorians. The growing use of guns in robberies—relatively few in number, it is true—also suggested that Britain was becoming more violent and less civilized. While it was true that some worrying crimes had all but disappeared (animal maiming generally and dog theft particularly are good examples), other crimes had emerged or become more common. In retrospect, the Victorian and Edwardian years saw an increase in security, but a vicious burglary in the neighborhood, an audacious robbery from a local warehouse or bank, or even a violent strike or political protest was a reminder of the thin veneer of civilized society. Further, the growth of popular and sensational journalism impacted on public perceptions. It is not implausible to argue that (as in Britain today) people accepted that they lived in a relatively secure local environment but believed that crime was rising elsewhere, even though the official statistics said otherwise.

CHAPTER FOUR

SEX AND DRUGS

B loody murders and daring robberies bulked large in the popular perception of crime, but the law and policing was about much more besides. The criminal justice system as it developed during Victoria's reign was as much (if not more) concerned with regulating the lives of ordinary citizens as it was with combating high-profile crime. The annual crime statistics, even allowing for their shortcomings, clearly reveal the tip of the iceberg that was serious crime, but it is at a local level that the contrast can best be appreciated. In Edwardian Middlesbrough, a boom town that still had something of a reputation as a frontier town, there were, on average, one or two homicides, two or three serious assaults, and one rape prosecuted each year. These figures were not out of line with the coroner's returns that showed six cases of willful murder and four of manslaughter between 1908 and 1913, though there were a further 20 open verdicts as well as 54 officially recorded suicides, not all of which were totally beyond doubt. Even if all these were in reality homicides (an unlikely assumption), the number of people charged with offenses resulting in death was no more than 20 a year. If all offenses against the person are included the figure rises to around 70. At the same time, in the same town the same number of people, about 70 a year, were prosecuted for obstruction, just over 100 for playing football in the street and some 150 for gaming. A similar number were brought to court for offenses against the Education Acts. Offenses against local bylaws ran at some 400 per annum, exceeded only by prosecutions for drunkenness, which averaged around 1,000 a year.[1] In other words, the maintenance of order and decorum in public places was a major concern of the law and the police. These were the arenas—the streets, the town squares, the public parks, and so forth—in which a growing number of people, especially young working-class men, came into contact with the criminal justice system. Further, it was contact and conflict in these arenas that gave rise to some of the greatest hostility to the police as front-line enforcers of a law that was often seen as an alien imposition. The situation was starkly summed up by Stephen Reynolds, writing in collaboration with the Woolley brothers.

> The police are charged . . . with the enforcement of a whole mass of petty enactments, which are little more than social regulations bearing almost entirely

on working-class life. At the bidding of one class, they attempt to impose a certain social discipline on another. In every direction, inside his own house as well as out, the working-man's habits and convenience are interfered with, or his poverty is penalized by the police. Whether or not he comes into collision with them is more a matter of good fortune than of law-abidingness, and he is a lucky man who does not find himself in their hands at one time or another in his life. Nor can it very well be otherwise, since the duties of the police have been made to tally with upper-class, as opposed to working-class, notions of right and wrong; so that a working man may easily render himself liable to arrest and all sorts of penalties from hard labour to the loss of a day's work, without in the least doing what is wrong in his own eyes or in the opinion of his neighbours. For that reason alone, there is hardly a man who cannot, from the working-class point of view, bring up instances of gross injustice on the part of the police towards himself or his friends or relations—to say nothing of cases that are plainly unjust from any point of view.[2]

The scale of police powers by the late 19th century was extensive and impinged on the most mundane aspects of everyday life. Boys and girls obstructing the footpaths by playing with tops or behaving noisily at ice cream vans fell foul of the police. People were prosecuted for throwing orange peel on the flags, throwing stones, flying kites, chalking on the pavement, cycling in public parks, swearing in public, disturbing the peace (even by the Salvation Army band), playing football on a Sunday, and so on, and so on. There were somewhat weightier matters concerning education and public health that led to legal action being taken, but the most contentious issues surrounded sex, drugs (overwhelmingly in the form of alcohol), and (in the absence of Victorian rock 'n' roll) penny gaffs and other forms of popular entertainment.

PROSTITUTION, SEXUAL ABUSE, AND HOMOSEXUALITY

Prostitution, the great social evil for so many Victorians, was a cause for continuing concern and yet was never made illegal. As with drinking and gambling there was a recognition that prostitution was long established and resilient and not something that could be eradicated. Again, there was no consensus of opinion on the subject, although vociferous pressure groups were highly prominent throughout Victoria's reign. The outcome was a messy, if not outright hypocritical, compromise. Restrictions were imposed on the places in which prostitution took place, those who lived off immoral earnings were increasingly criminalized, more attention was focused on public order and decorum (which meant that prostitution for the wealthy was largely untouched), and many unfortunate women were marginalized, turned into an outcast group by the unintended consequences of the very legislation that was supposed to help them.

It is impossible to speak precisely about the numbers of women involved in prostitution in Victorian and Edwardian Britain. The figures that were bandied about were, at best, honest "guestimates"; at worst, they were propagandistic exaggerations intended to force reluctant authorities into action. Understanding was also confused by the habit of many Victorian social observers, including those not unsympathetic to the realities of working-class life, such as Henry Mayhew, to describe cohabiting but unmarried women as prostitutes. The situation was further compounded by the fact that prostitution was a complex and diverse trade that stretched from the apparent luxury of the courtesans, who were to be found in royal and aristocratic circles, to the undoubted squalor of those who provided a service (a "fourpenny touch" or a "knee trembler") in the back streets of Whitechapel, by the docks, "over the border" in Middlesbrough, or in the lanes surrounding various military establishments. It was also a very mobile occupation in two important ways. First, for reasons to do with age, the onset of disease, and sheer luck, a working woman's fortune could change literally overnight. Second, such was the insecurity of life for many working-class women that there was a short- or medium-term movement in and out of prostitution, particularly in the earlier years of Victoria's reign.[3] And this leads to a further general point: precisely because of the complexity of the trade in sex, contemporary explanations couched in terms of aristocratic seduction or alien-run trafficking in women misrepresent the motives that led the vast majority of women to become prostitutes and fundamentally distort our understanding of this aspect of 19th-century life.

Attitudes toward prostitution fluctuated over time. The early years of Victoria's reign coincided with a resurgence of antivice sentiment. The sensational findings of Dr. Michael Ryan relating to London—"not less than 80,000 prostitutes exist . . . a great proportion of whom are of tender years"— were reinforced by the somewhat more temperate findings regarding Edinburgh by another medical man, William Tait.[4] The growth of population and its concentration into burgeoning towns and cities ensured that the presence of prostitutes in public places was increasingly visible. Parliament considered a bill to suppress brothels, introduced by the Bishop of Exeter in 1844, but rejected it; however, a bill to deal with "the practices of entrapping, by unfair arts, young and unsuspecting females," introduced by the evangelical Bishop of Oxford, finally succeeded in 1849. If public opinion was not wholly sympathetic to the calls of moral reformers, the police and magistrates, for the most part, took a relaxed view, considering prostitution as a public order issue rather than a matter of morality.[5] Existing legislation dealing with either drunken behavior in public or vagrancy was commonly used against street prostitutes. Attitudes hardened in the 1850s, not least because of the panic surrounding sexually transmitted diseases that followed the revelations about the disease-ridden state of the armed forces during the

Prostitutes in the Haymarket, c. 1860. The Haymarket, especially outside the Theatre Royal, was notorious for night-time prostitution; Regent Street was the day-time equivalent. (Courtesy Mary Evans Picture Library)

Crimean War, where it was estimated that one in three cases of sickness were due to syphilis or gonorrhea. Prostitution was reconceptualized, particularly in the writings of William Acton, as a question of public health.[6] The shift in emphasis had two important consequences for workers in the sex trade. First, more generally, the antiprostitute discourse became distinctly harsher. These women were increasingly presented as the seducers of young men, the corrupters of morals, and the carriers of disease.[7] Second, and more specific, the Contagious Diseases Acts of the 1860s heightened the sense of stigma and brought state regulation to certain aspects of prostitution.[8] It is difficult to determine the extent to which working-class sympathy for prostitutes was eroded by the general shift in attitude, which was largely a middle- and upper-class phenomenon, or by the workings of the Contagious Diseases Acts. However, there were increasing risks to respectable reputations for those ordinary men who came to the assistance of working women (or other women) who fell foul of the suspicions of those mature Metropolitan policemen who were selected to enforce this legislation. There was a striking change in imagery. The women were dehumanized as they became "Curragh wrens" or "Aldershot bushrangers," allegedly living like rabbits in warrens. The upshot was the creation of an outcast group, more isolated and more vulnerable than had previously been the case.[9] The impact of the Contagious Diseases

Acts was geographically restricted, but in cities such as York, untouched by the Acts, a similar process of marginalization was in process.[10] The gap between prostitutes and their wider communities was further increased by later legislation, such as the Industrial Schools Amendment Act of 1885 and especially the Criminal Law Amendment Act of the same year. By the late 19th century the modern model of prostitution, with a pimp running a number of women, was established. The reasons for this are complex and include wider social and economic changes that had a supply-side impact, but as Walkowitz has so forcefully argued, "legal repression" played a key role in this transformation.[11]

The enthusiasm with which some policemen enforced the Contagious Diseases Acts, highlighted in the brave campaign of Josephine Butler and her supporters, contrasts with the more general police approach to prostitution.[12] Butler came from a privileged background. For a lady to discuss prostitution was shocking; to do so in public was scandalous. She challenged the conventional view of prostitutes as "fallen women" and saw them as victims of male exploitation. Her intervention in political campaigning led to vitriolic verbal abuse and physical attacks. Stones were thrown through the windows of hotels at which she stayed and on one occasion the room in which she was speaking was set on fire. For the most part, prostitution was not seen as a major priority for the police. Further, interventions could be counterproductive, and the police, particularly those in the lower ranks, were all too aware of the need to maintain a *modus vivendi* with the communities they policed. In London, where the existence of large-scale and highly visible prostitution was a recurring source of concern, policing practices fluctuated over the years and were largely the outcome of a four-handed tug-of-war between outside pressure groups, such as the Society for the Suppression of Vice, magistrates, officials at the Home Office, and the Metropolitan Police Commissioners.[13] Despite growing anxiety with the scale of blatant prostitution, especially in places such as the Haymarket or Cremorne Gardens, and the impact of the 1869 Beerhouse Act, which had the unintended consequence of increasing street prostitution as disreputable beerhouses were closed down, commissioners Mayne and Henderson were very reluctant allies in the fight against vice.[14] The White Slave Trade panic of the 1880s led to greater police action, but this came to an abrupt end when a respectable dressmaker, Elizabeth Cass, was arrested and charged with soliciting even though there had been no complaint made. There were concerns not simply that the police abused their powers over prostitutes but also arrested respectable women. Commissioner Warren, despite his known dislike of prostitution, instructed the men of the Met to proceed with extreme caution. There were limits beyond which the police could not go without public support. The lesson had to be learned again in the early 20th century. Another crusade against prostitution, driven by the social purists on the London County Council, resulted in some successes, such as the closure of the Empire, Leicester Square in 1894.[15] Increased police zeal also resulted in the arrest of Madame Eva d'Angely in 1906. A respectable married woman, d'Angely was seen as a victim of improper police action. The fact that it was "well known" that some policemen accepted bribes, or favors in kind, from known prostitutes added to the controversy surrounding the case.[16] Given these pressures and their attendant dangers, policing of prostitution was pragmatic, a compromise that saw a degree of unofficial regulation.

Tensions were not confined to the capital. Indeed, the worst conflict came in Liverpool in 1890 when Watch Committee issued instructions to "proceed . . . by way of prosecution . . . against all brothels at present known to the police without any delay."[17] The Head Constable argued for a discretionary approach—the stance adopted for several years—but was forced to comply. Interestingly in this case, the outcry against the increase in police prosecutions was based largely on the unintended consequences of this crusade and their economic consequences. "[T]he raids on immoral houses only serve to increase the social evil by distributing it over a wider area and that the raiding of such districts . . . disorganises business and will prove financially disastrous to shopkeepers."[18]

Other cities attempted to find an alternative between state regulation (the Contagious Diseases Acts) and an essentially laissez-faire approach that focused on the criminal consequences of prostitution. In Glasgow from the 1870s (and Edinburgh a decade later) the approach was a combination of repression (via the police) and reform (via Lock Hospitals and Magdalene Institutions) that was intended to effect "the moral clearance of the streets."[19] Brothels and soliciting were subject to repressive policing that fell heaviest on working-class districts. Despite the claims made by advocates of the Glasgow "solution," change was less dramatic. Brothels were closed down (but opened elsewhere), while prostitutes either moved out as well, or, if they stayed, became less blatant in plying their trade. Further, the effect of the policy was to create a somewhat smaller but hardened core of professional prostitutes, not dissimilar to sex workers elsewhere in Britain.

Similar problems surrounded attempts to suppress brothels via the 1885 Criminal Law Amendment Act, which had been passed in the wake of a panic about the White Slave Trade that owed much to the sensationalist journalism of W. T. Stead and the publication of "The Maiden Tribute of Modern Babylon" in the *Pall Mall Gazette*. In practice the act was counterproductive. Brothels were driven underground—there was a proliferation of dubious massage, manicure, and chiropody parlors—prostitution was further professionalized, pimps and bullies became more common and working women placed in greater danger. And, to add insult to injury, the White Slave Trade was largely fictitious and had grown out of a general fear of racial degeneration and a more specific anti-Semitism aimed at the East European refugees who had come to London in particular following pogroms in Russia.[20]

The early years of the 20th century saw a shift in perception that reflected a wider worry about the problem of the feeble-minded in Britain. Prostitutes were increasingly described as "moral imbeciles," feeble-minded creatures incapable of protecting themselves. Prey to sexually predatory males, the myth of the prostitute-as-victim was reconstructed to chime with the anxieties of Edwardian Britain. As a result many young women who had the misfortune to become pregnant at an early age found themselves incarcerated for life in huge mental institutions.[21]

Victoria's reign saw the growing professionalization of prostitution as the result of a variety of socioeconomic and legal changes, but one thing remained unchanged: given male demand for commercial sex, prostitution remained a real option, particularly for the poor. However, whereas at the start of Victoria's reign it was not simply possible but quite common for women to move into and out of prostitution, by the end of her reign this was much less the case. The poor and vulnerable were more likely to be trapped in a lifestyle that set them apart from working-class (let alone middle-class) society and increased their dependence upon the men who ran the trade. And they were not likely to receive a sympathetic response from the police as two unusual cases in autumn 1895 reveal. An Oxford professor of anatomy, Edwin Lankester was charged with disorderly behavior and resisting the police on October 7 and found guilty of obstruction. Lankester did not let matters rest and wrote to *The Times*, complaining both of the treatment he received but also of the brutality of the police in arresting a prostitute. A month later George Alexander, manager of the St. James's Theatre, was involved in a similar incident.[22] But these were exceptions, and even Lankester's demand for an inquiry led to nothing. Here again, the practice of magistrates in accepting unquestioningly the evidence of a policeman led to popular resentment.

The late Victorian years saw an increase in prosecution for sexual offenses, though this did not necessarily mean that there was a significant and real shift in actual behavior. Changing attitudes toward childhood and redefinitions of "acceptable" masculinity led to condemnation of behavior that had once been acceptable and to demands for new codes of (predominantly male) behavior toward infants and young children, particularly young girls. As well as seeking to change patterns of behavior, reforming groups, such as the National Society for the Prevention of Cruelty to Children or the National Vigilance Society, sought changes in the law as part of their campaign. There were a number of spectacular scandals associated with baby farming (or "angel making" as it was known in France), which led to the passing of the Infant Life Preservation Act in 1872. The late 19th century saw a number of high-profile executions of women found guilty of mass child murder. Glasgow-born Jessie King was executed in Edinburgh in 1889 for killing two children; Rhonda

Willis in Cardiff in 1907; but the most scandalous were the Finchley Baby Farmers, Amelia Sach and Annie Walker, executed in 1903.[23]

From the 1860s onward there was a more general awareness of the sexual abuse of children, though there was a growing percentage of young victims in the late Victorian years.[24] The age of female consent was raised to 13 (from 12) in 1875 and again to 16 a decade later, the latter being a compromise between reformers who advocated 21 and those who saw no need for further change. The 1885 Criminal Law Amendment Act also made carnal knowledge of a girl aged between 13 and 16 a misdemeanor and a felony if the girl was less than 13 years of age.[25] Finally, incest was made a criminal offense in 1908. The changes in the law in themselves made illegal actions that previously had been legal, but the heightened awareness, if not outright moral panic of the mid-1880s, led to a greater determination to prosecute actions that were already illegal. Although the absolute numbers of prosecutions increased, they were still relatively few in number. Crimes committed within the family were hidden by a conspiracy of silence. The myth of "stranger danger," which has distorted the understanding and treatment of child abuse, has its roots in these years, but even some stranger danger crimes did not reach the courts and were dealt with informally by community sanctions, including severe physical chastisement.

Sexual abuse was seen to be the action of brutes and savages; sexual abusers were seen to come from the unreconstructed residuum of Victorian society. Considerations of class, gender, and respectability had an impact on the prosecuting of sexual offenses. Unskilled, uneducated working-class men (99% of all defendants were male) were more likely to be prosecuted and found guilty of sexual abuse. Respectable working-class men, who could demonstrate they were good fathers and husbands, were less likely to be found guilty than dangerous strangers, while middle-class offending was almost inconceivable: the "implausibility of a vicar committing such abominable acts, especially having come from a funeral" led to the dismissal of a case by a London magistrate in 1895.[26]

The Labouchère amendment, the 1899 Vagrancy Act, and the 1912 Criminal Law Amendment Act were important elements in the creation of a second outcast group—homosexual men.[27] Homosexual acts had been criminalized for centuries. The death penalty for buggery was tacitly abandoned from the mid-1830s but was not formally abolished until 1861 in England and Wales and 1889 in Scotland. The Labouchère amendment was part of a wider series of homophobic panics in the 1880s and 1890s, of which the trials of Oscar Wilde were the culmination. These panics were driven by concerns for racial degeneration and imperial decline, but also reflected a more general crisis of masculinity and fears for Victorian patriarchy. The impact of the "blackmailer's charter," as the Labouchère amendment came to be known, is difficult to judge. Relatively few men were brought to trial, but for those who were the result was public humiliation, if not worse; for those who were not there was the ever-present threat of prosecution and condemnation.[28] The high-profile trials of Oscar Wilde, which created the stereotype of the effete, dandified homosexual, may well have had the unintended consequence of allowing gay men—the vast majority of whom did not live flamboyant lives—to escape detection and prosecution.

DRINK AND DRUGS

The Victorians, like later generations, struggled with the philosophical and practical problems involved with the use (and misuse) of drugs. The use of mind-altering and addictive drugs (with a range of physical consequences as well) had a very long history and was deeply embedded in a wide range of sociocultural activities to be found in all classes of society. Many of the issues that the Victorians wrestled with have a very contemporary ring to them. Did the state have a right or responsibility to intervene in individual activities where those activities might (and did) have a harmful effect on the individual? Should the state intervene when the actions of individuals brought harm to society at large, for example, in the form of antisocial or criminal behavior? Should government take cognizance of other interests—the well-being and efficiency of the economy; or the ability to defend the nation and its imperial interests? If intervention were justified, what limits should be imposed? Did the answer lie in prohibition, or should encouragement be given to "responsible" usage? Should restrictions be placed on private establishments as well as public places? If yes, could and should the police be able to enter a private home if they suspected drunkenness? And what of the practicalities? What were the political and economic costs to the government of restricting the trade in different drugs? Could the police enforce legislation? Unsurprisingly, there was no consensus among Victorians on these (and other related) questions, and the outcome was a series of compromises of varying degrees of effectiveness.

As part of the redefinition of masculinity that took place during Victoria's reign, there was a growing emphasis on self-control and rational behavior.[29] This involved, among other things, a distancing from an earlier masculinity in which heavy drinking was highly prized. Drunkenness was associated with brutishness and a variety of unacceptable forms of behavior, and it was a major factor in the incidence of crime and immorality. James Greenwood was not alone in seeing drink as "the crowning curse" that ruined so many working-class lives.[30] Many Victorian social reformers (not all of middle-class origin) saw alcohol to be at the root of the myriad problems of working-class society and sought to curb or even eradicate its consumption. The forces opposing such reformers were considerable. Drink was a deep-rooted and ubiquitous element in popular culture; there were powerful commercial interests, brewers obviously but also important elements of the agricultural interest, with a direct and indirect interest in the liquor trade. Government also benefited, and not just in terms of the revenue it raised from drink.[31] But there was also a principle at stake. Some politicians, Liberal radicals and, later, Labor, believed the state had a responsibility at least "to make virtue easy and . . . vice difficult," as T.H. Green, the Oxford University philosopher and Liberal activist, put it. Others, and not simply doctrinaire free-marketers, emphasized the importance of educational and social reform and warned against the dangers of restricting individual liberty. The Whig bishop William Connor Magee, no supporter of free trade in alcohol, was unequivocal that "[i]t would be better that England should be free than that England should be compulsorily sober. I would distinctly prefer freedom to sobriety, because with freedom we might attain sobriety; but in the other alternative we should eventually lose both freedom and sobriety."[32]

Despite pressures from ardent reformers, there was never an attempt to make alcohol consumption illegal. Rather, governments (and local authorities) concerned themselves more with where and how alcohol was sold and consumed. Thus were constructed the hypothetical figures of the "responsible landlord" and the "responsible drinker." Various acts were passed restricting the opening hours of beerhouses and public houses from the 1830s onward, of which probably the most important were the Licensing Acts of 1872 and 1874. Enforcement fell upon the not always willing shoulders of the police. Responses varied considerably across the country, but there were recurrent complaints about police indifference, or worse acceptance of bribes, particularly in the large cities. Few cases of bribery and corruption were actually proved—though this in itself does not mean that such activities did not go on—and, despite some real difficulties in enforcing the legislation (how did one identify a drunk in a crowded bar of drinkers?), the police and local magistrates did a reasonable job in weeding out those badly run public houses and clubs where the law was most blatantly being broken.

The individual "abuser" of alcohol was also targeted. The 1872 Act for the first time made it an offense to be drunk on the highway or in a public place, though drunk and riotous behavior was already an offense under the Town Police Clauses Act. The zeal with which such legislation was enforced depended very much on local circumstances, such as the composition of the local watch committee, the attitudes of local magistrates, as well as the priorities of a chief constable, any one of which could influence the level of local police activity. It would be unwise indeed to assume that changes in the statistics relating to drunkenness reflect actual changes in the incidence of inebriation. For the most part the police were reluctant enforcers of such moral laws. Many constables had little sympathy with restrictions on alcohol and were well aware of the practical difficulties. At its simplest there were too many drunks, too few policemen and too little cell space. Marriot's *A Constable's Duty and How to Do It* (first published in 1893) gave the following unambiguous advice.

> A person found drunk on any highway or public place, but going quietly about his business, should not be interfered with or summoned; but a person found drunk and incapable of taking care of himself may be apprehended, provided the offender is unknown to the constable, but if he is known it is best to see him home and report the case.[33]

Probably more important consideration for the ordinary policeman was the awareness of the very real dangers of intervening with drunks. Marriot's advice here was equally clear in advocating caution. "Although the [1872] Act gives a constable power to apprehend offenders [who are drunk and disorderly in the highway or a public place] *it is absolutely necessary for discretion to be used.*"[34]

Not all constables used their discretion well, others were more zealous in upholding the law, and not all drunks wanted to be escorted home. A perusal of the local press makes abundantly clear that closing time was a fraught period when a large number of assaults upon police officers were inflicted by drunks, acting on their own or in gangs. One such case was reported from Clerkenwell, London in 1843 under the heading: "Brutal Assault on a Police Constable." From one perspective it was a straightforward story. "[A]n immense mob of men and women, all Irish . . . were creating a great disturbance" when the unfortunate constables Lawrence and Marsh tried to arrest a man who had struck out at them on being asked to move on. In the "general rush . . . made by the mob," Lawrence was struck on the back of the head by a large stone that fractured his skull.[35] Despite the "brutality of the prisoner in which he was actively aided by his companions [and] frequent attempts at rescue . . . made by the mob," P. C. Marsh and an unnamed colleague succeeded in "dragging their prisoner through the crowd and conveying him to the station house." The disparity between the violence of the large mob and the single- (or double-) handed success of the police suggests an alternative reading in which a boisterous group of Irish people, on their way home from the pub after a good night out, met two overzealous policemen who did not exercise discretion and provoked a violent response. The truth of this incident (whatever it might be) will never be known, but it highlights the problem of determining when one person's legitimate good night out becomes a nuisance to others. Tensions between the police and the working classes were further exacerbated when cases were brought to court. Police evidence that an individual was drunk and disorderly nearly always resulted in conviction. But there was a persistent belief that many constables, singly or together, abused their standing in court.

The late 19th century also saw a legal assault on the habitual drunkard. Many of these were women, which gave an extra twist to a more general debate about physical and moral degeneration. In practical terms little was achieved. The legislation was flawed and difficult for the police to implement, even when magistrates were willing to use it, and the regimes of the inebriate reformatories failed to tackle the root causes of the problem.[36] Nonetheless, though for other reasons, the consumption of alcohol declined in the last quarter of the 19th century, and the liquor trade was better regulated than it had been when Victoria first came to the throne. Equally important, by the early 20th century drink was no longer seen as the crowning curse.

Alcohol, being the most widely used drug, was the most problematic one with which Victorian authorities had to deal, and not least because of the complex social, economic, and political milieu associated with it, there emerged a compromise, a wavering middle way between the extremes of free trade and prohibition. Sales of this (legal) drug were controlled and taxed and the excessive behavior of its users punished by law. It was not the only problem drug of the period. In an age in which we supposedly wage war on drugs such as heroin, cocaine, and cannabis, it is easy to overlook the fact that for much of the 19th century such substances were legally consumed and attracted little attention or concern. Opium was widely viewed as a medicine. Its derivatives, notably laudanum, were praised in medical books of the day. William Gladstone and Florence Nightingale were both users. Poppy-head tea was a time-honored folk remedy, especially in the Fens of eastern England, but it also appeared in such products as *Hemmings' Syrup of Poppies* or *Battley's Sedative Solution*. Opium was particularly valued for its soothing effects on children. Victorian mothers could buy *Street's Infant's Quietness* and, best known of all, *Godfrey's Cordial*. The wholesale and retail drug trade was not subject to legislative control until the 1868 Pharmacy Act, reflecting more a public health concern with adulteration and overdosing. The mid-century Opium Wars (in which Britain fought for free trade in the substance, let it not be forgotten) brought a new image with lurid tales of opium slavery among the Chinese, but it was only in the early 20th century that a fundamental shift in perception took place. This paved the way for the criminalization of opium and opium derivatives, including heroin, which had been seen as a miracle drug ("a hero among cough remedies" according to the publicity of its manufacturers, the German pharmaceuticals company, Bayer) in the late 1890s. It was in these years that opium became almost exclusively identified with the Yellow Peril. Lurid and misleading accounts of Chinatowns with their opium dens and drug fiends can be found in Dickens (*The Mystery of Edwin Drood*) and Conan Doyle (*The Man with the Twisted Lip*), but it was the social inquirers and East-end missionaries of the 1870s and 1880s who first drew attention to a problem that could be linked to wider anxieties of the day. The enervating effect of opium, which had so ruined the once great

Chinese empire, could (or so it was feared) accelerate the imperial decline that was besetting late Victorian Britain. The racial stereotyping—"oriental cunning and cruelty," coexisting with "dazed and helpless addicts jabbering in an incoherent manner"—resulted in opium being transformed into an alien and threatening substance.

Although there were only local initiatives on opium consumption in Britain before 1914, the tide of opinion was beginning to turn.[37] The desire to curb the international trade in drugs was the subject of important meetings in Shanghai (1909) and the Hague (1911–1912, 1913, and 1914) but it was World War I that was to catalyze change, leading to the 1920 Dangerous Drugs Act.[38]

Cannabis, though reputedly used by the Queen herself, was largely unknown in 19th-century Britain. The official view was benign, particularly

An East End Opium Den, 1870. The illustration by Gustave Doré is from G. Doré & B. Jerrold, *London: A Pilgrimage*. (Courtesy Mary Evans Picture Library)

after the large-scale Royal Commission of 1893–1894 found no link between the consumption of Indian hemp and crime and noted its medicinal qualities.[39] Again, outside events drove a more punitive agenda. The early 20th century witnessed an international panic over cannabis, and the campaign for control was led by countries such as Egypt. Similarly, there was limited knowledge and use of cocaine in Britain for much of the 19th century. The 1880s saw the "discovery" of cocaine, not least thanks to the work of Freud. It became something of a pharmaceutical phenomenon, not least because of its importance as a local anesthetic, but it also became an important element in patent medicines such as Vin Mariani and Coca Cola (and its imitators Koka Nola, Celery Cola, Rocco Cola, and Dope Cola!). In the literary world both Dr. Jekyll and Sherlock Holmes used cocaine, but there was no great concern about potential damage. In contrast, America saw a "coke fiend" panic in the 1900s, associated with young men returning from the Spanish-American War, but also the "coke-crazed nigger" who allegedly threatened rapine and murder in the southern states. The panic spread to wartime Britain. As with opium and cannabis, cocaine was proscribed under the 1920 Act.

Recreational and quasi-medical uses of drugs were to be found in many sections of prewar British society. Attitudes were not constant, and an image of the enervated and depraved drug-taker was becoming more common and fed into a wider debate about imperial decline. Insofar as there was a drugs scene, it was small and a largely aristocratic and upper-middle-class activity, with only limited links to a demi-monde of crime. This perhaps as much as any other single factor explains the relative calm with which it was treated by the authorities. But not all commentators were so relaxed. In an observation that has considerable relevance today, an anonymous contributor to *Blackwood's Magazine* in 1901 commented thus on the availability of opium: "in their failure to legalize the trade, all parties conspired to foster its attendant evils. That," he continued, "is abundantly clear to us now."[40] There were, however, more serious threats, not least gambling, to preoccupy reformers and legislators in prewar Britain.

LEISURE ACTIVITIES AND GAMBLING

There was an attempt, never consistent and not always concerted, to create a new leisure ethic to go alongside the work ethic of industrializing Britain, and the class bias of much of this activity, including legislation and its enforcement, was clear at the time. Working-class leisure, particularly if left unregulated, could easily lead to laziness and crime—the devil, after all, made work for idle hands! Most popular leisure activities, from the traditional "Statty" (statute) fairs that continued to flourish in the early years of Victoria's reign, to the theaters, music halls, and penny gaffs of her later years, were associated with heavy consumption of alcohol, the suspension of the normal constraints and codes of "respectable" behavior. As such in the eyes of many middle- and upper-class Victorians, these activities posed a threat that had to be met in a variety of ways—through religion and education but also through the force of the law. However, at the same time these activities were much prized by ordinary men and women and as such to be defended from an onslaught that threatened to criminalize their leisure activities.

Much respectable fear centered on the threat to public order. The crowds that so delighted Dickens at Greenwich Fair scared many of his contemporaries. The huge crowds that assembled for Shrove Tuesday football matches or to celebrate Guy Fawke's Night threatened both person and property in those towns and cities that still enjoyed such traditional activities. Equally, large crowds attending the new sporting activities, association football and rugby football in particular, could lead to disturbances that suggested traditional intervillage rivalries had been reinvigorated and that a new barbarism was developing on the terraces.

A second concern was with immorality and crime. The penny gaffs that so shocked Mayhew in the mid-19th century appeared to be scenes of unlicensed debauchery that corrupted boys and girls of often tender years and even young mothers with babes in arms. The music halls, particularly in places such as Hoxton, that shocked Mrs. Ormiston Chant a generation later were scarcely any better.[41] But—and not for the first or last time—not all Victorians shared these concerns. Many were indifferent, especially if they were not disturbed in their immediate neighborhood. Others, entrepreneurs of leisure, had a vested interest in the continuation of these various leisure activities. Yet others disapproved but did not feel it appropriate for government and the law to interfere. Nonetheless, popular leisure activities were increasingly subject to legal constraint. The resilience with which certain customary activities were defended (for example, the bull running at Stamford, Nuneaton folk-football, or the Guy Fawkes celebrations in Guildford) shows a determination to resist reform in general and the police in particular. And where there was failure, there was often a sense of real loss. John Binns, writing in 1882 about Batley in the West Riding of Yorkshire summed up the feelings of many. He noted how

the first policeman came into our midst, to plant the thin edge of the wedge which was to revolutionize our manners and customs . . . we have lost all traces of mummery; all traces of Lee Fair . . . most of our Mischief Night; as nearly all the peace eggers; for what are left of the latter are of another mould to those of my childhood days . . . If mummers were to be seen upon the street now, the police would interfere. I put a deal of this severance from ourselves of old customs down to the advent of the policeman in uniform.[42]

Not all lamented the passing of the old. Indeed, many traditional activities were abandoned from within rather than suppressed from without. However, the key point is that plebeian leisure, old or new, was a contentious area. Furthermore, precisely because so many people were involved, the constraining and criminalizing of leisure was one of the most commonly felt ways in which the criminal justice system impinged upon ordinary day-to-day life.

GAMBLING

Gambling, like drinking, was a well-established feature of British life irrespective of class. Likewise, concerns with the detrimental effects of gambling, especially on the lower classes, were not unique to the Victorians. However, from the 1880 onwards there was a growing worry about this "grave national concern," in Churchill's words. Gambling was seen to undermine both the individual and the family, to provide a further encouragement to crime, and to impair economic efficiency at a time of growing competition. As with the drink question, there was no consensus of opinion, and unsurprisingly, the laws relating to gambling were selective, flawed, and hypocritical. Their enforcement was patchy, many policemen of all ranks had little sympathy with the legislation, but the very existence and implementation of these laws added to the hostility many working-class men and women felt toward their superiors and their enforcers in blue.

Racecourses continued to be a haven for bookmakers and punters at a time when there was a clamp down on betting at football matches and even cycling events. Gambling at racecourses was not affected by the 1853 Betting Houses Act, which in London at least, had the effect of driving betting and bookmakers onto the streets. The 1872 Act had a similar effect as gaming and betting in public houses was made illegal. Prosecutions for street gambling could be made under the 1873 Vagrant Act and other legislation dealing with obstruction. In contrast, gentlemen's clubs, whose primary purpose (technically, at least) was not gambling, could provide a haven for upper- and middle-class gamblers. There were many bogus clubs, and Robert Anderson, assistant commissioner of the Metropolitan police, tried to restrict them. It is a measure of the difficulties facing him that he had to resort to a piece of 16th-century legislation (the Unlawful Games Act of 1541) and, despite a series of raids in the 1890s and 1900s, effected few prosecutions. Anderson was the exception; few, if any, other officers shared his zeal. But there was growing pressure to deal with the problem of street gambling, which meant working-class gambling. The 1906 Street Betting Act was a blatant piece of class legislation. *Gambling* per se was criminalized, and anyone making a wager in the street was liable to prosecution with severe penalties, rising to £50 ($80) or six months' hard labor for a third conviction. Police powers were increased. They could arrest without warrant anyone loitering in the street "for the purpose of betting or paying or receiving money in respect of bets." But this increased tensions on the street and led to increasing allegations of subterfuge and entrapment as well as of bribery and corruption. In fact, police enforcement varied considerably. In Manchester there was a concerted attempt to implement the act; in Leeds and Middlesbrough it was largely a pretense. Many policemen disliked enforcing this law. As one told Lady Bell: "I feel ashamed sometimes to think what I spend my time in doing and what I am after. I am neglecting my other duties."[43] There emerged a tacit understanding between police and street gamblers that enabled the former to carry out raids but with sufficient forewarning for the latter to escape! As a chief constable of one northern industrial town ruefully noted, "though bookmakers have practically ceased to frequent the streets, there is no doubt that the practice of betting is still carried on to a considerable extent, and many are the devices resorted to for the purpose of escaping detection by the police."[44]

But what he did not note was the sense of alienation created by police action. Robert Roberts, commenting on his experiences in another northern industrial town, was quite clear.

> And in the heart of the group [of older teenagers], shielded by lounging bodies, a small card school would sit contentedly gambling for halfpence. Suddenly one hears a shriek of warning. The gang bursts into a scatter of flying figures. From nowhere gallop a couple of "rozzers," cuffing, hacking, punching, sweeping youngsters into the wall with a swing of heavy folded capes. The street empties, doors bang. Breathing heavily the Law retires bearing off perhaps a "hooligan" or two to be made an example of. The club is over for another night, leaving its young members with a fear and hatred of the police that in some perfectly law-abiding citizens lasted through life and helped colour the attitude of a whole working-class generation towards civil authority.[45]

Official concern with gambling was heightened by its association with police corruption. The high-profile Turf Fraud trial of five senior Met detectives in 1877 for accepting bribes and suppressing evidence was the tip of the iceberg; nor was it confined to London. Policemen from Merthyr to Middlesbrough were disciplined and dismissed for too close acquaintance with the gambling fraternity. The fact that the police who connived with some criminals prosecuted ordinary working-class men for minor gambling offenses that were not popularly seen as crimes added to the frustration and anger at the hypocrisy and selectivity of the law and its enforcement.

CONCLUSION

This and the preceding two chapters have been necessarily selective; for example, there has been no detailed discussion of white-collar crime nor of regulatory offenses. These chapters have two aims: first, to provide an insight into the nature of the various crimes that were brought to trial in Victorian and Edwardian Britain; and second, to give an indication of how these crimes were understood and "experienced" at the time. The spectacular murders and robberies were experienced indirectly, by all but a very few. They were refracted through the cultural constructions of the press or other writings, fictional as much as nonfictional. Often the coverage tells more about wider anxieties in society at large than about the intrinsic qualities of the crimes themselves. Indirect experience also applied but to a lesser degree to the more routine assaults and thefts, which by the end of Victoria's reign were dealt with summarily. But there was a greater immediacy about these crimes. These were mundane crimes that took place in every neighborhood, every week of the year. They were the stuff of local gossip as much as of press reportage. There were more perpetrators, more victims, and more family and friends to recount the tales, but sadly, they have left but little in the way of historical record. For most Victorians and Edwardians, knowledge and direct experience of crime was overwhelmingly concerned with petty offenses, so often neglected by later historians for being too insignificant or too unexciting. Yet through these unfashionable offenses many people had direct experience of and interaction with the criminal justice system and its various agents, whether as complainants about unacceptable noise and antisocial behavior on the streets of their town or village, or as recipients of a policeman's cuff about the ears, or of a summons to appear in court for scrumping apples, swimming naked, or begging. Occasionally, as in the writing of Robert Roberts or the Woolley brothers, or the oral histories collected by historians such as Stephen Humphries, we get a direct "view from below" that puts the hooligans of the popular press into a different perspective.

PART II

EXPLAINING THE CRIMINAL

CHAPTER FIVE

THE MALEVOLENT MALE

Thomas Plint, reflecting on the state of crime in the mid-19th century, highlighted the rapid urbanization that had taken place in Britain, particularly in the two previous decades and the "larger growth of the criminal or dangerous classes [that included] not only the professional thief or burglar, but the whole rabble of the vagrant and dissolute classes, who labor by fits, and eke out subsistence by pilfering, and who are ever on the verge of a more serious breach of the laws."[1] Writing some 50 years later, Major Arthur Griffiths, an ex-soldier and prison inspector, a man with considerable experience of the prison system, located the essence of the criminality of the country "in that group of habitual criminals, the outlaws, overt and undisguised against society . . . who persistently defy the law and refuse to abide by the rules and regulations that society makes, and which are respected by honest people."[2]

The notion of an alien "other" comprising a group of people "who wage such ceaseless warfare" against society was a continuing theme throughout Victoria's reign. Intimately linked to this was the belief that crime was the product of a moral decline that could start with the failure to listen to parental advice or to attend church on the Sabbath but then led inexorably through minor to serious crimes and, finally, the gallows—a theme that was echoed in numerous popular ballads and broadsheets.[3]

Numerous variations were played upon it, but at their core was the comforting (if not wholly accurate) belief that there was a minority of law-breaking "them" that threatened but was distinct from the majority of law-abiding "us." There was nothing new in this way of thinking. Eighteenth-century writers, couching their analyses in the language of the "body politic," characterized crime and criminals in terms of life-threatening diseases that had to be cut out by the sword of justice.[4] Victorian social commentators, however, went to considerable lengths to dissect and classify the component parts of this alien group and used the new language of class and conflict to explain to their readers the threat that lurked in the dark quarters of the burgeoning towns and cities.

Probably the best known account of the criminal class is fictional. In *Oliver Twist* Dickens described a corrupted and corrupting nether world that was inhabited by a variety of threatening characters, notably Bill Sikes, the Artful Dodger, Nancy, and above all, Fagin. Their environment was characterized by dirt and disorder. "Crazy wooden galleries common to half a dozen houses, with holes from which to look upon the slime beneath . . . rooms so small, so filthy, so confined, that the air would seem too tainted even for the dirt and squalor which they shelter . . . dirt-besmeared walls and decaying foundations; every repulsive lineament of poverty, every loathsome indication of filth, rot and garbage; all these ornament the banks of Folly Ditch."[5]

Of all the criminals that Oliver meets, Nancy is the most sympathetically portrayed as "there was something of the woman's original nature left in her still," but her life had been squandered "in the streets and among the most noisome of the stews [brothels] and dens of London" and she was "adept . . . in all the arts of cunning and dissimulation."[6] In comparison her partner and partner in crime, Bill Sikes, has no redeeming characteristics. A house-breaker, a threatening figure of considerable physical strength and prone to sudden outbursts of violence, he is—in a nice English touch—first introduced to the reader mistreating his dog. His violence is not confined to his dumb friend. Fagin and Oliver are threatened on several occasions, and his violence climaxes in the brutal murder of Nancy. Fagin, however, is the dominant figure who sits like a malevolent spider at the center of his criminal web. Dickens is scathing in his description of the man. He was "a very old shrivelled Jew, whose villainous-looking and repulsive face was obscured by a quantity of matted red hair." Here was the epitome of evil, an alien figure in whose mind existed "every evil thought and blackest purpose."[7] Here was a family patriarch but the very antithesis of Victorian respectability. Although presented as unequivocally Jewish, Fagin also combined elements of another threatening outsider—the Italian *padrone*.[8] Dickens would not have been unaware of the fact that the area in and around Little Saffron Hill, in which Fagin and his boys operate, was commonly known as Little Italy.

Nowhere is the process of classification clearer than in the writing of Henry Mayhew, who was at pains to ensure that his readers "should no longer confound the honest, independent working men, with the vagrant beggars and pilferers of the country" but rather that they should appreciate that "the one class is as respectable and worthy, as the other is degraded and vicious."[9] Using language not dissimilar to that used by Dickens in his portrayal of Bill Sikes in *Oliver Twist*, Mayhew described one of his ventures into criminal London.

> On entering into a public-house in another alley near Union Street we came to see one of the most dangerous thieves' dens we have visited in the course of our rambles. As we approached the door of the house we saw a dissipated-looking man stealthily whispering outside the door to the ruffian-looking landlord, who appeared to be a fighting man, from his large coarse head and broken nose . . . We went to another outhouse beyond, where some thirty and forty persons were assembled around a wooden enclosure looking on, while some of their dogs were killing rats. They consisted of burglars, pickpockets, and the associates of thieves, along with one or two receivers of stolen property. Many of them were coarse

and brutal in their appearance, and appeared to be in their element as they urged their dogs to destroy the rats . . . The men apparently ranged from twenty-two to forty years of age. Many of them had the rough stamp of the criminal in their countenances, and when inflamed with strong drink, would possibly be fit for any deed of atrocious villainy.[10]

Alongside such formidable characters coexisted "common thieves . . . often characterised by mental imbecility and low cunning . . . lazy in disposition and lack[ing] energy both of body and mind," but the threat they posed to "decent" society was equally beyond dispute.[11] Unlike Dickens, Mayhew went beyond description to classification. These "strange members of the human family," as he called them, "as distinct as the Malay is from the Caucasian tribe," belonged to "the several natural orders and species of criminals" which were "in a scientific point of view, as worthy of being studied as the varieties of animalcules."[12] He then proceeded to present a detailed analysis that produced, for example, a three-fold categorization of thieves (based on the means whereby they operated) each of which was then duly subdivided. The reader is presented with a mysterious but ordered world with its own language to describe its nefarious specialisms: *rampsmen*, *bludgers* or *stick slingers*, *prop nailers*, *thimble screwers*, *sawney hunters*, and *dead lurkers* were terms intended to send a frisson of fear down the back of the respectable reader.[13] But at the same time it was a rhetoric of reassurance. The "elite" construction of the criminal classes gave the reader a sense of superiority and eased some of the worries that arose from the unknown.

Such superiority was reinforced by his descriptions of the criminal districts of London. This criminal world was inhabited by grotesque figures, scarred both physically and morally; who wore the badge of crime on their very faces. The language used to describe this world emphasized both physical squalor and lack of orderliness ("sickening smells," "heaps of filth," "noisome and offensive," "tumbling houses," "lairs and holes") and moral failings ("most improvident manner," "unprincipled parents," "indiscriminate admixture of the sexes," "gross depravity or impropriety"). The "underworld" mirrors the "overworld" in its highly complex structure, but in that mirror world the moral order has been subverted and good replaced by evil. Through a process of transference, all that is seen to be immoral, all that is feared in respectable bourgeois society, has been ascribed to the inhabitants of the slums and rookeries. In so doing, not only has an other or nether world been constructed but also the superiority of "respectable" values has been confirmed. Those intrepid domestic explorers discovering the East End of London were effectively involved in the same process of discovery and definition that Edward Said associates with the West's contact with the orient. [14]

Mayhew's descriptions of the police and the relationship with the criminal class were also reassuring. Although never eulogizing the Metropolitan Police in the way that Dickens did in "On duty with Inspector Field," his description of the police in action was positive. For example, on one occasion Mayhew accompanied men of the Metropolitan police to Bluegate Fields, which was "nothing more or less than a den of thieves, prostitutes and ruffians of the lowest description," and yet

> the police penetrate unarmed without the slightest trepidation . . . we proceeded to Brunswick Street, more generally known in the neighbourhood and to the police as "Tiger Bay" . . . We entered No. 6, accompanied by two policemen in uniform, who happened to be on duty at the entrance to the place . . . We afterwards searched two houses on the opposite side of the way . . . When the magic word "Police" was uttered, the door flew open, as the door of the robbers' cave when Ali Baba exclaimed "Sesame."[15]

Reassurance was also to be found in the journalism of Dickens who contrasts the almost comical inadequacies of the criminal with the moral and physical strength of the policeman. In one of his best known pieces he notes how

> [c]oiners and smashers droop before him; pickpockets defer to him; the gentle sex (not very gentle here) smile upon him. Half-drunken hags check themselves in the midst of pots of beer, or pints of gin, to drink to Mr. Field . . . One beldame in rusty black has such admiration for him, that she runs a whole street's length to shake him by the hand; tumbling into a heap of mud by the way, and still pressing her attentions when her very form has ceased to be distinguishable through it.[16]

Having painted a grim picture of Rat's Castle at the beginning of the piece, Dickens was able to reassure his readers with the conclusion that "[b]efore the power of the law, the power of superior sense—for common thieves are fools beside these men—and the power of a perfect mastery of character, the garrison of Rats' Castle and the adjacent Fortress make but a skulking show indeed when reviewed by Inspector Field."[17] The threat from below is less than we (poor, frightened reader) had imagined; the forces that protect us are stronger and in control. Sleep easy, gentle reader; sleep easy as Inspector Field and his men guard the streets and houses in which you live!

But not all mid-Victorian writers painted such a comforting picture. William Hoyle was appalled by the fact that Britain was more criminal in 1871 than ever before despite the positive changes that had taken place in the preceding 20 or 30 years, which should have reduced crime.[18] Even more worrying was Plint's observation that the criminal and dangerous classes were not geographically separated from the respectable working classes. "The criminal classes live amongst, and are dove-tailed in, so to speak, with the operative classes, whereby they constitute so many points of vicious contact

with those classes—so many ducts by which the virus of a moral poison cir-
culates through and around them. They constitute a pestiferous canker in
the heart of every locality."[19] Put another way, the criminal class were "in
the community, but neither of it, nor from it" and thus "isolated from the
other classes." This strengthened, rather than weakened, his earlier observation that this "pestiferous canker" has the effect of revolting the sensibilities,
and lowering, more or less, the moral status of all whom come in contact with
them. "Their very presence, and the daily commission of offences by them,
is an evil, because it so habituates society to the loathsome spectacle of the
one, and the constant recurrence of the other, that the sensibilities become
blunted, and the judgement benumbed and stupefied."[20]

The worrying fluidity between social boundaries was well captured by
John Hollingshead. Another investigative journalist, Hollingshead was com-
missioned by the *Morning Post* to report on the distress that beset ordinary
Londoners in the severe winter of 1860–1861. The series of articles, titled
"Horrible London," were reprinted later as *Ragged London in 1861*. Recognizing the "many different degrees of social degradation and unavoidable poverty," he noted how "daily . . . one or more [of these outcasts] drop through
into the great pit of crime."[21]

More specifically, and more spectacularly, violent street crime gave
rise to a moral panic over garroting in the 1860s, which brought to the
surface fears of the threat posed by another outsider group, ticket-of-
leave men, who had been the center of criticism since the phasing out of
transportation in the 1850s. *The Times* was clear that the streets of London were less safe than they used to be as "[m]en are garotted and robbed
in the most public and well-frequented thoroughfares, not in the dead of
night, but while the streets are full."[22] Less prominent was its coverage of
attacks elsewhere, though it did note briefly that "the system of garotting"
had spread to the provinces.[23] Describing the November Session of the
Central Criminal Court at which a number of garroters were on trial, *The
Times* leader-writer waxed eloquent on the "predatory expeditions on a
system resembling the Indian 'thuggee'" carried out by the "impudent
and defiant . . . pirates of the streets" who were likened to "the sanguinary fa-
natics of the French Revolution."[24] Nor was *The Times* alone. *The Era* fueled
fears, arguing that the streets of London had been made a penal colony and
claiming that "it is whispered that the Police are *afraid* to encounter some of
the desperate ruffians who prowl along our streets."[25]

The fear of crime diminished without ever disappearing in subsequent
years, helped in no small measure by the tougher prison regimes introduced
by Edmund Du Cane. However, the considerable social and political tur-
bulence of the 1880s worried the elite fearful for the stability of society.
George R. Sims, a popular journalist, expressed concern at the "mighty
mob of famished, diseased and filthy helots . . . [whose] lawless armies"

threaten to bring to London "a taste of the lesson the mob has tried to teach now and again in Paris" and bemoaned the fact that there was no longer a physical gap between "respectable" and "dangerous" classes.[26] Rioting in the center of London created a near panic in parts of respectable society. Describing the events of February 1886, C. T. Clarkson and J. H. Richardson wrote of "a straggling mob [which] the police were powerless to resist . . . picking up flints from the roadway, smashing plate-glass windows, and finally looting the shops."[27] The presence of a red flag added to the sense of menace as "free fights ensued . . . as the guerrilla warfare" between police and protesters extended beyond Trafalgar Square and into Northumberland Avenue. It was not until nightfall that "the victory was won and the cause of law and order triumphed."[28] But this victory came only after the "inflammatory harangues" of the leaders of the Social Democratic Federation had been put into practice by "a mob of roughs and ruffians" who left an indelible memory of "brutal violence and infamous rapine."[29] November 13, 1887, saw further scenes of violence that were quickly dubbed Bloody Sunday. Looking back on events over a decade later, W.L.M. Lee, the first historian of the metropolitan police, recognized the significance of the fact that the Metropolitan police had lost control of the streets, albeit briefly, for the first time since their inception.[30] The alien threat from within (the Social Democratic Federation) had to be contained to prevent contagion spreading among gullible working men.

The specter of the Red Flag—the threat of revolutionary socialism, the possibility of a repeat of the butchery of the Paris Commune but this time on the streets of London—was frightening enough, but there were other causes for fear in these difficult years; not least the realization that a serial killer was butchering prostitutes in the East End of London in 1888. The term *East End* to describe the large working-class district east of the City of London was relatively new, and its negative connotations were clear from the first usages in or around 1880, but the construction of the East End as a hell of poverty and crime can be traced back to Mayhew and Dickens at least. The mob that invaded central London was drawn from this district, and its brutalized inhabitants could as easily turn on themselves as on respectable society. Sensationalist writing created an image of people besotted with drink and prone to random acts of violence. Murder and suicide were seen as unexceptional, an almost too predictable consequence of the squalid surroundings in which East Enders lived. But even the most hyperbolic description of the intrepid journalists who visited such parts of darkest England could not prepare people for the shocking horrors of the Whitechapel murders. In little more than three months, six women were brutally murdered and their bodies mutilated in a manner that still shocks.

Determining the identity of Jack the Ripper has become an industry in its own right, but of equal interest, in the hundreds of accusations, suspicions, and confessions of the time, is the light that contemporary speculation throws upon prevailing notions of criminality. The threatening outsider was a time-honored and common explanation. It was reported that mysterious foreigners had been sighted, and at least one, Charles Ludwig, arrested. A Russian anarchist, Nicolai Vassilyev, was named in an article in the *East London Advertiser*, while a Polish-born Jew, Jacob Pizer, was strongly suspected, despite each having strong alibis. Anti-Semitic outbursts were reported in the *East London Observer*, which noted repeated assertions that no Englishman could have committed such a crime and that "such a horrible crime . . . must have been done by a *Jew*."[31] Assistant Commissioner Sir Robert Anderson, head of the Criminal Investigation Department, held similar views.

Concerns with "Jewish criminality" continued after the initial Ripper media frenzy had died down. With tens of thousands of Jewish refugees flooding into Glasgow, Leeds, Manchester, and especially the East End of London as the result of pogroms in Eastern Europe there was growing concern with their economic and moral impact. Jews were accused of teaching "home-grown" hooligans how to use knives. They were linked with the rise in burglaries and particularly with gambling, prostitution, and the (alleged but also entirely nonexistent) white slave trade. The high-profile Lipski murder trial in London in 1887 and, even more so, the Oscar Slater trial in Glasgow in 1909 appeared to give substance to these concerns.[32]

Old scapegoats were juxtaposed with new. Literature (and the stage) in the immensely popular form of *Dr. Jekyll and Mr. Hyde* revealed the monstrousness that existed in man. Seizing on the ideas of the new positivist criminology, some writers found the answer to why such atrocities took place in heredity and the underdeveloped brains (akin to those of bears, according to one Professor Benedict) that allegedly characterized murderers. But more radical social critics, heirs of Engels such as William Morris and the Social Democratic Federation leader H. M. Hyndman, argued that the root causes were the social evils that grew out of the gross inequalities of a capitalist society. Though unwilling to accept the full implication of such a critique, the newly formed London County Council effectively accepted an environmentalist explanation of crime when it instigated housing reforms for the East End.

These competing explanations of the Whitehall murders show the extent to which perceptions of the criminal and explanations of criminality were changing. Early and mid-Victorian discourses were complex, but with very few exceptions, the experts of the day were clear that the criminal (in whatever form) was an active agent, exercising his or her free will, consciously making decisions, and responsible for the actions that were taken. Explanations of criminal behavior were couched in individualistic and moral terms. While there was a recognition that many criminals lived precarious lives in deprived parts of Britain's towns and cities, this was seen more as a *consequence* than a *cause* of their criminality. Further, many influential commentators explicitly denied any causal link between poverty and crime. Peel made this clear to parliament in his speech introducing the Metropolitan Police Bill, and Chadwick likewise was convinced that "the notion that any considerable proportion of crimes against property are caused by blameless poverty or destitution we find disproved at every step."[33] Parental neglect, disregard for the Sabbath, the pernicious effects of the ale house, and popular entertainments were seen to be the root causes of crime. Insofar as harsh economic circumstances had a part to play, it was a precipitating factor. Jellinger Symons conceded that "bad trade is sure to drive a portion of that large class into the actual commission of crime" but immediately added that these were people "always hovering on its [crime's] verge and who have not sufficient moral restraint or self-respect to deter them." He confidently told his audience, most of whom were respectable bourgeois citizens, that "want will not make a good Christian man criminal, be he ever so poor."[34]

By placing responsibility squarely on the individual, attention was diverted away from the inequalities and injustices in early and mid-Victorian society, which probably had a more direct impact on criminal behavior than the contemporary dominant discourse allowed. There was an alternative perspective, but it was one that was confined to the margins. Frederick Engels, now the best-known critic of early Victorian social conditions but of limited impact at the time of writing his *Condition of the Working Class in England in 1844*, saw crime as the product of "sheer necessity." He drew clear causal links between the growth of capitalism, which pauperized and dehumanized the working class, and the rise of crime, which he saw as a revolt against an unjust system.[35] Chartist thinking ran along similar lines and even the *Economist*, zealously advocating free trade, offered a not dissimilar analysis. Interestingly, the most sustained radical critique was to be found among commentators on rural life. William Cobbett, notably in *Rural Rides, Punch* at the time of the Swing Riots, and Thomas Campbell Foster, whose articles in *The Times* during the outbreaks of incendiarism in southeastern England in 1844 provoked outrage among readers, linked both poverty and a sense of injustice with the commission of crime. The radical critique, however, was too subversive and raised too many uncomfortable questions about the organization of the society and economy of Britain. The thought of stout John Hodge (the archetypal agricultural laborer) thinking for himself and taking action against those who exploited him was too frightening for Britain's elites to contemplate. Rather, such ideas were seen as preposterous. More comforting was the thought that rural crime was due to the pernicious effect of politically motivated outsiders who turned the minds of honest but dim laborers. Mysterious men in gigs, Frenchmen bringing their revolutionary ideas across the channel, and homegrown political extremists such as Cobbett and his followers were more acceptable explanations of the Swing Riots that peaked in 1831.

And that response to the laborers' revolt was a microcosm of a more general response to crime. The evidence of the courts, which showed a significant overlap between the criminal population and the population at large, was too close for comfort. Far better to believe in the stereotypes of Fagin, Bill Sykes, and Nancy: superficially frightening, such figures were fundamentally reassuring. That way the criminal world could be compartmentalized and controlled.

Early and mid-Victorian explanations of crime were overwhelmingly couched in individualistic and moral terms, but there was a minority that looked to science for an understanding of delinquent behavior. Phrenology, largely discredited by the 1850s, enjoyed considerable popularity in the early years of Victoria's reign. It is easy to mock a so-called science that sought to discern the character and aptitudes of an individual from the measurement of his or her skull, but the scores of death masks of notorious criminals made in these years bears testimony to the belief that the key to criminality was the mental constitution of the offender and, as such, something to be studied scientifically.

A more lasting medicalization of crime was to be found in the writings of Henry Maudsley. In his *Body and Mind*, first published in 1873, Maudsley wrote of the "evil ancestral influences . . . [the] flaw or warp of nature that all the care in the world" would not prevent the unfortunate individual from becoming vicious, criminal, or insane. Bleakly he wrote: "No one can escape the tyranny of his organisation; no-one can escape the destiny that is innate in him, and which unconsciously and irresistibly shapes his ends, even when he believes that he is determining them with consummate foresight and skill."[36]

Free will was illusory in such an analysis. Further, liberal notions of punishment were as inappropriate as liberal arguments of individual culpability. Punishments should fit the criminals not their crimes. And this was one of the conclusions that derived from the analysis of the founding father of positivist criminology, Cesare Lombroso. *Criminal Man* appeared in 1876 and was presented as the first scientific, as opposed to philosophical, explanation of crime. Central to Lombroso's argument was the claim that he had identified a distinct anthropological type, the born criminal, which was a product of moral and physical atavism. The born criminal was effectively a throwback in the evolutionary chain and as such akin to the savage and primitive people of much earlier ages. Lombroso's ideas attracted considerable attention across Europe and America but were not universally accepted. In Britain, the events of 1888 as much as his popularizers, such as Isobel Faord and Havelock Ellis, gave credence to the notion of the born criminal, a throw-back to a less civilized time.

The Home Office was unconvinced but felt it necessary to take action. It was decided that Home Office funding should be made available for a major

Lombrosian Criminal Types, 1895. From C. Lombros, *L'Uomo Delinquente*, 1876. (Courtesy Mary Evans Picture Library)

empirical study, to be conducted by the Broadmoor doctor, Charles Goring. Goring was himself part of the wider eugenics movement with its belief in biometrics. The outcome was *The English Convict*, published in 1913. The thoroughness of the investigation and the overwhelming mass of statistical tables made it a work more read *of*, than read. Nonetheless, Goring's conclusions were important and do not sit comfortably with the belief that English thinking remained firmly in the hands of the empiricists and had not fallen under the pernicious influence of continental criminological thought. On the basis of a study of almost 2,500 prisoners and a similar noncriminal population, drawn largely from undergraduates from Oxford and Cambridge, a company of Royal Engineers and residents of Middlesex hospitals, Goring concluded that the Lombrosian anthropological criminal type did not exist. He was equally scathing about sociological explanations, arguing that (once again) his detailed statistical analyses had revealed no meaningful links between a range of social disadvantages and the commission of crime.

> On the other hand, between a variety of environmental conditions examined, such as illiteracy, parental neglect, lack of employment, the stress of poverty, etc., including the states of a healthy, delicate, or morbid constitution per se, and even the situation induced by the approach of death—between these conditions and the committing of crime, we find no evidence of any significant relationship. Our second conclusion, then, is this: that, relative to its origin in the constitution of the malefactor, and especially in his mentally defective constitution, crime is only to a trifling extent (if to any) the product of social inequalities, of adverse environment, or of other manifestations of what may be comprehensively termed the forces of circumstances.[37]

Criminals, he concluded, were characterized by their defective physical and mental constitution. Rather confusingly, he accepted that mental defectiveness—a heritable condition—was "the principal constitutional determinant of crime."[38]

Such academic analysis has to be set against more popular discussions of crime and the criminal. The long-term decline in the recorded crime rate and the findings of Charles Booth that the "criminal residuum" was smaller than it had been in midcentury brought some calm. *The Times*, for example, claimed that "at the present rate of decrease the professional burglar and pickpocket will soon disappear." Not everyone was comforted. Indeed, the *Pall Mall Gazette* dismissed Booth's report as "too much like a complacent and comforting bourgeois statement of the situation." Class A might be small, but it was not totally disassociated from the numerically larger Class B, and as Booth himself conceded, the members of these classes threatened to contaminate more respectable members of working-class society. Second, one should not overlook a potentially more worrying finding of Booth's, namely that "every social grade has its criminal": a conclusion that strengthened the fear that there was an "enemy within."[39]

The late Victorian and Edwardian debate about crime, while sharing certain features in common with earlier discussions, took a distinct turn. In part, this was a product of the growing awareness of the problem of recidivism and the existence of a class of persons for whom crime was a way of life; in part, it was the product of new, *scientific* explanations of criminal behavior, which cast doubt on classical explanations of criminality based on the notion of free will. More specifically, the problem of the professional or career criminal was at the heart of the late Victorian and Edwardian concerns.

Perhaps the most prolific writer on the career criminal and the most high-profile (though not the most sophisticated) campaigner in the crusade against professional crime was Sir Robert Anderson who, although best known as an experienced policeman, came from a legal family and was himself a trained lawyer. A prolific writer (he wrote almost two dozen books on theology), he first made his name when he was transferred to the Home Office as adviser on Fenian affairs in 1876.[40] He was subsequently appointed to Scotland Yard where he headed CID from 1888 to 1901. Pessimistic in outlook, he believed that without "statutory morality" men had no "incentive to virtue" and nothing to hold them "back from vice." This was particular the case with "the hopelessly depraved" for whom Anderson's solution was "social tutelage," which meant placing habitual criminals "permanently under police supervision." After he left the force, Anderson produced a series of highly publicized articles (subsequently brought together in book form) in which he sought to foreground the victims of crime and further "the protection of society" through the introduction of indeterminate sentences, which, notwithstanding the emotive arguments of "the humanity-mongers" in society, was the only way (in his mind) to tackle the problem.[41]

Anderson's ideas were not universally welcomed at the time of publication (he was variously described as simplistic, crude, and sensationalist) and have received little praise from later historians ("a hotchpotch of old and new theories . . . embroidered with religious quotations and written in a highly inflammatory way").[42] Many contemporaries (let alone later historians) found him an unsympathetic character, while his beliefs and mode of expression antagonized many. However, that does not mean that his ideas did not resonate in certain important quarters, nor that he lacked influence both in the general sense of shaping the public perception of the career criminal and in the specific sense of influencing legislation.

Anderson never doubted there was a general decline in crime—"the judicial statistics afford indisputable proof"—but he constantly reiterated that "professional crime is on the increase." Like Mayhew before him, Anderson acknowledged a larger group of "weak" professional criminals: "those who are so utterly weak or so hopelessly wicked that they cannot abstain from crime," but he focused his attention on the "hard" professional criminal who adopted a calculative attitude and "who pursue a career of crime deliberately, with full appreciation of its risks."[43] These were the men who were responsible for the increase in burglary and housebreaking and for inflicting suffering upon "honest and peaceful citizens," and who were ignored by his pet hate, "the humanity-mongers." Such "professionals," he argued, were "numerous enough to keep the inhabitants of our large cities in a state of siege." To give substance to his general contention, he paraded before the reading public the likes of Henry Marchant, as a typical example of the desperate, professional burglar.

The prisoner under several aliases, has had a remarkable criminal career. In 1869 he had four months' imprisonment for theft; in 1872 two months'; in 1874, twelve months' for housebreaking; and in 1879, seven years' penal servitude for larceny. Soon after his release on ticket-of-leave he was captured in the act of breaking into a house in Canning Town, when he tried to use a revolver on his captor. Liberated on heavy bail, he absconded, and when re-arrested at Manchester he was in possession of a revolver, a complete burglar's outfit, numberless skeleton keys, and articles of jewellery, the proceeds of robberies in Manchester and Liverpool. He was tried at the Old Bailey and sentenced to ten years' penal servitude. By good conduct in gaol he again obtained a remission of sentence, and in 1896 he was caught housebreaking at Bow for which offence he was ordered twelve months' hard labour and sent back to complete his former sentence. When released again . . . he obtained employment and worked regularly for the greater part of the week, but carried out marauding expeditions on Saturday and Sunday evenings . . . [Arrested February 1901] in his pocket he had a powerful jemmy and some skeleton keys, and in his room were found jewellery and other stolen property.[44]

Such men were self-professed "outlaws" who had by their actions forfeited their right to liberty. Challenging conventional wisdom of "measuring his sentence by his latest offence," he argued that "the question should not be what the prisoner did . . . but *what he is.*"[45] Only by introducing indeterminate sentences could society be protected: only such incarceration of the hardened criminals would create the necessary geographical separation that would offer general protection to respectable society and also ensure that the criminal's trade was not taught to the next generation. Anderson's construction of the career criminal was intended to exploit fears of an increase in serious crime, but as with Mayhew before him, there was a message of reassurance in his writing. The hard core of career criminals, he was telling his audience, was known to the astute detective, such as Anderson. These men, who held society to ransom, could be apprehended and (with a change in the law) could be dealt with effectively. Society could be kept secure by the indeterminate incarceration in a single prison for the few hundred "outlaws."

It would be tempting to dismiss this as the ranting of an embittered and isolated policeman with but a crude grasp of Lombrosian criminology— tempting but not wholly accurate. Anderson received support from and was quoted with approval by a number of eminent figures. Major Arthur Griffiths, a man with considerable experience of the prison system, adopted a very similar line of argument. For such people, who wage such ceaseless warfare against society, the only answer was "indefinite detention."[46] Dr. R. F. Quinton, a eugenicist also with direct experience of the prison system as governor and medical officer of Holloway prison (and also a defender of Edmund Du Cane), was another to inveigh against the "person who deliberately adopts crime as his profession" and demanded indeterminate sentences.[47] Support was not confined to the professionals from the prison service. Mr. Justice Wills wrote to *The Times* in 1901 supporting Anderson and later referred to the man's "remarkable work." Faced with the threat of the calculative repeat offender, the "ideal system of punishment . . . would be the indeterminate sentence," and Wills looked to the Home Office "to hold its own against the outcry which at present seems sure to be evoked by any wholesome severity, however well deserved and however necessary for the protection of those amongst us who neither murder, steal, nor knowingly receive stolen goods."[48] Similar sentiments were echoed by Mr. Justice Darby (notably in the case of *R v Woodman*), while Hugh Gamon, who had written an extensive and (from a working-class perspective) largely sympathetic study of the London Police Courts, financed by the Toynbee Trust, painted a more alarming picture than Anderson. Focusing on the serious crimes of burglary, housebreaking, and shopbreaking, he noted that the "ratio of apprehensions to crime is lowest," a result of such criminals being "more skilful in eluding arrest," and he argued that "these are emphatically the crimes of the professional criminal."[49] Thus, an early 20th-century Bill Sikes was recreated, not through the writing of the novelist but through the writing of senior policemen, prison officers, and judges. But whereas Bill Sikes was duly punished (though not through the courts), his latter-day counterpart was effectively encouraged and nurtured by what Anderson termed the "absurd system of punishment" that prevailed.[50]

It is difficult to assess the precise impact of these writers on opinion in the early 20th century. Their analysis of the problem, and more so their prescription for it, aroused considerable opposition. The correspondence columns of *The Times*, as well as the pages of such publications as *The Law Times*, *The Law Magazine and Review*, *The Law Journal*, *The Law Quarterly Review*, *The Nineteenth Century and After*, *The Edinburgh Review*, and *The Humane Review*, contained a vigorous debate with strongly expressed arguments on both sides. Nonetheless, a concern with the hardened professional criminal and the perceived need for a new form of punishment gained momentum and resulted in an important piece of legislation: the Prevention of Crime Act of 1908.[51] In presenting the bill to parliament Herbert Gladstone gave official sanction to the construction of the career criminal, a small but threatening band of men, who at relatively mature ages and in an apparently calculating manner chose a life of burglary or shop-breaking, thereby terrorizing the law-abiding property owners of any class. Gladstone accepted (or exploited) other elements in this construction by asserting in a manner that would have pleased Anderson that such men mocked the present "absurd system" of punishment. There was a "large number of hardened, determined, persistent criminals, who rejoiced at only getting three years, because in two years and eight months they would be on the job again with health recruited and able to enjoy themselves again."[52]

Not everyone in parliament (or outside for that matter) accepted Gladstone's argument. As he (like others in the ongoing debate) had to concede the habitual criminal could not be simply characterized as a strong-minded and calculative individual who deliberately chose to use his strengths and skills to pursue a life of crime. There were also a large number of criminals whose lifestyle was the product of weakness rather than strength. In many respects, the habitual criminal as an inadequate individual, suffering from both physical and mental weaknesses (probably inherited), was a more widely recognized figure in Edwardian Britain. Concern with the degeneration of the country's urban population dated back into the last third of the 19th century, but this concern received further stimulus during and after the problematic second Anglo-Boer war when a significant minority of would-be recruits were shown to be physically unfit to fight and die for their country. The subsequent growth of the "national efficiency" movement in the 1900s strengthened the concern with and fear of the "weak" habitual criminal who seemed to embody, quite literally, the very physical and moral deficiencies that were undermining the standing of the nation.[53]

Even Anderson, for all his preoccupation with the hardened, professional criminal, had nonetheless recognized the existence of "the poor wretch who, begotten and born and bred in crime, has not the moral stamina to resist when opportunity for theft presents itself," for whom the proper institution was "the asylum prison, where his life can be spent in useful labor, with every reasonable alleviation of his lot."[54] Similar views could be found among his critics. Indeed, for a growing number of commentators this was the more important element in the problem, not simply because of their greater numbers (Gladstone estimated there to be 5,000 calculative professional criminals compared with the 60,000 weak-willed habituals "wandering about the roads and cities in a state of semi-vagrancy and crime"), but also because of the more insidious threat they posed. The concern of people such as Anderson with the "calculative" professional criminal was of a piece with mid-Victorian commentators in the sense that they claimed to have identified a distinct and threatening group that preyed on respectable society. While such predators no longer inhabited a separate geographical location, they were a definable "other," set apart from honest men and women. With the weak-willed habitual, the situation was less clear cut.

From the 1870s onward more and more social commentators had noted the growing number of urban degenerates, particularly in the great cities such as London and Manchester. The Reverend Osborne Jay, for example, had no doubt that in places such as Shoreditch there were to be found a "submerged and semi-criminal class" who were in that position precisely because of their "physical, mental and moral peculiarities." These were "drunken, besotted" creatures with "inherited defects of will and taints of blood" who existed in squalid conditions, little better than animals.[55] While "skilled criminals are recruited not from the mentally inferior stocks of the proletariat," as W. C. Sullivan, the medical officer of Holloway Prison, wrote in 1909, but "some criminals are of bad or degenerate stock."[56] The presence of such human flotsam and jetsam, incapable of work but out-breeding respectable, law-abiding society, was an ever-increasing source of worry in a country whose economic and imperial dominance appeared to be under yet greater threat with every

passing year. By a process of displacement, both the relative economic decline of Britain and the challenges to its imperial power are seen to be the
product of a defective and criminal residuum. Fears about the health of the
nation were focused on the most visible manifestation of degeneration—
that is, the physically and mentally weak habitual criminal.

Given the threat they (literally) embodied it was imperative to identify
clearly these problem groups and prevent them from contaminating the rest
of society. While rejecting Lombrosian ideas of the born criminal, Charles
Goring waxed eloquent on the need for a crusade against crime that would
involve an educational dimension, to modify "inherited tendency"; segregation and supervision of the unfit to reduce the opportunity of passing on their
"taint" to future generations; and the regulation of "the reproduction of those
degrees of constitutional qualities—feeble-mindedness, inebriety, epilepsy,

A British Rough, 1875. By William Small in *The Graphic*,
1875. (Courtesy *Illustrated London News Ltd*/Mary Evans
Picture Library)

deficient social instinct etc.—which conduce to the committing of crime."[57] Goring did not provide details of how the latter would be achieved, but others were less reticent about the benefits of castration.

Goring's preoccupation with feeblemindedness is particularly worthy of attention. He was not alone in associating crime with the "feebleminded." Mary Dendy, writing in *The Lancet* in 1902, observed that "hooligans, or corner-lads, criminals, paupers and drunkards—all are these frequently only because they are feeble-minded." Sullivan identified the criminally inclined "bad or degenerate stock" were a specific group "within the great pathological class of the feeble-minded."[58] But what was particularly disturbing was the fact that much crime (and especially much seemingly purposeless crime) was committed by those "semi-insane intellects" who inhabited the "borderland." The desire to categorize and compartmentalize (never far from the surface at any time) was particularly strong among a scientific community that saw identification and classification via new scientific and statistical methods as a necessary step in the battle against degeneration. But the very confidence that allowed such men and women to distinguish between morons, cretins, and imbeciles was undermined by the discovery of a "borderland" of feeble-mindedness wherein identification was highly problematic.[59] There was a real dilemma for those grappling with the problems of "diagnosing the border-line of cases of feeble-mindedness." On the one hand, "to commit an individual who shows no very clearly marked signs of mental defect to a semi-penal institution would be a gross infringement of the liberty of the subject." But on the other, it could not be "too strongly impressed upon our notice that every imbecile, especially the high-grade imbecile, is a potential criminal, needing only the proper environment and opportunities for the development and expression of his criminal tendencies."[60] The enemy was well and truly in the midst of society and sufficiently well camouflaged to escape detection. The threat of crime was taking on a new and deeply disturbing form. War was being waged on decent society, not only by self-evident villains with the marks of infamy on their faces, but also by the seemingly innocent. In the days of Mayhew, or even Charles Booth, there was a relative comfort to be derived from the fact of having a clearly identified group of "barbarians" at the gates of, or even encamped within, respectable society. In the early 20th century this was being replaced by a growing anxiety generated by the seemingly respectable, the fifth-columnist (had such a term been invented at the time) who passed himself off as a normal member of society, whereas in reality he was a criminal time-bomb just waiting to go off.

CONCLUSION

The changing perceptions of the criminal tell us much about the beliefs and concerns of elite figures in Victorian Britain, but they do not necessarily provide an accurate insight into the nature of the criminal and the cause of crime. Indeed, it is tempting to dismiss many of these perceptions as myths, mere phantoms that haunted an easily frightened populace. Undoubtedly, there was an element of caricature in some of the descriptions of 19th-century criminals, and not just in the pages of the popular press and sensationalist story! But there were also elements of truth—Fagin, for example, was probably based on the real-life Ikky Solomons—without which the stereotypes would not have had any credence, but trying to discern the elements of truth and building up a more realistic picture of the Victorian criminal is far from easy given the evidence that has survived.

There is little evidence to support the widespread contemporary belief in the existence of a distinct (and male-dominated) criminal class. In part this was simply a matter of scale. With the possible exception of London, where sheer geographical size made it possible, it is difficult to find clear-cut criminal ghettos and a distinct criminal class. At most there were notorious crime spots, "dangerous districts," especially in the larger towns and cities; places such as the China district of Merthyr, the old town area of Middlesbrough, or even Castlegate in Huddersfield. Moreover, within such districts there were people, like John Sutcliffe, the "King of Castlegate," who relied heavily upon the proceeds of crime to survive and even a few professional gangs who made a living out of organized theft, but this is not the same as saying there was a distinct criminal class. Even in the late 19th century, when the prison population was visibly aging, these "hardened and perhaps experienced" criminals did not, contrary to Anderson and others, constitute a class of their own. On the contrary, the evidence of the courts points more to the conclusion that criminals, particularly in the early Victorian years, were drawn from a wide section of society (predominantly, but not exclusively, working class) but with an over-representation of the more insecure, the more marginalized, and the more stigmatized. For contemporary commentators, aware of the details of the criminal statistics, this was an uncomfortable fact that raised profoundly difficult questions about the social and economic organization of the country. Not for the first, nor the last, time commentators sought to explain crime in terms of corrupting influences: alien figures, notably Jews and gypsies; inappropriate and immoral entertainment, such as penny gaffs and penny dreadfuls; and the absence of appropriate role models. But there was something Orwellian about the Victorians' ability to hold two contradictory pieces of information in their minds at the same time. One simple example encapsulates this ability. The worthy inhabitants of Middlesbrough regularly complained of the criminal activities of itinerants whose nefarious activities allegedly boosted the town's criminal statistics. They also read, year on year, in the chief constable's annual reports, published in full in the local press, that the majority of crimes were committed by residents of the town, most of whom were long-term residents to boot!

By the late 19th century, however, the criminal population, as well as declining as a percentage of the overall population, was less representative of the inhabitants of the country as a whole. By the last decades of the 19th century it was abundantly clear that "those who stole by habit or had to steal to survive were more and more conspicuously the most depressed and least literate in the population."[61] The criminal in the dock was more likely to be physical or mentally less able. Furthermore, he was likely to have a string of often petty offenses that started when he was in his teens, if not before. Criminological explanations of the habitual offender couched in the language of degeneration may jar on the modern ear but appear to contain a truth that could be verified by any Victorian who cared to visit a court or consult the annual crime statistics. The official figures do confirm contemporary fears about the habitual criminal. Between 1860 and 1890 the percentage of male prisoners who had previously been committed to jail rose from 26 to 46.[62] Local evidence brings out the point starkly. John Campbell, found guilty of theft in Middlesbrough, was a 28-year-old engineer who had been incarcerated for the first time at the age of nine. From Reformatory School he graduated to prison and was sent down a further 15 times, as well as receiving 9 fines for petty offenses, before he appeared at the Northallerton Quarter Sessions in April 1884. An even greater "failure" was the 62-year-old laborer George Clay. Found guilty in 1887 of stealing 12 rabbits in Marton, he was sent to prison for the 32nd time since 1860.[63] However, a note of warning needs to be sounded. The people who were prosecuted in the second half of the 19th century were not necessarily a random sample of the criminal population. Employers and others based their judgments of whom to prosecute on prevailing stereotypes of the "criminal." Thus, selective prosecutions, based in part on preconceived notions, may well have helped to create (or at least reinforce) the older, habitual criminal, rather than simply reflect his existence.

One fact does seem to be beyond dispute: crime was largely and increasingly a male activity. The majority of criminals appearing before the courts were male. For serious crimes tried at assize or quarter session the national average was about 80 percent, but there were considerable local variations. Men accounted for 95 percent of those tried at assize in Sussex in the first half of the 19th century and 89 percent of those tried at quarter session; in Gloucestershire the corresponding figures were only slightly lower, while in the North Riding of Yorkshire men accounted for just under 90 percent of all prisoners indicted for trial at quarter session. In contrast, women accounted for approximately 20 percent of all prisoners at the assizes in London between 1810 and 1850, though in some industrial areas the percentage of women was even higher: 25 percent in the Black Country and 30 percent in Middlesbrough.

Occupational status is of central importance but not easy to establish. The court records contain information, but it is often of too general. However, the fact that as many as 9 out of 10 people defined themselves as laborers is not without significance. As far as one can tell the unskilled manual worker, in his various guises, was a disproportionately frequent figure in the mid-19th-century court records. Some occupations were heavily overrepresented—canal boatmen in the midlands, for example, hawkers, tramps, and rag-pickers almost everywhere—as were certain ethnic groups, most notably the Irish. Depressions, short-term or long, in local industries reflected themselves in the crime figures. The appearance in court records of out-of-work blastfurnacemen in Middlesbrough, victims of sharp short-term downturns in their trade, or of furniture makers in High Wycombe and handloom weavers in south Lancashire, victims of longer term declines in their trades, bear witness to the links between economic misfortune and crime. Skilled workmen and craftsmen, whose skills and scarcity value brought higher wages and greater economic security than the less skilled, were underrepresented, as were, to a greater degree, shopkeepers, professionals, and gentlemen, though the latter may have escaped prosecution because of a neglect of white-collar crime and, when detected, a preference for informal sanction. The criminal population clearly did not reflect accurately the wider population, but there was a much greater overlap between the two, especially in the early Victorian years, than various exponents of the "criminal class" thesis allowed for. Most occupations were represented, although the less well-paid occupations and the more vulnerable workers were more likely to end up in court. Only by the 1880s was it possible to argue for a clear distinction between the respectable, law-abiding working classes and the rough, law breakers, and even then the borderline between the two could still be blurred.

Even though the adult male criminal had become a more common figure in the courts of late Victorian and Edwardian Britain and was the subject of much analysis by contemporary experts, it is important not to overlook the existence of female and juvenile criminality—phenomena that were, in many respects, qualitatively more frightening.

CHAPTER SIX

HARLOTS AND HOOLIGANS

Criminality was largely discussed in terms of male offenders, but they were far from being the only cause for concern. Criminal women, in certain respects, aroused greater fears. Male offending, however threatening, could still be construed in terms of prevailing gender stereotypes but not so female offending. Mary Carpenter had no doubt that "the very susceptibility and tenderness of woman's nature render her completely diseased in her whole nature when thus perverted to evil; and when a woman has thrown aside the virtuous restraints of society, and is enlisted on the side of evil, she is far more dangerous to society than the other sex."[1] Equally scathing was Mrs. Owen whose judgment revealed the racial as well as gender assumptions that prevailed at the time. Her judgment was unequivocal. "Criminal women as a class are found to be more uncivilised than the savage, more degraded than the slave, less true to all natural and womanly instincts than the untutored squaw of a North American Indian tribe."[2]

Such writers were merely giving voice to the widely held belief that humankind in general was innately sinful and that this wickedness could manifest itself more dangerously in women if freed from moral restraint. Thus, even before Victoria's reign commentators, including sympathetic figures, such as Elizabeth Fry, had stressed the moral and physical defects of female criminals. They were irreligious and immoral (almost by definition they were seen as harlots), and this moral corruption was made manifest on their bodies. Their ugly, almost subhuman appearance was visual proof of their wickedness; their slovenliness ("uncombed hair"), their lack of cleanliness ("unwashed dirty faces"), their lack of modesty ("no bonnets and not a 'kerchief over the half exposed bosom"), their coarse language; their drunkenness and lack of self-control; and their cruel, violent behavior confirmed them as beyond the pale of respectable society. There was little sympathy for these "soiled doves," even though there was a widespread view (among the middle classes at least) that these women were victims either of libertine aristocrats or, in a xenophobic variation, of debauched foreigners.

A persistent strand of Victorian analysis emphasized the moral failings and the absence of an appropriate upbringing and education among criminal women. "Drunken and ungodly parents" who failed to provide an appropriate domestic environment were seen to be responsible for sending impressionable girls into a corrupt and corrupting world. Worse still some parents were accused of forcing their daughters into prostitution and petty thieving. Lacking the necessary moral defenses these girls and young women easily succumbed to the immorality of the outside world—the factories or the workhouses with their promiscuous intermixing of the sexes, the penny gaffs and cheap theaters with their inappropriate, immoral entertainments, and above all the public house and the "demon drink" threatened the morality of the strongest, let alone the defenseless waifs from the slums who had been so betrayed by their parents. Although some writers and commentators, notably Dickens, showed a degree of sympathy for women who were victims of dire circumstances and male exploitation, there was still a powerful fear that once fallen, such women posed a threat to the very fabric of society. There was little new in this discourse, but it gained in intensity in the 1850s as Victorians became increasingly preoccupied with and fearful of crimes of morality.

Poverty, drunkenness, and prostitution were seen to go hand in hand. Although not an offense in itself in Victorian Britain, prostitution was a particular cause for concern. Drink helped a woman overcome her "natural" resistance to a life of sin and, or so it was argued, consoled her once she had succumbed.[3] Attitudes toward prostitutes, harsh enough in the 1830s, hardened in the following decades as the concerns with immorality were overlain with fears about disease. In no small measure due to the writings of men such as William Acton, mid-Victorian respectable society saw itself faced with the hideous threat of the diseased and disease-spreading harlot who (with breath taking hypocrisy) was seen to be the corrupter of young men and the spreader of loathsome diseases (syphilis in particular), which threatened the innocent and pure wife and even the unborn child of the unfortunate man led astray by the siren qualities of the lady of the night.[4] Following the passing of the Contagious Diseases Acts in the 1860s, prostitutes became an outcast group, demonized but more exposed to male exploitation than before. Sadly, the "protective" legislation of the 1880s exacerbated this problem.

However, there was also a sense in which working-class female criminals became to be seen to be victims of their environment. In a rapidly urbanizing world the provision of cheap accommodation for the working classes had serious moral consequences. As Foster Rogers, the assistant chaplain at Westminster House of Correction noted in 1850: "The indiscriminate herding together of the poor of all sexes and ages . . . has a necessary tendency to sap that instinctive modesty and delicacy of feeling which the Creator intended to be the guardian of virtue, and which are more especially necessary for the defence of the female character."[5]

The rediscovery of poverty, especially in London, in the 1880s, reinforced such concerns. Andrew Mearn's *Bitter Cry of Outcast London*, with its shocking allegation of widespread incest among the overcrowded working classes of the East End, had little doubt that such conditions led "young girls [to] wander off into a life of immorality."[6] In a variation on this argument, some writers, such as Havelock Ellis and W. D. Morrison, sought to explain female criminality in terms of their greater participation in the public sphere in late—Victorian Britain.[7] And—in the eyes of such critics—nowhere was this more clearly seen than in the wholly unfeminine antics of the suffragettes, agitating for votes for women, whose hysterical and extremist behavior threatened the whole of patriarchal society, or so it was said.

Environmentalist explanations of crime remained an important element in the debate, but later Victorian and Edwardian writings on female criminals reflected other wider themes in criminological thinking. Recidivism was a particular source of worry. Statistics for 1880 suggested that more female prisoners were likely to have had a previous conviction than their male counterparts (53% compared with 33%). Worse still a higher percentage of women prisoners (15% compared with 3% of males) had 10 or more previous convictions. The habitual drunkard, more commonly a woman than a man, was a bogey figure of late Victorian Britain. Exceptionally, as in the writing of Thomas Holmes, these women were treated sympathetically and their "appalling crimes" rendered intelligible in terms of misfortunes that had thrown them off the path of respectability. More commonly, such women were seen as unattractive and unnatural. Cyril Burt's dismissive description of "a burly, fierce-looking maiden, with a puckered scowl on her forehead and a square, under-shot resolute jaw [and] a policeman's blood literally moist upon her knuckles" summed up all that was wrong.[8] The language was indistinguishable from that of Carpenter and Owens over 50 years earlier.

In particular, female criminality was subject to medicalization. Henry Maudsley in the 1870s wrote of the "hysterical melancholy" brought on by puberty in girls and the recurrent "mania" brought on by menstruation.[9] Ellis was equally convinced of the link between any crime committed by a woman and menstrual cycle, while even later Burt warned his (male) readers of the dangers of that "monthly crisis" that led women "to roam the streets and accost young men" or to commit "such crimes as shop-lifting."[10] The alleged peculiarities of the female body and mind could work to the advantage of some criminal women. Courts, for a variety of reasons, were reluctant to find mothers guilty of murdering their young infants, and it was possible to maintain the image of devoted motherhood by appealing to puerperal mania and the trauma of childbirth as the cause of such an unmotherly act as child murder. The same sympathy however did not extend to "wicked" stepmothers or to baby farmers.[11]

The decades around the turn of the 20th century saw a coming together of long-established perceptions of female criminality, in which external physical "defects" mirrored internal, moral failings, with the latest continental positivist criminology. Having identified a degenerate type of female criminal, Ellis offered a breathtaking explanation of the long-term decline in the numbers of female criminals. "Masculine, unsexed, ugly abnormal women—the women, that is, most strongly marked with the signs of degeneration and therefore the tendency to criminality—would be to a large extent passed by in the choice of a mate, and would tend to be eliminated."[12] Late Victorian males must have found considerable satisfaction (and great relief) in the knowledge that their discernment in the marriage market was solving the awful problem of female crime!

Even starker was the analysis of Lombroso and Ferrero, whose book appeared in translation as *The Female Offender* in 1895. Like her male counterpart, the female criminal was atavistic. Unfortunately, Lombroso and Ferrero had difficulty in distinguishing between the characteristics of criminal and noncriminal women, though the former did tend to be more virile and coarse-voiced. Never willing to let facts get in the way of a good theory, they decided that as all women were, because of their biological inferiority to men, atavistic to a degree, then the differences between noncriminal and criminal women would be less marked than for noncriminal and criminal men! That is, with the exception of the prostitute who was the very embodiment of primitive woman—masked only by her make-up.[13]

Despite (or perhaps because of) their rarity, murderesses were the most reviled of female criminals. Often represented as ugly and masculine (notwithstanding the fact that the likes of Maria Manning or Florence Maybrick were indisputably feminine in appearance), these "creatures" had transgressed both the law and femininity. They posed a threat to society itself. Not for nothing was the murder of a husband (uxoricide) deemed to be petty treason. Some writers, notably John Stuart Mill and Harriet Taylor, spoke out on behalf of women as victims of harsh domestic circumstances, but the more common response was to excuse men for their violence against "nagging wives" while denying sympathy to a woman who responded in a similar fashion to an unreasonable husband. Still less was there any sympathy for the woman who resorted to that "most hideous wickedness," as *The Times* described it in 1849, the use of poison.[14] Although exceptional, the murderess highlighted a particular concern for Victorian society. Such creatures ought not to exist, given the dominant beliefs about the "natural" qualities of women, but they did, and this posed real difficulties in both explaining their offending behavior and dealing with it within the criminal justice system. As Knelman graphically expressed it, "Murder by a woman was so unthinkable in the patriarchal ideology of Victorian England that it had to be explained away as the action of a whore, witch, monster or madwoman."[15]

A radically different perspective was offered by a number of Victorian feminists (not that the term was used at the time) who challenged the gender-natured and double standards of Victorian society and appealed to women across class lines. The campaign against the Contagious Diseases Acts enabled women such as Josephine Butler to identify with the despised prostitutes and to argue that all women were, to a greater or lesser degree, victims of male exploitation. All women could fall foul of these discriminatory laws, but in a more general and more shocking sense, there was much in common between working-class and middle-class women. The former were often forced into prostitution; the latter into that legalized prostitution that was marriage.[16] "Call them *knocked-down* women, if you will but not fallen!"[17] Some men sympathized, most did not.

As well as being worrying in their own right, how (many Victorian and Edwardian experts asked) could such women take on their natural responsibilities for the care and moral training of their children? Not surprisingly, concern with the failures of working-class parents (but mothers in particular) led to exaggerated fears about the criminal propensities of the next generation. Criminal youngsters, some of whom were seen to be part of criminal gangs, others to exist in a near feral state, aroused fears in many quarters. The idea of children trained to a life of crime was not confined to the pages of *Oliver Twist*. Fascination and fear combined in the accounts of the "street Arabs," "English kaffirs," "human vermin," and "ownerless dogs" that were to be found in the literature of the 1840s. Fagin and his gang of child-thieves were among the less scaremongering representations of the early Victorian years. For some like the Earl of Shaftesbury the threat from the dangerous classes was compounded by the presence of political "extremism" in the form of Chartism. Even for a sympathetic observer, such as Mary Carpenter, for whom the very term *juvenile delinquent* was both an anomaly and a dreadful evil, saw something unnatural in young offenders who exhibited "in almost every respect qualities the very reverse of what we should desire to see in childhood; we have beheld them independent, self-reliant, advanced in the knowledge of evil."[18]

Unsurprisingly, contemporaries explained such deviant behavior in terms of defective parenting and corrupting influences, exacerbated by the squalid conditions in which so many juvenile offenders existed. Walter Buchanan was scathing, if fearful.

> There are many hundreds—perhaps I may safely say thousands—of such children in this Metropolis who have been thieves from their infancy, and who have no other pursuit . . . In the densely crowded lanes and alleys of these localities [such as St. Gile's, Seven Dials, Hoxton, Wapping and Ratcliffe] wretched tenements are found, containing in every cellar and on every floor, men and women, children both male and female, all huddled together, sometimes with strangers, and too frequently standing in very doubtful consanguinity to each other. In these abodes decency and shame have fled; depravity reigns in all its horror . . . Almost all are of the lowest and vilest grade and character. Such then are the progenitors of our young thieves and mendicants; and in such dark holes and noxious corners are they brought into life.

Juvenile Offenders, c. 1840. A relatively sympathetic representation of the "street Arabs" that terrified early Victorian Britain. (Courtesy Mary Evans Picture Library)

In such circumstances there was no hope.

> During these ten, twelve, or fifteen hours [during the day when their parents seek their "precarious" living] their unfortunate offspring are not only suffered to roam at large, but are often let to beggars by the day or hour, or in many instances compelled to beg and plunder in order to satisfy the cravings of hunger; moreover forced to bring to their parents or associates some fruits of their purloining and begging . . . and are cruelly beaten and maltreated for failing or neglecting to do so.

Mistreated by their parent, these unfortunate children lacked the saving grace of religion.

> These abandoned children have never offered up a prayer; have never been inside a place of Worship, nor at school; they swear most disgusting and profane oaths; they indulge in the worst passions; they are abominably wicked . . . Such then are the fruitful *first causes of juvenile crime*.

For Buchanan there was an inevitable Hogarthian slide into criminality.

Then follow idleness; corrupt association with other boys, and with prostitutes as young as themselves, who often aid them to rob; the joining of gangs for the sole purpose of thieving; the facility of finding purchasers for their illicit gains; the resorting to low public-houses and gin-shops and penny theatres; the gaming for pence, or shillings, or drink, or divers other causes of corruption;—all conspire to form adept thieves at a precocious age.[19]

Even more dramatic was Samuel Phillips Day's denunciation of the corrupting influence of popular culture.

Equally, if not more vicious, dissolute, and demoralizing are the low play-houses known by the unfashionable epithet of "Penny Gaffs" . . . Having reached the pit, I found it literally crammed with boys, to the number of several hundred, all dirty and untidy . . . Amongst the group were a few men and girls of the lowest class, seemingly delighted with the scenes that were being enacted before them. The yelling, hideous screams, and other horribly noises that arose from this part of the house, were truly deafening, which combined with the close atmosphere, made still more intolerable by the smoke from tobacco-pipes, rendered the place anything but agreeable, or indeed, supportable.

The absence of a respectable adult figure was worrying enough but the subsequent events confirmed Day's worst fears.

The evening's entertainment commenced with a series of low tumbling tricks . . . Next followed a comic vocalist, who illustrated, in character, *Jack Rag*, the crossing-sweeper, by a variety of *pose plastique* antics, some of which were harmless enough, but others had a decided tendency not only to bring sacred historical personages, but even the Holy Book itself, into ridicule . . . The curtain, having now arisen [after a break], a pantomimic play was produced, which, from my very slight acquaintance with the history of that notorious robber and highwayman, *Jack Sheppard*, I knew to be elucidatory of his life and acts. I never witnessed such unrestrained enthusiasm as repeatedly greeted the hero of this piece.[20]

Day was not the only critic of the penny gaffs. Mayhew had been equally worried by the sights that he had witnessed but saw the roots of criminality in other forms of entertainment.

Dancing and singing saloons are another source of mischief, and not only predispose, but in many cases directly lead to juvenile delinquency . . . A further cause of juvenile delinquency arises from the demoralizing publications, the number of which, from the immense circulation they obtain, it is difficult to compute. One thing is certain, that they are fraught with great evil to the community. Under this head may be particularly mentioned the lives of notorious robbers and highwaymen, such as *Jack Sheppard*, *Dick Turpin*, etc., who have been apotheosized by their injudicious biographers, and ridiculously elevated to the ranks of heroes! Such productions are read with avidity, even by those who peruse nothing else . . . Hence we find that many of our juvenile criminals possess little or no education beyond that of being able to read, or being otherwise familiar with those disreputable and demoralizing memoirs.[21]

Particular condemnation was reserved for that "class of publishers and vendors [who] pander to the grossest and most corrupt tastes, by issuing alleged biographies of notorious women of disrepute, spurious physiological treatises, penny numbers of letter-press obscenely illustrated, immodest and highly colored prints and photographs, numbers of which are imported from France."[22] Not for the first or last time, the corrupting influence of the French struck at the heart of England!

In a less dramatic and more sympathetic account, Captain W. J. Williams, Inspector of Prisons, told the Select Committee on Criminal and Destitute Juveniles in 1852 that "[j]uvenile criminals are inevitably from the lowest orders—parents are not always neglectful but they are placed in a certain condition of life in which it is impossible to have control over [their children]."[23] But lacking parental supervision and with time on their hands such children were prey to the less scrupulous for whom young children were ideal as pickpockets or beggars. Did not the devil find work for idle hands? Real-life Fagins were to be found in many parts of the country. In a passage that could have been taken from Oliver Twist, Henry Mayhew described how

[y]oungsters are taught to be expert thieves . . . a coat is suspended from a wall with a bell attached to it and the boy attempts to take the handkerchief from the pocket without ringing the bell . . . Another method is for the trainer to walk up and down the room with a handkerchief in the tail of his coat and the ragged boys amuse themselves by abstracting it until they learn to do it in an adroit manner.[24]

Contemporary commentators believed, as they would given the dominant explanations of juvenile crime, that a combination of improved elementary education and specialist institutions for the "perishing and dangerous" classes had brought about a reduction in juvenile crime, but new fears emerged as the old were laid to rest. A particular cause for concern in the last quarter of the 19th century was the violent young man—the scuttler or the hooligan. Scuttlers were members of adolescent gangs, particularly in and around Manchester and Salford. Gangs such as the Forty Row from Ancoats gained considerable local notoriety in the 1880s. A generation later, their successors, recalled by Robert Roberts in Salford, were known as Ikey Lads. Reports of their activities were frightening. Allegedly some 500 to 600 youths were involved in the Newton Heath scuttle of 1890. Most incidents involved smaller numbers, but the fact that fatalities occurred on more than one occasion emphasized the threat from rampaging youths.[25] Other cities could boast their gangs—Peaky Blinders or Sloggers in Birmingham, the Grey Mare Boys from Bradford, or the High Rip gangs of Liverpool, for example.[26]

And these gangs found an outlet for their activities in the rapidly growing spectator sport of association football. Players and officials were assaulted while rival gangs fought it out near the ground or at the nearby railway station. In exceptional circumstances, such as the 1888 association football cup semifinal between the two leading teams of the day, Aston Villa and Preston North End, troops were on standby throughout and had to intervene to control the crowd at the end of the match. Conflict between rival fans and with the police gave rise to a variety of injuries and, very occasionally, a fatality. At the 1896 Gloucestershire Assizes three men were charged with the murder of a police sergeant and the attempted murder of a constable.[27] In certain cities, notably Glasgow but also Liverpool, religious intolerance reared its ugly head in conflicts between fans of Orange and Green, Protestant and Catholic. The most serious rioting took place after the Scottish Cup Final of 1909 between Rangers and Celtic. With an estimate crowd of 60,000 in the ground, the police found it almost impossible to control the angry scenes that followed the final whistle. Ironically, the disturbances were sparked by the mundane fact that the authorities had made no provision for extra time in the case of a draw, despite the fact the teams had drawn the match a week before. But football violence was not confined to the large cities: Norwich supporters went on the rampage after a match against Chelsea in 1913, while a relatively small town such as Luton, with a team in the humble Southern League, saw scenes of violence from visiting fans from Tottenham in 1898 who took exception to the referee's decision to disallow a goal. In the two decades before the Great War the Football Association cautioned 17 clubs—including Burnley, Glossop, Loughborough, Middlesbrough, and Sunderland—and closed the grounds of 7 others—including Arsenal Bradford City and Notts County. Sheffield Wednesday had the dubious distinction of the only club to be cautioned and have its ground closed.[28]

The "football yob" became subsumed by a new folk devil that appeared in London in the 1890s: the hooligan. With his distinctive dress—"trousers very tight at the knees and loose at the foot" and "the substantial leather belt heavily mounted with metal [but] not intended for ornament"—and distinctive Mohican hair-cut and donkey fringe, here was a figure to put fear into the heart of respectable folk. With a strong sense of local identity, the Chelsea Boys or the Waterloo Road Gang became involved in high-profile pitched battles. The August Bank Holiday of 1898 was best known for the brawl that took place in the Old Kent Road, involving (it was said) 200 to 300 young men variously armed with boots, belts, knives, catapults, and iron bars.[29] *The Times* feared not simply that the hooligan was replacing the fast-disappearing pickpocket but that hooliganism effectively meant that the "larrikin" had arrived in London—an early case of the Empire striking back.[30]

Many explanations of such juvenile delinquency were couched in traditional terms. Lack of parental discipline and the corrupting effect of popular culture figured large in explanations of antisocial and often violent behavior. And yet there was a glimpse of promise in these explanations. Wayward young men misusing the strength and energy could be turned into good citizens—or so the advocates of organizations such as the Boys' Brigade and Scouting argued. There was also a shift of emphasis regarding environmental factors. Slums bred criminals; slum-clearance removed the breeding grounds for future criminals. The Liverpool *Daily Post* reflected on the circumstances that gave rise to gang violence in the city.

> Let anyone walk . . . into the dark, dismal streets and courts lying between Scotland Road and Vauxhall Road; let him witness the narrow lives of the inhabitants . . . their sole relief to the constant offence against sound and sight and scent to which they are ever exposed being the coarse animal pleasure offered by the gin palace; let him picture a lad born in the midst of this wild welter of misery, knowing nothing of nature except under her most perverted and degraded forms . . . always at odds with the representatives of law and order, and with all this, having to fight against hunger and ill-usage—imagine all these conditions, reader, and you have the explanation of the existence of the "High Rip Gang."[31]

A far more depressing explanation came from those preoccupied with the alleged degeneration of the English race. Somewhat perversely in the light of oft-reported scuttles and brawls, there were those who characterized the juvenile offender as weak.[32] Repeat juvenile offenders, according to Cyril Burt, were "frail, sickly, infirm"; they were the embodiment of racial degeneration that worried so many commentators of the 1890s and 1900s. But it was not simply a case of physical weakness. Reflecting a more general awareness of feeble-mindedness, there were a number of scandalous cases of juvenile crime that shocked Edwardian society. The worry that this could engender is well captured in an article written in 1910 by G. Auden, the medical superintendent of the Birmingham Education Committee, on "Feeble-mindedness and Juvenile Crime."[33] Auden cited a number of cases of youthful offenders, all of whom he identified as "moral imbeciles." He then quoted approvingly and at length Sir J. Crichton-Browne's definition in a manner that might be taken to imply that the dangerous *moral imbecile* is a definable and hence detainable individual who can be identified and removed before inflicting damage on others.

There is, however, one highly problematic case that is described in detail, which well illustrates contemporary beliefs.[34] The background to this case was the murder by some person or persons unknown of a "little toddling mite" aged 15 months, who had been found half-buried in rubbish on waste ground in an unspecified part of the north of England. A week later a mother missed her own baby, who had been playing on the door-step, and, on instituting a search, found him in the arms of an eight-year-old boy who had almost reached the fateful waste patch, the scene of the previous murder. He was accompanied by another small boy who was known to be mentally deficient. The [first] boy then made the following statement.

> He had been in the street a week previously, and seeing the little boy crying, had picked him up. As he carried the child about it fell asleep in his arms. He carried it into the field and laid it down while he made a hole with his hands in the débris from the disused ironworks. As he laid the baby on its back in the hole it woke and cried "Mummy! Mummy!" He described how it struggled and kicked while he piled the rubbish, brick ends and a large stone upon the living grave. Having done this, he went home, totally unconcerned, to his tea.

The sense of shock created by this "youthful fiend" was magnified by the fact that

> Every detail of this tale of horror was retailed without the slightest sign of compunction or regret, and he admitted that it had been his intention to repeat his exploit with the baby now found in his arms, though he said that he and his companion (the mentally-deficient child above referred to) had discussed whether they should bury this one or vary their method by drowning it.[35]

The most worrying feature of this whole case for Auden, however, was the fact that the double child killer "had as yet shown no such signs of mental deficiency as had already marked out his companion of his second and fortunately unsuccessful attempt." If there was any consolation to be found in the case it resided in a police officer's report on the boy. Recognizing that the prisoner, though "not very bright" was "not insane," he noted that the boy was illegitimate and had a mother who led "a very immoral life." Clearly such indicators offered some *prima facie* evidence of feeble-mindedness in the family.

CONCLUSION

As with male offenders, Victorian and Edwardian explanations of female and juvenile crime reveal as much, if not more, about contemporary values and fears than they do about the realities of such criminal behavior.

Many Victorians found the very thought of a female criminal frightening—a contradiction in terms that should not exist in a civilized society—but while there were a number of high-profile cases, the fact was that (in terms of court appearances) women were something of a vanishing species. In the early years of Victoria's reign there had been a worryingly high percentage of female offenders in court. In contrast to London, where women accounted for approximately 20 percent of all prisoners at the assizes between 1810 and 1850, in some industrial areas the percentage of women was even higher: 25 percent in the Black Country and 30 percent in Middlesbrough. The latter figure obscures a dramatic change in little over a decade. In the early 1840s women from Middlesbrough accounted for 10 percent of all prisoners appearing at the Northallerton Quarter Sessions. A decade later the figure had risen to 25 percent of the total, reaching 55 percent in 1855.[36]

However, by the late 19th century there had been a sharp reduction in the percentage of women appearing in court, most clearly seen in London, though perversely this had the effect of heightening the sense of threat that surrounded those notorious women who did fall foul of the law, especially those whose convictions ran into the scores and more. The statistics for reoffending for women gave cause for great concern. Between 1860 and 1890 the percentage of female prisoners who had previously been committed to jail rose from 42 percent to 63 percent.[37] Few were as well known as the unfortunate Jane Cakebread, and few came close to matching her record of 280 court appearances on charges of drunkenness, but there were well-known local cases.[38] In north Yorkshire Mary Fentiman, a 24-year-old married woman found guilty of stealing a purse and £7.15.0 ($12.30) at Middlesbrough in 1883, achieved a degree of local notoriety, having been imprisoned 16 times in the previous nine years for a variety of offenses ranging from indecency, drunk and riotous behavior, to theft. So too did 22-year-old Mary Ann Smith, who appeared in court at Northallerton in June 1886 but had been imprisoned on 16 previous occasions for a range of offenses, including using obscene language, prostitution, drunk and disorderly behavior, willful damage, and theft. Again, a note of warning needs to be sounded about the selectivity of prosecutions that created a self-fulfilling prophecy.

Concerns with juvenile delinquency were ever close to the surface of Victorian society, but assessing the age of criminals is problematic. Compulsory registration of births was not introduced until 1836, and in addition to those who genuinely did not know, there were those who falsified their age in the belief, well-founded or otherwise, that this would bring them more lenient treatment. The official figures are likely to overstate the scale of juvenile crime, although one can but speculate on the precise scale of this problem.[39] Exaggerated or not, Victorians were much exercised by young offenders, and at least one historian (Tobias) has argued that the increase in criminal activity was largely associated with young offenders; the official statistics lend only qualified support to this point of view. Forty percent of offenders in the period 1834–1841 were aged 21 or under, and 30 percent were under 20 in the period 1842–1847. Yet, according to the 1841 census 46 percent of the population was aged under 20. The greatest overrepresentation was for people in their late teens and twenties, but there was also a disproportionate number of people in their thirties.[40]

A further point needs to be made about juvenile delinquency over the course of the 19th century. The criminalization of relatively petty offenses that previously went unnoticed by the law and the extension of summary justice to cover more juvenile crimes probably led to an increased willingness to prosecute young offenders.[41] Similarly, the problem was also "manufactured" by other changes. The growing number of policemen and the extension of their discretionary powers led to youngsters appearing before the courts for such heinous offenses as playing cricket in the street, flying kites, and bowling hoops. Finally, magistrates were driven by a belief that children, particularly in towns, were so precocious and depraved that they were capable of acting criminally at any age. Certainly, there was a decline in the presumption of *incapacitas* for those under 14 years of age. Thus, the fear of juvenile criminality became self-fulfilling.

The prison returns of the late 19th century, relating to both indictable and summary offenses, show an aging criminal population in which young offenders were relatively less important. In 1861 about 30 percent of male offenders were aged 20 or under and almost 40 percent were 30 or over. By 1891 the contrast was even greater. Fifty percent of offenders were 30 or over but only 20 percent were 20 or under. The contrast for female offenders was even greater. In 1861 25 percent were 20 or under and just under 40 percent were 30 or over. By 1891 some 60 percent were 30 or over, but only 10 percent were 20 or under.

From 1893 the annual statistics distinguished by age group those convicted of indictable offenses. The figures point to a decline in serious crime among juveniles. In 1895 40 percent of the total number convicted for indictable offenses were aged under 21. By 1905 the figure had fallen to 35 percent. More striking, was the decline in the number of juvenile offenders as a percentage of the relevant age group. Between 1895 and 1905 the number of offenders aged from 12 to 16 fell from 261 per 100,000 to 218, a decline of 17 percent, while for those aged 16 to 21 the fall was from 321 to 275, or 14 percent.

The vast majority of convicted criminals, women more so than men, were drawn from the least educated sections of society. The percentage of female prisoners who could neither read nor write was in the low to mid 40s in the mid-19th century, falling somewhat but still in the mid to upper 30s thereafter. In contrast, the percentage of men in this category remained largely constant from 1840 to 1880, hovering in the low 30s and dropping sharply to the low 20s by 1890. However, this has to be set in the context of steadily improving literacy rates in the population at large. This is consistent with the view that the late Victorian prison population was drawn more from the illiterate and unskilled than had been the case in the early Victorian years.

Despite the recurring preoccupation with uncontrolled sexuality, there is little hard evidence to show that this was the predominant cause of female crime. The most common offenses for women were associated with prostitution, which although not a crime in itself was seen as a step to a life of crime, but few women became prostitutes because of their unbridled sexual urges. Nor, contrary to another popular explanation, were the vast majority of "fallen women" the victims of seduction and abandonment. Poverty was the most important factor. For many working-class women so few and precarious were the opportunities to earn a living that prostitution was seen as an almost in-evitable phase through which many young women would pass. Indeed, despite the obvious and well-known health hazards, prostitution offered a woman the opportunity to earn much more than would otherwise be the case and, at least until the 1860s, also offered her some independence and a degree of control over her life in a way that other jobs did not. This was to change in the late 19th century as prostitutes became more of an outcast group and prostitution became more male controlled.[42] As for those other women who came before the courts, their crimes also related more to poverty. This was particularly true of seamstresses and milliners and those working in the sweated trades gener-ally. Servant girls stealing from their mistresses and widows stealing from the people who employed them as charladies are recurring figures in the courts. Receiving was also more of a female crime, but again its explanation is not to be found in the peculiar sexuality of the women concerned.

It is easier to reconstruct what Victorian commentators thought about the causes of crime than to identify the determinants of offending behavior. Contemporary beliefs were often misplaced and simplistic at best, evasive at worst. But the 21st-century observer, living in a society experiencing levels of crime that would have shocked our Victorian forebears and still grappling unsuccessfully to explain this criminality, should sympathize with, rather than criticize, the failures of pundits in the past. They struggled to explain a problem. The most perceptive explanations of the day now appear to later generations as blinkers that hampered rather than helped their quest for an explanation, but in a very real sense Victorian criminals were constructed by the dominant beliefs of the day. Working-class men and women were more likely to be seen as criminal than middle- or upper-class people. Men and women who were deemed not to be respectable were more likely to appear in court. Women who worked in factories were more likely to be labeled as prostitutes, and women who walked alone at night were self-evidently so! Youths in gangs, walking the streets or hanging around street corners were (as now) targets for the law, even when they were guilty of little more than boisterousness. Itinerant hawkers and traders, indeed anyone of no fixed abode, as well as gypsies were under greater suspicion of criminal behavior than the resident population, as also were the Irish. These were the people who were kept under more general scrutiny and who were more heavily po-liced. Unsurprisingly, more of them were brought before the courts, but in a self-fulfilling prophecy, this confirmed that the initial "judgment" was cor-rect and the need to keep such "lawless" groups under control reinforced. This was not a failing peculiar to the Victorians. The criminal, as much as his or her crime, remains to a very large extent a social construct. Thus, it is not only easier but, in some respects, more valuable to discover what a society decides to be unacceptable and what steps it takes to prosecute such behavior than to seek to discover what makes the criminal man or woman.

PART III

COURTS AND COPPERS

CHAPTER SEVEN

CREATING CRIMINALS

Victorian Courts

A t the center of the Victorian criminal justice system stood the courts of law. Those found guilty in them became criminals, to be faithfully recorded, along with their punishments, by the clerks of court who were part of a wider bureaucracy that measured the health of the nation. And when Victorians thought of courts of law, they thought of the assizes or quarter sessions where trial by jury was to be seen by all who attended, and for the most part, they shared the confidence expressed by Blackstone that "trial by jury ever has been and . . . ever will be looked upon as the glory of the English law . . . [I]t is the most transcendent privilege which any subject can enjoy . . . that he cannot be affected either in his property, his liberty or his person but by the unanimous consent of twelve of his neighbours and equals."[1]

Rooted in the past but relevant to the present, trial by jury was part of a wider constitutionalism that guaranteed liberties in Britain in a way that was not found on the continent of Europe—or so it was popularly believed. This Whiggish view of history was comforting but misleading. Putting aside the dismissive attitude toward alternative legal systems and the failure to appreciate different pathways to civil liberties, such a complacent view overlooked significant changes as well as important shortcomings in this "grand bulwark" of liberties. Miscarriages of justice will be considered later, but first it is important to examine the role of magistrates or police courts and the changing nature of the trial by jury in the criminal justice system.

The rapid growth in summary justice from the 1840s onward, discussed in earlier chapters, meant that the most common trial experience in Victorian and Edwardian Britain was in a local magistrate's or sheriff's court. The situation at the start of Victoria's reign was less than satisfactory. There was no obligation to hold sessions in public, and in some areas the press was routinely excluded. In addition, there were no clearly defined procedures. Petty sessions took place in a wide variety of locations as returns collected in 1845 clearly showed. Local workhouses, national schools, even "a private room, lately sold as a straw hat warehouse," and "my office" were among the stranger locations

"*HIS FIRST OFFENCE.*"

MR. DEVINE SPEAKING FOR THE
PRISONER.

Court Scene, 1891. A juvenile offender faces "the beak." (Courtesy Mary Evans
Picture Library)

in England and Wales. Public houses, such as the King's Arms, Ampthill, the
Saracen's Head, Beaconsfield, or the White Hart Inn, Welwyn, were widely
used. In a county such as Norfolk petty sessions were twice as likely to be
held in an inn or public house as in a town hall or other public place. In the
North Riding of Yorkshire and Westmoreland, to take but two examples, the
balance between public house and public building was roughly even, while
in the more industrialized counties of the West Riding of Yorkshire and Lancashire over 60 percent of petty sessions were held in official buildings.[2] Some
returns made no attempt to disguise inadequacies. At Newport Pagnell the
justices used "an incommodious room at the Swan Inn," while on Anglesey,
use was made of "a parlour in the House [of the Panton Arms Tavern] of
very small dimensions and unsuitable for carrying on the great business of
the district."[3] The Petty Sessions Act of 1849 set about tackling the problem of unsatisfactory premises but more important (and more immediate in
its impact) was Jervis's Summary Proceedings Act of 1848, which required
magistrates to sit in open court and prescribed a procedural code. The 1879
Summary Jurisdiction Act extended summary justice but also gave to those

who faced on conviction a sentence of three months or more the right to elect for trial by jury.

Magistrates were for the most part unpaid amateurs. As a consequence an important but oft-time overlooked figure in the magistrate's court was the clerk to the justices upon whom they relied. Prior to 1877 there was no requirement for a clerk to have any legal training; hence the importance of handbooks, most particularly, Burn's *Justice of the Peace* and Stone's *Justices' Manual*, which became the standard work by the end of the 19th century. The quality of the justice dispensed was questionable. It was widely believed in the first half of the 19th century that rural magistrates used the Game Laws to protect their interests, while their urban counterparts similarly exploited the Factory Acts and similar legislation. The 1835 Report of the Royal Commission on the Municipal Corporations of England and Wales had no doubt as to the "evils resulting from the ignorance and inefficiency of the borough magistrates."[4] Spectacular examples of class bias can easily be found, but it would be unwise to generalize from the exceptional. Undoubtedly the greater openness after 1848 improved matters, but magistrates' courts retained a reputation for almost unquestioning support for the police and a tendency toward harshness toward the working classes. Gamon, commenting specifically on London in the early 20th century, had no doubt. "The police court . . . bears an evil reputation, and it is easy to see why."[5]

There were a small but growing number of stipendiary magistrates. The best known were to be found in London, dating back to the late 18th century. In the mid-19th century there were 13 courts and 26 magistrates; by the early 20th century the numbers had risen to 14 and 27. Manchester and Salford appointed paid magistrates in the first decade of the 19th century, and the 1835 Municipal Corporations Act allowed a municipal borough to appoint a stipendiary magistrate. Legislation in 1863 allowed towns of over 25,000 to do the same.

Little attention has been given to the detailed work of magistrates' courts, particularly outside London. Certain specific issues, notably the enforcement of labor legislation, have been explored in a number of localities. There is evidence, mainly from the west midlands in the mid-19th century, suggesting that the newer magistrates, drawn from the ranks of iron-masters and industrialists, were unwilling to enforce such legislation as the Truck Act and took a very partial stance when enforcing the Master and Servant Act.[6] It is in London that the full range of activities of the police courts can be appreciated. Further, the workings of the courts throw valuable light onto the implementation of the law. The London magistrates had considerable powers under the 1839 Police Act, which were extended by the legislation of the 1850s. The courts dealt with a large number of cases—some 100,000 a year in the mid-19th century—but were also involved in providing adjudications as well as advice and charity.[7] As one magistrate expressed it, "the value of an effective magistrate does not consist more in the strict legal performance of his judicial and administrative duties, than in the exercise of sound discretion, and in the considerate application of the principles and feelings of humanity as an adviser, an arbitrator and a mediator."[8]

This dual approach was essential to win public support for the judicial system. An awareness of the harsh realities of working-class life enabled some magistrates to intervene on behalf of the poor when they fell foul of the educational or poor law authorities, but there were limits to the extent to which they could act as champions of the poor. This was particularly the case when the police brought prosecutions, as they increasingly did. It was rare indeed for a magistrate not to accept without question police evidence given on oath. H. T. Waddy, looking back on his experiences as a police court magistrate, ruefully observed: "There are two unfortunate impressions as to the police court which exist widely in the minds of the working classes. One is that the policeman is both witness and prosecutor, and the other is that the magistrate is the creature of the police."[9]

The work of the police court throws up other interesting perspectives. It was undoubtedly the case that employers made use of the courts in their attempt to combat theft by their employees, but this tended to be the last rather than the first resort. Informal methods, including dismissal and blacklisting, were effective (and cheaper) deterrents, except perhaps in times of full employment. Employer discretion—a very 18th-century practice surviving well into the 19th—undoubtedly distorted the official crime figures. As one might expect, shopkeepers prosecuted shoplifters and landlords prosecuted defaulting tenants, but it would be wrong to suggest that prosecutors were middle class and the prosecuted working class. It is quite clear that members of the working classes made increasing use of the courts but again in a complex and selective manner. Informal sanctions continued to be used where appropriate, and prosecutions were stopped short of formally pressing charges—again, practices associated more with 18th-century justice. The difference was that the easier access to the law in the mid and late 19th century led to a redrawing of the boundary between unofficial and official sanction.

Despite the growth of summary justice, the "grand bulwark" of English liberties, in Blackstone's words, that is trial by jury—at quarter sessions or assizes—continued to attract considerable attention. The form of that trial, particularly in London, had changed significantly before Victoria ascended the throne. The old face-to-face confrontation of an earlier age had been gradually replaced by the "modern" adversarial trial. Driven initially by the determination of major institutions, such as the Royal Mint and the Bank of England, prosecution lawyers began to invade the Old Bailey in the late 18th century. Later merchants and shopkeepers began to follow suit. The "invasion" continued with defense lawyers appearing, though less frequently, as a response to the imbalance created by the use of prosecution lawyers.[10] However, the extent of change can easily be exaggerated. Not all London trials involved lawyers, and this was more so the case outside London. Furthermore, the emergence of the full adversarial trial was held back by the restrictions on defense counsel that were not removed until 1836. Even then concern with the dangers of an irresponsible defense counsel had a dampening effect. Nonetheless, the criminal trial was being reconceptualized and reformed. The trial of the Rugeley poisoner, William Palmer, in 1856 was a turning point. It was greeted as a triumph for adversarialism in which the emphasis was on testing the prosecution case rather than simply evaluating the performance of the accused.[11] The Palmer case was fiendishly complex, not least in the scientific detail. Palmer's defense was zealous and ingenious, but it was the bravura performance of the prosecution counsel, Sir Alexander Cockburn, that evoked admiration. A respected and influential writer on legal matters, Fitzjames Stephen, was at the trial and was convinced that "it exhibited in its very best and strongest light the good side of English criminal procedure."[12] Thereafter the adversarial trial became increasingly common.

The passing of the Prisoner's Counsel Act in 1836 was an important development.[13] Defense counsels now had the rights in all felony cases that previously had been restricted to treason cases only. It is not clear that concern for prisoners' rights was a major factor in driving reform. On the contrary, it was a desire to increase successful prosecutions that was paramount. The restriction on defense counsel was seen to be unfair, and juries (or so it was feared) gave defendants the benefit of the doubt. The limitations of the act—the low quality of defense counsels taking the dock brief—soon became apparent. Well-to-do defendants, such as Constant Kent or Florence Maybrick, had little difficulty in gaining the advice of a solicitor from the outset. Not so the poor. As a correspondent to the *Law Times* commented in 1851, the Prisoner's Counsel Act was "a cruel aggravation of the distinction between the man who had a guinea or friends and the man who had not."[14] There were some stark examples of the poverty of defendants, even in murder cases. William Distin, who was subsequently hanged despite a recommendation for mercy, was described as "entirely friendless . . . at the trial, no solicitor being retained on his behalf."[15] Thomas Wheeler was only marginally more fortunate in that he was represented at his trial but unfortunately "[p]risoners counsel intimated that he would not call any witnesses or present any evidence for the defence."[16] Demands for reform were limited before the 1880s, and it was not until 1903 that the Poor Prisoner's Defence Act accepted the principle that prisoners without means should not be disadvantaged, but legal assistance was conditional on disclosure of defense at the committal stage. This was particularly unhelpful as the best legal advice to defendants remained to reserve one's defense. To make matters worse, before 1914 judges took a very negative attitude in their interpretation of the act.

The defendant was also not permitted to give evidence on oath. This became the subject of considerable debate in the late 19th century. Proponents of reform argued that the defendant was disadvantaged by enforced silence in court to the extent that innocent people were convicted. Others felt that exposure in the witness box would weaken the position of the defendant, particularly if he or she were easily confused, liable to outbursts of temper, or prone to lying. The formal caution—"You are not obliged to say anything unless you desire to do so but whatever you do say will be taken down in writing and may be given in evidence against you at your trial"—introduced in 1848 was intended to prevent self-incrimination by accused, who Stephen later described as "poor, stupid and helpless."[17] Eventually legislation was passed in 1898, though, once again, this probably owed more to a desire to secure convictions by subjecting the defendant to cross-examination than to any wish to strengthen the rights of the accused or prevent miscarriages of justice.[18]

A number of important changes followed from the new style trial. The pre-trial interrogatory role of the magistrate declined and was formally abolished in 1848. Similarly, the role of the Grand Jury diminished, though, there were demands for abolition in the 1830s, but it had still played a part, rejecting just under 10 percent of homicide bills in the second half of the 19th century. Trials themselves changed and became more formalized. Judges were more distanced from court proceedings, trials became longer, though most late 19th-century trials were decided within a day.

Despite doubts about certain cases, there was general confidence for much of the early and middle years of Victoria's reign—best expressed by J. S. Mill during the debate on capital punishment in 1868 but reasserted by William Harcourt in 1881—that miscarriages of justice simply did not occur. Attempts to establish a court of criminal appeal failed six times between 1853 and 1864. This sat uncomfortably with the fact that the Home Office had granted a dozen pardons because of clear miscarriages of justice in the period 1857 to 1882. The trial and execution of Israel Lipski in 1887 and, even more so, the conviction of Florence Maybrick in 1889 aroused considerable public protests at perceived miscarriages of justice, but these cases also revealed the problematic state of ad hoc investigations by the Home Office.[19] Still nothing happened. Then, not long after Victoria's death, two high-profile scandals shattered the complacency and inertia regarding the question of criminal appeal. In 1904 it emerged that Adolph Beck had been wrongly accused and convicted not once, but twice. The detail of the case highlighted some major weaknesses in the administration of the criminal law. The background to the case was a series of frauds perpetrated in 1877 by a man called Thomas Smith on respectable but gullible women whom he persuaded to part with their jewelry. The crimes stopped when he was imprisoned and started up again in his release in 1891. The unfortunate Beck was arrested and "identified" by several women who had been defrauded and also by the police officers, now retired, who had arrested Smith in 1877. A key element in the prosecution case was a series of letters allegedly written in Beck's disguised handwriting. The judge ruled that defense counsel could not cross examine the handwriting experts, which meant that Beck's alibi—he was in Lima, Peru, in 1877—could not be established at the trial. Beck was sentenced to seven years' penal servitude. During his time in prison he petitioned the Home Office 16 times to have his case re-examined but to no avail. He was released in 1901 but three years later was arrested on charges very similar to those for which he was originally found guilty. Again he was found guilty. The judge, however, had some doubt and reserved sentence to enable further enquiries to be made. Fortunately for Beck, Thomas Smith was arrested and confessed to all the frauds. Beck was granted two free pardons and compensation of £5,000 ($7,950).[20] The committee of inquiry established to examine the case accepted that major errors had been made by the judge at the original trial and later by the Home Office, which had failed to act on the information it received in 1898 that Smith was circumcised and Beck not!

Even more scandalous was the case of George Edalji, a young Birmingham solicitor, the son of an Anglican clergyman of Parsee descent, living in Staffordshire. Accused via anonymous letters of disemboweling a horse, he was arrested, tried, found guilty, and sentenced to seven years' penal servitude in 1907. There were several problematic aspects to the case. First, George had an alibi from his father. Second, given his extremely poor eyesight, it was unlikely that he could have found his way through a stormy night to the paddock where the crime had taken place. Third, incidents of animal maiming continued after his arrest and imprisonment. Some 10,000 people signed a petition on his behalf only for it to be ignored by the Home Office. In 1906 the case was taken up by Sir Arthur Conan Doyle and such was the publicity engendered by the creator of Sherlock Holmes, demonstrating that Edalji could not have committed the crime for which he was incarcerated, that the Home Office finally gave way. A special inquiry determined that the conviction was unsound, but because the evidence did not positively establish innocence, it did not recommend a pardon. Eventually Edalji was pardoned, but shamefully in a case that had already been disgraced by racial prejudice, no compensation was awarded.[21]

Belatedly politicians reacted, and a Criminal Appeal Act was passed in 1907, some 50 years after Fitzroy Kelly and William Ewart first introduced a reform bill in parliament. The act allowed for appeal to a new court that would decide whether a conviction would stand, be modified, or set aside. The original sentence could be confirmed, reduced, or increased, but there was no power to order a retrial. The Home Office still retained responsibility for exercising the prerogative of mercy.[22]

The workings of the Victorian and Edwardian courts cannot simply be understood in terms of the legal changes just discussed. Wider social and intellectual pressures played an important part in the evolution of court procedures and practice. The impact of developing scientific thought and changing gender assumptions will be considered to illustrate this point.

A key consideration was the fitness of the accused to stand trial. Rationality was certainly key. Quite simply, if a person was not of sound mind, how could he be held responsible for his actions? In the 1800 landmark trial of Hadfield, who had shot at George III, Erskine had argued that "it is THE REASON of man that makes him accountable for his actions; and . . . the deprivation of reason acquits him of crime."[23] From that time, the Home Office had the power to hold all people deemed to be criminally insane—the so-called Queen's Pleasure lunatics. The early Victorian years saw a number of high-profile cases that were to have a profound long-term influence. In 1840 Edward Oxford shot at the Queen. At his trial medical experts diagnosed "hereditary moral insanity," and he was acquitted and committed to Bethlem Asylum. Three years later Daniel McNaughten killed Sir Robert Peel's private secretary. He also was found not guilty by reason of insanity. Not only had nine medical experts been called in his defense, but the highly talented Alexander Cockburn made a highly effective plea to "listen with patient attention to the evidence of men of skill and science . . . [because] modern science has incontrovertibly established that any one of these intellectual and moral functions of the mind may be subject to separate disease, and thereby man may be rendered victim of the most fearful delusions, the slave of uncontrollable impulses impelling or rather compelling him to acts such [as murder] . . . now under your consideration."[24]

Victoria was alarmed at both trial outcomes and wrote to Peel expressing her worries. The upshot was the so-called McNaughten rules, strictly a test of criminal responsibility rather than of insanity, which laid down that "to establish a defence on the ground of insanity, it must be clearly proved that at the time of committing the act the accused was labouring under such a defect of reason, from disease of the mind, as not to know the nature and quality of the act that he was doing; or if he did know it, that he did not know he was doing what was wrong."[25]

Not all worries were allayed by the new rules. Judges in particular were resistant to change in the mid-19th century. None more so than Baron Alderson, who in 1844 kept a jury locked up without food, water, and heat (as was his right) for almost a whole day until the jury rejected an insanity defense and convicted a wife-killer of murder. To underline the strength of his feeling, he recommended the home secretary to uphold the sentence of death on the grounds that "this plea of madness is a palliative of unruly passions leading to murder and is very dangerous."[26] In these years there was but a slight increase in the number of verdicts of not guilty by reason of insanity, and not many death sentences were not upheld on appeal on grounds of insanity. Nonetheless, the arrival of the forensic-psychiatric witness was a significant development.[27] The McNaughten rules, although intended to close down debate, merely set the ground for later discussion among medical and legal experts. As psychiatric and psychological knowledge developed in the forthcoming years the McNaughten rules came under increasing attack from both those who saw them as too broad in application and those who saw them as too narrow in definition of insanity. Influential figures, such as the medical advisor to the Home Office Dr. William Guy, argued that the mentally abnormal or deficient had a propensity toward violence, and others stressed the role of an "irresistible impulse" in violent crime. There was a tension between the Home Office and the new breed of "alienists," but an accommodation was reached and the Home Office increasingly used medical experts, such as Dr. Alfred Swayne Taylor and Dr. William Thompson, from the late 1860s onward.[28] This and the opening in 1863 of Broadmoor as an institution for the criminally insane help explain the growing number of criminally insane, though other factors, not least the growing restrictions on provocation defenses, played a part.

The number of people declared insane or not fit to plead increased from 99 in the 1860s (15 percent of the total committed for murder) to 232 (34% of the total) in the early 20th century.[29] There was also an increase in the number of special verdicts, that is those "not guilty by reason of insanity" before 1883 and "guilty but insane" following the 1883 Trial of Lunatics Act. Special verdicts accounted for around 5 percent of the total number committed for trial for murder in the 1860s but almost 40 percent by 1900.[30] In a number of cases the Home Office was happy to save money by short-circuiting expensive trial procedures when there was a strong likelihood of an insanity verdict, provided there was no opposition from family or friends.[31] The individuals, declared insane before trial, became known as the "Secretary of State's lunatics." But not everyone was happy with this trend. Justice Wills for one complained to the Home Office about "the extreme and growing frequency of the [insanity] defence in murder cases."[32]

In fact, most capital cases involving insanity were relatively straightforward and could be explained in terms of congenital idiocy, senile dementia, physical damage to the brain, or epilepsy, and the existence of persistent delusions also allowed an argument to be made for temporary insanity. The latter was highly problematic, not least because of class-based assumptions—temporary insanity was not something from which a "rough" working-class man would (even could) suffer. The near-contemporaneous cases of laborer Richard Addington and the Rev. John Selby Watson, former headmaster of Stockwell Grammar School, London, and a homicidal historian, illustrate the point well. A self-absorbed and somewhat eccentric schoolmaster, Watson was nonetheless a respectable middle-class figure. Out of the blue, he savagely beat his wife to death with a pistol and concealed the body for two days before attempting suicide. Watson obtained the services of a solicitor immediately after his arrest and a defense of insanity was prepared with the help of, among others, two eminent figures, Dr. Henry Maudsley as chief witness for the defense and Mr. Serjeant Parry as defense counsel. The jury found Watson guilty but recommended

mercy on account of "his age and previous character." Following several petitions for mercy and an unusual delay, Watson was reprieved and sentenced to
penal servitude, but the Home Office notes suggest that the home secretary,
the permanent under-secretary at the Home Office, and the trial judge all
assumed that the *middle-class* Watson was temporarily insane, even though
Maudsley never made this explicit in his evidence. In a not dissimilar earlier
case, Aldington, a farm laborer, had murdered his wife with a cobbler's knife,
but neither the jury nor the Home Office was persuaded by a plea of insanity,
even though Dr. Thomas Pritchard of the local asylum gave evidence that this
case was one of homicidal mania and persistent delusion.[33]

Psychiatric explanations were particularly important in the case of infanticide. All women, it was believed, were liable to "puerperal mania" following childbirth, and there was also the risk of "lactational insanity."[34] As
A. Herbert Safford noted in 1866 "that a mother should be capable of killing
her infant is a fact that even the strong intellect of a man cannot compass,
and we consequently rarely find a jury that returns a verdict of willful murder
against a woman so accused."[35]

But attitudes were tempered by both the age at which the child was killed
and the age of the mother. Selena Wadge was 27 years old when she killed
her illegitimate son by throwing him down a well so that she could run off
with another man who would not accept the child; she was found guilty
and the Home Office found no reason to intervene. She was executed in
August 1878.[36] Emma Wade was more fortunate, but the fact that she was
only 17, the daughter of a local policeman, and seduced by a local shop assistant helped; so too did the fact that she intended to kill both herself and her
baby but forgot to shake the bottle containing the strychnine-based "Battle's
Vermin Killer."[37]

There were other ways in which "scientific" developments impacted on
trials. Fingerprinting was established as a legitimate source of evidence in the
first decade of the 20th century. In September 1902 Henry Jackson had the
dubious honor of being the first person to be convicted through such evidence.
More importantly, in 1909 the court of criminal appeal upheld a conviction
based solely on fingerprint evidence in *R v Castleton*, in contrast to the decision in *R v Chadwick* a year earlier. But the breakthrough, as much in public
perception, came with the Deptford tragedy of 1902—a double murder of
husband and wife during a night-time robbery—and the subsequent trial and
conviction of the Stratton brothers in 1905. Although not the sole evidence,
the existence of a right thumb print on a cash-box till at the scene of the
crime was a key piece of evidence. The performance of Detective-Inspector
Collins, who presented the forensic evidence, was critical, though he was
helped by the fact that the expert witness for the defense, Dr. J.R. Garson,
had also offered his services to the prosecution; an action which led the judge
to describe him as "an absolutely unreliable [independent] witness."[38]

Equally significant and far more sensational was the Crippen trial of 1910. The case itself had every element of a melodrama. The popular, sociable American Dr. Crippen was married to an ex–music hall singer Belle Elmore, otherwise Cora Crippen. Crippen told friends that she had returned to America to nurse a sick relative, and later mysterious reports of her death appeared; Crippen fled England with a new young lover, Ethel Le Neve, masquerading under the name of Mister and Master Robinson. The police, who originally had not suspected murder, ordered a thorough search of Crippen's empty house and found the partial and mutilated remains of a woman who had been poisoned. Crippen was sought in France, Spain, and Portugal but was sighted on a steamer in the Atlantic. Here was the first wonder of the case—the use of "the powerful agency of wireless telegraphy." In breathless tones a special correspondent of *The Times* wrote that there was "something intensely thrilling and weird" in the fact that two people believed they were traveling in secret safety when the information about them and their whereabouts was being "flashed with certainty to all quarters of the civilized world." Inspector Dew of the Metropolitan Police took a fast ship to Canada and was able to arrest the couple, amid frenzied scenes, thus bringing about the "end of a long and picturesque police chase," when the SS Melrose docked in Canada. *The Times* delighted in the fact that Crippen and Le Neve "have been encased in waves of wireless telegraphy as securely as if they had been in the four walls of a prison."[39] A further twist came when the couple were brought back to London under the Fugitive Offenders Act of 1881. The trial revealed the second wonder—the "surgical and medical evidence" and the advances in "forensic medicine."[40] In particular, the evidence given by Bernard Spilsbury was outstanding. With only a small piece of skin and flesh he was able to demonstrate that, from the presence and arrangement of certain muscles, it was from the wall of the abdomen. Further, via microscopic examination, he showed that there was a scar consistent with a known operation of Belle Elmore.[41] Consciously echoing the Palmer trial, *The Times* concluded that "the trial from first to last showed English criminal justice at its best."[42]

The developing science of ballistics also impacted upon the courts. In 1860 Thomas Richardson was found guilty of the "dastardly deed of shooting a policeman" based on a match between the paper wadding found at the site of the murder (and in the second barrel of Richardson's shot gun) and a newspaper recovered from his home.[43] A more significant advance came some 20 years later, following the murder of another policeman in London. Thomas Orrock was found guilty when gun maker James Squires was able to identify three bullets as being of the type fired from the pin fire cartridges used by the gun Orrock had bought via *Exchange and Mart*.[44] However, only limited reference was made to the ballistic evidence at the trial. The most significant development, whereby a bullet was linked to a specific gun, came in 1912 at the Eastbourne murder case. Again there had been a police fatality. Initially, another gun shop owner, Robert Churchill, was able to identify the bullets recovered at the crime scene as being from a .25 automatic pistol. The police found parts of such a gun hidden on Eastbourne beach. Churchill refitted the gun and test-fired it and was able to show that the test bullets had the same rifling pattern as the bullet that had killed Inspector Walls. At the trial of George McKay, Sergeant William McBride, a police photographer at Scotland Yard, used close-range photography to show the pattern of grooves on the bullets. Also, in a striking *coup de theatre*, he produced wax castings from the gun barrel which showed the same pattern as that of a bullet fired from the gun.[45]

The impact of changing gender assumptions, particularly the redefinition of masculinity in late Victorian Britain, can be seen in the decisions of the courts. Allegations about gender bias in the criminal justice system abound. For example, *the Woman's Herald* in 1892 contrasted the harsh treatment meted out to Florence Maybrick, who was sentenced to 20 years' penal servitude for a crime about which there was considerable doubt, with the leniency showed to George Baker James Cooper, who was sentenced to 10 years' penal servitude for the manslaughter of his wife, whom he stabbed to death with a penknife. The explanation, it was argued was "juries, influenced by sex-bias . . . [that] excuse in a man what they hold inexcusable in a woman."[46] Similar arguments were advanced by late 20th-century feminist historians. Yet, at the same time, it was also argued that women appeared to be more leniently treated at all stages of the criminal justice system. The contradiction can be resolved by recognizing, firstly, that one cannot generalize about criminal men and women, as if they were homogenous categories; secondly, that criminal activities were gendered before they entered the criminal justice system, thereby making differential treatment unsurprising; and finally, that the effects of gender differences developed in complicated and, at times, inconsistent ways rather than as the outcome "of anything as simple as deliberate gendered discrimination."[47] With these points in mind, it is time to consider some of the more important developments that took place in Victorian Britain.

There was a growing intolerance of male violence that can be traced back at least to the beginning of the 19th century.[48] By the beginning of Victoria's reign there was a greater willingness to bring manslaughter cases to trial rather than, as had been the custom in the past, to seek reconciliation outside court; and punishments became more severe. Given the importance attached to self control, it is not surprising to find the many Victorians determined to maintain the principle that people should be held responsible for the consequences of their actions. Increasing reliance was placed on the notion of "the reasonable man," even before this was explicitly spelled out in 1869. Mr. Justice Keating, referring to cases of homicide, made it clear that "the law is that there must exist such an amount of provocation as would be excited by the circumstances in the mind of a reasonable man, and so as to as to lead the jury to ascribe the act to the influence of that passion . . . [such as] a severe blow—something which might naturally cause an ordinary and reasonably-minded man to lose his self-control and commit such an act."[49]

However, notions of self-control and reasonable behavior excluded acts carried out in a state of inebriation. "Drunkenness," in the words of Justice Hill, "is not [and] cannot ever in this country be allowed to be a mitigation of the crime of murder."[50] By the 1880s and 1890s a drunken defense was much less likely to succeed than in the 1830s and 1840s, but that said, opinions still varied, and it was not unknown for juries as late as the 1860s to hand out lenient sentences of a week, even a day, for manslaughter.[51]

More interesting was the change in attitude toward sexual violence. More prosecutions took place, particularly after the death penalty for rape was removed. Sexual assaults, including rape, were seen increasingly as violations against the woman, rather than an offense against another man's rights of property. The shift from "without her consent" to "against her will" similarly reflect the new seriousness with which the Victorians viewed rape. For the first time in 1869 Burn's *Justice* informed clerks of court and magistrates that there was a difference between submission and consent. Weiner concludes his detailed study of sexual violence on a positive note. "By the late years of Victoria's reign and even more by the beginning of World War I, a greater proportion of a larger number of prosecutions for sexual assaults were resulting in convictions than ever before."[52] However, it needs to be stressed that, important as these changes undoubtedly were, they reflect a greater determination to reform masculinity (especially "rough" working-class masculinity) than a desire to protect women per se. "Wife murder," in particular, became a scandal for mid-Victorians. Men charged with the manslaughter of their spouses or partners were treated more severely than men who killed men. Where the charge was murder the situation became harsher still. In the third quarter of the 19th century, prosecutions for wife murder doubled; convictions trebled and acquittals fell.[53] Indeed, in the late 19th century, when sentences generally were becoming shorter, this was not the case for convicted wife murderers. However, once again, it is important to recognize the limits of change. Some judges, notably Barons Alderson and Vaughan, were particularly hostile to male violence, but juries were often more lenient than judges, especially in the case of "nagging" wives. Judges had to tell juries in the 1850s that words, however provocative, could not reduce a murder charge. Equally, husbands of wives or partners who failed to meet the new feminine ideal—through drinking or, worst of all, infidelity—were treated more sympathetically. Jacob Riegelhuth stabbed his wife to death in 1866, but the jury recommended mercy "on the grounds of his youth [he was 23] and her drunken habits." Commissioner Monro provided a report for Godfrey Lushington, the permanent under-secretary at the Home Office, which drew attention to the "wretched story of the deceased woman's bringing up, surroundings and married life." The Liberal Home Secretary, H.C.F. Childers, had no doubt about reprieving Riegelhuth, commenting, that "[b]etween ourselves I do not think the case was a bad one. There was no premeditation. The stabs, of which one was fatal, were inflicted in a moment but there was not more moral guilt in it than in many cases of wounding which do not end fatally."[54]

Similarly, John Key, a 58-year-old printer who brutally murdered his wife with a flat iron, was found guilty but subsequently reprieved. Lushington observed that it was "[a] clear case of murder . . . he having killed her in bed without any provocation. His real provocation was the miserable life she had led him by her drunkenness and he himself appears to have been a respectable man."[55]

However, not all cases followed this pattern as the "sad story" of George Hall illustrates.[56] There was no doubt that Hall murdered his recently married wife, Sarah Ann, but even her mother thought she had behaved inexcusably in sleeping with another man and that Hall deserved to be reprieved. The trial had been melodramatic with a passionate plea from the defendant that was followed by his dead faint. As a respectable, hard-working, and (at least before the fateful night) nonviolent young man, Hall appeared an ideal case for clemency, but it proved difficult to gain him a reprieve. The judge did not endorse the jury's recommendation of mercy, and the head of the judiciary, Lord Chancellor Selbourne, concluded that he felt "compelled to say that the interests of society require that there should not be a commutation of the sentence."[57] The Home Secretary, Sir George Grey, accepted Selbourne's judgment, but faced with a tidal wave of petitions and letters, including one from the Lord-Lieutenant of Warwickshire, noting "the strong feeling among all classes in the county," finally gave way at the last minute.[58] The scaffold had been erected and trains bringing spectators were arriving when Hall's sentence was commuted to life imprisonment. The frustration and anger of those deprived of the spectacle of a hanging was more than offset by the relief of those who felt that, in this case at least, the execution of a wife-murderer would have been unjust.

The tensions aroused by this and similar cases throw an interesting light on changing attitudes in Victorian Britain. This was particularly so when a man murdered his wife's lover. Intent to kill was at its clearest, but provocation at its worst—how should the courts respond? Judges took a hard line; juries and public opinion took a more "tolerant" line of this form of male killing. The Home Office, not noted for its willingness to reprieve guilty murderers, did just that in the three cases it considered of men found guilty of murdering their wives' lovers. Indeed, in the second half of the 19th century there were 38 reprieves for wife murderers on the grounds of provocation compared with only 3 for man-on-man violence.

Nonetheless, in broad terms, the provocation defense, even *in extremis*, lost its force in the last quarter of the 19th century. Lord Chancellor Selbourne noted that "[cases] of adultery occur constantly & often under circumstances of the greatest provocation to the injured husband *but* it would be of the most dangerous consequences to society if such provocation were accepted as a reason for not capitally punishing the husband when he commits a coolly premeditated murder."[59] However, it is perhaps no coincidence that there was an increase in insanity defense pleas.

However, murder and rape were exceptional crimes. Assaults were much commoner, and the evidence, insofar as it has been studied, points in a similar direction. Male assault defendants were more likely to be convicted, especially if fighting another man; female assault defendants to be bound over or have their case dismissed, particularly if it was an all-female fight. More importantly, men were much less likely to be bound over on conviction and more likely to receive long sentences, that is seven days or more, especially if found guilty of assaulting a woman. Whereas women received a "just measure of pain," men were more likely to receive a deterrent amount, even in those highly deviant incidents, for the Victorians and Edwardians, of drunken women brawling with one another. In other words, in contrast to the "doubly deviant" argument that women were more often convicted and more heavily punished, it would appear that male violence was treated more seriously, which fits with the broader "dangerous masculinities" arguments found in Weiner and Emsley, and the perceived need to civilize "brutal" men.[60]

CONCLUSION

Much work remains to be done on the working of the courts in Victorian and Edwardian Britain, but it is clear that important changes took place in these years. Trials at quarter session and assize became more formal following the "invasion of the lawyers," important reforms took place, often motivated by a desire to improve prosecutions, which benefited the defendant. The courts also became more professional: magistrates and clerks, after the 1877 Justices' Clerks Act, were required to have some legal training, and medical and other scientific experts played an increasing role in proceedings.[61] Further, the courts, at all levels, played a number of important roles in redefining expectations and behavior, most notably in the case of "brutal" males. Most important, the courts played a key role in establishing and maintaining the legitimacy of the criminal justice system. To a large extent they succeeded, but if early interpretations overstated working-class hostility to the law and its various enforcement agents, there is a danger of going too far in the opposite direction and underestimating the underlying resentment and hostility to the police and the courts that were still to be found on the eve of World War I. "Begrudging and instrumental acceptance" is perhaps the best way of summing up popular responses.

CHAPTER EIGHT

THE CREATION
OF A POLICED SOCIETY

I n the early 20th century *The Times* spoke in glowing terms of the police in
general and the Metropolitan Police in particular. "The policeman . . . is
not merely guardian of the peace; he is an integral part of its social life. In
many a back street and slum he not merely stands for law and order; he is
the true handy-man of the streets, the best friend of a mass of the people
who have no other counsellor or protector."[1] Reflecting on his childhood in
Edwardian Salford, Robert Roberts had a somewhat different view. "[N]obody
in our Northern slum, to my recollection, ever spoke in fond regard, then or
afterwards, of the policeman as 'social worker' and 'handyman of the streets.'
Like their children, delinquent or not, the poor in general looked upon him
with fear and dislike. When one arrived on a 'social' visit they watched his
passing with suspicion and his disappearance with relief."[2]

Beyond dispute was the fact that Edwardian Britain was a policed society
in a way that it had not been when Victoria ascended the throne. In dispute
was (and remains) the nature of that policed society and the responses of the
policed to the "boys in blue" who had become an integral part of society in
town and country alike.

The history of modern policing in Britain has often been presented as a
relatively unproblematic, if somewhat belated, progression from the creation
of the Metropolitan Police in 1829, through the 1839 Rural Constabulary
Act, to the County and Borough Police Act of 1856: the reality was more
complex and less Anglo-centric and certainly less London dominated. The
origins of the new police, as they are often called, can be found as much in
Scotland and Ireland as in England; but perhaps the most important feature of the development of policing in the first half of the 19th century was
its patchiness, which in turn reflected the persistence of traditional forms of
parish-based policing.

The development of policing in Scotland has for too long been overlooked, but some of the earliest developments in modern policing took place
"north of the border," and the nature of policing and its development during
the 19th century show an alternative route to modernity that has not been

The Kind-Hearted Policeman, 1864. An early representation of the policeman as "handyman of the streets" from the
British Workman. (Courtesy Mary Evans Picture Library)

sufficiently recognized by police historians preoccupied with England.[3] The
first point to stress about policing in 19th-century Scotland is the persistence
of an older and broader concept of policing as "an instrument of urban administration" rather than being restricted to crime control and the maintenance
of public order.[4] Closely related to this was the fact that until late in the
19th-century local initiatives and local forms of management—assisted by
a degree of indifference at Westminster to certain Scottish matters—added
to the distinctiveness of Scottish policing. Finally, and in no small measure
due to this strength of localism, the development of policing in Scotland was
more evolutionary and, with certain exceptions, less confrontational than
in England. Indeed, such was the gradual nature of police reform that the
distinction between old and new police—itself problematic in the English
context—becomes almost meaningless.[5]

Rapid urban growth and its associated problems, notably vagrancy and petty crimes, was a key driver in police reform. It is no coincidence that the earliest initiatives were to be found in Glasgow (1800) and Edinburgh (1805) and in burgeoning trading centers such as Greenock (1801), Port Glasgow (1803), Leith (1806), and Dundee (1824), though smaller towns, such as Arbroath and Montrose, also improved policing provisions. Not all burghs participated. Kirkcaldy, Perth, and Peterhead, for example, excluded watching provisions from their improvement acts.[6] The growth of police forces was encouraged by legislation that allowed existing royal burghs to establish a police force without recourse to a local act of parliament. Thirty-six burghs adopted the 1833 Burgh Police (Scotland) Act, of whom 18 adopted the act in full (such as Kirkwall, Kelso, Thurso, and Mussleburgh), and a further 8 partial adopters (such as Arbroath, Elgin, and Hawick) included watching provisions from the outset.[7] Further legislation in 1850, which updated the 1833 Act, allowed "populous places" of 1,200 inhabitants and more to become police burghs; while the lower limit was reduced to 700 in 1862. Once again, there was some resistance to reform, often because of the expenses involved. Of 53 burghs adopting the 1850 Act, 18 excluded policing provisions.

Not surprisingly, Scottish urban policing in the mid-19th century was varied in both quantitative and qualitative terms. Some three-quarters of burgh forces employed 10 or fewer constables. Four cities—Aberdeen, Dundee, Edinburgh, and Glasgow—accounted for 75 percent of all constables in Scotland: Glasgow alone accounting for 43 percent. Police/population ratios were almost certainly lower than in England at this time. There were also many inefficient forces. According to the returns of the Inspector of Constabulary for Scotland in his first report (1858–1859), 37 forces were "inefficient" and only 20 "efficient." The former included Aberdeen and Dundee (both with populations over 70,000 in 1851) as well as Airdrie, Dumfries, Inverness, Kilmarnock, Montrose, and Perth (whose populations ranged from 12,000 to 22,000). The latter included the two major cities, Edinburgh and Glasgow (whose combined populations exceeded 400,000 in 1851), and the large urban centers of Perth and Greenock. It was the Inspector's view that "low pay and want of discipline" were the major weaknesses across the country, though poor quality clothing and "wretched accommodation" were all too common. Even the Edinburgh force, though deemed efficient, was neither smart nor well-disciplined, and the constables were "insufficiently instructed in their duties."[8]

The second half of the 19th century saw a gradual improvement in policing north, as well as south, of the border. Already detectable in the mid-19th century, town councils in Scotland increasingly took over responsibility from police commissioners set up under earlier legislation. Once again the big cities led the way: Glasgow in 1846, Dundee in 1851, Edinburgh in 1856, and Aberdeen in 1871. This contributed to greater efficiency, but smaller burghs hung on longer to old practices; Maxwelltown police commission surviving until 1892.[9] The persistence of small burgh forces was a major problem—"the weak point in the police of Scotland," according to the 1869 annual report—that had not been resolved by the end of the period. Maxwelltown was one of a number of persistently inefficient forces in burghs that were "clinging to the power of appointing their one or two constables who are in some cases the men who clean the streets and perform other menial tasks inconsistent with the position of police constables of the present day."[10]

The other major and persistent problem related to remuneration. Levels of pay were too low for much of the period, particularly given the demands of the job, and the problem of superannuation (or its absence) was not solved until 1892. However, other problems, such as the standard of police accommodation and facilities, uniforms, and discipline diminished, though often "improvements . . . were most wanting where they were most required."[11]

County policing developed earlier with over 20 county forces being established in the 1830s and 1840s, from Aberdeenshire to Berwickshire, with the all-important commissioners of supply taking advantage of the 1833 Rural Police (Scotland) Act and the 1839 County Police Act. Those who had not done so, such as Lanark and Ross-shire, were required to establish forces by the Police (Scotland) Act of 1857. Recent research on the development of policing in the borders reveals another variation in the pattern of development that reflected the practical problems facing a small force responsible for a large geographical area.[12] Alfred John List was an experienced officer before he came to the borders. Influenced by Mayne and the Metropolitan model, in regular contact with Edwin Chadwick, he developed a two-tier system, suited to the particular needs of the border counties, in which full-time district constables, stationed at strategic points throughout the county, worked with part-time parochial officers in every parish. The parochial officers acted as the eyes and ears of the system, providing intelligence that was augmented by the activities of the district constables in a system of close surveillance remarkable for its time.[13] As in other parts of Britain, vagrancy was a major cause for concern, but the fortuitous survival of the notebooks of Constable Alexander Sharp, a district constable stationed at Melrose, show just how much time was devoted to the problem. The formal reports included in the County Information Book show vagrants accounting for only 20 percent of individuals, but the notebooks reveal that Sharp spent most of every day noting the presence and movement of vagrants in his area. The shortcomings of county forces must not be overlooked—some, like Ross-shire, struggled for years to achieved efficiency in the eyes of the inspector of constabulary—but early and important developments took place outside the great cities and towns of Scotland.[14]

Although there were important differences between police developments north and south of the border, there were also similarities. Urban policing in provincial England developed in fits and starts. The Municipal Corporation Act of 1835 led to a surge in numbers as new forces were established, for example, in Banbury, Bedford, Cambridge, Canterbury, Gloucester, Kidderminster, Northampton, Shrewsbury, and Poole. In all, just over 120 new forces were created between 1835 and 1838. Large forces were created in cities such as Birmingham, Liverpool, Manchester, and Bristol, but the majority of new forces, even in growing towns, were relatively small: Doncaster had a force of only 5 men, Wigan 7, and Bolton 10. Not surprisingly, the ratio of police to population could vary markedly. In Liverpool and Hull there was 1 policeman for approximately every 400 persons; in Manchester and Birmingham 1 for every 600. At the other end of the scale there was, at one point, 1 policeman for every 6,200 people in Walsall, though this fell to 1 for every 2,200 by 1844. The burgeoning industrial towns of Lancashire were badly served. The police/population ratio in Stockport was 1:3,800, in Wigan 1:4,000, and Bolton 1:4,800.[15]

The development of rural policing was also patchy. Various experiments with subscription forces were tried in parts of Hertfordshire, Gloucestershire, and Norfolk, and in other parts of Norfolk, Essex, and Lincolnshire improved policing came via the 1833 Lighting and Watching Act. The 1839 Rural Constabulary Act, a piece of permissive legislation, was an important staging post in the ongoing debate about provincial policing. The decision to appoint county police forces rested in the hands of local magistrates, who met to debate a variety of constitutional and financial considerations.[16] Adoption of the act was predictably patchy. Thirty-five counties adopted the act (though in some cases for only part of the county), and, of these 22 did so within two years of the act being passed.

In some cases there is a link between recent disturbances and the creation of a police force. Several Lancashire magistrates, for example, made it clear that recent Chartist troubles had convinced them of the need for reform, though the fact that the initiative was taken by magistrates from the thinly populated and rural northern hundreds of Lonsdale North and Lonsdale South suggests that direct experience was not necessary. At the same time, magistrates in Staffordshire and the West Riding of Yorkshire decided not to adopt the act, notwithstanding the considerable disturbances they had experienced. Proximity did not automatically lead to adoption. Indeed, the reverse may well have been true in some cases. Of the English counties to adopt the act in 1839 and 1840, neither Bedfordshire, Cambridgeshire (Isle of Ely), Cumberland, Essex, Gloucestershire, Hampshire, Herefordshire, Hertfordshire, Norfolk, Northamptonshire, Suffolk (East), Sussex (East), Warwickshire, Wiltshire, nor Worcestershire could be seen as hotbeds of industrial unrest. Nor is there convincing evidence of a strong link between Swing disturbances and the adoption of rural police forces. Of the 10 most riotous Swing counties, 5 adopted the act and 5 did not. The impact of anti-poor law disturbances may have been greater but of 10 counties that experienced both Swing and anti-poor law troubles, 5 rejected the act, including the much troubled counties of Kent and Berkshire. Such variations in response should not come as a complete surprise given what we now know of the variety of policing options available in the 1830s. Indeed, one might even expect to find a relationship between the innovative counties of the 1830s and the adopters of the 1839 Act. Among the innovative counties, Hampshire adopted the act while Kent did not, while among the noninnovative counties Wiltshire was keen to adopt while Somerset was not.[17]

Cost was clearly an important consideration in nonadoption in certain districts such as the West Riding of Yorkshire, Buckinghamshire, and Lincolnshire. In Derbyshire the magistrates actually resolved to adopt the act but were forced to change their decision in the face of ratepayer opposition. Preventative policing, "watching and suspecting," was seen to be too expensive and ran contrary to a tradition of using the police, for example, under the Special Constables Act, as an ad hoc response to specific problems. However, it would be simplistic to see opposition simply in financial terms, even when those financial considerations implied a model of policing. Equally important was the fear of centralization. Opposition to Chadwick's centralizing proposals that would have curbed the powers of local magistrates is well known and given exaggerated importance in police histories. When critics of the Rural Constabulary Act expressed their fears of centralization they had in mind the demise of the individual justice with the removal of authority from petty sessions to quarter sessions where, it was feared, the lord lieutenant and the larger landowners of the county held greater sway. Finally, differing assessments of the threat to social order will have played a part in the decision-making process alongside ideological beliefs and pragmatic political considerations.

While the 1839 Act was important, it did not sound the death knell of parochial policing. Notably in Kent, there were magistrates seeking to develop and strengthen traditional forms of policing. However, it became increasingly clear in the 1840s and early 1850s that there were limits to parochial-based policing. In a society that was changing rapidly and in which expectations of security were rising, it was becoming apparent that, in the words used about London by Sir Robert Peel in 1829, the country had "outgrown its police institutions."[18] A more coordinated approach was needed and this finally came about through the 1856 Act, which required all counties and boroughs in England and Wales to establish police forces, which would be eligible for Treasury support subject to a satisfactory annual review by the newly created inspectors of constabulary. Here was a framework, but if 1856 represented the end of a period of experimentation in different forms of policing, it also marked the beginning of a new period in which the practices of modern policing were to be developed.

The establishment of new police forces was an important first step, but there was much still to do. The creation of a functioning policed society required the creation of an efficient and effective constabulary, which in turn required the recruitment, retention, and training of bodies of men capable of carrying out the varied and often highly sensitive tasks assigned to the police. This was not easy. Policing was not an occupation that was held in high esteem by working men. It was for many a stop-gap; a job that paid until something better turned up. For iron and steel workers in south Wales, on Clydeside, or in the northeast of England, policing provided an alternative when trade depressions brought large scale lay-offs "at the works"; for craft workers in Lancashire and Hertfordshire made redundant by technological change it provided a safety net; for the unskilled agricultural laborer, new to town, it provided employment, a uniform, and some rudimentary training that would prove useful when moving on to become a railway porter. Few men joining the constabulary in the early years of Victoria's reign thought that they would make a career of policing. Many came and left almost immediately, serving a few months, a few weeks, and in some cases barely a few days. This should not be a cause for surprise. The job was demanding and dangerous. The new police constable was meant to be the walking embodiment of order and decorum. As such he was subject to restrictions on his dress and appearance (some forces banned beards, others insisted upon them; some tolerated facial hair but regulated the gap between sideburns and moustache); and to restrictions on his behavior. He was not to enter a public house, nor accept a drink while on duty; he was to attend church on Sunday (in some forces more than once), and his manner and speech was to be discreet and polite no matter the provocation he might face. Further, he needed to provide proof of his independence before marrying, while his wife (assuming the woman in question was a suitable partner for the upholder of law and morality) could not take in washing or lodgers, no matter how stretched the family budget might be. In other ways the policeman's lot was not a happy one: the hours were long, trudging the streets and lanes in all weathers, and the holidays few and far between in the early years. The flat-footed copper found on the music hall stage was not a figment of the imagination. While the tedium of beat duty was frequently broken it often took the form of danger—a fire, a runaway horse, or dangerous dogs to be seen to. And to cap it all, there was the suspicion and outright hostility with which he was viewed by his working-class fellows. Recruited from the ranks of labor, domiciled and working among them, he was "in" rather than "of" the working classes. The fact that his remit impinged on both the work and leisure activities of the poor, particularly in the towns and cities, ensured a constant tension and suspicion. For street-traders, such as the costermongers of London, the decision of a policeman to move them on or to divert them off a main thoroughfare could have major economic repercussions. The fact that the same man might also seek to restrict their leisure activities (or arrest them for having indulged in them) merely added insult to injury. It was little wonder that young costers fought a daily battle with the police and took pride in "serving out" one of Peel's Blue Locusts. Likewise, the Irish, many of whom had fled dire poverty in their home land to live in squalor and penury in mainland Britain, faced an often prejudiced public and a police force that could enhance their reputation by being tough on society's marginalized people. The policeman, far from being a reassuring figure, was "the peregrinating embodiment of tyranny and oppression."[19] It is not surprising that many men felt that the regular wage associated with police work was not sufficient to offset these demands. Indeed, more surprising is the fact that there was a steady supply of men willing to give a try to policing early Victorian Britain.

The high turnover rates that characterize these years were not simply the result of disillusioned recruits leaving for other jobs; it also reflected the dissatisfaction of their employers with the failure of recruits to develop the appropriate characteristics and behavior patterns expected of a police constable. As a significant minority of recruits resigned in large numbers, often after the briefest of spells in uniform, a larger minority were dismissed for various failings. Drunkenness, on and off duty, was the commonest reason for dismissal, but men lost their jobs because of insubordination, fighting (variously, each other, their superiors, and members of the public), failing to turn up for duty, falling asleep while on duty, and for acting in a variety of criminal or immoral ways. It was the exceptional policeman who tried to poison his wife or who seduced the daughter of his commanding officer, but most offenses that gave rise to dismissal were relatively mundane: an over familiarity with a local publican, or members of the gambling fraternity, not to mention certain ladies of the night ended the careers of young (and not so young) policemen across the country.[20]

But some stayed, serving for 10 years and more. And the numbers becoming career coppers increased as the years passed. As late as the 1860s only approximately 5 percent of police recruits went on to draw a pension. A generation later, this figure had increased to just over 20 percent as some of the worst features of early Victorian policing were ameliorated. Overall statistics suggest that average police pay increased by a third between 1860 and 1890, and this at a time when prices were falling by as much as 40 percent. In addition to this there were the unofficial perks (the free tram rides, entry to the theater, and so forth) that probably increased over time, the opportunity for promotion, and the unchanging security of regular employment, irrespective of seasonal fluctuations or trade cycles that affected other occupations. Work conditions were less harsh. There was a shorter working day with recognized meal breaks as well as rest days and holidays. Popular hostility almost certainly declined in the late Victorian years, and policing was seen by a growing number of people to provide a valuable service, though suspicion remained, particularly among the more marginalized and less "respectable" elements in society. Finally, there was a growing *esprit de corp* among the police themselves. A positive self-image of the guardian of society, watching while others slept, developed. There was growing professional pride as experience accumulated and was handed on to new recruits and as training improved, albeit from a very low level.[21]

Gradually from the mid-Victorian years onward, there was a series of interrelated changes taking place that contributed to the creation of the recognizably policed society of the Edwardian era. Scientific advances such as the use of photographs and fingerprints slowly changed the image of the police.[22] Other developments, such as the improvements in experience and training, were also essentially qualitative in nature, but others were simply quantitative. At its simplest the overall number of policemen increased, thereby cutting the police/population ratio by about a third in little more than a generation. At the same time the scope of police work increased. Police forces took on a wide range of responsibilities, including the oversight of lodging houses, responsibility for checking weights and measures, and checking the storage of dangerous substances. In addition, the growth of local bylaws as well as changes in national legislation increased the role and responsibility of the police and ensured that they played a greater, necessarily more intrusive, part in everyday life.

The creation of new forces across the United Kingdom was the product of a complex interplay of factors, the balance of which varied considerably between and within the four home countries. There were, however, common concerns. The threat (real or imaginary) posed by petty criminals, ticket-of-leave men, poachers, and vagrants underpinned action in many places. The threat posed by large crowds, particularly if politically motivated, bulked large, particularly in the thinking of authorities in towns and cities. In addition, the police were increasingly seen as an essential component of good governance, "as necessary to the proper management of a town as gas lighting," in the words of the *Brighton Examiner*.[23] The uniformed bobby was to be seen as the embodiment of decency and order, the man whose quiet control ensured the smooth running of the streets and the safety of respectable citizens as they went about their lives. Writing in 1890, James Monro, recently assistant commissioner of the Metropolitan police, painted a picture of the police that encapsulated not simply the views of the police themselves but also of a majority of the middle and upper classes. It was a picture of a special relationship with the public that transcended class. "Weak in numbers as the force is, it would be found in practice altogether inadequate were it not strengthened, to an extent unknown, I believe, elsewhere, by the relations which exist between the police and the public, and by the thorough recognition on the part of the citizens at large of the police as their friends and protectors," he wrote and continued, perhaps protesting too much, that the "police, in short, are not the representatives of an arbitrary and despotic power, directed against the rights or obtrusively interfering with the pleasures of law-abiding citizens: they are simply a disciplined body of men, specially engaged in protecting the 'masses,' as well as 'classes' from any infringement of their rights on the part of those who are not law-abiding—a force which is felt to be only a terror to the evil-doer and for the praise of them that do well."[24]

It was a comforting interpretation that presented the constabulary as an essential part of the smooth running of London life. Who could not be reassured when they read the following?

> The police touch all classes of the public at many points beyond the performance of the sterner duties as representatives of the law, and they touch them in a friendly way. Few crossings in crowded thoroughfares can be got over by the nervous and timid without an appeal to the courteous help of the policeman; no marriage party in the West End is complete without the attendance of Scotland Yard to quietly look after the safety of costly wedding gifts; the laborer in Whitechapel depends upon the early call of the man on the beat to rouse him for his work; the police bands often cheer the spirits of unfashionable audiences in the East End, and the police minstrels are cordially welcomed at concerts for charitable purposes. Many a homeless wanderer has to thank the watchful patrol for guiding her to a "refuge" for the night, and it is no uncommon sight

Constable on Traffic Duty in London, 1895. The image of the constable controlling city traffic captured middle-class perceptions of the police and their role in society. (Courtesy Mary Evans Picture Library)

to see a little child, lost in the streets, trotting contentedly by the side of a burly guardian of the peace in a custody as kindly as it is secure. [25]

While there were elements of truth in Monro's comment, it was a partial picture but one that was recognized by those who, before the advent of the motorcar at least, had little or no direct experience of being policed, and for whom the police were essentially servants. Such a top down perspective was not shared by those who, while not criminals narrowly defined, found themselves on the receiving end of routine policing. For many members of the working classes, the police viewed from the bottom up were far less benign.

Given the wide remit of the new police forces across the United Kingdom, there was a constant friction between police and policed. This was most obvious in the early years as the new police sought to establish themselves. There were serious antipolice riots in the 1840s in Colne and Leeds, but in some parts of the country the advent of the new police was relatively unproblematic. This was certainly the case in established market towns such as Exeter and York. More surprisingly, there was little large-scale opposition in southern ports, such as Portsmouth and Southampton, and even in such industrial towns as Halifax and Huddersfield in the West Riding of Yorkshire. However, there were other rapidly growing industrial towns, particularly those with a large Irish presence, such as Manchester and Wolverhampton, where the establishment of a police presence involved large-scale and often drawn out opposition from sectors of the local working classes.[26] Some of the worst problems were to be found in the fast growing but heavily male iron and steel communities in the northeast of England or the south of Wales, such as Middlesbrough and Merthyr Tydfil.[27]

At times there were high-profile and violent outbursts directed at the police as they were drawn into political or industrial disputes. On March 6, 1848, Glasgow witnessed large-scale rioting by a crowd of 5,000 unemployed men who had been "addressed by various speakers in an inflated style on the exciting topic of the day, and called upon to assert their rights, and do a deed which would rival the heroism of their Republican brethren of France."[28] A mob, allegedly comprising "the most wretched-looking men . . . [and] a great number of women," ransacked bakers' shops despite the presence of the city police led by their superintendent. Immediate economic hardship exacerbated deeper-rooted antipolice feelings. Cries of "Murder the bastards; kill every one of them!" were heard in the streets of Glasgow.[29] Additional forces, including special constables, the cavalry, and a small number of "Foggies" (as the army pensioners were known locally) were used. March 7th saw a further mass demonstration that was barely contained by the police and the Foggies. Faced with an angry crowd throwing sticks and stones, and with one of their number severely injured, the authorities sought to arrest ring leaders but were forced to fire upon the crowd. One man was killed instantly, two more died of their wounds, and a further two were injured. Concern with the police was not confined to popular hostility. Following an inquiry by the local magistracy, the chief superintendent of police, William Pearce, resigned.[30] The scale of the disturbances in Glasgow put these troubles into a class of their own, but anti-police violence was to be found elsewhere. In Kelso in 1854, for example, rioters destroyed the tollgates, repulsed the local police, and were only subdued when the town was swamped with cavalry, infantry, and outside constables. Two years later the town's police were subject to further attack at the August St. James' Fair.[31]

Such troubles were confined neither to Scotland nor the early years of Victoria's reign. Proposed legislation to curb Sunday Trading in 1855 gave rise to a series of public protests in Hyde Park, which culminated in a mass demonstration, involving some 40,000 people, on July 1. The events of that Sunday severely damaged the reputation of the police not only among the working classes, who were the intended victims of the proposed legislation and also on the receiving end of police baton charges, but also among the middle classes, some of whom had witnessed firsthand the overzealous police tactics used to clear the park. *The Times* carried a number of critical reports, and the *London Illustrated News* carried a front page that focused unambiguously on police violence.

The passage of the second reform act was accompanied by serious rioting in London, while protests by the unemployed in central London in 1886 and 1887 led to rioting in and around Trafalgar Square. On February 8, 1886, the police temporarily lost control of the streets in the face of extensive rioting. In the following year serious fighting took place between demonstrators and the police on Bloody Sunday, November 13, 1887, that resulted in over 200 casualties including 3 fatalities. The crowd was faced by some 5,000 constables, including 300 mounted officers. Trafalgar Square itself was cordoned off by 1,500 police constables, but they were unable to control a crowd rush in the late afternoon. An estimated 20,000 people forced their way into Trafalgar Square where vicious fighting took place. *The Times* was quite clear where responsibility lay. "So far the people had gone quietly and rather exultantly on their way towards Trafalgar Square; but at this point matters took a serious turn. The police, mounted and on foot, charged in among the people, striking indiscriminately in all directions . . . The blood in most instances was flowing freely . . . and the spectacle was indeed a sickening one."[32] The police were subsequently criticized for handing out summary justice, having allegedly been ordered not to make arrests. Order was finally restored by the military, members of the Life Guard, and the Grenadier Guards, who were cheered as heartily as the police were booed and hissed.[33]

Industrial disputes, leading to bloody clashes between police and protesters, especially in 1911, were a source of great anxiety for the authorities in Edwardian Britain. The rioting during the Liverpool dock strike led to

A View of the Brutal Attack
ON AN UNARMED, RESPECTABLE, AND PEACEABLE MULTITUDE
OF BOTH SEXES, AND ALL AGES, MADE BY A
DESPOTIC POLICE,
IN HYDE PARK, ON SUNDAY, JULY 1st, 1855.
DEDICATED TO LORD G——R AND ALL THE SAINTS.

[London:—Printed and Published by MARKS, Long Lane, West Smithfield, and Houndsditch.]
ONE PENNY PLAIN.   TWO-PENCE COLOURED.

Despotic Police! Hyde Park, London, 1855. *The Illus-trated London News* made clear its disapproval of the way in which the Metropolitan Police in general and of Superintendent Hughes in particular handled the protest meeting against the Sunday Trading Bill in Hyde Park, July 1, 1855. (Courtesy Metropolitan Police Authority/ Mary Evans Picture Library)

unprecedented action by local and national authorities. Some 4,000 special constables were recruited locally, additional police were sent from Birming-ham and Leeds, infantry and cavalry troops were sent by Churchill who, fol-lowing a request from the city's Head Constable, also ordered a warship to be sent to the Mersey. August 13, 1911, became known as (another) Bloody Sunday. The Riot Act had to be read on 10 occasions; the police came under sustained attack during major riots spread over the weekend of August 12–13. Police were lured into side streets where they were met with volleys of slates and brickbats from Liverpudlians sitting astride the roofs of terraced houses, who took the side of the strikers.[34] Two people were killed and many injured as the police and army cleared the streets. Armed troops had to patrol the streets to maintain order. The Head Constable conceded that there had been "scenes of great violence" in which "it is probable that many innocent persons received injuries."[35] Antipolice sentiment, widespread among parts of the working-class community before the strike, was strengthened by the events of that unfortunate weekend.[36]

Perhaps even more virulent and long-lasting was the conflict in the South Wales coalfield where the police openly supported the colliery owners in a bitter struggle against trade unionists that lasted for much of the first quarter of the 20th century. The partisan stance of chief constable Captain Lionel Lindsay alienated many working men and women who were further angered by reports of heavy-handed policing. In one incident in November 1911, the police "with a dervish yell and batons drawn," according to one account, "dashed out between 80 and 90 strong from the colliery yard . . . and scores of the rioters were struck down like logs with broken skulls and left on the ground. The agony cries of the injured, the sharp hissing clash of baton against pick handle and other weapons, the sickening thud of skull blows, and the howling of the mob maddened with rage is better imagined than described . . . scores of batons were broken in this fight . . . and the local supply of staffs had been completely exhausted."[37]

The Metropolitan police came in for much criticism in many quarters. In Tonypandy they were stoned; but they also received some unexpected praise.

> At Gelli, Rhondda Valley, where 1,000 of Messrs. Cory Brothers' miners are out, everything is quiet in marked contrast to the situation at Tonypandy and Llwynypia. The Metropolitan police have shown great tact in carrying out their duties, and it is not an unusual thing to see the men playing with the children returning from school. The police gave a practical proof of their sympathy by subscribing to the fund to supply children with food. That this is appreciated by the workmen was demonstrated at the mass meeting of the strikers on Saturday. They appointed a deputation to wait upon Inspector James of the K Division who was in charge, and conveyed to him the following resolution:-
>
> That a hearty vote of thanks be given to the Metropolitan police for their kindness to the children and the sympathy shown the men during the present lock-out.[38]

It is important to recognize the variations between different parts of the country—Swansea was more like Liverpool, characterized by conflict, but Newport and Cardiff were more like Hull, characterized by conciliation— as well as variations within districts, but the reporting of violent conflicts between police and striker confirmed and perpetuated suspicions that had surrounded the new police since their introduction. For many trade unionists and political activists, men as much as women, there was a deep-rooted, and far from unwarranted, dislike of the police.

Political demonstrations and industrial actions were the exception rather than the rule. The public interaction with the police took place in more mundane, but not necessarily less fraught, situations. Costermongers in London, like street traders across the land, found their activities restricted by police "move on" tactics. Henry Mayhew was told in no uncertain terms that "[t]o serve out a policeman is the bravest act by which a costermonger can distinguish himself."[39] There was a state of near warfare between the police and the young costers who informed Mayhew that

> [s]ome lads have been imprisoned upwards of a dozen times for this offence; and are consequently looked upon as martyrs . . . The lads endeavour to take the unsuspecting "crusher" by surprise, and often crouch at the entrance of a court until a policeman passes, when a stone or brick is hurled at him . . . Their love of revenge, too, is extreme—their hatred being in no way mitigated by time; they will wait for months, following a policeman who has offended or wronged them, anxiously looking out for an opportunity of paying back the injury.[40]

The feeling that police attention was unduly and unfairly focused on the poor was found in many parts of the country. An editorial in the *Middlesbrough Weekly News* in 1868 criticized the "systematic contempt and disregard for the rights and feelings of poor people simply because they are poor."[41] Popular hostility was manifest in a series of assaults upon various members of the local constabulary, including on one occasion the superintendent of police himself, some large-scale attacks on the police, and some crowd rescues involving several hundred angry townsfolk.[42]

However, in Middlesbrough, as in the country at large, the number of assaults on the police fell in the last third of the 19th century. This did not necessarily mean that the police had won working-class hearts and minds in the manner suggested by Monro. Writing in 1907, the Oxford don H.R.P. Gamon commented on the coexistence of two conflicting views of the police in London—"the Western and Eastern views." The Western view was essentially that of the middle and upper classes who know

> nothing of the P.C. as an individual man. To it he is always, not this or that P.C., but *the* P.C. simply . . . He is the prosecutor of all wrongdoers; to boot, an exceedingly civil and obliging servant of the community; a gallant simple fellow with a warm heart and a strong sense of duty. The papers give reports of his exploits and his deeds of daring; others tell of his little acts of charity, his gifts of buns and pence to children. The order of the streets and squares in Bayswater bear testimony to his efficiency . . . There is no doubt of his popularity down West.

The Eastern, or working-class, view was very different.

The police down East are no longer the servants of the community. they are masters; at the best kindly champions, at the worst tyrants . . . [The P.C.] is a man
of power in the days of peace. He tells one bus-driver to stop, and he stops; and
another to go on, and he goes on. He hastens costers forward or turns them up
side streets. He moves on knots gathered at the street corners. He speaks and he
expects to be obeyed. He has not only the court of law behind him, but he exer-
cises a summary jurisdiction of his own, which requires in him a judicial discretion, if it is not to be abused . . . And that judicial discretion he does not always
possess in a marked degree . . . Lack of self-control and overweening insolence
on the part of the police is at the bottom of a large number of police assaults.[43]

There followed an unflattering list of police shortcomings: discrimination against the poor, corruption, sexism, and petty favoritism. The working
classes "fear the power of the police; they feel that they are under a despotism; and however beneficent that despotism may be, it is more sudden than
judicial."[44] Although "they see the frailties and failures of the police and exaggerate them," such sentiments were not confined to the criminal class but
included "the view of the more or less respectable father of a family, several
classes higher up social scale."[45] Similar sentiments were expressed about the
police in Salford and their heavy-handed actions in dealing with petty offenses, such as street betting.

And in the heart of the group itself, shielded by lounging bodies, a small card
school would sit contentedly gambling for halfpences. Suddenly one hears a
shriek of warning. The gang bursts into a scatter of flying figures. From nowhere
gallop a couple of "rozzers," cuffing, hacking, punching, sweeping youngsters
into the wall with a swing of heavy folded capes. The street empties, doors
bang. Breathing heavily the Law retires bearing off perhaps a "hooligan" or two
to be made an example of. The club is over for another night, leaving its young
members with a fear and hatred of the police that in some perfectly law-abiding
citizens lasted through life and helped colour the attitude of a whole working-
class generation towards civil authority.[46]

Gambling was but one example of "a whole mass of petty enactments,
which are little more than [bourgeois] social regulations bearing almost entirely on working-class life."[47] As a consequence, in the view of an outspoken
Edwardian social critic,

In every direction, inside his own house as well as out, the working-man's
habits and convenience are interfered with, or his poverty is penalized by the
police. Whether or not he comes into collision with them is more a matter
of good fortune than of law-abidingness, and he is a lucky man who does not
find himself in their hands at one time or another in his life. Nor can it very
well be otherwise, since the duties of the police have been made to tally with
upper-class, as opposed to working-class, notions of right and wrong; so that a
working man may easily render himself liable to arrest and all sorts of penalties

from hard labour to the loss of a day's work, without in the least doing what is wrong in his own eyes or in the opinion of his neighbours. For that reason alone, there is hardly a man who cannot, from the working-class point of view, bring up instances of gross injustice on the part of the police towards himself or his friends or relations—to say nothing of cases that are plainly unjust from any point of view.[48]

The existence of such negative views of the police (and the law that they enforced) among otherwise respectable members of working-class society is an important indicator of the nature of the policed society that had been created by the later years of Victoria's reign and the limitations to police legitimacy. However, it remains the case that the police had become a permanent feature of town and country life across the United Kingdom. Only in highly exceptional circumstances, such as those in Colne in 1841, could the police be driven out, but even then only for a very short time. Suspicion and criticism remained and to a greater degree than supporters of the police conceded, but even the most outspoken critics, such as Edward Carpenter, while warning of the dangers of a Russian-style police state, argued for the curtailing of police powers and not for their abolition. Individual policemen were still hated, and certain collective police activities (notably the mishandling of strikes) provoked considerable anger, but the *idea* of the police per se was not questioned. The reasons behind this creation of a viable policed society, this establishment of a sufficiently broad-based and rooted police legitimacy, are varied. Some had to do with the way in which the police went about the work, developing skills and tactics over the years; others, more important ones, had to do with changes in the wider circumstances in which the police operated.

There can be little doubt that the police authorities, from the very outset, sought to win over popular support and to establish their legitimacy in the eyes of the public at large through a variety of strategies intended to dispel the fear that the police were a despotic force, working against the interests of the majority. Great emphasis was given to presenting an image of professionalism. Officers were to be trained and disciplined to be "well-regulated machines"; their "dress, deportment and discipline" was to be such that they were the embodiment of respectability as well as of authority. And senior officers had an important role to play in weeding out those recruits who failed to make the grade. In part, the high dismissal rates of the early years of Victoria's reign reflect a zealousness born of a perceived need to enforce high standards of police behavior. Behavior that had led to dismissal in the 1850s and 1860s was more commonly punished by a fine or demotion in many forces in the early 20th century. The impartiality of the police officer was emphasized in a variety of ways. The rhetoric of equality before the law was an important legitimizing argument. The police were both enforcers of and subject to an allegedly impartial law, though this was not always obvious to the policed. However, the fact that much police attention was directed at those on the fringes of society (and presented as threats to mainstream society), such as gypsies, navvies, and other itinerants, and later, aliens, enabled the police to present themselves as defender of "decent" society by working with the prejudices of that society.

Similarly, the nonmilitary nature of the new police was stressed. Cutlasses and pistols were to be carried only in exceptional circumstances; the truncheon was to be used for self-defense. Police tactics, notably "moving on," were intended to diffuse tension. Force was to be used sparingly and in proportion to the seriousness of the situation. In theory, the principle of minimal force sounded very attractive, but the reality was less clear cut and positive. The use of the baton charge was not obviously appropriate "minimal force" to those on the receiving end who saw police action as unprovoked violence.

More generally, the police took on a range of responsibilities that enabled them to be presented as servants of the community at large. Some of these responsibilities (such as those for inspecting weights and measures or the storage of petroleum and other dangerous substances) were formal and in some cases had been inherited from earlier forms of policing. Others were informal. It is easy to parody the policeman as the finder of lost children and stray animals, or as the helper of old ladies flustered by the busy streets of urban Britain, but such activities did take place and did have some tempering effect on the public's image of the police. More so did the action of the police in emergencies. Helping in floods and fires; stopping runaway horses or enraged cattle; even organizing boot clubs and soup kitchens brought positive responses from working men and women. And how many people enjoyed listening to the police band as it performed on a Sunday afternoon in the local park?

Most important of all was the apparent effectiveness of the new police in combating crime. The decline in serious crime was presented as proof of the success of the police. The realities were undoubtedly more complex, but as long as people believed the police were becoming more effective that was an important "fact" in its own right. Indeed, the evidence of the courts, particularly the lesser courts, suggests that there was a growing use of the criminal justice system by working-class men and women as well as their middle- and upper-class counterparts.

In a fundamental (but not cynical) sense, successful policing depended upon carrying off a number of confidence tricks. Acceptance of the police depended upon a belief that the police were (by and large) irresistible, impartial, and effective. The realities were different. In simple physical terms, the police could be outnumbered and the control of the streets wrested from them. This rarely happened. Indeed, one of the most important aspects of the Trafalgar Square riots of 1886–1887 was the potential damage to the reputation of the police as the "mob," albeit briefly, held control of parts of central London. Similarly, the police enforced a law (or more accurately a series of laws) that was heavily focused on (if not biased against) the working classes; and they often enforced the law in a way that assumed the poor were criminals and the wealthy not.

But this did not matter as long as such sentiments were not sufficiently wide-spread, public, and organized to undermine public confidence in the police.

Important as were these changes from within, their impact depended in large measure on circumstances beyond the control of the police. A number of important changes took place from the mid-Victorian years onward that greatly eased police work. Gradual improvements in working-class living standards, particularly in the last third of the 19th century, reduced the numbers living on the economic margins for whom the slightest downturn in economic activity brought hardship of a degree that made petty pilfering a necessity in the struggle for survival. The decline in crimes against property probably had as much to due with this long-term amelioration of working-class living standards as it did to improved policing. In a different manner, economic progress for the working-class elite, the skilled laborers, and the resultant accumulation of small-scale property meant that such people now saw real benefits in the police and courts. Similarly, the police were probably more beneficiaries than instigators of the long-term decline in violence that characterized these years. A final factor was the gradual incorporation of organized labor into the political nation. This was most clearly seen in the extension of the franchise in 1866 and 1884–1885, but there was also a greater willingness to accept that trade unions had a legitimate role to play. The point must not be overstated. Many men were effectively disenfranchised in Edwardian Britain, and a growing number of those that did have the vote were becoming disillusioned with the established parties, Liberal and Conservative, and were looking for independent representation. More importantly, the continued resistance to demands for the enfranchisement of women gave rise to a militant movement and bitter clashes with the police in the Edwardian era. Recognition of trade union legitimacy was also patchy, and as noted previously, some of the worst clashes with the police took place in industrial disputes in which employers were seeking to destroy the unions that represented their employees. Nonetheless, some of the structural tensions that lay behind the often violent protests of the 1830s and 1840s had been eased. Thus, taken together, these broader socioeconomic and political changes created an opportunity for the police to reduce opposition and even win over support. Their ability to win positive support was overstated by men such as Monro, but their ability to reduce opposition (subject to the various limitations discussed earlier) was a real achievement.

Generalizing about popular responses to the police is fraught with difficulties. The complexities of Victorian and Edwardian society and the varied ways in which individuals and groups experienced the police meant that there was not a single middle-class or working-class perspective. Indeed, at an individual level experiences of the police could be contradictory. A relatively well-to-do artisan welcomed police protection for his hard-earned property, but the same police at a picket line, allowing access to nonunionized "scab" labor, were hated. With this in mind, the following observations probably held true. Middle-class opinion was overwhelmingly but not uncritically supportive. The most common concern was with value for money, but there were occasions when police actions were criticized. Excessive violence, picking on innocent women, or corruption led to condemnation. And there was a small fringe of middle-class critics who, often because of their left-wing politics, took a more sustained and wide-ranging opposition to the extension and misuse of police powers.

In contrast, the number of working-class men and women who positively welcomed the police in the way that their middle-class counterparts did was small. Some did, and others were positive for more calculative reasons. They had property to protect and they benefited from the smooth and orderly running of the streets. However, the fact remained that for many working-class men and women in late Victorian and Edwardian Britain, the police were begrudgingly accepted. Suspicion was commonplace; mistrust and hostility were not far from the surface. But this was tempered by a recognition that the police were a fixture and were no more likely to be swept way than the once-hated and never loved factory or mill in which many found employment. But an insight into working-class attitudes can be found in the representation of the police in popular culture, the music hall songs and melodramas. Blanchard Jerrold described a visit to the Garrick Theatre in Leman Street Whitechapel in the early 1870 where a performance of "The Starving Poor of Whitechapel" was underway. "[A]t the moment of our entry the stage policemen were getting very much the worse of a free fight, to the unbounded delight of pit and gallery."[49] Almost 40 years later, H.R.P. Gamon made a similar observation.

> The P.C. frequently figures in the melodrama. He has characteristics that eminently fit him to be the hero. But he is always, not indeed the villain in chief, but a minor villain—a common knave with a sadly atrophied moral sense. He drinks; he cadges; he is a coward and a fool; and his mouth is full of despicable sentiments.

Perceptively, he concluded:

> No doubt the P.C. in action is too common a sight to be readily idealised, and it is a privilege to be able to laugh at the caricature when it is forbidden to laugh at the reality. But is it fanciful to believe that genuine distrust and dislike of the police lie behind the hisses and laughter that point the moral for the ridiculously vicious character on the boards?[50]

And not just in London: the Chief Constable of Glasgow, giving evidence about community relations to the 1908 Royal Commission on Police, spoke for every city, town, and village when he ruefully noted that "in the rougher localities the feeling [towards the police] is hostile and always in favour of the arrested person."[51]

PART IV

PUNISHMENT

CHAPTER NINE

THE DEATH PENALTY

Dismantling the Bloody Code in Early Victorian Britain

GENERAL INTRODUCTION

On the morning of August 13, 1868, Thomas Wells, a young man of 18 years, engaged to be married later that month, made history. Dressed in the velveteen suit of a railway porter in a desperate effort to retain dignity to the last, mumbling a half-remembered hymn from happier childhood days to give himself support in time of trial, hunched and crouching as he walked, his hands convulsively clasped together, he went to his death in Maidstone Gaol: the first man to be executed behind prison walls rather than in front of a gallows crowd. The *Daily Telegraph* proclaimed that this "the first private execution mark[ed] the beginning of a new and most important chapter in the history of English civilization."[1] Queen Victoria probably gave little thought to the demise of the unfortunate Wells, but she was well aware that the death penalty was now confined, to all intents and purposes, to the crime of murder, and its imposition had been removed from the public gaze. In contrast, the world into which Victoria had been born was one in which the death penalty applied to a wide range of crimes and in which the theater of execution was a central element in the process of justice. To appreciate the extent of the changes that had taken place in both principle and practice and to understand why they came about, it is necessary to look back some 50 years.

THE BLOODY CODE AND ITS DEMISE

Joseph Hunton was executed on December 8, 1828, one of many people hanged for a nonviolent crime against property. Hunton's offense was forgery. This was somewhat unusual—the more common offenses that brought men and women, old and young, to the scaffold were thefts, often of a relatively minor nature—but his death attracted much attention and a large crowd outside Newgate because he was wealthy, "a person of good repute," and a Quaker.[2] By the early 19th century Britain had the most severe and sanguinary criminal code in Europe. There were well over 200 capital offenses (no one knew the precise total), the most recent, dealing with the destruction of colliery machinery, having been added to the statute book in 1816. To its contemporary critics (and many later historians) the so-called Bloody Code was irrational, arbitrary, and ineffective, an affront to a civilized society. Despite being "monstrous and ineffectual," in the words of *The Times*, many able and intelligent men of the time believed in the virtues of a broad-based capital code and in the efficacy of public executions.[3] Religious justification for the execution of murderers was easily found, but it required the Bishop of Salisbury, Gilbert Burnet's *Exposition on the Thirty-Nine Articles*, and the secular writings of John Locke, notably the *Second Treatise on Government*, to provide a rationale for execution for crimes against property. The highly influential Locke was unambiguous. In maintaining peace and security and advancing the public good, the state had the "right of making Laws with Penalties of Death, and consequently of all lesser penalties, for the Regulating and Preserving of Property."[4]

The most influential, and certainly the most quoted, defender of the Bloody Code was Archdeacon William Paley. For Paley, in "Of Crimes and Punishments," part of *The Principles of Moral and Political Philosophy*, first published in 1785, there was a choice between two approaches. The first was characterized by a limited number of capital offenses and the rigid enforcement of the law, while the second was characterized by a wider range of capital offenses and the exercise of discretion in the application of the law.[5] He had no doubt that the latter was superior for the simple reason that it enabled juries and, more particularly, magistrates to consider the particular circumstances of each offense and each offender thereby ensuring that justice was done. To treat all offenses in the same manner would be to deny justice by ignoring the individuality of specific crimes and specific criminals. Thus, in Paley's thinking, society was offered protection against a wide range of offenses through the threat of the application of selective terror.

Further, justice (quite literally) was seen to be done when those found guilty and sentenced to death paid the ultimate penalty on the scaffold. There was a theater of execution, a morality tale for the uneducated populace at large, in which every participant, from the victim, through the attendants on the scaffold, to the crowd itself, had a part to play. The repentant criminal exhorted the crowd not to do as he (or she) had done in ignoring their parents and the church and indulging in the gambling, drunkenness, and immorality that had sent them tumbling down the slippery slope that had brought them to such a sorry fate on the gallows. The crowd, suitably moved, would see the awful fate that befell a criminal and would be strong in its resolve to resist temptation and crime. That was the theory—and there is evidence that some confessions were genuine and that some crowds watched respectfully as the law took its rightful course—but increasingly questions were being asked about both the principle and the practice of the Bloody Code. Doubts were raised about its morality and rationality and, perhaps more importantly, about its effectiveness.

Underpinning the growing concern with the Bloody Code was the seemingly inexorable rise in crime that dated from the 1790s, if not before. Initially much of the evidence was anecdotal or, where more rigorous, confined to specific areas, most notably London. Nowhere was this more clearly seen than in the writings of the merchant and magistrate Patrick Colquhoun.[6] However, the collection and publication of annual statistics relating to serious crime across the country as a whole, from 1810 onward, fueled concerns and appeared to give them a more solid basis. In fact, as some contemporaries were aware, much of the increase was due to an increase in prosecutions rather than an increase in crime itself. In 1828 a parliamentary Select Committee found that "a great part of the increase in the number of Criminal Commitments arises from other causes than the increase in Crime. Offenses that were formerly either passed over entirely, or were visited with summary chastisement on the spot, are now made occasions of commitments to gaol and regular trial."[7]

Nonetheless, there was a growing feeling that the existing approach to crime simply did not work. The debate that ensued provided an opportunity for would-be reformers, frustrated by the conservatism of wartime Britain in the first decade of the 19th century, to advocate new principles, notably proportionality of punishment, deterrence through the certainty of punishment, and the reform of criminals in "new" prisons. They were also able to highlight both the absurdity of the existing criminal code (the defacing of Westminster Bridge, for example, was technically a capital offense) and its counterproductive nature. It was widely believed that criminals calculated that their chances of execution were remote, while prosecutors and juries were deterred by the fear that a person might be executed for a relatively minor crime against property.

While, in hindsight, the critique of the Bloody Code might appear overwhelming, change came slowly. Influential figures, not least the "furred homicides," as Dr. Parr described the judges in 1808, resisted change. Formidable figures such as Lord Chief Justice, Ellenborough, and Lord Chancellor Eldon, as well as an array of lesser lights, such as Baron Hotham, noted more for their mediocrity than their mercy, fought a bitter rearguard action to preserve the Bloody Code.[8] But rearguard action it ultimately proved to be. Concern with the blatant failure of the Bloody Code did not easily or immediately translate itself into support for the reduction in the number of capital offenders. Reformers, notably Romilly, were aware of the need to proceed cautiously, and even then the pace of change was slow; so slow, in fact, that Romilly, in despair at the limited success he had achieved, took his own life in 1820. A turning point came with the publication of the report of a House of Commons Select Committee on the criminal law in 1819. Cautiously worded, it explicitly reaffirmed "the right of the Legislature to inflict the punishment of Death, wherever that punishment, and that punishment alone, seems capable of protecting the community from enormous and atrocious crimes." However, it concluded that "many [capital] statutes . . . might be safely or wisely repealed."[9] In the following decade there was growing acceptance, from all but a rump of die-hard ultraconservatives, that the status quo was indefensible and that some degree of reform was required; but the extent of that reform was a matter of debate. One extreme, the maximalist position, looked to the total abolition of the death penalty, even in the case of murder, as a matter of principle. The other, the minimalist position, looked to do away with anomalies and anachronisms but to preserve the principle and practice of capital punishment for a range of serious crimes, not just murder. In the middle, opinion varied as to which crimes merited the death penalty. For some protagonists, serious crimes against the person, notably rape, or against property required the ultimate sanction of death; for others, only murder and treason were of sufficient gravity to warrant it.

REFORM IN THE 1820S AND 1830S

During the 1820s the key figure was the Home Secretary, Robert Peel. Best known for the introduction of the Metropolitan Police, he had a reputation as the leading reformer of the criminal justice system. He had a holistic approach that embraced the reform of trial procedures, prisons, as well as the police. His approach to capital punishment was part of this broader agenda, but it was essentially conservative in nature. Peel was well aware that the presence on the statute book of capital offenses that were either absurdly anachronistic or unjustifiably out of proportion brought the criminal justice system into disrepute. This was compounded by the glaringly obvious shortcomings of a system in which victims of crime were unwilling to prosecute and juries unwilling to return guilty verdicts in the face of strong evidence because of the severity of punishment, particularly for range of relatively minor property offenses, which might be imposed. As a consequence, the rate of pardoning had risen to such levels (over 95% in London and 90% in the country at large) as to make a mockery of the argument that the death penalty was a deterrent. Finally, and to make matters yet worse, the Bloody Code was not a code but an ad hoc collection of capital offenses that had come onto the statute book in piecemeal fashion, particularly over the course of the 18th century. This last feature provided Peel with an easy first step. The scale of the Bloody Code could be reduced through the simple expedient of bringing together like offenses, such as the defacing of bridges in the capital. Similarly, the removal of anachronistic, and rarely used, offenses could be achieved with little opposition and, more importantly, with little danger of losing the initiative to those who were looking for root-and-branch reform.

On the surface Peel's record was impressive. His self-proclaimed commitment "to remove, in all cases where it was practicable, the punishment of death" led to the repeal of 278 old statutes and their replacement with a mere 8 acts.[10] However, appearances can be deceptive. As one contemporary critic tartly observed, Peel's reforms were "superficial and delusive."[11] He had pruned away the dead wood but (like some judicious gardener) had intended the essential bush to survive and flourish. Hanging was still, in his opinion, the rightful punishment for forgery or the theft of livestock. Abolishing the capital offense of impersonating a Greenwich pensioner or of consorting with Egyptians, even raising the value of goods stolen from a dwelling house at which the death penalty was prescribed from £2 ($3.20) to £5 ($8), was a price worth paying to ensure that highway robbers and burglars as well as forgers and coiners went to the gallows. It is a measure of the change brought about by Peel's reforms that in 1824, before his reforms were introduced, the number of people executed was 49, while after his reforms in 1829 and 1830, the numbers executed were 74 and 46 respectively.[12] Peel, no doubt, was undismayed.

Throughout, Peel's main concern had been to restore credibility and to improve the effectiveness of a "hanging regime" that encompassed serious crimes against both person and property. However, his success was short-lived. Indeed, the conservative reformer of the 1820s was very much the father of the more radical reforms that came to the fore in the 1830s. The signs were there as early as 1830 when an amendment proposed by Sir James Mackintosh, that forgery be punished by transportation, was carried despite the staunch opposition of the Home Secretary himself. The advent of a Whig government opened the way for further and more fundamental change that swept aside the Peel's pragmatic conservative compromise. The new government set up a Royal Commission on criminal law that met between 1833 and 1836. Its reports were to have a profound effect on the course of reform. The second report of 1834 ruthlessly exposed the weaknesses of current practices: the self-defeating outcome of a "want of discrimination" between different offenses; the counterproductive outcome of executing but a small percentage of convicted criminals, the failure to deter criminals; the corrupting effect on prosecutors and juries devising "some stratagem to secure the escape of the offender," including suppressing facts or withholding testimony; and the corrupting impact of discretionary justice. Significantly, the commissioners concluded their observations on "the practice of discretionary selection" with a frontal assault on Paley's arguments.[13] Following their final report and recommendations, the Home Secretary Lord John Russell put before parliament a bill to abolish the death penalty for 21 of the remaining 37 capital offenses.

Astonishingly, an amendment to retain the death penalty for murder alone was defeated by a mere one vote.[14] By 1841 the number had been reduced to seven and by 1861 to four. Victorians were content to execute only murderers, traitors, violent pirates, and arsonists in Her Majesty's dockyards, though to all intents and purposes murder was the only capital offense. The site (and sight) of punishment had been changed profoundly as the old regime, centered on the scaffold, was replaced by a new regime centered on the prison.

By any standards this was dramatic change. Within a matter of years the practices and principles of previous generations dating back over centuries had been swept away. The reasons are far from straight forward. The simplest (and most comforting) explanation can be couched in terms of rational and humanitarian progress. The dismantling of the Bloody Code can be seen as a triumph over the barbaric and irrational as new ideas and new values spread through the educated and political classes of early 19th-century Britain. Certainly new ideas were in circulation from the late 18th century onward, especially following the publication (and the rapid translation) of Cesare Beccaria's *Dei Delitti delle Pene (On Crimes and Punishments)* in 1764. His readers and admirers in Britain included literary figures, such as Samuel Johnson and Oliver Goldsmith, but also influential politicians and writers, such as William Eden, William Wilberforce, Sir William Blackstone, and Jeremy Bentham, though the influence of the latter's voluminous writings should not be overstated.[15]

The idea that discretion should be at the center of a judicial system based on an individualized, ad hominem view of crime and punishment was challenged by rationalists who, appalled at the lottery of execution, wished to see uniformity in punishment. There was a longstanding and powerful belief in the deterrent effect of selective terror. Public execution was a clear demonstration of the power of the state and its determination to cut off "the gangrenous limb" for the good of "the body politic," that is, society as a whole. It was an attitude well summed up by Samuel Moody who wrote with commendable if brutal brevity. "The corrupt members of a community must be cut off by the sword of justice, lest by delay and impugnity the malignant disease spread further, and the whole be infected."[16] Such beliefs were gradually replaced by new notions of deterrence based on certainty of arrest and punishment; by new principles of punishment based on the idea of proportionality; and by a belief in the reformability of the individual criminal.

Similarly, it was the case that attitudes toward executions were changing as part of a wider change in sensibilities. New notions of masculinity, with greater emphasis on care and protection of the weak and less fortunate, were emerging. Violence in its various forms was (for some vocal sections of society, at least) now to be condemned. In the same way as bear-baiting and bull-running (the latter albeit confined to Stamford in Lincolnshire and Tutbury in Staffordshire) were condemned as being unacceptable in a civilized society, so doubts were cast on the brutality of hanging. Gratuitous violence was roundly condemned. It is no coincidence that the arguments used against dueling in the opening decades of the 19th century were repeated (almost to the word) in the 1820s and 1830s as part of the campaign against the widespread use of the death penalty. Perceptions of the execution (and its function) changed. The unembarrassed curiosity found in earlier generations had disappeared; the belief that an execution was a "grand moral example" was increasingly questioned. Executions—it could not be escaped—involved suffering. Even with the advent of the drop, death was not instantaneous and painless. Too long a rope could (and did) result in decapitation; too short in strangulation. Botched executions, especially when the executioner was old and drunk, as William Calcraft was in his latter years, were distressing; so too (almost without exception) was the dispatch of a young woman.

EXÉCUTION DE L'EMPOISONNEUSE MARY ANSELL

The Execution of Mary Ansell, 1899. The executions of women were often highly charged events. Twenty-two-year-old Mary Ansell was found guilty of poisoning her younger sister who was in an asylum. She was executed at St. Albans, Hertfordshire on July 19, 1899. (Courtesy Mary Evans Picture Library)

A particular case in point was the spectacle of 18-year-old Sarah Thomas being hauled, struggling and screaming, by six warders in 1849, to the scaffold at Bristol New Gaol where she pleaded for her life to the last. Her executioner, William Calcraft, was visibly affected by the spectacle and such was its horror that the prison governor fainted.[17] Less dramatic but exercising a greater impact was the execution of Elizabeth Brown outside Dorchester prison in 1856. Found guilty of the murder of her husband, this attractive woman, wronged by a brutal and adulterous husband, aroused considerable local sympathy, but the campaign for her reprieve failed. On Saturday, August 9, 1856, she walked from her prison cell to the scaffold in falling rain. Among the crowd, estimated to be between 3,000 and 4,000, watching from a good vantage point in a tree close to the gallows, was the 16-year-old Thomas Hardy. Brown became the inspiration for Tess of the D'Urbervilles, and Hardy continued to write about Brown's death even in his eighties.

Equally shocking was the execution of William Bousefield, who had been found guilty of the murder of his wife and three children in 1856. A disturbed individual, he had thrown himself into the fire in his condemned cell on the eve of his execution in an attempt to commit suicide. Brought to the scaffold with bandaged face, he had to be seated on a chair while the noose was put around his neck. The macabre turned to the horrific after the drop opened. To the astonishment of the crowd, the desperate man managed on three occasions to hook his toes on the edge of the platform and pull himself up. Finally, in desperation an allegedly drunken Calcraft hurled himself upon the unfortunate man to dispatch him.[18]

Botched executions, unsurprisingly, led to crowd anger at the incompetence of the practitioners of death, but even ordinary executions carried the very real danger, or so many feared, that attention would be distracted from the true message of the scaffold and improper sympathy evoked for the suffering victim. Richard Whately, Archbishop of Dublin, and a prolific writer on crime and punishment, captured this concern with "merely excessive and misplaced compassion . . . when compassion is withheld from the deserving and bestowed only on the undeserving [it becomes an] error as odious as it is practically noxious." The national character, he lamented, had changed for the worst and "one of the worst features . . . [was] that very little sympathy, comparatively, is felt, except for the guilty."[19] An influential example of such a sentiment can be seen in the observations of the writer William Makepeace Thackeray, who had seen Francois Courvoisier executed in 1840.

> The horrid gallows is perpetually before him [the condemned]; he is wild with dread and remorse. Clergymen are with him ceaselessly; religious tracts are forced into his hands; night and day they ply him with the heinousness of his crime, and exhortations to repentance. Read through the last paper of his; by Heaven it is pitiful to read it; see the Scripture phrases brought in now and anon; the peculiar terms of tract phraseology; one knows too well that such

language is learned—imitated from the priest at the bedside, eagerly seized and appropriated, and confounded by the poor prisoner.[20]

However, there is a danger of exaggerating the extent to which sentiments changed. While few still exhibited the enthusiasm for executions shown by Dr. Johnson's biographer, Boswell, there were many in the 1820s and 1830s who, like Thomas Carlyle, scoffed at the "mawkish sentimentality" and effeminacy of the critics of executions with their misplaced sympathy for the suffering of the criminal.

Reform owed much to simple pragmatism. Fears of a crime wave that were discernible in the 1790s continued into the new century. The ending of hostilities with France in 1815, the dislocation caused by a returning army, and the shift from a war to a peace-time economy added to those fears. The Bloody Code, notwithstanding its plethora of capital offenses appeared not to be working. Worse, it appeared to be counterproductive as youthful pickpockets learned their trade while their elders were euphemistically "launched into eternity" or, more pithily, "danced the Tyburn jig" above their heads. In the face of these problems there were those who argued that the law was too lax and that more rigorous enforcement was required. Once again, pragmatism had a part to play. The hanged of London and Dublin in particular were all too visible to the inhabitants of those cities. To increase the numbers going to the gallows would have led to an unacceptable number of corpses swinging in the wind. Yet more practical were the witnesses who gave evidence to the commissions. They wished to reform a system that failed to offer them and their property adequate protection.[21] But there was also a pragmatic concern that slowed the pace of reform. Behind the rhetoric of cautious reform there was a keen awareness that "men must be hanged because we did not know what else to do with them," but as Harriet Martineau continued, "such an avowal . . . could not be made by any government—either in decency or because no man could be hanged after such an avowal."[22]

Taken together these pragmatic and principled considerations throw light on the dominant attitudes of the early years of Victoria's reign and set the scene for a further debate on the appropriateness of the death penalty for any offense. But before looking at the campaign for total abolition it is necessary to consider one of the major concerns expressed by early and mid-Victorian critics of public executions: the gallows crowd as a threat to public order.

DEMONIZING THE GALLOWS CROWD

There was nothing new about this problem. In late 18th-century Dublin crowd troubles led first to the abandonment of hanging on St. Stephen's Green (and the associated hanging processions through the city) in favor of executions in front of Newgate prison in Green Street and then to the transfer of executions to within the prison walls to deny access to the mob.[23]

Similarly, the traditional place of execution in London, Tyburn, had been abandoned. Crowd troubles did not disappear but were simply relocated. Indeed, matters appeared to get worse in the third quarter of the 19th century. The recently formed Metropolitan Police devoted considerable resources to the maintenance of order at executions. A crowd of some 30,000, attracted by the novelty of a husband and wife double hanging, came to watch the execution of the Mannings in 1849. Five hundred policemen were on duty to ensure that a boisterous crowd did not wreak havoc in the vicinity of Horse-monger Lane Goal. Fifteen years later, a crowd estimated to be in excess of 50,000 assembled to watch the execution of Franz Muller, a German, responsible for the first railway murder and, to add further piquancy, the first man to be arrested through the use of the Atlantic cable. In the same year 300 constables from the City police force alongside 800 from the Met were on duty at the execution of the Five Pirates. The horrific nature of their crime attracted a large crowd for whom improved transportation in the capital—trams and underground trains—made access easier.[24]

Concerns were heightened by the blatant commercialization of executions. Again, there was nothing intrinsically new in the commercial exploitation of executions. The precise form changed, as did the scale of operations, but more importantly, perceptions also changed. The once acceptable was no longer to be tolerated by the respectable classes of mid-Victorian Britain. The sale of ballads, last-minute confessions, and true stories relating to notorious crimes, with a moral purpose, of course, was well established long before Victoria's time, as was the sale of gingerbread representations of lately executed criminals. Victorian entrepreneurs simply found new ways of tapping a seemingly insatiable market. Railway companies offered concessionary fairs to enable gallows watchers to reach previously inaccessible executions. A high-profile trial, such as that of the "Rugeley Poisoner," William Palmer, brought hundreds of eager spectators not just from Wolverhampton and Birmingham but also from London to watch his final moments on the scaffold in Stafford.[25] And for those wanting a more lasting memento, there were figurines to be bought. What could be better (or worse) than matching figures of the murdering duo, Mr. and Mrs. Manning, to set off the fireplace? And here was the nub of the matter for many respectable people in mid-Victorian Britain. The working-classes, especially the rough element that frequented executions, were not playing their proper part in the theater of execution. As Leech's cartoon for *Punch* so vividly showed, "the great moral lesson of the scaffold" had been corrupted and transformed into "the ruffian's holiday."[26]

The barbarous crowd had its depraved tastes fed by unscrupulous entrepreneurs in a downward, self-reinforcing spiral, or so it was portrayed!

The gallows crowd and those who pandered to its debased instincts were increasingly demonized in the mid-19th century. Nowhere can this be seen more clearly than in the writings of Charles Dickens. In a letter of 1846, after he had attended the execution of Courvoisier he wrote of the spectacle:

The Great Moral Lesson at Horsemonger Lane Gaol, Nov. 13.

"The Great Moral Lesson": The Gallows Crowd Outside Horsemonger Lane Gaol, 1849. The famous *Punch* cartoon by John Leech depicting the gallows crowd outside Horsemonger Lane Gaol, London, 1849 drawn soon after the execution of the Mannings. (Courtesy Mary Evans Picture Library)

From the very moment of my arrival, when there were but a few score boys in the street, and all those young thieves, and all clustered together behind the barrier nearest the drop—down to the time when I saw the body with its dangling head carried on a wooden bier into the gaol—I did not see one token in all the immense crowd; at the windows, in the streets, on the house-tops, anywhere; of any one emotion suitable to the occasion. No sorrow, no salutary terror, no abhorrence, no seriousness; nothing but ribaldry, debauchery, levity, drunkenness, and flaunting vice in fifty other shapes. I should have deemed it impossible that I could have ever felt any large assemblage of my fellow-creatures to be so odious.[27]

Even more outspoken was his letter to *The Times*, following the execution of the Mannings.

I believe the a sight so inconceivably awful as the wickedness and levity of the immense crowd collected at that execution this morning could be imagined by no man, and could be presented in no heathen land under the sun. The horror of the gibbet and of the crime which brought the wretched murderers [Mr. & Mrs. Manning] to it faded before my mind before the atrocious bearing of the assembled spectators. When I came upon the scene at midnight, the *shrillness* of the cries and howls that were raised from time to time, denoting that they came from a concourse of boys and girls already assembled in the best places, made my blood run cold. As the night went on, screeching, and laughing, and yelling in strong chorus of parodies on negro melodies, with substitutions of "Mrs. Manning" for "Susannah", and the like, were added to these. When the day dawned, thieves, low prostitutes, ruffians and vagabonds of every kind, flocked on to the ground, with every variety of offensive and foul behaviour. Fightings, faintings, whistlings, imitations of Punch, brutal jokes, tumultuous demonstrations of indecent delight when swooning women were dragged out of the crowd by the police, with their dresses disordered, gave a new zest to the general entertainment. When the sun rose brightly—as it did—it gilded thousands upon thousands of upturned faces, so inexpressibly odious in their brutal mirth or callousness, that a man had cause to feel ashamed of the shape he wore, and to shrink from himself, as fashioned in the image of the Devil. When the two miserable creatures who attracted all this ghastly sight about them were turned quivering into the air, there was no more emotion, no more pity, no more thought that two immortal souls had gone to judgment, no more restraint in any of the previous obscenities, than if the name of Christ had never been heard in this world, and there were no beliefs among men but that they perished like beasts.[28]

Dickens was not the only critic and London not the only cause for concern, but his outspoken criticisms of the scenes in the capital were at the forefront of a growing body of opinion that public executions had become unacceptable. Giving evidence to the Royal Commission in 1866, the Rev. S. G. Osborne gave full vent to his anger and abhorrence of

a crowd notoriously composed of those who are the scum of mankind, who go again and again to such scenes, each time to pollute the very air with their fearful language, people to whom it is a sort of gala day, men and women blaspheming, singing obscene songs, with half drunken jollity coming to riot below the gallows, . . . viewing the scene without one single display of one feeling that evinces sympathy with the law, screaming a kind of fiend's welcome to the hangman, . . . groaning at, or in their own way, encouraging "the victim," ordering "hats off" to "death" but damning each other's souls,—as they look upon it.[29]

And, as many critics, not least *Punch*, pointed out: executions did not deter.

More importantly, this upsurge of criticism coincided with and provided a backcloth to the debate on the total abolition of capital punishment, which came to the fore in the 1840s and was not resolved until the late 1860s.

CHAPTER TEN

THE DEATH PENALTY

The Abolition of Public Executions and the Failure of Total Abolition

THE CAMPAIGN FOR TOTAL ABOLITION OF THE DEATH PENALTY

The campaign for total abolition started with the foundation by the Quaker William Allen of the unambiguously titled *Society for the Diffusion of Knowledge Respecting the Punishment of Death and the Improvement of Prison Discipline* in 1808, with committees in both Dublin and London. It provided a vehicle for Sir Samuel Romilly to bring his arguments to a wider audience, but its direct political impact was negligible. A more effective pressure group was its successor organization, the *Society for the Diffusion of Information on the Subject of Capital Punishment*, formed in 1828 and chaired by William Allen. In 1830 it was responsible for a petition containing the signatures of 1,000 bankers, pressing for reform of the forgery laws. A more militant stance was adopted a decade later when younger and older abolitionists came together to form the *Society for Promoting the Abolition of Capital Punishment* in 1846.[1] With the example of the Anti-Corn Law League before them, men like Charles Gilpin, Thomas Beggs, and William Ewart conducted a nationwide tour to heighten awareness.[2] At the same time, successive Home Secretaries were lobbied, not least to press for the reprieve of condemned criminals. Members spoke in dramatic terms of their activities. Alfred Dymond talked of hunting down the Home Secretary like a deer, watching him "like revenue officers snaring a false coiner" and pursuing him on the way to parliament.[3] Assessing their real impact is more problematic. After his narrow failure to have capital punishment abolished for all but murder, Ewart introduced a total abolition bill in March 1840. It failed but almost 100 MPs had supported it. With influential support outside parliament from the likes of Charles Dickens, John Stuart Mill, Henry Mayhew, and Douglas Jerrold, a regular contributor to the abolitionist publication, *Punch*, and some distinguished political support within, not least John Bright, there was reason for believing that the abolitionist cause would triumph. It did not. The act of 1868, which did away with public executions, was a clear defeat for the abolitionists. The movement rapidly lost momentum. Abolitionist bills introduced in 1872, 1877, and 1878 were heavily defeated and, following the latter, *The Times* editorialized that the death penalty was no longer one of the "real questions of the day."[4]

THE DEBATE ON CAPITAL PUNISHMENT IN THE 1850S AND 1860S

To understand this outcome it is essential to distinguish between two related but very different issues. The first was the abolition of public executions; the second, the total abolition of capital punishment. While for many abolitionists the former was merely a means to achieve the latter, for retentionists the former was a necessary step to prevent the latter. The year 1868 saw the "abolition" of the execution crowd so that capital punishment might be retained. Unlike some later historians, William Ewart did not confuse the two issues. When the Bishop of Oxford, Samuel Wilberforce, persuaded the House of Lords to set up a Select Committee in 1854 by arguing that the abolition of public executions was essential for the continuance of capital punishment and that "private" execution would enhance the awfulness and thus the deterrent effect of the death penalty, Ewart, to avoid losing the initiative, sought to establish a similar Select Committee in the House of Commons but was defeated by 158 votes to 64.

The tide of events, however, was turning against the reformers. The phasing out of transportation and the ending of the Crimean War led to growing anxieties about rising crime and the threat posed by "ticket of leave men" (convicts released on license) and returning soldiers. Attitudes were hardening. There was a greater willingness to strengthen the state through police reform and a greater skepticism about the reformatory effect of the new prison regimes.[5] This was not the time for dangerous experiments. Prisons needed to be made more austere, and the deterrent of the death penalty needed to be retained, if not enhanced. One time abolitionists were beginning to change their minds. The Wilberforce Committee delivered its report in 1856 and concluded that public executions were undermining the credibility of the death penalty, making heroes of criminals and hardening or corrupting those who watched. The demonization of the crowd, with its "low jesting and indecent ribaldry [and its] morbid curiosity," was well under way.[6] Action was not immediately forthcoming. Powerful figures, notably the Chief Justice and Home Secretary, opposed the abolition of public execution and the question might well have disappeared from view had it not been for the worries aroused by the "uneducated and vicious mob [that] descended in parties on the scene of the execution as avidly for the Derby" to see the fate of the Five Pirates in 1864.[7] Ewart made a further attempt to persuade the House of Commons to set up a Select Committee, but this time he had the support of the Home Secretary Sir George Grey, who believed that a Royal Commission was the appropriate vehicle for an examination of the contentious question of executions.

For two years the Royal Commission took evidence but significantly ignored the leading abolitionist organization, the *Society for the Abolition of Capital Punishment*. At the same time a fierce debate broke out in the leading journals of the day.[8] While it is tempting to see this debate in terms of a clash between abolitionists and retentionists (and at heart this it was), it is important to recognize the degree of confusion that surrounded the issue. Some witnesses to the Royal Commission and journal contributors, including experts from the prison service and judiciary, argued for the retention of executions in public; others, also including experts from the same background, argued for executions to be conducted in private; and others argued for the total abolition of the death penalty. To make matters worse, there was lengthy discussion of the merits and practicalities of distinguishing between first and second degree murder. The final report recommended the division of murder into first and second degree and, by a seven vote to five majority, the abolition of public executions. Although it was abolitionist members of the Royal Commission who had voted against the second recommendation, the *Society for the Abolition of Capital Punishment* welcomed the report. Parliament was determined to act, but the first proposal (to introduce degrees of murder) was withdrawn after a tied vote in the House of Lords. The second proposal soon became law. On May 29, 1868, the Capital Punishment Amendment Act received the royal assent. Three days earlier the Clerkenwell bomber, Michael Barrett became the last man to be executed in public in mainland Britain.[9] Ironically, the crowd that assembled to watch the last public execution behaved impeccably! Nonetheless, the gallows, like the gibbet 30 years before, disappeared from the landscape.

THE TRIUMPH OF THE RETENTIONISTS

The decision to relocate executions within prison walls was a logical response to the perceived problems of the scaffold crowd. There were still those who argued that public executions ensured that justice was seen to be done (and injustices in private prevented), but such arguments, couched in the language of the theater of execution, appeared as echoes of an earlier, less educated time and were no longer seen to be relevant. Nonetheless, there was a fear that "secret extermination," as the radical *Eclectic Review* termed intramural executions, would undermine impartial justice and pave the way to tyranny. Insofar as there were legitimate fears that private executions would enable those with influence to escape death, new procedures to be put in place would ensure that the right person was duly executed.[10] The dominant view was that the relocation of state executions would restore legitimacy to a justifiable, proportionate punishment that was in danger of being degraded by the behavior of the uncouth mob. Further, the cessation of public executions would bring an end to the disruptive and disgusting scenes of brutish and depraved behavior that (allegedly) accompanied executions, as well as dramatically reducing the opportunities for the commercial exploitation of executions, though little did reformers imagine the ingenuity of the popular press to cater for the demands of an audience that reveled in the details of the final moments of criminals. Finally, the terror associated with the death penalty, and thus its (alleged) deterrent effect, would be enhanced by the absence of a supportive crowd, by the silence and solitude in which the condemned man or woman faced death.

Further explanation is required of the overwhelming triumph of the retentionists in 1868. For three or more decades critics of the death penalty had been in the ascendancy. Abolitionists, arguing for the sacredness and sanctity of all human life, condemning "state murder" and the moral corruption of hanging, were part of a wider movement for change that reached beyond Britain. By 1865 the death penalty had been abolished in Tuscany, Oldenburg, and Nassau and the American states of Michigan and Wisconsin without succumbing to anarchy and immorality.[11] The penitentiary and its reformative regimes appeared to offer a more civilized and more effective way of dealing with the problem of the criminal. The number of capital offenses had been dramatically reduced in little more than a decade, and in the years around 1850 it looked as if the hangman would become as redundant as the gibbet. But the hopes were thwarted, and it was not until 1965 that Britain finally abolished the death penalty.

In part the abolitionists were weakened by changing circumstances. There was a greater pessimism about the threat of crime and the inefficacy of prisons from the mid-1850s onward. One-time abolitionists changed their mind—Dickens and Mill being but two of the best known and influential apostates—and the tide turned in favor of those who argued for the death penalty for murder. The retentionist argument comprised strands of varying force. Most powerful was the assertion that the murderer, by the very act of murder, forfeits his or her right to life. This was not a simple Old Testament "eye for an eye" argument but one that fitted with more recent rationalist arguments that stressed the importance of proportionality. Such was the seriousness of the crime—depriving another of life—that death was the only appropriate and proportionate punishment. Closely linked to this was the belief that hanging was a unique deterrent.[12] On closer examination, as both contemporary and later critics pointed out, the force of this argument was severely weakened by the fact that a very high percentage of murders were carried out by family members (husbands more than wives) or close friends in a fit of passion and/or by an individual who subsequently turned out to be insane. In such circumstances, the presence of the death penalty was irrelevant. As Sir John Macdonnell later noted, "[m]urder is not generally the crime of the so-called criminal classes, but is in most cases rather an incident in the miserable lives in which disputes, quarrels, angry words and blows are common. The short history of a large number of cases . . . may be summed up thus:—domestic quarrels and brawls; fighting, blows; a long course of brutality and continued absence of self-restraint."[13]

A third argument emphasized the strength of the British judicial system in general, and the safeguards afforded the accused in particular.[14] There was no risk of a miscarriage of justice as the criminal justice system erred in favor of the defendant. Such claims, so confidently made in parliament by Mill, sat uneasily with a number of cases, some very recent, in which there were very real doubts (or more) about the guilt of the condemned. Edward Chalker went to his death in 1835 protesting his innocence of the murder of a gamekeeper. In 1842 an English soldier, on his deathbed in India, confessed to the crime. More recently Serafino Pellizzioni had been sentenced to death, following a Boxing Day incident in 1864.[15] Fortunately for him, his case was taken up by law-reformer William Ballantine who was convinced that the police witnesses had committed perjury. Eventually, the true culprit, Gregorio Mogni, was convicted after a private prosecution for manslaughter brought by Pellizzioni's friends. The execution of John Wiggins in London in 1867 raised "widespread apprehension" that an innocent man had gone to the scaffold.[16] However, in contrast to the 1950s and 1960s when concerns with miscarriages of justice (Evans, Bentley, and Hanratty being the best known examples) were a central element in the abolitionist campaign, in the 1850s and 1860s there was no such upsurge of concern for innocent victims of the hangman.[17] Retentionist arguments were also couched in terms of concern for the guilty: life imprisonment, it was argued was worse than execution. Ignoring the point that, if this were the case, then the unique deterrent effect of hanging is called into question, one suspects that a more pragmatic consideration (the cost of keeping murderers in prison for the remainder of their lives) was at work. Finally, retentionists also justified their position in terms of national moral fiber, arguing that the excessive and inappropriate sentimentality of abolitionists threatened to bring enervation and effeminacy to the "general mind of country."[18] Easy to mock in hindsight, such sentiments were not unimportant to the men who legislated for the continuance of capital punishment in 1868.

THE DEATH PENALTY AFTER THE ABOLITION OF PUBLIC EXECUTIONS

No longer one of the "real questions of the day," largely removed from the public gaze, capital punishment featured little in the debates of late Victorian and Edwardian Britain. Out of sight, out of mind—but not quite. Prison executions were witnessed, albeit by the select few, and rarely by members of the press after the mid 1890s, but they were routinely followed by coroners' inquests. Official information was in the public domain and found its way quickly into the pages of the burgeoning popular press. Unofficial information, unguarded words from a hangman or his assistant, not to mention more formal autobiographies, added to the awareness of what was going on behind prison walls. Despite assurances to the contrary, press reports could make uncomfortable reading for Home Office officials and prison governors alike who maintained that executions were now conducted with decorum, free of the sordid excesses described by Dickens.[19] Prison-gate crowds, smaller than before, it is true, still behaved badly on occasions, especially if the condemned was a foreigner. The execution at Usk in 1878 of the young Spanish sailor Joseph Garcia, who protested his innocence throughout, was marred by a jingoistic crowd cheering the hangman the length of his journey from the railway station to the jail. Crowd scenes followed the execution of John Boyle in Londonderry in 1893. The executioner, Scott, found himself pelted with rotten vegetables as he left for home. Executioners still behaved inappropriately, getting drunk and holding indiscreet levees in local public houses, telling gory stories and selling "trophies." It was to stamp out such unseemly behavior that the Home Office decided in 1891 that it would issue (and receive back) the paraphernalia of death, thereby ending "money for old rope," that is the hangman's "perk" of selling the rope, and other items, used at an execution.

More common, executions were still botched as equipment failed (as in the case of John Henry Johnson, who in 1877 had to wait for a new rope to be found after the first one snapped) or the hangman miscalculated the drop.[20] The early 1880s were not a good time for executions, and 1885 was a particularly bad year. Fifteen people were hanged that year, and three executions created a scandal and galvanized the government into action. On May 25 the executioner, the deeply religious former Bradford policeman and one-time shoe salesman, James Berry was due to execute 65-year-old Moses Shrimpton at Worcester. Berry took pride in the fact that he had advanced the executioner's art by devising a table of calibrated drops, which would show at a glance the necessary length of rope for the given weight of the condemned. Unfortunately, insufficient attention was paid to the poor physical condition of Shrimpton. The nine-foot drop was too long and, as a consequence, Shrimpton's head was torn from his shoulders to the horror of all who witnessed the event. On November 30th, Berry repeated his mistake when executing Robert Goodale at Norwich. The terror-stricken Goodale had to be carried to his death on the gallows. This was an un-nerving experience in itself for those officials involved, but their shock at his behaviour was compounded by the miscalculation that resulted in another decapitation.[21]

The third scandal involved an execution that did not take place. John Lee, a 19-year-old footman, was due to be executed at Exeter prison for the murder of his elderly employer, Mrs. Keyse. Found guilty of a "cruel and barbarous" crime, his conviction had raised some comment as the evidence was circumstantial, but this was as nothing as the events of February 23 unfolded. Pinioned and noosed, he stood on the drop. Berry pulled the lever but nothing happened. Despite the combined efforts of Berry and some prison warders stamping on the drop, it would not open. The unfortunate Lee was then led away while adjustments were made to the scaffold, which was now in working order. Lee was brought back, but for a second and third time the drop refused to open, at which point the prison governor postponed the execution. Lee's sentence was subsequently commuted to life imprisonment, and he achieved a degree of fame and fortune as "The Man They Could Not Hang."[22] It was commonly believed that heavy rain in the night before the execution had warped the wood so that the drop would not work once a weight was placed on it. Notwithstanding this failure, Berry was paid his full fee and learned the lesson that in future gallows should be tested with a weight on the drop. The nonevent became a *cause célèbre* reported across the national press. The *Pall Mall Gazette* condemned the Home Secretary's "sickly sentimentality," *The Times* thought the singularly "ill advised" decision to reprieve Lee owed more to "sentiment than justice," and one irate correspondent felt that executions should be announced "weather permitting."[23]

Such was the extent of governmental concern that Sir Richard Cross, the Home Secretary, set up a Departmental Commission of Inquiry in 1886 to look into existing practices to ensure that in the future "all executions might be carried out in a becoming manner." In light of the evidence heard by Aberdare's Committee, the decision to make the inquiry confidential was, in political terms at least, a wise one. The political risks were high, and there could be no guarantee that the abolitionists would be sufficiently strengthened to carry the day. As Henry Labouchère tartly commented:

> I would as soon see a murderer decapitated as strangled. If, however, we wish to remove the head of this class of criminal I trust that some more scientific way of effecting the operation will be speedily adopted than that of wrenching the head from the body with a rope, in the manner practised by M. Berry . . . At any rate, if some less disgusting method of execution is not soon devised, we shall certainly have to face before long a strong agitation against capital punishment, which I, for one, should be very sorry to see.[24]

Unsurprisingly, executions (as in 1868) were exonerated, and this time (in the absence of a crowd to demonize) executioners were blamed. New guidelines were introduced to improve the efficiency of hanging, and more incompetent figures, such as Bartholomew Binns and William Marwood, were removed from the government's list of approved executioners. Marwood had established himself as a highly capable executioner when he took over from William Calcraft. He once boasted that he executed people whereas Calcraft merely hanged them, but in his later years he was reportedly drunk after a number of executions.[25] Binns, by contrast, was an almost total disaster.[26] In December 1883 a combination of drunkenness and incompetence led to the botched execution of Henry Dutton, which led to an official protest by the prison governor to the Home Office. No action was taken, but returning to Liverpool in March of the following year where, for the second time in three months, he arrived drunk, he so mishandled the execution that the unfortunate Michael McLean took almost half an hour to die through strangulation. It is a measure of official concern with the problems attendant on hanging that consideration was given to a variety of "cleaner" alternatives, including the electric chair, lethal injection, the guillotine, and the garrote.

While matters improved somewhat as a result of the recommendations of the Aberdare Committee, things could still go wrong. James Berry continued to hold levees in various public houses in various towns, notoriously in Kidderminster in 1888, and was even accused of accepting bribes to take unauthorized people into prisons to act as his assistant. And the more rigorous Home Office approach to hanging equipment could not guarantee "becoming" executions. The execution of Henry Devlin, in Glasgow in September 1890, was unbecoming as the drop was too short, and death resulted from strangulation; that of John Conway in Liverpool in August 1891 was unbecoming because Berry got the drop too long! The Conway execution had attracted more than the usual amount of attention as Conway was a leading figure in the Seamen and Firemen's Union and at the forefront of the "new unionism." The case was also particularly disturbing, involving, the murder, mutilation, and dismemberment of a young boy. Berry had fallen out with the prison doctor over the appropriate rope length but had insisted on the longer drop that all but decapitated Conway. To compound matters his behavior prior to the execution had caused anger locally. On his arrival he had repaired to a local public house where he had put on "an exhibition of a not very entertaining kind."[27] Unaware that the Home Office had already decided not to employ him again, Berry offered his resignation, but once again the "villain" of the piece was the incompetent hangman, rather than the barbarous practice of hanging. The fact that he quickly published his autobiography, My Experiences as an Executioner, and went on to make something of a career in the music halls and the lecture theater, recounting his gruesome tales of death, demonstrated that he could act "in a manner calculated to discredit capital punishment" even after he had ceased to be an official of the state and thereby strengthened the belief that the problem lay with executioners rather than executions.[28]

Even when the execution itself was conducted without mechanical malfunction, there were still distressing scenes as distraught men and women found their courage failing as they took their final steps to the gallows. There were those who went to the gallows with indifference or good humor and bravery (feigned or otherwise), and every hangman had his "bravest man" who never flinched at the sight of the gallows;[29] but equally there were those like William Henry Palmer, executed at Leicester in 1911, who, protesting his innocence to the very end, had to be dragged kicking and screaming to the gallows, where he managed to land one last kick on his executioner as the noose was put around his neck. Likewise, Mary Ann Britland was carried screaming to the gallows in Manchester in 1886. John Henry Gibbs, wailing pitifully, had to be supported on the drop at Usk in 1874. Three years later, William Hassell cried bitterly as he ascended the scaffold at Exeter in 1877, while in the same year Charles Smith, overcome with terror, fainted as he stood on the gallows at Oxford. And other, more ordinary executions were nonetheless characterized by cruel ironies. Ebenezer Jenkins (executed in 1889) was so light that James Berry (well aware of the problems facing the hangman) attached 7 lb. weights to the man's legs to compensate for his lightness; Mary Ann Cotton went to her death at Durham in 1873 a mere five days after giving birth, while the lovers, John Gallagher and Emily Swann, were hanged together, standing back to back, at Leeds in 1903. Gallagher's last words were "Good morning, love," to which Swann replied, "Goodbye. God Bless You," just before the lever was pulled and the drop opened.

Finally, there was also some awareness in late Victorian Britain that there had been some serious miscarriages of justice, but much to the governmental relief, public anger, insofar as there was any, was displaced almost exclusively on to the executioners. Unlike 18th-century advocates of the death penalty, such as Paley, who unsqueamishly saw the victim of a miscarriage of justice innocently sent to the scaffold as comparable to a soldier laying down his life for the good of the nation, Victorian and Edwardian officials maintained the fiction that miscarriages of justice were impossible and simply did not happen. Yet several men and women went to the gallows protesting their innocence until the very end. In a number of cases the evidence on which they were convicted was far from strong. Periodically, public opinion was concerned by the possibility that justice had not been done, especially in a capital offense.

One man who died protesting his innocence, not well known to later historians, was Jeremiah Corkery. He and his friends had been involved in an incident involving two policemen in a Birmingham public house in which both officers were stabbed. Corkery, along with a number of other men, was paraded before the two officers as they lay in hospital but neither identified him. Corkery was released, only to be rearrested and charged with murder when some while later one of the policemen died. Despite a weak case— the victim, when taken to the hospital where the injured Corkery was lying, was unable to identify him as his assailant and there was no other evidence linking him directly to the crime—he was found guilty at Warwick Assizes in 1875 and sentenced to death. Stating that he was not seeking mercy, he pointed out to the court the lack of direct evidence linking him to the murder and claiming that he was the victim of a plot that was intended to ensure the release of others at his expense.[30] Very real doubts existed about his guilt; nor was this an isolated case.

The *Howard Association* drew attention to other cases—John Upton, executed in 1877 at Leicester, and Daniel Gorrie, executed in 1890 at Wandsworth. Similarly the conviction and execution of Israel Lipski in August 1887 led to numerous calls for the establishment of a Court of Criminal Appeal.[31] A little later there were even more appeals made following the conviction of Mrs. Florence Maybrick for the murder of her husband. Indeed, such was their volume that her sentence was commuted, though doubts remained about her guilt. Another indisputable victim of a miscarriage of justice was William Habron who along with his older brother John was tried at Manchester Assizes in 1876 for the murder of P. C. Nicholas Cock. John was acquitted but William sentenced to death, but he was subsequently saved by the Royal Prerogative. In this case Habron's unequivocal innocence of the crime with which he had been charged was eventually established. The man who was actually responsible—Charles Peace—had sat through the trial silent. However, having been tried and found guilty of murder at Leeds Assizes in 1879, Peace confessed to the murder of P. C. Cock. Habron, after two years' breaking limestone in Portland Prison, was released and awarded £800 ($1,377) in compensation. A similar case took place in early 20th-century Glasgow when Oscar Slater was found guilty of murdering an elderly woman. His sentence was commuted to life imprisonment, but he served 19 years in prison before his innocence was established. The case received much publicity when Arthur Conan Doyle became involved and published his book *The Case of Oscar Slater* in 1912. When eventually freed, he received £6,000 ($9,540) compensation but was required to pay the £1,500 ($2,385) cost of his appeal. Such cases were disconcerting but did not become part of a broad-based campaign against the death penalty. It was recognized that "men have been hanged before now on circumstantial evidence which has afterwards been disproved [and] the life has gone," but even among reformers there was rueful acceptance of the fact that such cases were "quickly hushed up and forgotten."[32]

Overall, with no public outcry about capital punishment per se to compare with the mid-19th (or indeed mid-20th) century, attention was focused not on the appropriateness of killing as a punishment for murder, but with its appropriateness for certain "problem" groups and the technicalities that surrounded the application of the law, particularly in regard to insanity.[33] With growing medical knowledge, it was no longer felt to be right or proper to execute insane murderers, but where should the line be drawn? Similarly, executing the very young was no longer acceptable, but the 1908 Children Act only gave formal recognition to practice since 1887 of not hanging under-16 year olds.

CONCLUSION

The changes that had taken place over the course of Victoria's reign were considerable and appeared to many contemporaries as a triumph for progress and civilization. Punishment was now, broadly speaking, directed at the mind rather than the body. Men and women were no longer strangled for a range of

The Execution of Sach and Walters, 1903. Known as the "Finchley Baby Farmers," Amelia Sach (29) and Annie Walters (54) were the first women to be executed at Holloway Gaol on February 3, 1903. Allegedly both women had to be carried to the drop protesting their innocence. (Courtesy Mary Evans Picture Library)

property offenses and crimes against the person, excepting murder. They were incarcerated in prisons, though particularly in the second half of the 19th century, their regimes appeared to grind men down, rather than (in the words of early Victorian reformers) to "grind men good." Along with the dramatic reduction in the number of capital offenses, executions in the late Victorian and Edwardian period took place outside the public gaze behind prison walls. The streets of London, Edinburgh, and Dublin in particular were no longer disrupted as crowds gathered around the gallows to watch the last moments of some wretched convict. The debasement of morals that had so shocked Dickens was no more. Respectable Victorian sensibilities had been eased, but the terror of the gallows had been increased by the isolation of execution. The process of execution itself was improved. Death was inflicted more scientifically; the victim was made less uncomfortable by various new pinions and belts; the anxiety of the last moments was reduced by having death cells only seconds' walk from the gallows.[34]

But the fact remains, miscarriages of justice apart, that the civilized rulers of the greatest Empire in the world still felt it fit and proper that murderers should die, many in terror, urinating and defecating, men ejaculating, women losing menstrual blood, their heads encased in a cloth bag. Such was the extent of the "civilizing process" in Victorian and Edwardian Britain. Oscar Wilde's bitter words still ring true.

> They hanged him as a beast is hanged!
> They did not even toll
> A requiem that might have brought
> Rest to his startled soul,
> But hurriedly they took him out
> And hid him in a hole.[35]

CHAPTER ELEVEN

PRISON AND THE PROBLEM OF SECONDARY PUNISHMENT

Grinding Men Good

In 1841 the chaplain of Preston Gaol, the Reverend John Clay, wrote in his annual report that the "experiment of *solitary confinement* has been tested by the experience of another year. I am more than assured of its value; and my conviction does not so much depend upon any abstract reasoning upon the matter, as upon the direct and decided evidence afforded by the language and demeanour of the prisoners subjected to its operation."[1] In the same year, a prison officer took a more pessimistic view of separate confinement, claiming that placing a prisoner in Pentonville for three or four years will tend to make a man a confirmed idiot rather than a good and useful member of society.[2] A worrying flow of evidence suggested that all was not well. Not untypical was the unnamed prisoner (DF 4920), who "five and a half months after admission was observed to be depressed in spirit and strange in his manner and conversation [suffering] from vague fears and apprehensions of impending evil."[3] Nighttime was worst. Men dreamt they saw snakes coiled round the bars of their cells, or that poisoned food was being forced upon them. Sobs, screams, and cries rent the air: the "awful tales of long suffering and deep mental agony," in Mayhew's words, behind the figures for "the breaking down of weaker minds" and, in the case of the most desperate, the self-destruction.[4] *The Satirist* campaigned vigorously in the 1840s on behalf of "the miserable wretches who are hurried to a premature grave by the infamous torture which is called discipline in the Model Prison Pentonville."[5]

Nor were these problems confined to the 1850s. A quarter century later a more harrowing case of suicide was reported. "A man opposite has hung himself by means of his braces . . . And he only had a letter from his little daughter yesterday, enclosing a lock of her hair. She was on her death-bed but the authorities would not let him have the little tress: 'tis against the Christian rules and regulations of English prisons."[6]

This was not how it was supposed to be. The prison (that most visible and lasting monument to the Victorians) was to have provided an enlightened and humane solution to the problem of rising crime. The new regimes, or so their advocates had argued over many years, would not only act as a deterrent to existing and would-be criminals, but would also lead to the reform of prison inmates, returning them to society as fit and proper persons. Unfortunately, the story of the Victorian prison is largely one of failure. To understand how this came about we need to look back to the early 19th century and the wider debate about punishment that was engendered by the growing concerns with the effectiveness of the Bloody Code before looking more closely at the practicalities of prison.

TRANSPORTATION

Even in the heyday of the Bloody Code in the 18th century, concerns had been expressed about the absence of an appropriate secondary punishment for those found guilty but for whom the death penalty was inappropriate. One solution, formalized in 1718, was transportation. Initially, the dumping ground had been the American colonies, but after 1776 a new location was required. The hiatus created by the American Revolution necessitated an immediate practical response. The short-term solution (which was to survive until the 1850s!) was the use of decommissioned warships, or Hulks, which were permanently moored on the Thames and other offshore sites.[7] There was also an opportunity to consider other alternatives, including the penitentiary. A Penitentiary Act was passed in 1779 to complement the 1776 Hulks Act, but there was limited commitment to investment in an expensive and largely untried approach to the problem of crime. Transportation remained the best option, and a new destination had been found for those whom the British authorities wished to banish from their shores—Australia.

Thus began in 1787 a unique experiment in which convicts were transported to found and to be punished in a new colony. Transportation appeared to hold out three benefits. First, by removing the most serious criminal elements, it would prevent the corruption of others; second, banishment to a distant land and a severe regime would act as a deterrent; and third, the experience in Australia would also provide training in new skills that would fit the convicts for the free life that would follow the end of their sentence. When Victoria came to the throne, transportation was at its peak, but it was also coming under fierce criticism both in Britain and Australia. Sydney Smith was scathing but witty in his condemnation. Writing to Sir Robert Peel in 1826 he parodied transportation in no uncertain terms. "Because you have committed this offence . . . you shall no longer be burdened with the support of your family. You shall immediately be removed from a very bad climate and a country overburdened with people to one of the finest regions of the earth, where the demand for human labour is every hour increasing."[8] But, somewhat perversely, he was pessimistic about the effects. "There can be but one opinion. New South Wales is a sink of wickedness in which the great majority of convicts of both sexes become infinitely more depraved than at the period of their arrival . . . It is impossible that vice should not become more intense in such society."[9]

Transportation had always attracted its critics, but hostility increased significantly in the 1830s when the Whigs came to power.[10] The turning point in parliamentary terms was the establishment of the Molesworth Committee, which was to deliver a devastating critique. Its Report, very much the case for the prosecution, painted an alarming picture of inefficiency, corruption, and economic incompetence and worse. Determined to horrify its respectable audience, the Report starkly stated that

> [i]t is difficult to conceive how any man . . . merely having the common feelings of morality, with the ordinary dislike of crime, could be tempted by any prospect of pecuniary gain, to emigrate, with his wife and family, to one of these colonies, after a picture has been presented to his mind of what would be his probable lot. To dwell in Sydney . . . would be much the same as inhabiting the purlieus of St. Gile's, where drunkenness and shameless profligacy are not more apparent than in the capital of Australia . . . [E]very kind and gentle feeling of human nature is constantly outraged by the spectacle of punishment and misery—by the frequent infliction of the lash—by the gangs of slaves in irons—by the horrid details of the penal settlements; till the heart of the immigrant is gradually deadened to the sufferings of others, and he becomes at last as cruel as the other gaolers of these vast prisons . . . [T]he whole system of transportation violates the feelings of the adults, barbarizes the habits and demoralizes the principles of the rising generation; and the result is, to use the expression of a public newspaper, "Sodom and Gomorrah."[11]

The reference to Sodom and Gomorrah was an unsubtle reference to the "unnatural practices" that allegedly flourished in the male-dominated penal colony. With a grand flourish the Report concluded that

> Your Committee . . . consider that they have submitted the most unquestionable proofs that the two main characteristics of Transportation, as a punishment, are inefficiency in deterring from crime, and remarkable efficiency, in not reforming, but in still further corrupting those who undergo the punishment; that these qualities for inefficiency for good and efficiency for evil, are inherent in the system, which therefore is not susceptible of any satisfactory improvement; and lastly, that there belongs to the system extrinsically from its strange character as a punishment, the yet more curious and monstrous evil of calling into existence, and continually extending societies, or the germs of nations most thoroughly depraved, as respects both the character and degree of

their vicious propensities. Your Committee, therefore, are of opinion, that the present system of Transportation should be abolished.[12]

Other influential writers, such as Charles Dickens and Harriet Martineau, contributed to the wider campaign in Britain, while in Australia the Anti-Transportation League mounted a highly moralistic attack on "the Stain" that blighted Australia. Historians might object to the one-sided picture created by the critics of transportation, but the contemporary political reality was that it was a discredited system.[13] Its demise was not immediate, but despite a rearguard defense by Lord Caernarvon, transportation to eastern Australia was phased out in the 1850s and to western Australia the following decade.[14]

THE RISE OF THE PENITENTIARY

The phasing out of transportation cannot be explained simply in terms of its own (perceived) failings. A better alternative had to be presented, and increasingly this was seen to be the penitentiary, or reformed prison, but the roots of the Victorian prison system can be traced back to the last quarter of the 18th century. The publication of John Howard's *The State of the Prisons* in 1777 caused a considerable stir, coming as it did at a time when the doubts about the Bloody Code and the need for an appropriate form of secondary punishment had been heightened by the transportation crisis. William Eden, responsible for solving the problem, forced through the Hulks Act in 1776, followed, three years later, by the Penitentiary Act, that envisaged the construction of separate prisons for men and women with a standardized approach to imprisonment. The Act expressed a clear reformist ideal. "Imprisonment, accompanied by well regulated labour, and religious Instruction, might be the means, under Providence, not only of deterring others from the Commission of the like Crimes, but also of reforming the Individuals, and inuring them to Habits of Industry."[15]

However, change was limited. This reflected in part the countervailing view that prisons had a limited role to play—holding people for trial or for execution—but also skepticism about the reformatory potential claimed by reformers and a pragmatic concern with the expense of prison building. The initiative of Sir George Onesipherous Paul led in 1791 to the opening of Gloucester Penitentiary, which was to be a national model, but the reality was that few new prisons were built, particularly during the 1790s and 1800s. Historians commonly point to the report of the Holford Committee in 1810 and the involvement of the government in financing Millbank (partially opened in 1816) as a turning point. In one sense this is clearly correct—the new convict prison in London, under direct government control, would exist alongside locally controlled prisons across the country—but in practical terms the problems and failings of this new penitentiary came close to discrediting the whole idea of the reformed and reforming prison.

THE WORKSHOP UNDER THE "SILENT SYSTEM" AT MILLBANK PRISON.

The Silent System: Associated Labor in the Workshop of Millbank Prison, London, 1862. From Mayhew and Binney, *The Criminal Prisons of London*, 1862. (Courtesy Mary Evans Picture Library)

From the outset Millbank had a sorry history. Massively over budget, its chosen site by the Thames was unhealthy. A poor dietary regime led to major health problems, such as scurvy, contagious diarrhea and, allegedly, cholera among prisoners, and the evacuation of the prison in 1823. To compound matters, despite being selected because they were deemed to be most responsive to a reform regime, several prisoners suffered from various forms of mental instability and some were driven to suicide. Others became rebellious. As early as 1818 Bow Street Runners had to be called in to restore order at gunpoint, after warders and other staff had been assaulted and cells wrecked. In 1822, the first year of full occupancy, there were further disturbances that were officially blamed on too good a diet for the prisoners! In 1826 another major outbreak occurred. Cells were smashed, fighting broke out in the chapel, warders were once again assaulted, and the prison cat hanged! Millbank ceased to be a penitentiary and in 1843 became a holding prison for those awaiting transportation.

The failure at Millbank was a serious blow to those prison reformers and in particular those who had advocated the "silent system" in which prisoners engaged in communal working but without communication. The silent system was predicated on the Enlightenment belief that man was a rational and perfectible being, whose mind was a *tabla rasa* on which would be inscribed beliefs and values as the result of a continual process of association between sensation and experience. Moral education, in general, was essential to ensure a positive association between wrongdoing and pain. For the convicted criminal, for whom wrongdoing had been associated with pleasure, prison was to be the corrective institution in which this inappropriate and antisocial association was to be reversed, while the convict also learned new habits of obedience and industry. In practice Millbank had followed a mixed regime that combined segregation and communal working, but the "evils of contamination" that resulted from the latter were seized upon by its critics, notably Crawford and Russell, for whom the root of the Millbank debacle was to be found in the failure to establish an effective regime around the notion of Christian reformation. This was to be achieved through the "separate system." Underpinning this approach was a set of religious arguments that recognized the natural sinfulness and disobedience of mankind (which was exacerbated by the rapid social changes that were beginning to sweep Britain in the late 18th century) but that also emphasized the divine forgiveness that held out the hope of redemption for all through Christian teaching. The prison was envisaged as a total institution, free from the taint and temptation of the outside world, in which the living presence of Christianity, embodied in the prison chaplain, would ensure punishment but also reform of a moral and practical nature. In more practical terms, prisoners would be held in single cells where they could contemplate their wrongdoings, exhorted to repent and reform by the chaplain and other prison officials but isolated from the contaminating influence of other prisoners, whether at work, prayer, or exercise. Inward contemplation and the awakening of conscience would be the first step to the acceptance and internalizing of new values.

The emergence of the concept of the separate system in the 1830s owed much to two men: William Crawford and Whitworth Russell. Crawford, like de Tocqueville, had been inspired by a visit to America. Specifically, he believed that the so-called Philadelphia system, the embodiment in penological practice of Quaker beliefs, provided a last solution to the problem of combining deterrence and reform. The attraction of the Philadelphia system of solitary confinement was that it combined terror (as the convict reflected on the awfulness of his crimes) with reform (as solitude prepared the mind for the reception of Christian truths) while carrying with it the subsidiary benefit of inculcating a work ethic. On his return he became an ardent and influential advocate. He was joined by the Reverend Whitworth Russell, ex-chaplain of Millbank Penitentiary. The Prisons Act of 1835, establishing a system of government inspection and report, was a crucial turning point. Crawford and Russell were appointed as inspectors for the Home Division and, as such, exercised a disproportionate influence until their deaths in 1847. In their role as inspectors they were in a position (which they seized) to change practice in local prisons that remained under the control of local magistrates.

Although the reform of the prisoner was a central concern, the regime was not intended to be a soft option. "The convicted prisoner," they argued has committed an offence; therefore he must be punished; he is depraved himself; he must therefore, not be suffered to corrupt others: he is capable of further depravation; he must, therefore, be secluded from all intercourse with such as may impart it; he is to return, at the expiration of his sentence, to society; he must, therefore, be trained to such habits, and be subject to the inculcation of such duties, as shall afford as strong a guarantee as possible to the community that he shall not be led to further violation of the law; or at least, that he shall be deterred from such violations, by a recollection of the privations, hardships, and discomforts of a prison.[16]

Elaborating upon their "tough love" views, they argued that

[u]pon the offender in his separate cell all the moral machinery is brought to bear with as much force and effect as if the prison contained no other culprit than himself. His submission then must be immediate and complete: he will be calm, for there is nothing to ruffle or discompose him; he will be disposed to self communion, for he has no companion but his own thoughts; he will be led to listen with attention and respect to the instruction, reproof or consolation, of his keepers and instructors, for almost the only accents of friendly intercourse are those which issue from their lips; and he will apply himself with ardour to the labour of his hands as a relief from the insufferable burden of idleness and ennui.[17]

They recognized that where sentences were short, as many were, moral reformation could not be achieved, therefore, "in these cases we must forego the hope of amendment; satisfied with intimidating, where we are unable to reclaim. In all cases, with reference to the places of confinement for the convicted, whatever may be the moral advantages, a prison should be a place from which both the public and the criminal recoil with more or less of dread: repugnant to the imagination of one, painful to the recollection of the other."[18]

A further Prison Act of 1839 was greatly influenced by the thinking of Crawford and Russell, not least in its emphasis on religious reformation, but it did not go as far as directing local prisons to adopt the separate system. Recognizing practical constraints—it would have been prohibitively expensive for some prisons to adopt the separate system in its entirety—the act facilitated separation wherever possible.[19]

Fired by a belief in the efficaciousness of the separate system, the government once again became involved in prison building. The outcome, "the Model," as Pentonville was quickly dubbed, was opened in 1842, the embodiment of the new thinking and meant as an example to others. Since 1839 all new plans for prisons had to be approved. The key figure, first as Home Office adviser, later as Surveyor-General of Prisons, was Joshua Jebb. Under his eye, and encouraged by Crawford and Russell, some 50 prisons came under the influence of the Pentonville model in the following decade. With its radial layout, and cells on each side of a central open corridor in each wing, close surveillance of inmates was achieved. The cells themselves (some 13 feet by 7 feet and 10 feet high) were designed to prevent communication between prisoners.

Here the individual prisoner slept, worked, and ate, leaving his cell, still under conditions of strict segregation, only to attend chapel or to take exercise.

Mountjoy Prison in Dublin, Strangeways in Manchester, and Armley in Leeds are but three examples of the transplanting of the Pentonville model. Nor was it restricted to British shores—Melbourne Gaol, for example, was one of many colonial prisons that adopted the same approach. However, the separate system did not sweep all before it. While roughly a third of 120 English provincial prisons, including most major cities, had fully implemented the

SEPARATE CELL IN PENTONVILLE PRISON.
WITH HAMMOCK SLUNG FOR SLEEPING, AND LOOM FOR DAY-WORK.

The Separate System: Prison Cell in Pentonville Prison, London, 1862. The cell contains a hammock and loom. From Mayhew and Binney, *The Criminal Prisons of London*, 1862. (Courtesy Mary Evans Picture Library)

separate system, another third had only adopted it partially, while the remainder either adopted the silent system or were unreformed. In part, for
example in Exeter, this was a reflection of the cost of changing existing buildings to implement the new system. Indeed, this burden of the past was most
starkly seen in Scotland, where, according to the first report of the Board of
Directors in 1839, there were some 70 lock-up houses comprising a single
room and a further 80 small burgh jails that were equally unfit for the new
purpose. However, there was also a resistance to London driven change. The
magistrates of Lancashire, for example, asserted their local control by rejecting the schemes of Crawford and Russell.[20]

Early visitors to Pentonville were impressed. An anonymous contributor to
the *Quarterly Review* could scarcely contain his enthusiasm for the new model
prison with its

> contrast to the pandemonium of associated criminals does the visitor perceive
> who enters for the first time the walls of the model prison at Pentonville! In-
> stead of the noise and bustle of the old Newgates —absolute stillness; a few silent
> warders only scattered here and there in the large and lofty corridors contain-
> ing a triple tier of cells, which range the whole length of these galleries! In spite
> of the blaze of daylight which should enlighten, and the scrupulous cleanliness

CONVICTS EXERCISING IN PENTONVILLE PRISON.

The Separate System: The Exercise Yard at Pentonville, 1862. As well as being
kept at a distance as they walk round holding the rope, the prisoners are wear-
ing masks to enhance their separation. From Mayhew and Binney, *The Criminal
Prisons of London*, 1862. (Courtesy Mary Evans Picture Library)

which should raise notions of comfort, it is impossible not to feel the oppression of resistless power . . . They [the prisoners] are fed at the same moment,
rest at the same hour, are out in masses in the open air. They are catechized in
the school, and respond in the chapel—yet man knows not man . . . A small
aperture is so contrived in the door of each cell as to permit the visitor to see
its inmate without himself being seen.

And there was a positive side to be seen.

All are profoundly engaged—one plying his trade, another busy with his slate,
a third fixed and motionless over his Bible. The shoemaker is squatting cross-
legged and stooping over his last; the tailor raised on his table with his imple-
ments and materials about him; the weaver hardly distinguishable amid the
frame-work of his active machinery; the basket-maker in his corner, distant an
arm's length from the heap of osiers from which ever and anon he is selecting
that to which he is about to give form and shape. It is not here, as in the solitary
occupations of the world, that the artisan can beguile his labour with snatches
of some favourite melody; nothing must break the silence of the cell. Its inmate
soon learns to concentrate all his energies on his work, which becomes to him
a consolation—a necessity.[21]

The Select Committee on Prison Discipline (commonly known as the Grey
Committee) gave the official stamp of approval to the separate system, believing it to be "more efficient than any other system which has yet been tried,
both in deterring from crime and in promoting reformation."[22] The reality
was more grim. Despite the good intentions of high-minded reformers, there
were major practical problems, some inherent in the separate system, others
more general to the running of any large institutions whose inhabitants were
unwilling residents. The catalog of mental anguish and breakdown, of self-
harm and suicide, brought about by separation that had started in Millbank
was continued in Pentonville and the other prisons modeled on the same or
similar lines. Maintaining separation as men moved from cells to chapel or
the exercise yard was time consuming and difficult. Preventing communication between prisoners proved impossible. Whether through messages tapped
on pipes or through forms of ventriloquism, prisoners learned how to cir-
cumvent the rules to meet a human need for interpersonal communication.
Prisoners were rendered docile or feigned an acceptance of religion as they
learned to play the game. Some were transformed, though they found it difficult to gain employment on their return to the outside world; but many others simply were not. Recidivism was a major problem that pointed clearly to
a central failure of the prison system. The underlying premise—that all men
could be ground good—was flawed. At a more basic level, it was difficult to
recruit suitably qualified and committed men to become warders. Not all were
brutal or corrupt—but many were. Maintaining the high standards expected
by the prison chaplain was not easy, and while the overt power relationship

appeared to heavily favor the prison authorities, it soon became apparent that a *modus vivendi* had to be found between prisoners and guards. Prisoners' lives were obviously circumscribed by their guards; but the actions of those self-same guards were also restricted by those they watched over.

Problems were not confined to the convict prisons of London. The new prison at Birmingham saw a regime of "remorseless tyranny" that only came to light following the suicide of the pathetic Edward Andrews, aged 15, who had been driven to take his life having been forced to work on the crank machine and then strapped in a "punishment jacket" for hours, during which time he was doused with cold water.[23] There was a similar scandal at nearby Leicester where prisoners, who were required to complete 1,800 revolutions of the crank machine to receive a breakfast, 4,500 for dinner, and 5,400 for supper, were reported to be showing signs of "weakness and fatigue"![24]

JOSHUA JEBB AND THE IRISH ALTERNATIVE

The heyday of the reformism surrounding the separate system was, in reality, short-lived. Major problems emerged within months and years of the opening of Pentonville (and other such prisons across the British Isles), but the ideological drive was significantly weakened in 1847 when in April, William Crawford, who was known to be in ill health but continued to drive himself to make a success of his pet project, Pentonville, died of a heart attack in its board room; then in August, Whitworth Russell, whose management skills had recently been criticized, committed suicide, shooting himself with a pistol in Millbank. Such are the ironies of history! There followed a period of pragmatism dominated by the figure of Joshua Jebb.

Jebb faced a three-fold task. The new prisons, driven by the doctrinaire zeal of Crawford and Russell, had not been an unqualified success, and more effective management was required. Second, the Hulks, that expedient of the 1770s that had survived until the 1840s, were under such fierce criticism that parliament had decreed that they should be replaced and an alternative location found for their thousand or so inmates; and third, transportation was also being phased out and accommodation was required for those who would now serve a term of penal servitude under the provision of the 1853 Act. A prison building program was essential and in due course new establishments were built at Portland, Dartmouth, Portsmouth, and Chatham. That was the easier part of the solution; more problematic was developing a workable regime. Jebb combined considerable experience with a pragmatic, largely non-doctrinaire approach. He took an enlightened view on a number of matters, rejecting the notion of "less eligibility" for prisoners, believing in the need to combine the moral improvement of prisoners with practical help both during and after sentence to help ex-prisoners return to society.[25] Above all, he advocated flexibility in the prison system with an emphasis on productive labor. The upshot was the progressive stage system, which was intended to combine "invigorating hope and salutary dread."[26] The first stage took the form of separate confinement, but the period was much reduced in light of the concerns that had been expressed, first to 12 months and later to 9. The second stage involved arduous communal public work on schemes that would benefit the wider public, such as the building or extending of dockyards or even, somewhat later, the building of Wormwood Scrubs Prison. The final and most contentious stage involved release on license before the expiry of the full sentence.[27] The "ticket of leave man" was to become a bogeyman in mid-Victorian Britain.

Jebb was unfortunate in that his pragmatic reformism came at a time when the tide of opinion was beginning to flow against reformist ideas. He was not helped by the high-profile problems in two of the new convict prisons. In 1855 there was a disturbance involving some 350 convicts at Portland, and in 1861 an even greater disturbance took place at Chatham involving 850 convicts.[28] In addition, there had always been critics who had poured scorn on the very idea of reform, insisting that prisons should be places of terror. Sydney Smith bitterly complained that the "cleanliness and order" of the new prisons undermined the salutary impact of "loathsomeness and misery." Indeed, he saw the new prison regimes as being counterproductive. "[T]he present lenity of jails, the education carried on there—the cheerful assemblage of workmen—the indulgence in diets . . . are one of the great causes of the astonishingly rapid increase in commitments."[29] *Punch* summed it up as the "Civilisation of the Roughs," whereby convicts received lessons from professors of dancing and deportment!

Mayhew and Binney, in their massive survey of London's prisons, were scathing in their criticisms of the efficacy of the various prison regimes. Classification, insofar as it could meaningfully be done, was counterproductive. "[H]ad it been the object to make provision for compulsory education in crime, no better plan could have been devised."[30] The silent associated system was labor intensive, ineffective in maintaining silence—"an act of refined tyranny, that is at once unjust and impossible of being thoroughly carried out."[31] The separate system—this "maniac making system," as *The Times* called it—inflicted unacceptable levels of physical and mental suffering, All systems suffered from the fundamental flaw that they associated work with punishment—hardly an appropriate preparation for an honest life outside prison. Thus, despite these experiments in reform, crime and the criminal population was on the increase—so much for deterrence. Further, of the prison population, a sizable number (over 30%) were recidivists, some having been recommitted on four or more occasions. "Thus we discover how utterly abortive are all our modes of penal discipline."[32] To make matters worse, the garroting panic of the early 1860s (street muggings in modern parlance) was wrongly blamed on "ticket of leave men." The presence of allegedly hardened, repeat offenders on the streets of London gave support to the growing belief that some habitual criminals were beyond reform. In a characteristically scathing passage, Thomas Carlyle described prisoners as "[m]iserable distorted blockheads, the generality: ape-faces, imp-faces, angry dog-faces, heavy sullen ox-faces; degraded underfoot perverse creatures, sons of indocility, greedy mutinous darkness, and in one word, of stupidity, which is the general mother of such."[33]

As opinion hardened in mainland Britain, on John Bull's Other Island an interesting and seemingly highly successful experiment was taking place. The man responsible for creating the stir was Walter Crofton. Inspired by Alexander Maconochie's brief experiment with a reformist regime on Norfolk Island, Crofton's Irish System, as it came to be known, was a variant on the progressive system found on mainland Britain.[34] A rigidly enforced nine-month period of separate confinement in Mountjoy Prison in Dublin was followed by a period of public work at Spike Island in the Bay of Cork. Here convicts passed through a series of stages, but in addition, a marks system was introduced that provided the convict with an opportunity to "work out his own redemption through his own toil."[35] Prisoners gained marks through their own labor, which enabled them to pass to the next stage. In practical terms, a prisoner sentenced to four years' penal servitude could reduce the length of the sentence by nine months if he passed through all the stages at Spike Island. For someone sentenced to 12 years, the reduction could be as much as 3 years.[36]

The distinctiveness of the Irish System lay in the next stage, which involved transfer, for all but those deemed to be incorrigible, to an intermediate prison—either at Smithfield (for artisan labor), Fort Camden (for mechanical labor), or Lusk (for agricultural labor)—for a period of "probationary and natural training." Transfer was dependant on receipt by Crofton of a favorable report on the convict. Here there were no prison clothes and no prison hair cuts. The emphasis was on "individualisation," and the convicts were treated like Christians with a future rather than untrustworthy criminals with a past. At every opportunity the convicts were exhorted to become honest citizens and, if at all possible, to emigrate. Evening lectures included such topics as "Conscientiousness Regarding Debt," "Swearing: its Evil Consequences," "The Advantages of Emigration to the Unfortunate," and "New Caledonia as a Field for Emigration."[37]

The convicts were given responsibility, running messages outside the prison and ultimately working outside and returning to prison at night. Convicts were prepared for their return to the outside world; but the immediate outside world was also prepared for the returning but reformed convict. On offer of employment the convict was released but under police supervision for the remainder of his sentence. He was required to report to the local police, who would monitor his life to ensure he did not slip back into idleness and worse. Every time he moved he had to sign on with the local police. Any breach of the conditions of the license resulted in a return to prison to complete the sentence. As a final encouragement to emigration, a free discharge was offered to the convict who left Ireland. Between 1856 and 1860 some 1,250 male con-victs were released on license, of whom 77 (or just over 5%) had their licenses revoked. Moreover, the overall prison population also dropped sharply.

Crofton's approach was seen to be a huge success and attracted consider-able attention from reformers across Europe. Matthew Davenport Hill visited Ireland three times and waxed eloquent on the virtues of the prison regime there. Similarly, Mary Carpenter and William Clay were enthusiasts advocat-ing the adoption of the Irish System in England. *The Economist* summed up the contrast in a single sentence: "Captain Crofton has succeeded beyond our most sanguine hopes . . . Colonel Jebb has failed beyond our worst fears."[38] The judgment was doubly wrong. Jebb was less of a failure than his critics made out, and Crofton was less successful than his admirers believed. The success of the Irish System owed much to the peculiar circumstances of the Famine. Of the Famine convicts who passed through the Irish System, more than one-third emigrated when they reached the end of the intermediate stage. Of the remainder, many never fell foul of the law again, but this had as much, if not more, to do with the more favorable economic conditions into which they were released. It became apparent in the 1860s that a different type of criminal (more akin to his English counterpart) was moving through the prison system, and the statistics painted a less rosy picture as the percent-age of repeat offenders increased sharply. In 1868 only a little over 10 percent of the men committed to Mountjoy (25 out of 185) were first-time offenders; the rest had at least one, and in several cases considerably more, previous committal to prison. Disillusionment set in, and Crofton was roundly (but unfairly) criticized. His system limped on, but in 1886 the once-famous Lusk prison was closed.

CHAPTER TWELVE

PRISON AND THE PROBLEM OF SECONDARY PUNISHMENT

Grinding Men Down

THE DU CANE REGIME

Jebb had been forced on the defensive as he came under attack from critics on both the left and the right. For the former he was doing too little to reform, for the latter too little to deter. His death in 1863 facilitated the swing to a more deterrent-focused approach to prison. Within parliament opinion was shifting in a pessimistic direction. The Caernarvon Committee, which looked at the whole question of prison discipline, concluded that penal servitude was "not sufficiently dreaded." Convicts, it was alleged, scoffed at a sentence of penal servitude. Appalled by the variations between prison regimes, amazed by the generous diets, and shocked at the absence of an agreed definition of hard labor, the committee agreed that there was too much emphasis on re-forming the unreformable and too little deterrence.[1] Furthermore, members of the committee "do not consider the moral reformation of the offender holds the primary place in the prison system, [nor] that mere industrial employment without wages is sufficient punishment for many crimes."[2]

A new, more deterrent centered on hard labor approach was needed and a new man to see it through. The 1865 Prisons Act enshrined the principles of uniformity and severity, and Edmund Du Cane was the man to put them into practice. Like Jebb and Crofton he had a military background before becoming a professional prison administrator. Starting as inspector of military prisons, he later became director of convict prisons before becoming the chairman of the prison commissioners. Although retaining a belief in the potential for reform of the juvenile offender, he was dismissive of reformatory regimes for adult, habitual offenders. They made up "a class of fools whom even experience fails to teach" and as such were beyond redemption. As a consequence, there was little point in putting either religion or education at the center of the prison regime. A believer in the merits of long sentences, Du Cane was determined that deterrence was to be the order of the day.[3] Harsh conditions—"hard fare, hard labour and hard bed"—were needed to achieve this. Further, the administration of the prison system was to be modernized by giving "due respect to scientific principles and practical knowledge" and also by ensuring uniformity of treatment. Du Cane advocated a four-stage system that linked good behavior, rewarded by marks, and progress through the system. Stage promotion required 224 marks. As the maximum daily award was 8, this ensured that the minimum time spent in a stage was 28 days, thereby ensuring that short-term prisoners, irrespective of their behavior, could not move out of the lowest stage.

Nowhere was this more clearly seen than in his approach to diet. Using the latest scientific advice, minimum levels of diet were established and enforced for all categories of work. Even the sick were included with appropriate reductions made for them. Furthermore, the food was to be plain and coarse—hard fare, indeed, with no more luxuries for prisoners! Prison diet would comprise bread, gruel, potatoes, suet pudding, and meat, but only those in the fourth class would have access to the full diet. The agreed daily diet in 1885 is shown in Table 1.

The class one diet was effectively a starvation diet with an estimated calorific content of 1730 compared with an ideal intake for an active adult male of 2,500 to 3,000 calories. Indeed only the class four diet, with approximately 3,000 calories, came close to recommended intakes.[4] And it was not as if the men sent to the convict prisons were in peak condition after a nine months' separation in which they did no hard work.[5] Diet was now being used for punitive ends. Unsurprisingly, the new diets were not met with universal approval, provoking prisoner revolts, including a refusal to work, at Portland and Chatham. Improved diets were introduced as a result, but the medical officer at Chatham believed they were "scarcely sufficient to make them [the convicts] effective for the hard labour of this place."[6] More generally, and contrary to Du Cane's claim that "the health of the prisons is certainly higher," convict prison diets proved to be inadequate and gave rise to an increase in health-related problems. Stories emerged of prisoners eating candles, boot oil, even snails and old poultices in desperation. In exceptional cases, such as that of John Nolan, prisoners died, in part because of the inadequacy of punishment diets.[7] Nolan's case created a scandal that revealed the harsh realities of prison life for the less fortunate of Victoria's subjects. A glass-blower by training, Nolan, a mere 18 years old and described by prison officials as "an overgrown boy," became unemployed and ended up living on the streets; he then was imprisoned for being a rogue and a vagabond. In two months in prison he was punished 18 times and was put on a bread and water diet

Table 1
Recommended Prison Diet, 1885

Adult Men at Hard Labour	Men not at Hard Labour, Women and Boys under 16 years of age
Class 1	
16 oz bread	16 oz bread
1½ pts stirabout	1½ pts stirabout
Class 2	
18 oz bread	15 oz bread
2 pts gruel	2 pts gruel
8 oz potatoes or suet pudding	8 oz potatoes or 6 oz suet pudding
Class 3	
22 oz bread	18 oz bread
2 pts gruel	2 pts gruel
8 oz potatoes	6 oz potatoes
¾ pt soup or 3 oz beef	¾ pt soup or 3 oz beef
Class 4	
24 oz bread	18 oz bread
2 pts porridge	2 pts gruel
8 oz potatoes	8 oz potatoes
1 pt soup or 4 oz beef	1 pt soup or 3 oz beef
or 12 oz suet pudding	or 10 oz suet pudding

Source: "Local Prison Code, 1885," cited in S. McConville, *English Local Prisons, 1860–1900: Next Only to Death* (London: Routlege, 1995), p. 307.

10 times. His offenses consisted of failing to pick his daily quota of oakum and for being incontinent at night and during the day. On November 8, 1878, the pathetic Nolan died of double pneumonia. Nolan's case was exceptional but not unique. The death of John Harvey from pneumonia, again at Coldbath Fields, was attributed to inadequate diet. *The Times* solemnly noted that "the mortality among short-term prisoners in this gaol [Coldbath Fields] is very large on account of insufficient food."[8] The majority lived but not without damage to their physical (and mental) well-being.

Hard labor was approached in a similar fashion. Physically demanding construction work was prescribed for fit prisoners. Docks were built by prison labor at Chatham, the existing dockyards at Portsmouth extended, and a breakwater constructed at Portland

Most strikingly of all, new prisons were built by convict labor at Woking, Borstal, and Wormwood Scrubs where prisoner labor was kept on site in the

Chatham Prison: Convicts Breaking Rocks, c. 1860. The harshness at Chatham led to a major prison riot. (Courtesy *Illustrated London News Ltd*/Mary Evans Picture Library)

very cells that they had built. The application of science was also evident in determining the use of the treadmill across the prison system. The 1865 Prison Act had stipulated that the first three months of a sentence of hard labor should be spent on the treadmill, but it did not specify a uniform task. In 1880 a six-hour treadmill task was introduced. Split into two equal shifts and with the wheel set at 32 feet per minute, prisoners could make the recommended maximum daily ascent of 8,640 feet within the given period and still have a five-minute break after every fifteen-minute spell on the wheel. For prisoners at Gloucester, who had been subject to a mere 6,800 feet, this was a clear worsening of conditions, but for those at Northallerton and Rutland, where the daily ascent was 12,000 and 15,000 feet respectively, the improvement was significant indeed.

In addition to the physical effort required on the treadmill there were very real dangers. Not for nothing was it colloquially called the "cockchafer." Strong men were reported to be led away weeping after a stint on the "mill." And there were other forms of approved hard labor such as shot drill, pumps and capstans, and the crank.[9] When not at such activities, prisoners sentenced to hard labor picked oakum. The tedium and futility of this activity was worse than the physical demands it made, but failure to meet the daily quota brought sanctions, as did failure to meet requirements elsewhere.

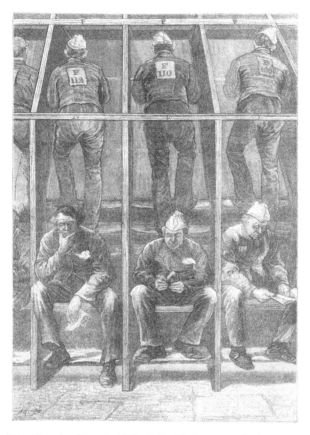

The Treadmill at Cold Bath Fields Prison, Clerkenwell, 1874. The treadmill had been invented by Sir William Cubitt, better known as a civil engineer. (Courtesy *Illustrated London News* Ltd/Mary Evans Picture Library)

The combination of inadequate diets and strenuous labor was sufficient to exhaust all but the sturdiest, but there was little respite or recovery at night. Physical hardship continued as the old hammocks and flock beds were replaced by wooden beds, coir mattresses, and minimal bedding; but worse was the psychological torment as men relived their daily tribulations in their dreams. As *One Who Has Suffered It* wrote:

He crawls back at night a beaten animal, in a worse plight relatively, than any animal under the heavens. He must at once divest himself of boots, outer shirt, trousers, and hat, and put these with the sweeping-brush outside the cell door. Then the door is locked upon him. Where no slippers are provided, he must walk on the flags in his socks, or, if he has no socks, with naked feet. . . . He

CELL, WITH PRISONER AT "CRANK-LABOUR," IN THE SURREY HOUSE OF CORRECTION.

Cell with Prisoner at Crank Labor in the Surrey House of Correction, 1862. Prisoners usually had to perform 12,000 revolutions a day, though some had "only 10,000." From Mayhew and Binney, *The Criminal Prisons of London*, 1862. (Courtesy Mary Evans Picture Library)

stretches the hammock, spreads the rugs, champs his dry bread, endeavours to drink the stewed tea. If there is gas, he can read for a couple of hours. If there is not, he must content himself as he may with the thought that, probably, he has gone to bed earlier than his babies. Here, then, arrives the grand occasion on which prison administrators delight to dwell—the "reforming" influence of thirteen or fourteen hours of darkness! Oh, the torture of those fearful nights wherein the hellish beleaguering of insanity must be strenuously repelled![10]

The general awfulness of prison was exacerbated by particular actions, events, or times. In John Galsworthy's research on the early 20th-century prison system, he discovered that assiduous officials put prisoners in sunken pits in work sheds to maintain separation. Weekends were more stressful times as there were less communal activities, be it work or exercise. And there was an obvious sexual element (or more accurately the absence of sexual contact) to cellular isolation that was largely kept from respectable

Victorians. However, Sir Godfrey Lushington told the Gladstone Committee of his concerns with the prevalence of "the solitary vice" (that is masturbation) in prison. Warning pamphlets, such as "The Narrow Way" and "The Pack of Lies" were distributed to male prisoners, and in extreme cases, young men caught in the act had their penises blistered. Finally, executions created tensions for days beforehand, while the event itself, especially if there was a suspicion that it had been botched, could give rise to collective protests, including the destruction of cell furniture.[11]

The prison system became ever more impersonal and mechanistic; efficiency was sought through uniform discipline and enforced order. Du Cane claimed that his approach was "the exact opposite of governing by mere fear of punishment . . . [and had] a reformatory effect" and claimed that "as a means of diminishing the necessity of more drastic forms of prison punishments, its success has been most marked," but the scale and range of punishments, often for relatively minor offenses, increased.[12] The threat of the dark cells, chains, and whips created an atmosphere of fear and repression.[13] The quasimilitaristic approach was enhanced by the increased use of ex-military men as warders. There was little commitment to notions of reform but rather an institutionalized distrust of prisoners, which was duly reciprocated. Outright resistance was very limited, but there were cases of major disturbances at Chatham and Portland. In the latter several convicts were shot dead in the battle, and in both cases the ringleaders were punished severely after order had been restored by the army. Less spectacular, but no less serious, individual warders continued to be attacked and a number killed throughout the period. Equally striking was the persistence of passive resistance in the form of malingering or self-inflicted injuries which bore witness to prisoner hostility. Chatham, which acquired the nickname of "the slaughterhouse," was particularly problematic and in the worst year of 1871 33 amputations resulted from self-inflicted injury. The extent to which the public was aware of conditions behind prison walls in the 1870s and 1880s is a matter of debate. Du Cane was both autocratic and secretive and kept civil servants in the Home Office (and their political masters) in the dark. To a degree this satisfied all concerned. The political response had been firm and the official view, as expressed by the Kimberley Commission in 1879, was positive, welcoming the fact that penal servitude had become more greatly feared.[14] What is more, prison numbers were falling Prison worked, or so it could be presented.

Historians have focused on the convict prisons of Victorian Britain for obvious and good reason, but the more common prison experience was in the local prison. The 1877 Prison Act brought all local prisons in England and Wales under the control of central government, as did legislation for Ireland and Scotland, though in Scotland the process of central control dated back to the creation of the General Board of Directors of Scottish Prisons in 1839. Du Cane's regime touched all prisoners. Sentences were shorter in local prisons.

The maximum was two years, but most sentences were shorter. In 1879 65 percent of the sentenced population served six months or less; in 1894 the figure had risen to over 70 percent. The regimes were more repressive and even less reformist than in the convict prisons. To use a catch phrase of a later age, this was the "short, sharp shock" treatment. Its deterrent value was limited; many came back, time and again, effectively serving a life sentence by installments. Jane Cakebread (imprisoned 280 times) and William Onions (imprisoned 175) became well-known examples of the failure of local prisons when their names and experiences gained widespread publicity, but they were far from unique. Thousands of men and women, whose names have long since been lost to posterity, saw their lives wasted via a steady succession of prison sentences. In the 1890s it was alleged that recidivism rates had risen from roughly a third to almost a half. The harsh conditions of the convict prisons were replicated in county jails. Oscar Wilde incarcerated in Reading bitterly lamented:

> Each narrow cell in which we dwell
> Is a foul and dark latrine
> And the fetid breath of living Death
> Chokes up each grated screen,
> And all, but Lust, is turned to dust
> In Humanity's machine.

In a letter to the editor of the *Daily Chronicle* he condemned the psychological pressures faced by prisoners.

> The present prison system seems almost to have for its aims he wrecking and the destruction of the mental faculties. The production of insanity is, if not its object, its result. Deprived of books, of all human intercourse, isolated from every humane and humanising influence, condemned to eternal silence, robbed of all intercourse with the external world, treated like an unintelligent animal, the wretched man who is confined in an English prison can hardly escape becoming insane.[15]

There was little comfort in the fact that the population of local prisons fell significantly in the last quarter of the 19th century from some 21,000 in 1878 to under 13,000 in 1892, and then rose slightly to 15,000 by 1900.

THE GLADSTONE COMMITTEE AND THE REACTION TO DU CANE

Du Cane oversaw a regime that was rarely criticized in the 1870s and 1880s. The Howard Association supported much of what was being done, and the Kimberley Commission had no doubt that "the system of penal servitude, as at presented administered, is on the whole satisfactory, that it is effective as a punishment, and free from serious abuse."[16] Du Cane could have hardly expressed it better.

In the last decade of Victoria's reign it appeared that there was a dramatic shift in opinion that led to a flurry of important legislative changes. A few remained optimistic—the *Daily Graphic* called Pentonville "the healthiest place in England," but few agreed.[17] Du Cane's rule was brought to an end in spectacular fashion and a reaction against the harshness of his regime took place, though the scale of that reaction remains a matter of debate. Two different things were taking place. First, there was a change in public opinion. Concern with the new "nationalized" prisons was not new but the volume of criticism slowly increased, and more importantly, there was a growing feeling that prison was not working in terms of either deterrence or reform. William Booth's *In Darkest England and the Way Out*, published in 1901, argued (among many other things) for a greater emphasis on reformation and the individual treatment of the prisoner, but the most influential figures were Henry Massingham, the editor of the *Daily Chronicle*, the voice of respectable Liberalism; the larger-than-life left-wing politician, John Burns, who had served a sentence in Pentonville in 1888; and the Christian-socialist activist, William Douglas Morrison, who was assistant chaplain at Wandsworth prison for eight years. A series of three articles in the *Daily Chronicle* titled "Our Dark Places" appeared in January 1894 and mounted a fierce critique of the current prison system in general and Du Cane in particular. Massingham mentioned both Burns and Morrison in very positive terms. Both had direct experience of prison conditions and could bear witness to the inappropriateness and ineffectiveness of Du Cane's approach, particularly for those prisoners who suffered from some physical or mental disability. In an article in the *Fortnightly Review*, Morrison spoke scathingly of the misleading claims of success made by Du Cane.

> If a prison does not succeed in deterring an offender who has had experience of its severity from coming back to it again and again, it is not likely to have much influence in deterring the criminally disposed from embarking on a criminal life. On the contrary, the spectacle of an offender going to prison for the fifth, the tenth, the twentieth time is calculated to encourage the peccant materials in the population rather than to deter them. . . . The statistics of recidivism are utterly hostile to the idea that we are more successful than our neighbours in dealing with the convicted population. Our system . . . is less deterrent, inasmuch as it produces a larger percentage of offenders who persist in a career of crime after repeated experiences of prison life.

Challenging the optimist spin put on the statistics for the prison population as a whole he continued:

A very great deal is made of the circumstances that the prison population and the number of committals to prison have exhibited a tendency to diminish within the last few years . . . But the real and simple explanation of the matter is never so much alluded to. Whilst the proportion of the prison population and of committals has been exhibiting this downward tendency, the proportion of convictions and of offences has been steadily increasing; and it is by the growth of offences and convictions that the criminal condition of a community must in the first instance be judged.[18]

Second, there was a more receptive audience within the political classes. In part this reflected the concerns and priorities of a new generation, men such as Herbert Asquith and Herbert Gladstone, influenced to a degree by T. H. Green at Oxford, and in part it was a "palace revolt" by civil servants, as much as politicians, who could no longer tolerate the secretive and autocratic manner of Du Cane. The outcome was the establishment in 1895 of a departmental committee, chaired by Herbert Gladstone, that, in effect, was charged with the responsibility for evaluating the Du Cane regime. Gladstone had no doubt that the prison system was his and that he (Du Cane) was "the embodiment of prison severities." In fact, the terms of reference of the committee were unhelpful and incomplete. Asked to consider consequences but to ignore causes, the committee was not asked to tackle the fundamental question of the purpose of prison.[19]

The committee's report was delivered in April 1895, but it was already clear that the Liberal Government was on its last legs and other matters dominated the political agenda. The report itself was an uneven and, at times, ambiguous document. Although there was praise for what had been achieved in the past 30 years, there was also condemnation. The principles that underpinned Du Cane's approach—uniformity, long sentences, and severe discipline—came in for heavy criticism. Perhaps the most damning criticism, largely accepted by the committee, came from Sir Godfrey Lushington.

I regard as unfavourable to reformation the status of a prisoner throughout his whole career; the crushing of self-respect; the starving of all moral instinct he may possess; the absence of all opportunity to do or receive a kindness; the continual association with none but criminals . . . the forced labour and the denial of all liberty. I believe the true mode of reforming a man or restoring him to society is exactly in the opposite direction of all these.[20]

Reverting to the optimism of an earlier age, the committee took a positive view of prisoners who "have been treated too much as a hopeless or worthless element in the community . . . too much as irreclaimable criminals, instead of reclaimable men and women" and declared that reformation should be placed alongside deterrence as one of the twin aims of the prison regime, so that "prison discipline should be more effectually designed to maintain, stimulate, or awaken the higher susceptibilities of prisoners, to develop their moral instincts, to train them in orderly and industrious habits, and wherever possible to turn them out of prison better men and women, both physically and morally, than when they come in."[21]

And to that end uniformity should be tempered, "the system should be made more elastic, more capable of being adopted [sic] to the special cases of individual prisoners."[22] As well as condemning the rigid separate system, the committee report also rejected useless hard labor in its various forms. Here was the essence of the report: temper the excessive severity of imprisonment and strengthen the elements of reform. Continuity was the order of the day—only excess was to be excised.

The response to the committee report was mixed in the press, within parliament, and among the prison commissioners. Under the chairmanship of Evelyn Ruggles-Brise, the commissioners gave a full but varied response, accepting some proposals, rejecting others, and simply ignoring yet others. Contrary to the view that there was a fundamental break with the principles and practices of his predecessor, their response was such that they gave the appearance of accepting the principle of reform while perpetuating the old system with the minimum of change. Sacrificing the use of the treadmill and the crank was a small price to pay for maintaining the principle of separate confinement.[23] And the subsequent Prisons Act of 1898 was also to be a triumph for Ruggles-Brise. In particular, the power to make prison rules, a matter of fundamental importance given the criticisms that had been leveled at Du Cane, was not vested in parliament. Reformers knew they had achieved little. Massingham bitterly observed that, despite some minor changes (or promises of change) regarding the form of hard labor, punishment in prison, and prison dietary, "the plank bed, the separate system, and the farce of prisoner education remain."[24] Ironically, as he was the principal victim of the Gladstone Committee, Du Cane could hardly have complained at the provisions of the 1898 Prisons Act.

The continued criticism of prison life also bears witness to the limited change brought about by the Gladstone Committee. Writing in language that echoed the 1890s critique of Du Cane, the socialist Edward Carpenter waxed eloquent in 1905. With undisguised indignation he asked his readers to

> [t]hink of a nation deliberately taking its weak, its half-witted, its ill-born, its children of the gutter, of drink and of extreme poverty—for of such stock are the majority of criminals—and then trying systematically what amount of added starvation of body and mind these unfortunates could bear.

Warming to his theme, he continued.

> Few people pause to think what these things mean. To be confined in a bare cell, with nothing but a stool to sit upon, for nearly twenty-three hours out of the twenty-four (for exercise and prayers occupy little more than an hour),

the mind turned in upon itself, gnawing itself in monotony and desperation, the stomach gnawing itself with hunger, no sign or word from any friends or relatives, no look of kindness or sympathy from any one, no chance of doing or showing a kindness towards anyone; if any work has to be done, that work probably consisting in turning the crank or picking oakum, work brutalizing and useless, from which every soul with a spark of manhood in it must revolt; and this to go on for days and weeks and months; could anything be imagined more debasing and stunting, more calculated to produce the hardened and hopeless "habitual criminal"? . . . It is a fact that, even now, in most prisons the windows (too small already for the needful amount of light) are placed so high up and in such a position that the inmate of the cell cannot see *anything* out of them . . . Yes, truly these prisons are outwardly clean and decent and orderly: but inwardly what are they but whited sepulchres full of dead men's bones?[25]

But the most powerful and influential critique came from an unusual source: a playwright. On February 21, 1910, John Galsworthy's new play *Justice* opened at the Duke of York Theatre, London. Galsworthy had visited Dartmoor, Lewes, and Chelmsford prisons several times, and his representation of what he had seen and heard had a stunning impact. The dramatic third scene of act three in which no word is spoken but in which the central character, Falder, who had been sentenced to three years' penal servitude for fraud, paces his cell like a caged animal before beating at his cell door with clenched fists was eclipsed only by the final scene in which Falder commits suicide. So shocked was the Home Secretary Winston Churchill that he intervened to reduce the period of separation to one month. Suicides were uncommon, but many inhabitants were ground down by "the silence, the separation and slave mentality" that made "senile and debilitated old men" of the many repeat offenders in the prison population.[26]

The Gladstone Committee played an important role in the introduction of a more controversial punishment: preventative detention. Critical of the one-regime-fits-all approach of Du Cane, it proposed the introduction of indeterminate detention to incapacitate the habitual prisoner. There was an appealing simplicity to the recommendation, but the practicalities proved more problematic, not least because the term *habitual criminal* was open to different interpretations. The prominent writer and publicist Sir Robert Anderson, one-time head of CID at Scotland Yard, had distinguished between weak habitual criminals, incapable of resisting temptation or learning from experience, and the hard professional criminals who, though small in number, were responsible for the majority of serious crimes. Only indeterminate sentences would protect society; a view shared by other experts such as Griffiths and Quinton.[27] However, not everyone accepted these ideas. Indeed, the influential Evelyn Ruggles-Brise advocated a hybrid scheme that combined penal servitude with preventive detention, though even this was opposed by several distinguished judges who disliked the very notion of an indeterminate sentence.

Herbert Gladstone, the Home Secretary, advocated indeterminate sentences in a speech to parliament in May 1908, which contained examples of habitual offenders that could have been drawn from Anderson; he laid great emphasis on "formidable offenders, men who are physically fit, who take to crime by preference, decline work when it is offered them, and refuse the helping hand."[28] Gladstone sought to shock the House of Commons with a list of men who had chosen crime as their profession.

> A., thirty-eight years of age, received his first conviction at twenty-five; had served sentences of two and six years' penal servitude; time actually spent in prison, seven and a half years; a well-educated man, a professional forger. B., forty-five years of age, received his first conviction at twenty-nine; served three terms of penal servitude and eleven sentences for stealing; now undergoing three years penal servitude for stealing and receiving; eleven and a half years in prison; C., forty years of age, received first conviction at twenty-seven; served thirteen sentences for stealing and housebreaking, now serving five years for larceny; nine years actually in prison. D., thirty-one years of age; first conviction eighteen; served nineteen sentences for stealing and shop-breaking; now serving three years penal servitude for stealing; seven and a half years in prison.[29]

Despite Gladstone's eloquence the bill was not accepted in its entirety. The notion of the indeterminate sentence was rejected, in part at least, for in its place was substituted preventive detention for a specified period of between 5 and 10 years. Camp Hill Preventive Detention Prison on the Isle of Wight was built for the purpose of housing prisoners subject to this new form of detention. There was, however, a lack of commitment in key places. The Home Secretary Winston Churchill was unsympathetic and sought to restrict use of these provisions; some judges were equally unconvinced; and the staff at Camp Hill had doubts about the new regime for which they were responsible. Preventive detention, not quite still-born, was a sickly child that barely survived infancy. Perhaps the greater surprise is that it survived into the interwar years rather than expiring sooner.

CHAPTER THIRTEEN

PRISON AND THE PROBLEM OF SECONDARY PUNISHMENT

The Treatment of Female and Juvenile Offenders

WOMEN

Although the Victorian prison population was dominated by adult men, there were others who fell foul of the criminal justice system and for whom appropriate punishment was required. Classification and the separation of prisoners into different categories had been the response to the criticism of indiscriminate imprisonment of men, women, and children in early 19th century jails, but modifications were necessary to take into account the essential differences that Victorians saw between men and women and children and adults.

Certain aspects of the new prison regimes—hard labor, particularly in public—were clearly inappropriate given prevailing gender beliefs, but more importantly, there was a deep-rooted belief that criminal women were more depraved in nature, more difficult to deal with, and more threatening to the wider moral order of society. Female criminals were doubly damned. Not only had they broken the law, but by their very criminality they had transgressed the norms of femininity. This laid them open to the criticism that they were at least uncivilized, if not unnatural. This had a profound effect on the nature of the regimes in women's institutions, which were concerned with the re-creation of appropriate patterns of female behavior as much, if not more than, as with punishment.[1]

Over 95 percent of women prisoners were held in local prisons, but little is known of the conditions in them. Before 1877 there was immense diversity.

In Tothill Fields, for example, despite increases in accommodation, there was never sufficient provision for separate cells for all. In the mid-19th century there were single cells for 56 percent of the female prison population, although this had risen to 93 percent by 1870. There were other problems, not least the shortness of sentences, that hampered the intended reform of prisoners. Seventy-five percent of sentences were less than one month, and 50 percent less than two weeks. Other circumstances were less than ideal: educational facilities were limited, the impact of the chaplain marginal, the usefulness of labor questionable, and the turnover of often low-quality staff high. Not surprisingly, "the realities of prison management clearly confounded the avowed aims of penal reformers."[2]

Two further factors highlight the gulf that existed between theory and practice. First, as in all prisons, the clear-cut distinction in theory between controllers and controlled (that is, warders and prisoners) was not replicated in practice. Prison management was often a matter of negotiation; compromise, rather than unquestioned control, was the reality. A variety of relationships between warders and prisoners developed. Some were quite mercenary—the bringing in of food, and so forth—but there is evidence of more intimate relationships, certainly emotional and possibly sexual, developing.[3] Discreet references to "tampering" cast a veil over incidents of lesbianism. Second, the assumption that prisoners wished to be reformed so as to avoid a return to prison was flawed. For some women prison was more of a refuge, a place to return to in times of trouble. It is a measure of the harshness of life for many working-class women in Victorian Britain that prison was seen as preferable to life outside. In prison there was a respite from the threat and worry associated with a profligate or violent partner. Facilities for pregnant women were often superior, and in a more general sense, prison was for some an attractive winter alternative in terms of accommodation and food. Nor was this confined to the mid-19th century. The prolific writer Mrs. Sarah Amos told the Gladstone Committee in 1896 that it was not possible to "make prison anything but a haven to very many."[4]

After 1877 the situation changed as the result of the nationalization of the prison system. The number of prisons holding female prisoners fell from 61 to 32, and there was a determination to impose more uniform regimes. Nonetheless, certain problems remained. A large percentage of women served very short sentences. In 1895 45 percent of women committed to local prisons served seven days or less, and almost three-quarters served no more than two weeks.[5] The quality of staff remained problematic, and little interest was shown in the vexed question of appropriate labor for women. It also became apparent that prison did not appear to be effective or appropriate for the large number of women repeatedly sentenced to terms of imprisonment for drink-related offenses.

The shortcomings of local prisons could be explained in part by the brief span of most sentences. The same could not be said of the convict prisons.

Millbank was the main prison for women sentenced to penal servitude, but in 1853, Brixton was opened as the first purpose-built women's prison.[6]

The number involved was small—some 2 percent of all women sentenced to terms of imprisonment—but the opportunity, in theory, was great because the average sentence was some seven to eight years.[7] However, the experience of women in convict prisons was bedeviled by doubts about the appropriateness of penal servitude, problems in devising an appropriate regime, and even greater problems in implementation.

Penal servitude was questioned on the grounds that women were constitutionally less able to withstand the rigors of long-term imprisonment. Perversely, it was also argued that the more emotional nature of women, combined with their more sedentary character, meant that penal servitude would not have the same impact upon them as it did on men. In more practical terms, the public-works stage, an essential component of the regime for men, was simply not appropriate for women, but finding an acceptable alternative

FEMALE CONVICTS AT WORK, DURING THE SILENT HOUR, IN BRIXTON PRISON.
[From a Photograph by Herbert Watkins, 179, Regent Street.]

The Silent Hour at the Female Convict Prison, Brixton, London, 1862. From 11 A.M. the women sat at their needlework for an hour outside their cell doors. From Mayhew and Binney, *The Criminal Prisons of London*, 1862. (Courtesy Mary Evans Picture Library)

proved to be an insoluble problem. A compromise stage system was devised. The first two stages were served at Millbank. A probation period lasting two months spent in almost total isolation with arduous work, such as picking coir matting or heckling old ropes, was followed, assuming good behavior, by promotion to the third class where work was lighter and visitors allowed. Satisfactory progress was followed by transfer to Brixton for the remainder of the sentence, though availability of accommodation as much as an individual's behavior determined the move. As well as working in silent association, a prisoner in the second class at Brixton received a small wage. Despite its centrality, attitudes towards work were ambiguous. Acceptable work, such as knitting or clothes-making, could lead to unfair competition with "free" labor outside. Cooking and laundry work had the advantage of reducing prison costs, though the latter was of such low repute that it was feared that the women would be returned to the contaminating environment that had led them astray in the first place.[8] A mark system was also operated, although, unlike men, women could gain marks for good behavior alone. In addition, educational and religious support was provided, though in practice both were marginal activities and often viewed with skepticism by the authorities. Many women did not progress beyond this stage, but those deemed to be reformable were promoted to the first class and, generally speaking, served the last year of their sentence in the less repressive atmosphere of Fulham Refuge, which was intended to prepare women for release by training them in useful, and appropriately feminine, skills such as cleaning and cooking.

The quality and commitment of prison staff was of great importance, perhaps more so than in male convict prisons, but convict prisons, like local prisons, suffered from a range of problems: the work was potentially dangerous, the hours long, and the pay relatively poor; unsurprisingly, turnover rates were high. Staffing levels were not ungenerous (averaging one staff member to every 15 prisoners) in light of the belief that women needed to be treated on a more individual basis than men, which further added to a less-regimented approach in the female convict prisons, but which made greater demands made of the staff. The most fundamental problem, not unique to female convict prisons, remained the fact that many prisoners were either unwilling or unable to be reformed in the ways that the authorities wanted. The history of the female convict prisons in the late 19th century was thus one of failure. Incidents of resistance, collective as well as individual, and the resultant use of a variety of forms of punishment was an obvious sign of failure. Even the normal conformity was probably little more than superficial. Less spectacular, but ultimately more telling, was the continuing problem of female recidivism.[9] By the late 19th century a growing body of opinion felt that both local and convict prisons were being asked to undertake a task for which they were not fitted. A large number of recidivists were socially inadequate, or even sick rather than threatening and sinful.

The late 19th century saw a growing concern with the habitual criminal in general and the habitual drunkard in particular, many of whom were women.[10] Here was a threatening character for a society believing it faced racial degeneration and a decline in world status. Here were new folk devils to scare respectable Victorians. Probably the best known was Jane Cakebread for whom "many were her challengers for notoriety, but they came and went, the grave closed over them, yet she held on."[11] In London in 1896, at the age of 67 she was charged for the 280th time with drunkenness, thereby exceeding the record of Ellen Sweeney, who, at Swansea in 1895, had received conviction number 279. Tottie Fay likewise attracted press attention, not least because of her peculiar dress in court: ball gown and satin slippers!

The medical press spawned a specialist literature dealing with the problem; the popular press spawned a moral panic; and parliament responded by passing new legislation. Unfortunately, the Habitual Drunkards Acts of 1872 and 1879 and the Inebriates Act of 1888 were ineffective, not least because inebriates had to volunteer to give up their freedom and then pay for their treatment. The Departmental Committee on the Treatment of Inebriates saw compulsory long-term sentences as the only hope for the country, if not for the individual. The 1898 Inebriates Act was scarcely more effective. It advocated a two-track approach: habitual drunkards were to be dealt with by philanthropic organizations and local authorities; those committing serious crime when drunk would be dealt with by the state. In practice, the private response was limited and the government reluctantly took over responsibility for provision in the early 20th century. Finance was again the stumbling block as local authorities were unwilling to contribute to maintenance costs.

The solution, or so it was thought, was to be found in another type of institution, the reformatory. Located in the more conducive conditions of the countryside, reformatories would provide model conditions for the unfortunate women sent their way. They were an unmitigated disaster. The regimes were ad hoc, and there was a strong and overt moral tone to the training, even though alcoholism was deemed to be a disease. The practical training was limited and inappropriate. Butter-making, bee-keeping, and hay-making were hardly usual skills for hardened inner-city women with little wish to be reformed! Disillusionment soon set in, and the emphasis shifted from hopes of reform to a preoccupation with containment and deterrence.

A new explanation of the habitual drunkard emerged in the early 20th century. Expert opinion now asserted that the cause was to be found in "feeble-mindedness" and "moral insanity."[12] These ill-defined concepts blurred the distinctions between mental illness, crime, and immorality but provided an alternative way forward. As the feeble-minded person was inadequate, irresponsible, and incurable, it was inappropriate to subject her to a prison regime. Instead, long-term incarceration in a special institution was the answer both for the individual, who because of her weakness was open to exploitation, and for the nation whose stock was threatened by the innate promiscuity and high fertility of the feeble-minded. Old morality was but thinly disguised by the new science of eugenics. It was "well-known" that women were peculiarly prone to mental illness; therefore it was not difficult to adjust to these new ideas.[13] The feeble-minded or morally insane woman, by definition, could not make responsible decisions to exercise sexual restraint. Pregnancy should only take place within marriage; therefore, pregnancy outside of marriage was "proof" of feeble-mindedness! Thus was born the 1913 Mental Deficiency Act with its four-fold classification of idiots, imbeciles, feeble-minded, and moral imbeciles, and thus asylums replaced prisons as the repository for these "deviants" until the 1970s.

YOUNG OFFENDERS

Victorians were also worried about the number of young offenders that bedeviled society with particular "panics" around the mid-century and again at the turn of the century when "the hooligan" was a particular cause for concern.[14] Special treatment in separate institutions was again seen as the way forward.

The early advocates of classification within prisons were concerned to prevent the contamination of the young, perhaps first-time, offender by older, more-hardened criminals, but the idea of separate institutions developed slowly. A prison hulk, *Bellepheron*, was given over solely to boy convicts in 1824. Some 18 months later the "specially fitted" *Euryalus*, at Chatham, was brought into service. In 1838 Parkhurst was opened as a prison where young offenders would serve a preparatory period before transportation. Numbers peaked at around 800 per annum in the late 1840s, falling to just over 600 a decade later and less than 350 in the early 1860s. Effectively undermined by the development of reformatory schools, Parkhurst closed as a juvenile prison in 1864. Deterrence and moral reformation were the twin aims, though complaints from the recipients of Parkhurst "graduates" sent to Australia do not suggest any long-term success was achieved.[15]

More significant developments took place in the 1850s with the passing of the legislation establishing reformatory schools in 1854 and industrial schools in 1857. Convicted children under the age of 16 could be sentenced to a period of from two to five years in a reformatory school, following a prison sentence. Industrial schools were intended to have a more educational purpose and were initially linked to the education rather than the prison system, catering for children between the ages of 7 and 14 who had been convicted of vagrancy. Although falling short of the demands made by such reformers as Mary Carpenter, who had advocated the need for special treatment for children of the "perishing and dangerous classes," the fact that the law recognized that such children were not wholly

Boys in the Exercise Yard at Middlesex House of Correction, Tothill Fields, London, 1862. From Mayhew and Binney, *The Criminal Prisons of London*, 1862. (Courtesy Mary Evans Picture Library)

to blame for their actions, and required treatment in distinct institutions, perceived as "moral hospitals," was an important development.[16]

The inculcation of new and "appropriate" patterns of behavior—of orderliness, punctuality, and industriousness—was central to the reformatories. In addition, the 1857 Industrial Schools Act gave the state the power, under certain circumstances, to take children (predominantly, if not exclusively, working-class) from their parents. A further act of 1866 extended the legislation and defined children in need of state care in broad terms to include not only those who had appeared before a court but also those deemed to be in danger of slipping into criminality, such as a child under the age of 14 found "begging or receiving alms . . . wandering, and not having a home or settled place of abode, or any visible means of subsistence, or [who] frequents the company of reputed thieves."[17]

Contemporary opinion was positive. Numbers fell and "the viciousness and premature depravity" detected in the late 1850s was no longer apparent in the mid 1870s, but later historians have painted a bleaker picture of harsh conditions, poor diets, inadequate training, and even brutality.[18] The inspectors' reports undoubtedly provide examples of authoritarian regimes using excessive corporal punishment, particularly on some of the Industrial Training Ships, but there is a danger of losing sight entirely of some of the positive aspects of some reform schools. The staff of the Linthorpe school, on the edge of Middlesbrough, "treated [the boys] with obvious kindness," according to the inspectors. Physical punishment does not appear to have been a central element in the running of the school. Indeed, there was a wide range of leisure activities, from brass bands and choirs to gymnastics. The boys themselves were not isolated but took part in a variety of activities within the town. Furthermore, the school had a good record in finding employment for its boys, albeit mostly in the armed services. The official records do not record the voices of the inmates directly, but the low levels of absconding and the well-attended reunions of "old boys" in the early 20th century suggest that this was not a tyrannous regime.[19]

Contemporary concern with young offenders diminished in the third quarter of the 19th century, though vicious attacks associated with city gangs reminded respectable Victorians that the problem had not been eradicated. Attitudes became even more pessimistic in the 1890s when the problem of hooliganism was seen as a blight particularly in London. Concern was given a new slant by the emerging belief, later given authority by the Gladstone Committee, that the making of the habitual criminal took place between the ages of 16 and 21, during the turbulent years of newly discovered adolescence.

Fears for the future of the nation's youth led to a variety of initiatives in late Victorian Britain. Youth movements dating from the 1880s, such as the Boys' Brigade, aimed to prevent young working-class men from offending, and some leaders, notably Baden-Powell, specifically looked to the hooligan element, believing that here was material with considerable potential for good.[20] However, there were also developments within the legal system. The apparent success of the reformatory schools, buttressed by reports of the experience of the Elmira Reformatory in New York State, led to active consideration of an alternative form of incarceration and treatment for "juvenile adults," that is young offenders over the age of 16. Despite the shadow of the Parkhurst failure, Evelyn Ruggles-Brise, who had visited America in 1897 and was impressed by what he saw at Elmira, initiated an experiment with eight selected young prisoners at Bedford in 1900 that led to its extension to Borstal convict prison in Kent in 1901 and Dartmoor in 1903. Ruggles-Brise was clear that he was intending to remove those of "dangerous" age, that is, 16 to 21 years old, out of the prison system and into reformatory institutions. In so doing he was effectively raising the age of criminal majority from 16 to 21.[21] Despite working with "the most difficult material imaginable," as Alexander Paterson described them, the results were sufficiently positive to justify a full-scale scheme.[22]

The Prevention of Crime Act of 1908 did precisely that. Part One of the act allowed for the sentencing of persons between the ages of 16 and 21 to "detention under penal discipline in a Borstal Institution." Feltham, originally an industrial school, was taken over by the Prison Commissioners in 1910 as another Borstal institution. In Scotland, Polmont (in Stirlingshire) was opened as a Borstal in 1911, and in 1914 Borstal departments were opened at Barlinnie and Duke Street prisons in Glasgow. The emphasis was on young male offenders, but young women were catered for in Aylesbury prison in England and Dumfries (the Jessiefield Institution) in Scotland. Although a part of the prison system, Borstal institutions were devised along lines that owed much to the practices of the public schools and organizations such as the boy scouts. Alexander Paterson, the leading figure, had an optimistic view of young offenders and sought to create a regime that would provide the necessary moral and physical training to bring out and develop the innate goodness that he believed was to be found in every boy.

The impact of the new system is difficult to assess, not least because of the outbreak of war in 1914, but contemporaries, both before and after the Great War, viewed the Borstal system as highly successful. Ruggles-Brise talked in glowing terms of the way in which the new Borstal institutions "are fulfilling in an admirable way the purpose for which they were created . . . [E]xperience is daily showing that all these things [i.e., the training] are having the effect of arresting in his downward career the young, and often dangerous, criminal between the ages of sixteen and twenty-one, who . . . [previously] served an apprenticeship in a succession of short sentences for trivial crimes in his early days, in order to qualify for entry into the ranks of habitual crime."[23] Similarly, Paterson, citing the fall in the number of adult prisoners as evidence, claimed that three out of every four boys were saved, while official figures produced in 1925 showed that two-thirds of ex-Borstal boys had not reoffended. These figures are overly optimistic, as were some contemporary reports. The realities were more prosaic, not least because of the relative inexperience of the staff in this new form of prison work.[24]

CONCLUSION: THE VICTORIAN AND EDWARDIAN PRISON REGIMES

The prison is central to the history of punishment in Victorian Britain. By the late 19th century there were some 70 local prisons and 10 convict prisons. However, the prison population fell in the last quarter of the 19th and first quarter of the 20th century. In 1878 the daily average of prisoners in local prisons was about 20,000 and 10,000 in convict prisons. By 1921 these figures had fallen to 8,000 and 1,400 respectively, though the most dramatic fall took place after 1914. But this fall in number coexisted with a continuing optimism in the prison as an appropriate institution of deterrence and reform, notwithstanding continuing evidence of failure.

The early Victorian developments, which have their roots in the late 18th century, were part of a wider response by political and intellectual elites to the profound social and economic changes that we term the Industrial Revolution. They drew on new ideas of the individual and her/his workings; of the relationship of the individual to society; and of the nature and purpose of punishment. Secular and religious ideas, relating to the natural roles of men and women and appropriate codes of behavior, contributed to the new penal system. Similarly the developments of the late 19th and early 20th century were the product of the interaction of a variety of factors. A number of external factors can be identified. Britain's relative economic decline, concerns about the long-term security of the Empire, and the discovery of greater-than-imagined poverty came together with scientific ideas derived from Darwin and others to create an atmosphere of pessimism about physical degeneration and the decline of the race. Internal forces played their part, too. There was a bureaucratic imperative that drove the prison system toward a more uniform, centrally controlled system. Further, the practical experiences of the prison system, the failure to reform, and the emergence of the habitual criminal added to the pressure to devise alternative approaches. Noncustodial alternatives, special institutions catering for specific subgroups of the criminal population, and the medicalization of specific problems were all part of the rationalization of the prison system in late Victorian and Edwardian England. Nonetheless, there was an underlying unity to the Victorian and Edwardian ages. There was no fundamental shift in thinking. The criminal was still seen to be largely responsible for his or her actions; punishments were accordingly handed out in a proportionate manner.[25]

Although imprisonment became the dominant form of punishment in the 19th and 20th centuries, it was subject to continuing accusations of failure. And, for the most part, the critics had a powerful case. Prisons did not have an appreciable impact on crime rates (even Du Cane conceded this point), they did not appear to be an effective deterrent, nor did they reform the criminal, and yet their "leniency" undermined the sense of punishment. In part, the sense of failure stemmed from the grandiose but naive claims of reformers. The idea that prison could provide an environment in which a criminal could be transformed was always optimistic: prison resources were too limited, prison sentences too short, and the wider environment to which the criminal, sooner or later, returned too unhelpful. Similarly, the noble view of the perfectibility of the individual paid too little attention to the grim realities of the character and lives of the majority of criminals. But if the advocates of reform were guilty of overoptimism, so too were the advocates of deterrence—and once again, the explanation lies in the failure to appreciate the circumstances and responses of the men and women who made up Victoria's prison population.

Even in periods of reformist optimism, there was no escaping the simple fact that prisons were places of unwilling incarceration. Prisoners were deprived of their liberty and subject to rules and regulations that determined how their time was spent but that were beyond their control.[26] For those in authority, time had meaning. It was the opportunity to awake the conscience of the convict for the advocates of reform; the opportunity for the convict to learn the costly errors of his criminal ways for the advocates of deterrence. But viewed "from below," time had a very different meaning, if it was meaningful at all. Time was something to be endured and survived. The extreme monotony and loneliness of life in the cells placed huge psychological pressures on prisoners. The tribulations of the well-educated are best known to posterity, but these were the people with the best resources to resist the mind-numbing, nay mind-destroying, experience of prison. Others less able to cope succumbed to a fatalistic acceptance that easily degenerated into apathy, even insanity. The present, and its mundane realities of eating and sleeping, took on disproportionate influence as time acquired an endless quality.

Such conditions were hardly conducive to reform. Undoubtedly there were some for whom conscience was awakened. Mayhew and Binney were reduced to tears by what they saw at a chapel service in Pentonville. The chaplain had spoken of the death of a convict's daughter when "some [convicts] buried their faces in their handkerchiefs . . . others sobbed aloud . . . telling of the homes they had made wretched by their shame . . . [and crying] aloud to their Almighty and most merciful Father that they had erred and strayed from his ways like lost sheep."[27] Others played the game. Owen Suffolk spent time in Millbank before being transported to Australia. Though not a religious individual,

I saw plainly that a sanctified demeanour was the best passport to favour . . . I came to the conclusion that the chaplain should have the honour of converting me, and that I would become a pattern prisoner in his eyes . . . Two days passed without a visit from the chaplain, but on the third he again entered my cell with a large bundle of tracts in his hand. After listening to the customary homily I took up my Bible and asked him to explain to me the meaning of some obscure passage. He gave the explanation, and told me he was glad that I had commenced to interest myself in the Book of Life. I requested him to be so good as to select a portion of scripture for me to commit to memory. This he did very readily, and was evidently much gratified with the change in my demeanour— which of course he attributed to his own persuasive eloquence.[28]

And many more simply saw the chaplain's visit as a marker in their weekly routine, something that broke up the monotony of the day.

Regulations had been a necessary part of prison life from the outset. Restrictions on communications in particular added to the difficulties of accommodating to the realities of serving a sentence. As the emphasis swung to deterrence, so the scope and burden of regulations increased. Michael Davitt, one of the best-known Irish political prisoners, summed up the situation well.

> [To] speak, sing, whistle, or walk; to attempt to ornament the cell; to offer to, or take from, a neighbour an ounce of bread; to exchange a book; to possess a needle or a pin; to stitch a button upon a garment without permission; to look out of the cell-window into the prison-yard; to protest against bad or light-weight food; to refuse to strip naked whenever the warder requires this to be done for the purpose of searching the prisoner—all this, with a hundred other nameless, irritating, ceaseless, mind-killing worries and degradations, is what separate cellular life and work means to a prisoner undergoing "reformation" by the Du Cane plan.[29]

This was a regime of "purgatorial expiation" that lacked discrimination or sensitivity and treated inmates "in a manner which mechanically reduces them to a uniform level of disciplined brutes."[30] Austin Bidwell, another ex-prisoner, captured the essence of survival in such a system.

> An English prison is a vast machine in which a man counts for just nothing at all. He is to the establishment what a bale of merchandise is to a merchant's warehouse. The prison does not look on him as a man at all. He is merely an object which must move in a certain rut and occupy a certain niche provided for him. There is no room for the smallest sentiment. The vast machine of which he is an item keeps undisturbed on its course. Move with it and all is well. Resist, and you will be crushed . . . Without passion, without prejudice, but also without pity and without remorse, the machine crushes and passes on. The dead man is carried to his grave and in ten minutes is as much forgotten as though he never existed.[31]

But many prisoners did resist because resistance itself gave some meaning, some sense of control of events, to men otherwise subject to the control of others. Malingering, assaults on fellow prisoners, and assaults on prison staff were more than evidence of the "incorrigibility" of hardened criminals. And this was recognized by some (if not all) prison warders who, for example, turned a blind eye to the early phases of fights between prisoners because it acted as a safety valve; but letting men let off steam merely ensured that matters did not get out of hand and become a full-scale disturbance. For some harm was inflicted, not on others, but on themselves and *in extremis* real-life Falders killed themselves. As one ex-convict wrote, among prisoners, separation gave rise to a "sullen hatred of themselves and everyone else" that frequently manifested itself in some form of violence.[32]

There was also a more pragmatic set of considerations that became more apparent with the passing of time. Particular management skills were required, from prison governor to the humblest warder, to maintain control of large-scale institutions in which the unwilling inmates heavily outnumbered the staff. Although the balance of power rested heavily (seemingly exclusively) with the authorities, the reality was that the actions of the warders, and other members of staff, was constrained to a greater degree than was initially imagined by the very prisoners whose liberty had been taken away and whose lives were subject to close regulation. There had to be a *modus vivendi* within prisons, in the same way as the police and those they policed had to strike some form of tacit bargain. That required a degree of trust and a degree of fairness acceptable to both sides. This did not always happen. There was small-scale corruption and victimization of prisoners by warders and other staff, and in some cases this gave rise to major disturbances. However, given the nature of the problems of prison management (and the limited experience, often acquired more by trial and error than any other way), the difficulties of recruiting high-quality men into the ranks of warders, and the underlying resentment within and unpredictable responses of the prison population, the surprise is that there was not more trouble in Victoria's prisons. This was success of a kind but not the achievement of reform or deterrence that were the main aims of the prison system.

An assessment of Victorian prisons cannot be made simply in narrow penological terms. In a wider sense, the prison was the acceptable and symbolic way in which unacceptable behavior was punished and which, in conjunction with other institutions, played an important part in maintaining the stability of Victorian and Edwardian England. Prisons played an important part in the identification of outcasts. They were the physical sites in which criminals were punished. The fact of having been imprisoned set certain men and women apart from their fellows in society. This contributed to the belief in the existence of a clearly defined and allegedly threatening criminal class that was distinct from law-abiding society. Further, this belief enabled "respectable" society to unite across class, though not necessarily ethnic, lines in its condemnation of the antisocial criminal. In turn, this brought a broader-based legitimacy to the criminal justice system as a whole. This is not to suggest a crude conspiracy theory whereby the working classes were divided and ruled, but rather to argue that the imprisonment of the habitual thief, as much as the murderer, was welcomed by a majority of the population. Not just members of the propertied classes, but also working-class victims of petty theft welcomed the protection of the law. Theft was not eradicated by the new police and the new prison, but the fact that a convicted thief did receive a prison sentence had a symbolic importance that is easily overlooked.

This argument can be taken a step further. By distinguishing between different types of criminals and, accordingly, proposing distinct treatment for each group, humanity could be seen to be grafted onto justice. The more scientific approach to the problem of the criminal, particularly from the late

19th century onward, was seen to have led to a more sophisticated and sensitive approach to the causes of crime, the needs of the criminal, and the needs of society. Nonetheless, legal processes, if not the law itself, often appeared to be biased against the working classes, and there was a widely held and well-founded belief that an element of luck was required, particularly for a young working-class male, not to fall foul of the authorities and end up in prison. Real resentments undoubtedly existed, but notwithstanding these problems, only a small minority of the population questioned the legitimacy of the criminal justice system as a whole in late Victorian and Edwardian England. To the extent that they played a part in this legitimizing of authority, prisons cannot be dismissed as unqualified failures.

CHAPTER FOURTEEN

AFTERWORD

The Edwardian criminal justice system was not the same as that of the early Victorian years. There had been a number of significant changes, most notably the expansion of summary justice, the creation of Borstals and juvenile courts, and the development of policing, but the fundamentals remained the same; and it was a system that would be recognizable to an early 21st-century observer in a way that the early 19th-century criminal justice system would not. The system, and its component parts, was often imperfect in theory; partial and hypocritical in terms of class, gender, and race; and imperfect in practice. The most visible and novel element of the new Victorian system, the prison, was a constant source of concern for its failure to deter and reform. Victorian and Edwardian understanding of the causes of crime and the motives of criminals was similarly partial and flawed. Too often the assumptions of rational, reasonable middle-class men were imposed on others who, for reasons that are more understandable in hindsight, acted in different ways and for different reasons but that made sense to them. At times, there was an almost willful denial of "reality." Myths were created about the irreligious criminal, led astray by the corrupting influence of popular theater or popular literature in early Victorian days; about prostitutes who were the victims of aristocratic seducers or foreign white slavers; about monstrous murderers and foul, brutal strangers who abused and assaulted women and children. And yet these myths are important. First, they are important for what they obscure—the underlying nature and causes of certain crimes—and for the negative impact that this had on dealing with such offenses; second, for what they tell us about the beliefs and priorities of our Victorian forebears. Their belief in the sanctity of the family and the decency of respectable men and women (irrespective of class) provided strong motivation for much that was good as well as for much that was bad (especially in hindsight); but it ill behooves our society, which hides behind its own convenient myths (some no different from those of a hundred years ago) and refuses to face up to some of the uncomfortable and difficult "realities" about criminal behavior, to condemn the shortcomings of the Victorians and Edwardians.

NOTES

PREFACE

1. "Straw moves to put victims first and says jail is for punishment," *The Guardian*, October 27, 2008.

INTRODUCTION

1. V.A.C. Gatrell, "Crime, Authority and the Policeman State, in *The Cambridge Social History of Britain*, vol. III, ed. F.M.L. Thompson (Cambridge: Cambridge University Press, 1993), p. 245.

2. Gatrell estimates the cost of reported burglaries in London in 1899 to be the equivalent of 3d. (little more than 1p or less than 2 cents) per head of the metropolitan population—a trivial sum. However, for victims of theft the loss of a relatively small sum of money (in our eyes) could have a significant economic, as well as a damaging psychological, effect on the victim that should not be overlooked. More significant is the fact that white-collar frauds, especially at the height of the railway mania, cost the country larger sums than everyday theft, and this burden often fell on small shareholders with very limited resources tied up in the high-risk investment.

3. See also V. Bailey, "English Prisons, Penal Culture, and the Abatement of Imprisonment, 1895–1922," *Journal British Studies* 36 (1997), 297–312. Historians have differed in their interpretation of the period c. 1895–1914. For an alternative perspective see D. Garland, *Punishment and Welfare: A History of Penal Strategies* (Aldershot: Gower, 1985).

4. The phrase "beyond reasonable doubt" is highly problematic being influenced by changing understanding of what constitutes knowledge and understanding. Similar difficulties surround the phrase "moral certainty" so often bandied about in discussion of capital cases.

5. Gatrell, "Crime, Authority," p. 280.

6. For a very brief introduction to Scottish law see D. Manson-Smith, *The Legal System of Scotland* (Edinburgh: HMSO, 1995). For the influence of English law on Scottish criminal law see L. Farmer, *Criminal Law, Tradition and Legal Order: Crime and the Genius of Scots Law 1747 to the Present* (Cambridge: Cambridge University Press, 2005).

7. References to the Lord Advocate acting as chief public prosecutor date from the late sixteenth century. See http://ww.procuratorfiscal.gov.uk/News/Historical/HistOffLordAdv.

8. The procurator fiscal was appointed by the sheriff in the 19th century and dealt with the bulk prosecutions, except for District Courts where local magistrates appointed prosecutors. The 1907 Sheriff Courts (Scotland) Act vested the right of appointment of procurators fiscal to the Sheriff Courts in the Lord Advocate. See http://www.procuratorfiscal.gov.uk/News/Historical/HistDevPF.

CHAPTER 1: CRIME IN VICTORIAN BRITAIN

1. T. Plint, *Crime in England: Its Relation, Character and Extent as Developed From 1801 to 1848.* (London: Gilpin, 1851), p. ii.

2. Anon, "Criminal Statistics, 1910," *Law Magazine Review* 27 (1912): 308–25. There is an important distinction between serious crimes, which are tried on indictment before a judge and jury or magistrate and jury, and petty crimes, which are the less serious offenses tried simply before a magistrate.

3. "Introduction to the Judicial Statistics for 1893," *Parliamentary Papers* 7725 (1895): 7. Famously, in 1892 Edmund Du Cane, Chairman of the Prison Commissioners, believed the judicial statistics showed a fall in crime; the Chaplain of Wandsworth Prison, W. D. Morrison, believed that crime was rising; and the Chief Constable of Staffordshire believed that there was no significant change either way. Summarized in J. J. Tobias, *Crime and Industrial Society in the Nineteenth Century* (London: Penguin, 1972), p. 19.

4. "Judicial Statistics for Scotland for the year 1899," *Parliamentary Papers* 107 (1900): 11.

5. Crimes were now categorized as: offenses against the person; offenses against property involving violence; offenses against property not involving violence; malicious offenses against property; offenses against the currency; and miscellaneous offenses.

6. "Introduction to the Judicial Statistics for 1893," *Parliamentary Papers* 7725 (1895): 5.

7. J. Archer, "The Violence We Have Lost? Body Counts, Historians and Interpersonal Violence in England," *Memoria y Civilización* 2 (1999): 171–90; H. Taylor, "Rationing Crime: The Political Economy of Criminal Statistics

Since the 1850s," *Economic History Review* 51 (1998): 569–90. R. M. Morris, "Lies, damned lies and criminal statistics: Reinterpreting the criminal statistics in England and Wales," *Crime, Histories & Societies*, 5 (2001): 111–27.

8. L. Radzinowicz and Roger Hood, *The Emergence of Penal Policy in Victorian and Edwardian England* (Oxford: Oxford University Press, 1990), pp. 818–24.

9. "Report of the Commissioners appointed to inquire into the operation of the Acts relating to Transportation and Penal Servitude," *Parliamentary Papers* 6457 (1863): 127 (cited in B. Abel-Smith and R. Stevens, *Lawyers and the Courts* (London: Heinemann, 1967), p. 31).

10. The 1870 Education Act enabled school boards to introduce bylaws to make elementary education compulsory; the 1880 Education Act made attendance compulsory for children aged between 5 and 10 years. Compulsory vaccination against smallpox was introduced by the Vaccination Act of 1853, which was subsequently strengthened in 1869. Following the report of a Royal Commission in 1896, a further Vaccination Act of 1898 reiterated earlier policy but included a conscience clause.

11. "Introduction to the Judicial Statistics," p. 7.

12. P. King, *Crime, Justice and Discretion in England, 1740–1820* (Oxford: Oxford University Press, 2000); D. Philips, *Crime and Authority in Victorian England, 1835–1860* (London: Croom Helm, 1977).

13. "Select Committee on Cause of Increase in Number of Criminal Commitments and Convictions in England and Wales," *Parliamentary Papers* 545 (1828).

14. Taylor, "Rationing Crime," p. 583.

15. B. Godfrey, "Changing Prosecution Practices and Their Impact on Crime Figures, 1857–1940," *British Journal of Criminology* 48 (2008): 171–89; D. Taylor, *Policing the Victorian Town: The Development of the Police in Middlesbrough, c. 1840–1914* (Basingstoke: Palgrave Macmillan, 2002), p. 145. Interestingly, there was a dramatic increase in reported cases of wounding in the town in the years 1910–13, but it is not clear whether this was a real increase or reflected earlier underreporting.

16. Godfrey, "Changing Prosecution Practices," p. 579.

17. Ibid., p. 586.

18. For example, Taylor, *Policing the Victorian Town*.

19. Godfrey, "Changing Prosecution Practices," p. 185.

20. This paragraph draws heavily on J. Davis, "A Poor Man's System of Justice: The London Police Courts in the Second Half of the Nineteenth Century," *Historical Journal* 27 (1984): 309–35, and J. Davis, "Prosecutions and Their Context: The Use of the Criminal Law in Later Nineteenth-Century London," in *Policing and Prosecution in Britain, 1750–1850*, ed. D. Hay and F. Synder (Oxford: Oxford University Press, 1989). But see also R. Swift,

"Another Stafford Street Row," *Immigrants and Minorities* 3 (1984): 5–29; R. Swift, "Heroes or Villains? The Irish, Crime and Disorder in Victorian England," *Albion* 29 (1997): 399–421; and Taylor, *Policing the Victorian Town*.

21. The London omnibus companies appear to have tolerated a system of low pay supplemented by employee theft until the late 1860s, after which employers redefined employee fraud as theft and used the courts to stamp out unacceptable practices. The introduction of the bell-punch and a rise in basic wages for conductors finally solved the problem. Davis, "Prosecutions and Their Context," p. 409.

22. D.C. Woods, "The Operation of the Master and Servants Act in the Black Country, 1858–1875," *Midland History* 7 (1982): 93–114; Philips, *Crime and Authority*; and Taylor, *Policing the Victorian Town*.

23. B. Godfrey, "'Policing the Factory': The Worsted Committee 1840–1880," *Criminal Justice History* 14 (1996): 87–107; B. Godfrey, "Law Factory Discipline and Theft," *British Journal of Criminology* 39 (1999): 56–71; and B. Godfrey, "Judicial Impartiality and the Use of the Criminal Law Against Labour: The Sentencing of Workplace Appropriators in Northern England, 1840–1880," *Crime, Histoire & Sociétés/Crime, History & Societies* 3 (1999): 56–71.

24. S. Petrow, *Policing Morals: The Metropolitan Police and the Home Office, 1870–1914* (Oxford: Oxford University Press, 1994), esp. Part III. See also Tobias, *Crime and Industrial Society*, London, Penguin, 1972, Appendix, for the impact of chief constables on crime figures in Leeds. For details of the Cass and d'Angely cases, see chapter 5.

25. Godfrey, "Changing Prosecution Practices," and H.R.P. Gamon, *The London Police Court, Today and Tomorrow* (London: Dent, 1907) p. 101.

26. Davis, "Prosecutions and Their Context," p. 425.

27. Taylor, "Rationing Crime"; Tobias, *Crime and Industrial Society*; and Rob Sindall, *Street Violence in the Nineteenth Century* (Leicester: Leicester University Press, 1990), chap. 2.

28. Sindall, *Street Violence*, p. 26.

29. To say the crime rate is artificially made is not the same as saying it is arbitrarily made. To the contrary, the distinction made between serious crimes and others is a deliberate one that gives important insights into the values of society. See K. Bottomly and K. Pease, *Crime and Punishment: Interpreting the Data* (Milton Keynes: Open University Press, 1986), p. 3.

30. The best introduction to 19th-century criminal statistics is V.A.C. Gatrell and T.B. Hadden, "Criminal Statistics and Their Interpretation," in *Nineteenth-Century Society: Essays in the Use of Quantitative Methods for the Study of Social Data*, ed. E.A. Wrigley (Cambridge: Cambridge University Press, 1972). See also V.A.C. Gatrell, "The Decline of Theft and Violence

in Victorian and Edwardian England," in *Crime and the Law: A Social History of Crime in Western Europe since 1500*, ed. V.A.C. Gatrell, B. Lenman, and G. Parker (London: Europa, 1980) and Philips, *Crime and Authority*, chapter 2.

31. The figures in this section are drawn largely from Gatrell and Hadden, "Criminal Statistics." It must not be forgotten that the reclassification of 1834 creates an important break in the statistics; as does the legislation of 1855 and 1856.

32. H. Perkin, *The Origins of Modern British Society, 1780–1880* (London: Routledge & Kegan Paul, 1969), pp. 162 and 167–68.

33. D. Hay, "War, Dearth and Theft in the Eighteenth Century: The Record of the English Courts," *Past & Present* 95 (1982): 117–60.

34. E. Dunning, P. Murphy, & J. Williams, *The Roots of Football Hooliganism: An Historical and Sociological Study* (London: Routledge and Kegan Paul, 1988).

35. J. Weeks, *Sex, Politics and Society: The Regulation of Sexuality Since 1800* (London: Longman, 1989).

36. These changes are charted in the annual judicial statistics. It is important not to exaggerate the scale of these developments, which account for a small percentage of the overall total.

37. The Education Acts are well-known, less so is the legislation relating to vaccination. Dating from the 1840s, effective compulsion dates from the acts of 1867 and 1871. Imprisonment could and did follow nonpayment of fines.

38. "Judicial Statistics for England & Wales for the Year 1900," *Parliamentary Papers* 953 (1902): 14.

CHAPTER 2: CRIME OF VIOLENCE

1. Gatrell, "Crime, Authority."

2. J.C. Wood, "'A Useful Savagery': The Invention of Violence in Nineteenth-Century England," *Journal of Victorian Culture* 9 (2004): 22–42.

3. J.C. Wood, "Criminal Violence in Modern Britain," *History Compass* 4 (2006): 77–90.

4. HMSO, *Select Committee on Capital Punishment* (London: HMSO, 1931), § 79. The judgment applies equally to Britain before World War I.

5. There is a wealth of literature of varying quality on Jack the Ripper but see P. Sugden, *The Complete History of Jack the Ripper* (New York: Caroll & Graf, 1995); P. Begg, *Jack the Ripper; The Definitive History* (Harlow: Pearson, 2005); and L. Perry Curtis, Jr., *Jack the Ripper & the London Press* (New Haven, CT: Yale University Press, 2001). T. Boyle, *Black Swine in the Sewers of Hampstead* (New York: Viking, 1989) covers the Palmer case and other sensations of the time. For Florence Maybrick and other female murderers, see M.S. Hartman, *Victorian Murderesses* (London: Robson, 1985) and

J. Knelman, *Twisting in the Wind: The Murderess and the English Press* (To-ronto: University of Toronto, 1998). For Courvoisier and Müller see H. Pot-ter, *Hanging in Judgment: Religion and the Death Penalty in England* (London: SCM Press, 1993). For the Mannings's case see M. Alpert, *London 1849: A Victorian Murder Story* (London: Pearson, 2004). For the Road Hill House case see K. Summerscale, *The Suspicions of Mr. Whicher* (London: Blooms-bury, 2008).

6. H. Walker, *East London, 1896*, cited in J. White, *London in the 19th Cen-tury* (London: Vintage, 2008), p. 129.

7. *East London Observer*, September 15, 1888, cited in W. J. Fishman, *East End 1888* (London: Duckworth, 1988), p. 217.

8. For a good introduction to the general question see E. O. Hellerstein, L. P. Hume, and K. M. Offen, eds., *Victorian Women* (Palo Alto, CA: Stan-ford University Press, 1981); and L. Davidoff and C. Hall, *Family Fortunes: Men and Women of the English Middle Class 1789–1850* (London: Hutchinson, 1987).

9. *The Times*, November 13, 1849, "The Bermondsey Murder," 4; and "The Condemned Convicts," 5.

10. Cited in R. Clark, *Women and the Noose: A History of Female Execution* (Stroud: Tempus, 2007), p. 123.

11. Crown Office and Procurator Fiscal Service, "The Strange Case of Jessie McLachlan," http://www.procuratorfiscal.gov.uk/News/Historical/JessMach.

12. H. B. Irving, *The Trial of Mrs. Maybrick* (London: Hodge, 1912), p. 110.

13. For a more detailed discussion of these issues see Knelman, *Twisting in the Wind*, chapter 10. See also Hartman, *Victorian Murderesses*, chapter 6.

14. L. Rose, *Massacre of the Innocents: Infanticide in Great Britain, 1800–1939* (London: Routledge & Kegan Paul, 1986).

15. For a full account see Summerscale, *Suspicions of Mr. Whicher*.

16. *Bath Chronicle*, July 19, 1860, cited in Summerscale, *Suspicions of Mr. Whicher*, p. 111. The case was extensively reported in the national and pro-vincial press. Similar sentiments were expressed, for example, by the *Bristol Mercury*, October 13, 1860, 2, but others focused more on the shortcomings of the rural police, for example, *Reynold's Newspaper*, December 2, 1860, 1, or of the coroner, for example, *Morning Chronicle*, January 31, 1861, 6.

17. The case, like that of the later Ripper murders, also aroused questions about police efficiency. Further, the unfortunate Detective Whicher was vili-fied for his intrusive behavior in the case.

18. R. Roberts, *The Classic Slum* (London: Penguin, 1973), p. 45.

19. S. Humphries, *Hooligans or Rebels? An Oral History of Working-Class Chil-dren and Youth, 1889–1939* (Oxford: Blackwell, 1983); G. Pearson, *Hooligan: A History of Respectable Fears* (London: Macmillan, 1983). A. Davies, "Youth Gangs, Masculinity and Violence in Late Victorian Manchester and Salford,"

Journal of Social History 32 (1998): 349–69, and A. Davies, "'These Viragoes Are No Less Cruel Than the Lads': Young Women, Gangs and Violence in Late Victorian Manchester and Salford," *British Journal of Criminology* 39 (1999): 72–89.

20. S. D'Cruze, *Crimes of Outrage: Sex, Violence and Working-Class Women* (London: UCL Press, 1998); E. Ross, "'Fierce Questions and Taunts': Married Life in Working-Class London, 1870–1914," *Feminist Studies* 8 (1983): 575–602; N. Tomes, "A 'Torrent of Abuse': Crimes of Violence Between Working-Class Men and Women in London," *Journal of Social History* 11 (1978): 328–45; C. Emsley, *Hard Men: Violence in England Since 1750* (London: Hambledon, 2005), esp. chap. 4.

21. See, for example, *The Times,* November 7, 1856, 9; December 1, 1862, 11; and July 2, 1877, 10; *Daily News,* November 7, 1874, 3; Reynold's *Newspaper,* October 1, 1876; *Plymouth and Cornish Advertiser,* December 24, 1840; and especially *Jackson's Oxford Journal,* December 19, 1840, August 16, 1851, August 22, 1868, July 7, 1877, May 27, 1882, and June 18, 1887. Rough music was also used to protest against adultery, over-hasty marriage following the death of a spouse, a marked discrepancy in the age of partners (especially an old man marrying a young woman), and also against unscrupulous shop owners and tradesmen. The best introduction is E. P. Thompson, *Customs in Common* (London: Penguin, 1993), esp. chap. viii.

22. Frances Power Cobbe, "Wife Torture in England," *Contemporary Review* 32 (1878): 55–87. The often very trivial incidents that precipitated many savage assaults are discussed in Tomes, "'A Torrent of Abuse.'" See also Ross, "'Fierce Questions and Taunts'" and her *Love and Toil* (Oxford: Oxford University Press, 1993).

23. Cited in C. Emsley, *Hard Men: Violence in England Since 1750* (London: Hambledon, 2005), p. 63.

24. M. E. Doggett, *Marriage, Wife-Beating and the Law in Victorian England* (London: Weidenfeld & Nicholson, 1992).

25. Anna Clark, *Women's Silence, Men's Violence: Sexual Assault in England, 1770–1845* (London: Pandora Press, 1987).

26. *The Times,* June 23, 1845, 8.

27. *The Times,* July 23, 1852, 7.

28. *The Times,* June 8, 1871, 11.

29. *Lloyd's Weekly News,* December 20, 1874, 1.

30. *The Times,* October 29, 1842, 6. See also *The Times,* March 29, 1852, 7; and June 3, 1893, 9; for similar cases in which a servant was raped by the son of a clergyman and a "respectable" journalist, respectively.

31. *The Times,* September 26, 1885, 6; October, 3, 1885, 6; and November 19, 1885, 6.

32. *The Times,* July 17, 1852, 7.

33. *The Times*, June 10, 1896, 16; *Newcastle Courant*, December 9, 1864, 2; *Western Mail*, October 5, 1869, 4.

34. *The Times*, December 6, 1856, 10.

35. *The Times*, February 28, 1868, 9. See also the rape by two soldiers of a "respectable" woman who had attended a music-hall at North Camp, Aldershot. *The Times*, December 31, 1888, 11.

36. *The Times*, January 2, 1864, 9.

37. "The Tottenham Outrage," *The Times*, January 25, 1909, 11.

38. Ibid.

CHAPTER 3: GARROTERS, BANK ROBBERS, AND POACHERS

1. For full details see the tables in Gatrell and Hadden, "Criminal Statistics," pp. 387–96; and Gatrell, "Theft and Violence," pp. 339–70.

2. Although now rarely heard, the once popular children's chant asserted that Taffy was a Welshman; Taffy was a thief. Taffy came to our house and stole a leg of beef.

3. G. Spraggs, *Outlaws & Highwaymen: The Cult of the Robber in England from the Middle Ages to the Nineteenth Century* (London: Pimlico, 2001); J. Sharpe, *Dick Turpin: The Myth of the English Highwayman* (London: Profile Books, 2004).

4. Sindall, *Street Violence*; J. Davis, "The London Garotting Panic of 1862: A Moral Panic and the Creation of a Criminal Class in Mid-Victorian England," in *Crime and the Law: The Social History of Crime in Western Europe since 1500*, ed. V. Gatrell, B. Lenman, & G. Parker (London: Europa, 1980).

5. Although strictly speaking garroting referred to strangulation by use of a rope, the term quickly lost its specific meaning and was applied indiscriminately to street assaults and robberies.

6. Remission of sentence in this manner had been a feature of the transportation for many years. After 1857 the principle was applied to penal servitude. Remission was not on merit but on the grounds that the convict's "conduct in prison should be such as not to deprive him of that indulgence." Tickets of leave could be revoked if the individual committed another crime, associated with criminals, led "an idle and dissolute life," or "had no visible means of obtaining an honest livelihood." "Report of the Penal Servitude Acts Commissioner," *Parliamentary Papers* 31 (1863): 12, 15.

7. *Spectator*, 19 July 1862, cited in Davis, "London Garrotting Panic," p. 199.

8. This did not stop; for example, the *Pall Mall Gazette* regaled and frightened its readers with a series of articles on often exotically named gangs (such as Prince Arthur's gang, the Monkey-parade gang, and the Jovial Thirty Two) that roamed the streets of London. See for example, October 13, 1888, 1.

9. Compared with a figure of 3.5 percent in 1810. Gatrell and Hadden, "Criminal Statistics," Table 2.3, p. 29.

10. *Reynold's Newspaper*, April 11, 1880, 6.

11. *Illustrated Police News*, March 13, 1886, 3; *Daily News*, January 14, 1897, 2; and *Illustrated Police News*, February 27, 1897, 2. See also the trial of the "worst gang in Clerkenwell" reported in *Lloyd's Weekly Newspaper*, February 5, 1888, 4.

12. Philips, *Crime and Authority*, pp. 246–47.

13. *Northern Echo*, April 28 1888, 3.

14. *Liverpool Mercury*, April 2, 1888, 5; and *Western Mail*, April 2, 1888, 3. There was also the suggestion that one of the accused had said "Let's chuck the b—— into the canal." For similar cases elsewhere see, for example, *Manchester Times*, April 24, 1880, 4; *Newcastle Courant*, July 9, 1880, 8; *Glasgow Herald*, August 30, 1880, 4, and August 18, 1897, 7; and *Western Mail*, September 8, 1888, 18. Small towns were not always safe. See *Bristol Mercury And Daily Post*, June 23, 1888, 3 for a similar attack in the small town of Bedminster.

15. *Leeds Mercury*, February 4, 1880, 2.

16. *Birmingham Daily Post*, July 31, 1888, 5.

17. *Birmingham Daily Post*, May 18, 1880, 4.

18. *Birmingham Daily Post*, July 30, 1889, 4; and *Ipswich Journal*, February 22, 1889, 5 and July 26, 1889, 8.

19. *Illustrated Police News*, January 22, 1866, 2.

20. These examples were taken from the *Police Gazette* for December 1866. A perusal of other editions reveals a similar pattern.

21. Philips, *Crime and Authority*, p. 239.

22. *Aberdeen Weekly Journal*, September 3, 1887, 6.

23. *Liverpool Mercury*, March 19, 1888, 8.

24. This case was widely covered, but see *Leeds Mercury*, October 26, 1889, 5; and *Birmingham Daily Post*, October 25, 1889, 8.

25. *Illustrated Police News*, March 13 1897, 7, and July 24, 1897, 8; *Daily News*, June 7, 1897, 3, and July 1, 1897, 2; *Lloyd's Weekly Newspaper*, June 13, 1897, 7.

26. *Newcastle Weekly Courant*, March 23, 1895, 3.

27. *Lloyd's Weekly Newspaper*, May 26, 1893, 6. A similar snatch raid took place at a London branch of the National provincial bank in 1891 when £12,000 was taken. *Daily News*, February 17, 1891, 4. In another case reported in *The Illustrated Police News*, February 25, 1893, 4, a messenger was distracted by a man enquiring if a piece of paper on the floor belonged to the messenger. As he bent down to check, the messenger had his wallet containing almost £12,000 snatched!

28. *Daily News*, January 26, 1899, 5

29. *Birmingham Daily Post*, August 31, 1900, 4.

30. *Glasgow Herald*, August 26, 1882, 2.

31. *Birmingham Daily Post*, November 27, 1883, 4, and November 28, 1883.

32. This paragraph owes much to G. Robb, *White Collar Crime in England, 1845–1929* (Cambridge: Cambridge University Press, 1992).

33. Ibid., pp. 147, 150.

34. D. Taylor, "The Antipodean Arrest: Or How to Be a Successful Policeman in Nineteenth-Century Middlesbrough," *Bulletin of the Cleveland and Teesside Local History Society* 58 (1990): 26–30.

35. Taylor, *Policing the Victorian Town*, pp. 47–49.

36. C. Dickens' *Dombey and Son* and *Martin Chuzzlewit* are but two of the more obvious examples.

37. Archer stresses the importance of the invention of the lucifer match in 1829–1830, which greatly facilitated the work of the arsonist. At the same time, worsening socioeconomic conditions, and in particular the 1834 Poor Law Amendment Act, led to an intensification of hostility in the countryside. Not all the evidence points in this direction, however. Thomas Overman, a farmer of Maulden, Bedfordshire, giving evidence to the 1838 Select Committee on the Poor Law Amendment Act, commented on "night-poaching, setting fire, cutting and maiming of animals and such like depredations" *before* 1834. N. E. Agar, *The Bedfordshire Farm Worker in the Nineteenth Century*, Bedfordshire Historical Record Society 60 (1981): 92.

38. Some incidents of animal maiming had more to do with ritual magic and others, involving the poisoning of horses, appear to have been the result of overzealous actions by grooms.

39. *The Times*, "Incendiarism in Suffolk," July 29, 1844, 6.

40. The death penalty for these offenses was replaced by a mandatory sentence of life transportation under the 1832 Punishment of Death Act.

41. For Sussex and Gloucestershire see G. Rudé, *Criminal and Victim: Crime and Society in Early Nineteenth-Century England* (Oxford: Oxford University Press, 1985), chap. 2. The Northallerton Quarter Session records reveal a very similar picture for the North Riding of Yorkshire. See also Taylor, *Policing the Victorian Town*.

42. *Johnson's Oxford Journal*, March 10, 1863. The author's maternal grandmother stole turnips, which she ate raw, such was her hunger, as she went to school in rural Warwickshire in the last years of Victoria's reign. It is no coincidence that poaching prosecutions peaked in the winter months when employment and food were scarcer.

43. See Philips, *Crime and Authority*, p. 201.

44. J. Rule, *The Experience of Labour in Eighteenth-Century Industry* (London: Croom Helm, 1981); and C. R. Dobson, *Masters and Journeymen: A Prehistory of Industrial Relations 1717–1800* (London: Croom Helm, 1980). See also Godfrey, "Policing the Factory," "Law, Factory Discipline and Theft," and "Judicial Impartiality."

45. Taylor, *Policing the Victorian Town*.

46. P. King, "Gleaners, Farmers and the Failure of Legal Sanctions in England, 1750–1850," *Past & Present* 125 (1989): 116–50.

47. J. E. Archer, "Poachers Abroad," In *The Unquiet Countryside*, ed. G. E. Mingay (London: Routledge, 1989); H. Hopkins, *The Long Affray: The Poaching Wars in Britain* (London: Macmillan, 1986); P. B. Munsche, *Gentlemen and Poachers* (Cambridge: Cambridge University Press, 1981); R. Wells, "Sheep Rustling in Yorkshire in the Age of the Industrial and Agrarian Revolutions, *Northern History* 20 (1981): 127–45.

48. "Select Committee on the Game Laws," *Parliamentary Papers* 13 (1872): 258.

49. *Oxford Chronicle*, March 3, 1852, 4; J. Hawker, *A Victorian Poacher* (n.d., ca. 1930; repr., Oxford: Oxford University Press, 1961). See also Lilias Rider Haggard, ed., *I Walked by Night: Being the Life & History of the King of the Norfolk Poachers written by HIMSELF* (1935; repr., Oxford: Oxford University Press, 1982).

50. Hopkins, *Long Affray*, p. 237.

CHAPTER 4: SEX AND DRUGS

1. Taylor, *Policing the Victorian Town*, esp. chap. 8.

2. S. Reynolds, B. Woolley, and T. Woolley, *Seems So! A Working-Class View of Politics* (London: Macmillan, 1911), 86–87.

3. It was not uncommon for many working-class young women to spend a brief time, maybe up to two or three years, as a prostitute before setting up or marrying. Such behavior was not widely stigmatized in working-class districts. It is worth emphasizing the economic attraction of prostitution to semiskilled or unskilled women for whom life could be one of abject poverty. Notwithstanding the well-known risks of disease, prostitution—especially as a short-term measure—was an attractive option. And this uncomfortable truth is not unique to Victorian Britain.

4. M. Ryan, *Prostitution in London with a Comparative View of That of Paris and New York* (London: Bailliere, 1839); and W. Tait, *Maddalenism. An Inquiry into the Extent, Causes and Consequences of Prostitution in Edinburgh* (Edinburgh: Rickard, 1852).

5. Magistrates came under attack for their unwillingness to act. See report in *The Times*, May 17, 1844, 3, detailing complaints of inhabitants of Castlechurchyard ward in London.

6. W. Acton, *Prostitution Considered in its Moral, Social and Sanitary Aspects, in London and other Large Cities: With Proposals for the Mitigation and Prevention of its Attendant Evils* (first published 1856, 1870 edition; repr., London: Cass, 1972).

7. For further details see the excellent J. R. Walkowitz, *Prostitution and Victorian Society: Women, Class and the State* (Cambridge: Cambridge University

Press, 1980). See also P. McHugh, *Prostitution and Victorian Social Reform* (London: Croom Helm, 1980); F. Mort, *Dangerous Sexualities: Medico-Moral Politics in England since 1830* (London: Routledge & Kegan Paul, 1987); L. Mahood, *The Magdalenes: Prostitution in the Nineteenth Century* (London: Routledge, 1990); P. Bartley, *Prostitution: Prevention and Reform in England, 1860–1914* (London: Routledge, 2000).

8. The Acts of 1864, 1866, and 1869 were intended to check the spread of syphilis in garrison towns and ports in the United Kingdom. By 1869 there were 18 so-called subjected districts.

9. Walkowitz, *Prostitution*, chap. 10.

10. F. Finnegan, *Poverty and Prostitution: A Study of Victorian Prostitution in York* (Cambridge: Cambridge University Press, 1979).

11. Ibid., esp. pp. 212–13.

12. As well as Walkowitz, *Prostitution*, see also M. Forster, *Significant Sisters: The Grassroots of Active Feminism, 1839–1939* (London: Penguin, 1984); O. Banks, *Faces of Feminism* (Oxford: Blackwell, 1986); B. Caine, *Victorian Feminists* (Oxford: Oxford University Press, 1992); and J. Jordan, *Josephine Butler* (London: Murray, 2001).

13. Petrow, *Policing Morals*.

14. Sir Richard Mayne was the first commissioner of the Metropolitan police, serving from 1829 to 1868. Sir Edmund Henderson succeeded Mayne and was commissioner from 1869 to 1896. Henderson was criticized for playing down the significance of corruption among his detective force in the late 1870s and resigned following his failure to act decisively during the Trafalgar Square riot of 1886.

15. It is a measure of the polarized attitudes of the time that this was greeted as the "Great Defeat of Lust and Licence and Lying" by the *Methodist Times*, November 8, 1894, and as "The Triumph of Cant" by the *Sporting Times*, October 13, 1894.

16. It is difficult to know how many cases of wrongful arrest took place. Cass was fortunate to have an employer willing to stand up for her, and d'Angely was an exceptional woman. Others, less fortunate or less forceful, may well have suffered, but no record survives.

17. Cited in M. Brogden, *The Police: Autonomy and Consent* (London: Academic Press, 1982), p. 67. Interestingly, between 1836 and 1872 only 5 percent of demands from the city Watch Committee to the police were concerned with brothels and prostitution, compared with 16 percent concerning violation of the Sabbath and 25 percent concerned with disorderly behavior in the streets.

18. *Liverpool Review*, January 17, 1891, cited in ibid.

19. Mahood, *The Magdalenes*. 52.

20. There are similarities with the current preoccupation with sex trafficking in Britain. "Sex, Lies and Trafficking: The Making of a Moral Panic," *Guardian*, October 20, 2009, 6–7.

21. Bartley, *Prostitution*, part III. More generally see M. Jackson, *The Borderland of Imbecility: Medicine, Society and the Fabrication of the Feeble Mind in Late Victorian and Edwardian England* (Manchester, UK: Manchester University Press, 2000). One of the author's great-aunts, by no means feeble minded, fell pregnant at the age of 15 and was therefore incarcerated. Thanks to a determined family she was finally released, though several years of incarceration undoubtedly had an impact on her mental condition in later life. She was one of a lucky few.

22. Cited in T. Fisher, *Prostitution and the Victorians* (Stroud: Sutton, 1997), pp. 145–49.

23. King was a baby farmer suspected of killing several children. She was found guilty of murdering two. Both had been drugged with whiskey and then strangled. Willis became a baby farmer after falling on hard times and was paid £6 to adopt a child, which she then smothered. Amelia Sach was the proprietor of a nursing home and refuge for unmarried mothers. She offered to take unwanted children in return for a fee. The children were then put in the "care" of Annie Walker, who smothered and dumped the children in the River Thames or on local rubbish dumps. Walker gave the game away by twice telling her landlord that a child she was looking after had died suddenly. Her landlord was a policeman and became suspicious.

24. G.K. Behlmer, *Child Abuse and Moral Reform in England, 1879–1908* (Stanford: Stanford University Press, 1982); L.A. Jackson, *Child Sexual Abuse in Victorian England* (London: Routledge, 2000).

25. Perversely the age of consent for indecent assault had been set at 13 by the 1880 Assault of Young People Act.

26. Jackson, *Child Sexual Abuse*, p. 130.

27. In contrast, lesbianism was never criminalized. Indeed, in many circles it simply was not discussed.

28. Weeks, *Sex, Politics and Society*; J. Weeks, *Coming Out: Homosexual Politics in Britain from the Nineteenth Century to the Present* (London: Quartet Books, 1977); R. Davenport-Hines, *Sex, Death and Punishment: Attitudes to Sex and Sexuality in Britain Since the Renaissance* (London: Fontana, 1990). Much has been written about the Wilde cases, but see H.M. Hyde, *The Trials of Oscar Wilde* (New York: Dover, 1982); E. Cohen, *Talk on the Wilde Side* (London: Routledge, 1993); and P. Hoare, *Wilde's Last Stand: Decadence, Conspiracy & the First World War* (London: Duckworth, 1997). HMSO, *The Trials of Oscar Wilde, 1895* (London: HMSO, 2001) is a good collection of documents.

29. These changes were already under way when Victoria came to the throne. See particularly Davidoff & Hall, *Family Fortunes*; R.B. Shoemaker, *Gender in English Society, 1650–1850* (London: Longman, 1998); J.A. Mangan & J. Walvin, eds., *Manliness and Morality: Middle-Class Masculinity in Britain and America, 1800–1940* (Manchester, UK: Manchester University Press, 1987); and J. Tosh, *A Man's Place: Masculinity and the Middle-Class Home in Victorian England* (New Haven, CT: Yale University Press, 1999).

30. J. Greenwood, *The Seven Curses of London: Scenes from the Victorian Underworld* (1869; repr., Oxford: Oxford University Press, 1981), p. 213.

31. See B. Harrison, *Drink and the Victorians: The Temperance Question in England, 1815–1872* (Keele, UK: Keele University Press, 1994), esp. chap. 2.

32. Cited in Ibid.

33. Ibid., p. 78.

34. T. Marriot, *A Constable's Duty and How To Do It*, 2nd ed. (London: Reeves & Turner, 1894), p. 76. Italics added.

35. *News of the World*, October 1, 1843, 4.

36. The attempts to deal with female inebriates are well covered in L. Zedner, *Women, Crime, and Custody in Victorian England* (Oxford: Oxford University Press, 1994), part III.

37. Although much coverage was sensationalist, for example, "The Terrors of the Opium Den," *Chums*, 23 November 1892, *The Times*, 25 November 1913, 6, noted the orderly nature of London's Chinatown and compared it favorably with American counterparts. See also *Pall Mall Gazette*, September 17, 1900, 3.

38. V. Berridge, *Opium and the People: Opiate Use and Drug Control in Nineteenth and Early Twentieth Century England* (London: Free Association Books, 1999); L. Foxcroft, *The Making of Addiction: The "Use and Abuse" of Opium in Nineteenth Century Britain* (Aldershot: Ashgate, 2007); M. Jay, *Emperors of Dreams* (Sawtrey: Dedalus, 2000); J. H. Mills, *Cannabis Britannica: Empire Trade and Prohibition* (Oxford: Oxford University Press, 2003); D. Streatfield, *Cocaine* (London: Virgin, 2001); T. Madge, *White Mischief: A Cultural History of Cocaine* (Edinburgh: Mainstream Publishing, 2001); M. Booth, *Opium: A History* (London: Simon & Schuster, 1996); M. Kohn, *Dope Girls: The Birth of the British Drug Underground* (London: Granta, 2001); and R. Davenport-Hines, *The Pursuit of Oblivion: A Global History of Narcotics, 1500–2000* (London: Wiedenfeld & Nicholson, 2001).

39. This was welcomed by *The Times*, 22 April 1895, 9, which saw alcohol as a much greater threat.

40. "The English in China," *Blackwood's Magazine*, January 1901, p. 68, cited in Foxcroft, *Making of Addiction*, p. 75.

41. Laura Ormiston Chant, parodied by *Punch* as Mrs. Prowlina Pry, is best known for her social purity campaign against immorality in London music halls but she was also a campaigner against the Contagious Diseases Acts and an advocate of female suffrage.

42. J. Binns, *From Village to Town* (Batley: Fearnsides & Sons, 1882), p. 139.

43. Lady Bell, *At the Works: A Study of a Manufacturing Town* London: Edward Arnold,1907; repr., Newton Abbott: David & Charles,1967), p. 255.

44. Annual Report of the Chief Constable of Middlesbrough, 1909, p. 16. Published in Minutes of Middlesbrough Borough Council, 1879–1914, Cleveland County Archive (Middlesbrough), CB/M/C, 1/70.

45. Roberts, *Classic Slum*, p. 162.

CHAPTER 5: THE MALEVOLENT MALE

1. Plint, *Crime in England,* p. 144.

2. A. Griffiths, *Fifty Years of Public Service* (London: Cassell, 1905), pp. 385–86.

3. This explanation of crime was most famously depicted in Hogarth's *Rake's Progress.*

4. See, for example, Samuel Moody's exhortation that "the corrupt member of a community must be cut off by the sword of justice, lest by delay and impunity the malignant disease spread further, and the whole be infected." *The Impartial Justice of Divine Administration* (1736), cited in R. McGowen, "The Body and Punishment in Eighteenth-Century England," *Journal of Modern History* 59 (1987): 662.

5. C. Dickens, *Oliver Twist* (1838; repr., London: Collins, 1954), p. 381.

6. Ibid., pp. 305 and 338.

7. Ibid., pp. 72 and 357.

8. There was a flourishing Italian boy trade in early Victorian London. Sons of impoverished peasants were all but slaves to their "employers" or "masters." See S. Wise, *The Italian Boy: Murder and Grave-Robbery in 1830s London* (London: Jonathan Cape, 2004).

9. H. Mayhew and J. Binney, *The Criminal Prisons of London* (1862; repr., London: Cass, 1968), p. 87; H. Mayhew, *London Labour and London Poor,* vol. 4 (1862) cited in P. Quennell, ed., *London's Underworld* (London: Hamlyn, 1969), pp. 204–5.

10. Quennell, *London's Underworld,* pp. 204–5.

11. Ibid., p. 134.

12. Mayhew and Binney, *Criminal Prisons,* p. 45.

13. *Rampsmen* were plunderers by force, such as burglars or footpads; *bludgers* or *stick slingers* robbed in the company of low women; *prop nailers* stole pins and brooches; *thimble screwers* wrenched off watches; *sawney hunters* stole cheeses and bacon from cheesemongers' doors; and *dead lurkers* stole from passages of houses. The term *bludger* is still current in Australia but refers to a scrounger and has nothing to do with Harry Potter!

14. E. Said, *Orientalism: Western Conceptions of the Orient* (London: Routledge & Kegan Paul, 1978).

15. Quennell, *London's Underworld,* p. 63.

16. C. Dickens, "On Duty with Inspector Fields," reprinted in *London Crimes,* ed. N. Aisenberg (Boston: Rowan Tree Press, 1982), p. 61.

17. Ibid.

18. W. Hoyle, *Crime in England and Wales in the Nineteenth Century: An Historical and Critical Retrospect* (London: Effingham Wilson & Co., 1876), pp. 87–89.

19. Plint, *Crime in England,* p. 146.

20. Ibid.

21. J. Hollingshead, *Ragged London in 1861* 1861 (repr., London: Dent, 1986), pp. 23 & 24.

22. *The Times*, November 7, 1862, 5.

23. *The Times*, November 24, 1862, 10. In fact garroting incidents were being reported in the provincial press well before this. *Reynold's Newspaper*, July 27, 1862, 2 was critical of the government for ignoring the problem when victims were ordinary citizens.

24. *The Times*, December 1, 1862, 8. *The Times* seized upon these incidents to highlight the inadequacies of existing penal practices and the need for tougher measures against these "professed enemies of the human race." *The Times*, December 30, 1862, "The criminal classes," 7. Joshua Jebb unsurprisingly came in for vociferous criticism. *The Times*, February 16, 1863, 8. See also chapter 12.

25. *The Era*, September 7, 1862, 9. See *Liverpool Mercury*, November 13, 1862, 6, for similar views. For further details see Sindall, *Street Violence in the Nineteenth Century*; J. Davis, "The London Garrotting Panic of 1862."

26. G.R. Sims, *How the Poor Live* (London: Chatto & Windus, 1889), p. 44.

27. C.T. Clarkson & J. Richardson, *Police!* (London: Field & Tuer, Leadenhall Press, 1889), p. 200.

28. Ibid., p. 205. In fact there was further fighting between police and protesters the following day.

29. *The London Illustrated News*, February 13, 1886, 4.

30. W.L.M. Lee, *A History of the Police in England* (London: Methuen, 1901), p. 337. Lee similarly saw the importance of Bloody Sunday residing in the success of the police in clearing Trafalgar Square and enforcing order.

31. *East London Observer*, 15 September 1888, cited in Fishman, *East End 1888*, p. 217. See also A. Palmer, *The East End: Four Centuries of London Life* (London: John Murray, 2000.

32. P. Knepper, "British Jews and the Racialisation of Crime in the Age of Empire," *British Journal of Criminology* 47 (2007): 61–79; B. Braber, "The Trial of Oscar Slater (1909) and Anti-Jewish Prejudice in Edwardian Glasgow," *History* 88 (2003): 262–79.

33. "Report of the Commissioners on the Best Means of Establishing an Efficient Constabulary Force," *Parliamentary Papers* 169 (1839), 67.

34. J. Symons, "Crime and Criminals," *The Law Magazine* 10 (1849): 260.

35. F. Engels, *Condition of the Working Class in England in 1844*. Translated by W.O. Henderson and W.H. Chaloner, (London: Macmillan, 1973), 242.

36. H. Maudsley, *Body and Mind* (London: Macmillan, 1870), p. 76.

37. C. Goring, *The English Convict: A Statistical Study* (London: HMSO, 1913), p. 371.

38. Ibid., p. 372.

39. Cited in G. S. Jones, *Outcast London: A Study in the Relationship Between Classes in Victorian Society* (London: Penguin, 1976), p. 321.

40. Irish Nationalists were commonly termed Fenians (from the old Irish *Fianna*, the legendary Irish warriors) and were organized as the Irish Republican Brotherhood in Ireland and Clan na Gael in America.

41. See the following, all by R. Anderson: "Our Absurd System of Punishing Crime," *Nineteenth Century and After* 49 (1901): 268–84; "The Punishment of Crime," *Nineteenth Century and After* 50 (1901): 72–92; "More about Professional Criminals," *Nineteenth Century and After* 52 (1902); "The Crusade Against Professional Criminals," *Nineteenth Century and After* 55 (1904): 811–21; *Criminals and Crime: Some Facts and Suggestions* (London: J. Nisbet, 1907); "Criminals and Crime," *Law Magazine Review* 33 (1908): 129–40, 257–64; and "The Prevention of Crime Act," *Nineteenth Century and After* 65 (1909): 241–50.

42. Petrow, *Policing Morals*, p. 105.

43. Anderson, "Our Absurd System," p. 271.

44. Ibid., pp. 274–75.

45. Ibid.

46. Griffiths, *Fifty Years of Public Service*, pp. 385–86.

47. R. F. Quinton, *Crime and Criminals, 1876–1910* London: Longman, 1910, 75; and R. F. Quinton, "The Need for Preventive Detention," *Edinburgh Review* 220 (1914): 167–79.

48. A. Wills, "Criminals and Crime," *Nineteenth Century and After* 62 (1907): 893.

49. H. R. P. Gamon, "The Punishment of Crime and the Indeterminate Sentence," *Law Magazine and Review* 35 (1910): 192–93.

50. Anderson, "Our Absurd System." For further discussion see chapter 12.

51. See chapter 11.

52. *Parliamentary Debates*, June 12, 1908, col. 498.

53. G. R. Searle, *The Quest for National Efficiency: A Study in British Politics and Political Thought, 1899–1914* (Oxford: Oxford University Press, 1971) is the essential starting point.

54. Anderson, "Our Absurd System," pp. 278–79.

55. O. Jay, "The East End and Crime," *New Review* 11 (1894): 401–8, 403, 406; A. Morrison, *A Child of the Jago,* was a fictionalized account of the Old Nicol where Jay worked. More generally on the Old Nicol, see S. Wise, *The Blackest Streets; The Life and Death of a Victorian Slum* (London: Vintage, 2009).

56. Dr. W. C. Sullivan, "Eugenics and Crime," *Eugenics Review* 1 (1909): 120.

57. Goring, *English Convict*, p. 373. Goring did not expand on the practicalities of his proposal, but others were less reticent about the benefits of castration. See, for example, R. R. Rentoul, *The Proposed Sterilisation of Certain*

Mental and Physical Degenerates (London: Walter Scott Publishing, 1903), esp. pp. 17–23.

58. Sullivan, "Eugenics and Crime," p. 116.

59. Jackson, *The borderland of imbecility*.

60. Ibid, 141–12.

61. Gatrell and Hadden, "Criminal Statistics," p. 379.

62. Ibid., p. 382.

63. D. Taylor, unpublished analysis of Northallerton Quarter Session, 1835–1893. Copies of the original records are held on microfilm at the North York-shire Record Office, Northallerton.

CHAPTER 6: HARLOTS AND HOOLIGANS

1. Mary Carpenter, *Our Convicts*, vol. 1 (London: Longman, Green, 1853), pp. 31–32.

2. M. E. Owen, "Criminal Women," *Cornhill Magazine* 14 (1866): 152–60, quote at p. 153.

3. See, for example, the chaplain of Millbank Prison, Rev. G. P. Merrick, *Life Among the Fallen as Seen in the Prison Cell* (London: Ward Lock, 1891).

4. Acton, *Prostitution*.

5. Cited in Zedner, *Women, Crime and Custody*, p. 52.

6. A. Mearns, *The Bitter Cry of Outcast London* (1883; repr., London: Frank Cass, 1970), p. 10.

7. H. Ellis, *The Criminal* (London: Walter Scott, 1890), p. 217; W. D. Morrison, *Crime and Its Causes* (London: Swan Sonnenschein, 1891), p.157. Morrison also argued that southern women were more criminally inclined because of their greater freedom compared with their northern counterparts.

8. C. Burt, *The Young Delinquent* (London: University of London Press, 1925), p. 444.

9. Maudsley, *Body and Mind*, pp. 79–89.

10. H. Ellis, *Man and Woman* (London: Walter Scott, 1904), p. 293; and Burt, *Young Delinquent*, p. 224. Later conventional wisdom saw menopause as the cause of female shoplifting.

11. R. Smith, *Trial by Medicine* (Edinburgh: Edinburgh University Press, 1981); J. P. Eigen, *Witnessing Insanity: Madness and Mad-Doctors in the English Court* (New Haven, CT: Yale University Press, 1995).

12. Ellis, *The Criminal*, p. 217.

13. C. Lombroso and E. Ferrero, *The Female Offender* (1895; repr., New York: Philosophical Library, 1958). See particularly chap. viii, "The Criminal Type in Women and Its Atavistic Origin," and chap. xii, "The Born Criminal."

14. *The Times*, August 8, 1849, 4.

15. Knelman, *Twisting in the Wind*, p. 230. See also Hartman, *Victorian Murderesses*.

16. Walkowitz, *Prostitution and Victorian Society*; Forster, *Significant Sisters*; Caine, *Victorian Feminists*; and Jordan, *Josephine Butler*.

17. Unnamed female philanthropist cited in Zedner, *Women, Crime and Custody*, p. 74.

18. M. Carpenter, *Juvenile Delinquents: Their Condition and Treatment* (London: W. & F. G. Cash, 1853), p. 17.

19. W. Buchanan, *Remarks on the Causes and State of Juvenile Crime in the Metropolis* (London: Taylor, 1846), pp. 49–51.

20. S. P. Day, *Juvenile Crime: Its Causes, Character, and Cure* (London: Reeves, 1851), p. 32 and pp. 283–85.

21. H. Mayhew, *London Labour and the London Poor* (London: Giffen, 1851), 1:28. See also "Of the 'Penny Gaff.'"

22. Ibid., pp. 285.

23. "Select Committee on Criminal and Destitute Juveniles," *Parliamentary Papers* 21 (1852): 7.

24. Quennell, *London's Underworld*, pp. 133–35 and 180–83. See also *Manchester Guardian*, May 28, 1821, for a northern example and the evidence of John Clay, chaplain of Preston House of Correction to the 1852 "Select Committee on Criminal and Destitute Juveniles," *Parliamentary Papers* 23 (1852–53).

25. See for example reports in the *Manchester Times* on February 14, 1880, 4, 7; October 2, 3, and 9, 1880, 5; July, 19, 1884, 7; October, 4, 1884, 8; October, 18, 1884, 19; November, 8, 1884; November, 29, 1884, 5; December 13, 1884, 8; May 2, 1885, 6; January, 9, 1886; November 27, 1886, 5; November 12, 1887, 7; May 4, 1889, 8; and June 22, 1889, 3; July 13, 1889, 2, 3; November, 2, 1889, 2; and November 9, 1889, 3.

26. Pearson, *Hooligan*, esp. part two; Davies, "Youth Gangs, Masculinity and Violence"; A. Davies, "Youth Gangs and Violence, 1870–1900," in *Everyday Violence in Britain, 1850–1950*, ed. S D'Cruze (London: Longman, 2000); A. Davies, *The Gangs of Manchester* (Preston: Milo Books, 2008); and M. MacIlwee, *The Gangs of Liverpool* (Preston: Milo Books, 2006).

27. P. Murphy, J. Williams, and E. Dunning, *Football on Trial* (London: Routledge, 1990), p. 102. See also Murphy, Williams, and Dunning, *The Roots of Football Hooliganism*.

28. Murphy, Williams, and Dunning, *The Roots of Football Hooliganism*, p. 52. These figures represent the tip of an iceberg of over 250 reported incidents of crowd disturbance.

29. *The Times*, August 17, 1898, 7.

30. *Larrikins* were Australian "roughs" particularly associated with Melbourne. See L. T. Hergenham, ed., *A Colonial City: High and Low Life, Selected Journalism*

of MARCUS CLARKE (St. Lucia: University of Queensland Press, 1972); J. Grant and G. Serle, *The Melbourne Scene, 1803–1956* (Melbourne: Melbourne University Press, 1957).

31. *Daily Post,* September 4, 1886, cited in MacIlwee, *The Gangs of Liverpool,* 201.

32. An exception to this is C. Rook, *Hooligan Nights* (1899; repr., Oxford: Oxford University Press, 1979).

33. G.A. Auden, "Feeblemindedness and Juvenile Crime," *The Medical Officer* 4 (1910): 375–78.

34. There are obvious parallels with the high-profile case of Jamie Bulger almost a century later.

35. Auden, "Feeblemindedness," 375.

36. Rudé, *Criminal and Victim,* pp. 41, 45, and 51; Philips, *Crime and Authority,* p. 147; D. Taylor, "Crime and Policing in Early Victorian Middlesbrough, 1835–55," *Journal of Regional and Local Studies* 11 (1991): 59.

37. Gatrell and Hadden, "Criminal Statistics," p. 382.

38. *The Times,* 29 January 1896, 14. Her plight was sympathetically described by the police-court missionary and secretary to the Howard Association, Thomas Holmes. See T. Holmes, *Pictures and Problems from London Police Courts* (London: Edward Arnold, 1908).

39. Philips found that repeat offenders in his sample gave ages that were consistent with the age they claimed to be on their first appearance before the courts. This may simply show that Black Country criminals were consistent liars!

40. Gatrell and Hadden, "Criminal Statistics," Table 7, p. 384.

41. It is an exaggeration to claim Robert Peel as the father of juvenile delinquency, but changes in legislation, such as the 1824 Vagrant Act and the 1827 Malicious Trespass Act, greatly increased the number of juvenile offenders.

42. See especially Walkowitz, *Prostitution and Victorian Society.*

CHAPTER 7: CREATING CRIMINALS

1. William Blackstone, "Of The Trial by Jury," in *Commentaries on the Laws of England,* Book 3, Chapter 23, http://www.lonang.com/exlibris/blackstone/bla-323.htm.

2. "Return of Description of Buildings in which Justices of Petty Sessions Districts in England and Wales Hold Usual Sittings," *Parliamentary Papers* 606 (1845). Taken from all returns for relevant counties.

3. Ibid, p. 2 and 44.

4. "Report of Select Committee on the State of Municipal Corporations in England and Wales," *Parliamentary Papers* 344 (1833): 40.

5. Gamon, *London Police Court,* p. 47.

6. D. Philips, "The Black Country Magistracy 1835–60: A Changing Elite and the Exercise of Its Power," *Midland History* 3 (1976): 161–90; Woods, "The Operation of the Master"; and R. Swift, "The English Urban Magistracy and the Administration of Justice During the Early-Nineteenth Century: Wolverhampton 1815–60," *Midland History* 17 (1992): 75–92. This was not always the case elsewhere. Magistrates in Middlesbrough, despite being drawn from the dominant trades of the town, were less inclined to use the law to protect their interests. It is also not clear if such practices continued into the late 19th century in the midlands.

7. Davis, "A Poor Man's System"; Davis, "Prosecutions and Their Context"; and J. Davis, *Law Breaking and Law Enforcement: The Creation of a Criminal Class in Mid-Victorian London*, Ph.D. dissertation, Boston College, 1984.

8. Mr. Murray, magistrate, evidence to "Select Committee on Metropolitan Police Offices," *Parliamentary Papers* 15 (1838): 118, cited in Davis, "Poor Man's System," p. 315.

9. H. T. Waddy, *The Police Court and Its Works* (London: Butterworth, 1925), p. 26.

10. J. H. Langbein, *The Origins of the Adversarial Criminal Trial* (Oxford: Oxford University Press, 2003); A. N. May, *The Bar & the Old Bailey, 1750–1850* (Chapel Hill: University of North Carolina, 2003); D. T. Andrews and R. McGowen, *The Perreaus & Mrs. Rudd: Forgery and Betrayal in Eighteenth Century London* (Berkeley: University of California Press, 2001).

11. D.J.A. Cairns, *Advocacy and the Making of the Adversarial Criminal Trial, 1800–1865* (Oxford: Oxford University Press, 1998).

12. J. F. Stephen, *A General View of the Criminal Law*, 2nd ed. (London, 1890), p. 269, cited in Cairns, *Advocacy*, p. 164.

13. The Criminal Procedure Act, 1865, further strengthened the position of the accused by giving defense counsel a closing address to the jury at the conclusion of the defense evidence.

14. Cited in A. H. Manchester, *Modern Legal History* (London: Butterworth, 1980), p. 100. Barristers were obliged to accept dock briefs for which service a defendant paid a fee of one guinea, plus the clerk's fee, to obtain the services of counsel.

15. *The Times*, November 4, 1880, 11.

16. *The Times*, November 9, 1880, 10.

17. J. F. Stephen, *History of the Criminal Law*, vol. 1 (London: Macmillan, 1883), p. 442.

18. W. R. Cornish, "Criminal Justice and Punishment," in *Crime and Law in Nineteenth Century Britain*, ed. W. R. Cornish and J. Hall. (Dublin: Irish University Press, 1978), p. 58. G. Parker, "The Prisoner in the Box—The Making of the Criminal Evidence Act, 1898," in *Law and Social Change in British History*, ed. J. A. Guy and H. G. Beale (London: Royal Historical Society, 1984).

19. R. Chadwick, *Bureaucratic Mercy: The Home Office and the Treatment of Capital Cases in Victorian Britain* (London: Garland, 1992), p. 192.

20. R. Pattenden, *English Criminal Appeals, 1844–1994* (Oxford: Oxford University Press, 1996), chap. 1; Chadwick, *Bureaucratic Mercy*, pp. 211–16; HMSO, *The Strange Story of Adolph Beck* (London: HMSO, 1999), is a good collection of documents drawn from the 1904 official enquiry into the case.

21. Pattenden, *English Criminal Appeals*, pp. 30–31. The case has recently received wider coverage in Julian Barnes, *Arthur & George* (London: Jonathan Cape, 2005).

22. The prerogative of mercy was used, albeit sparingly, to find an acceptable way between the strictness of Common Law and changing popular perceptions of guilt and culpability. See Chadwick, *Bureaucratic Mercy*.

23. J. P. Eigen, *Witnessing Insanity: Madness and Mad-Doctors in the English Court* (New Haven, CT: Yale University Press, 1995), 49–51.

24. Cited in M. J. Weiner, *Reconstructing the Criminal: Culture, Law and Policy in England, 1830–1914* (Cambridge: Cambridge University Press, 1990), 87.

25. Radzinowicz and Hood, *The Emergence of Penal Policy*, pp. 683–84.

26. *The Times*, 9 and 10 May, 1844. Quoted in M. J. Weiner, "Judges v Jurors: Courtroom tensions in Murder Trials and the Law of Criminal responsibility in Nineteenth-Century England," *Law and History Review* 17 (1999): 498.

27. Eigen, *Witnessing Insanity*.

28. The Home Office also sought specialist ballistics advice for the trial of Charles Peace in 1879.

29. Chadwick, *Bureaucratic Mercy*, p. 399.

30. Ibid., p. 400.

31. Ibid., p. 50.

32. Cited in Weiner, *Reconstructing the Criminal*, p. 275.

33. *The Times*, January 13, 1872, "The Trial of Dr. Watson," 9; Chadwick, *Bureaucratic Mercy*, pp. 239–53; Weiner, "Judges v Jurors," pp. 498–500.

34. "Climacteric insanity" was another female malady associated with the onset of menopause.

35. A. Herbert Safford, "What Are the Best Means of Preventing Infanticide?" *Transactions of the National Society for the Promotion of Social Science* (1867), p. 224.

36. *The Times*, July 29, 1878, 4.

37. *The Times*, May 1, 1879, 4.

38. *The Times*, May 6, 1905, 19.

39. *The Times*, August 1, 1910, 7 and also at 10.

40. *The Times*, October 24, 1910, 4 and 5.

41. *The Times*, September 17, 1910, and October 21, 1910, 6. Spilsbury's arguments have not gone unchallenged, and recent attempts have been made to overturn them through DNA testing.

42. *The Times*, October 24, 1910, 11.

43. Quite why Richardson kept the copy of *The Times* for March 27, 1854, from which he had torn strips of paper to use as wadding remains a mystery. *Oxford Journal*, December 29, 1860, 6; *Daily News*, November 10, 1860, 2; *Manchester Times*, December 15, 1860, 6.

44. The murder took place in 1882, but it took a colleague of the deceased policeman two years to find a bullet embedded in a tree on Tottenham Marshes where Orrock had practiced. This bullet was shown to be the same type as two found in the body of P.C. Cole. *Birmingham Daily Post*, August 23, 1884, 4; *Lloyd's Weekly Newspaper*, August, 24, 1884, 7, and September 21, 1884, 7. Orrock was in Coldbath Prison for burglary when he was arrested for murder. He was hanged at Newgate on October 6, 1884, along with Thomas Harris, a father of 11 children, who had cut the throat of his wife.

45. McKay was tried under the (false) name of John Williams and achieved notoriety as the "Hooded Man" as he entered court with his face shrouded. He was hanged at Lewes on January 29, 1913. *The Times*, October 28, 1912, 3, and December 13, 1912, 54. See also http://www.historybytheyard.co.uk/pc_gutteridge.htm.

46. *The Woman's Herald*, November 26, 1892, 3.

47. D. Palk, *Gender, Crime and Judicial Discretion, 1780–1830* (London: Boydell, 2006), p. 157.

48. See particularly M.J. Weiner, *Men of Blood: Violence, Manliness and Criminal Justice in Victorian England* (Cambridge: Cambridge University Press, 2004); and Emsley, *Hard Men*.

49. *The Times*, October 29, 1869, 9; Weiner, "Judges v Jurors," p. 484.

50. Cited in Weiner, "Judges v Jurors," p. 492.

51. Weiner, *Men of Blood*, p. 52.

52. Ibid., p. 121.

53. Ibid., p. 165.

54. Cited in Chadwick, *Bureaucratic Mercy*, p. 316.

55. *Manchester Times*, July 10, 1880, 5.

56. M.J. Weiner, "The Sad Story of George Hall: Adultery, Murder and the Politics of Mercy in Mid-Victorian England," *Social History* 24 (1999): 174–95.

57. Weiner, "The Sad Story of George Hall," 187.

58. Ibid, p. 187.

59. Cited in Chadwick, *Bureaucratic Mercy*, p. 362. Italics added.

60. Very little work has been done on local courts. The exception is the important article by B.S. Godfrey, S. Farrall, and S. Karstedt, "Explaining Gendered Sentencing Patterns for Violent Men and Women in the Late-Victorian and Edwardian Period," *British Journal of Criminology* 45 (2005): 696–720, which analyzes minor assault cases in 10 English magistrates' courts.

61. The 1887 Coroner Act also resulted in a more professional approach to inquests.

CHAPTER 8: THE CREATION OF A POLICED SOCIETY

1. *The Times*, "The Metropolitan Police: Part III," December 28, 1908, 6.

2. Roberts, *The Classic Slum*, p. 100.

3. For examples one need look no further than my own earlier writings on the subject.

4. D.G. Barrie, *Police in the Age of Improvement: Police Development and the Civic Tradition in Scotland, 1775–1865* (Cullompton: Willan, 2008), p. 270.

5. Ibid.; and D. Smales, *The Development of the New Police in the Scottish Borders, c. 1840–1890*, unpublished Ph.D. dissertation, Open University, Milton Keynes, UK, 2008.

6. Barrie, *Police in the Age of Improvement*, chap. 4. There were also a small number of late 18th-century improvement acts that included watching provisions. Improvement Acts were also used in England, but this has been somewhat overlooked in older police histories.

7. Ibid., Table 7.1, p. 176.

8. "1st Report of the Inspector of Constabulary, 1858–9," *Parliamentary Papers* 40 (1859). The comments on Edinburgh are at p. 38.

9. For details see Barrie, *Police in the Age of Improvement*, chapters 7 and 9.

10. "7th Report of the Inspector of Constabulary, 1864–5," *Parliamentary Papers* 311 (1865): 3–4.

11. "4th Report of the Inspector of Constabulary, 1861–62," *Parliamentary Papers* 310 (1862): 3.

12. Smales, "Development."

13. Ibid., chap. 4.

14. Barrie, *Police in the Age of Improvement*, is critical of the claims made by Carson and Idzikowska, but Smales's recent work supports them.

15. For further details see D. Taylor, *The New Police in Nineteenth-Century England* (Manchester, UK: Manchester University Press, 1997), chapter 2, pp. 31–6. See also D. Taylor, *Crime, Policing and Punishment in England, 1750–1914* (Basingstoke, UK: Macmillan, 1998), chapter 4.

16. D. Philips and R.D. Storch, *Policing Provincial England, 1829–1856: The Politics of Reform* (Leicester, UK: Leicester University Press, 1999).

17. Taylor, *New Police*, chapter 2, pp. 24–31.

18. House of Commons, April 15, 1829, Metropolis Police Bill, col. 868. For a general discussion of the debate on new policing see Taylor, *New Police*, 12–43.

19. "Editorial," *Middlesbrough Weekly News*, May 6, 1864, 4. Similar sentiments could be found expressed by members of the Irish communities in London, Liverpool, Glasgow, Wolverhampton, and York. See Taylor, *New Police*, chapter 3.

20. For a detailed case study see Taylor, *Policing the Victorian Town*.

21. Taylor, *New Police*, chapter 3.

22. This was true of other forces. See D. Wilson, *The Beat: Policing a Victorian City* (Beaconsfield, Victoria: Melbourne Publishing, 2006) for an Australian example. One should not exaggerate the ability of the police to identify criminals. For a discussion of the various methods used by the Metropolitan Police and their limitations, see T. G. Stanford, *The Metropolitan Police, 1850–1914: Targeting, Harassment and the Creation of a Criminal Class*, unpublished Ph.D. dissertation, University of Huddersfield, Huddersfield, UK, 2008.

23. Cited in S. H. Palmer, *Police and Protest in England and Ireland, 1780–1850* (Cambridge: Cambridge University Press, 1990), 510.

24. J. Monro, "The London Police," *North American Review* 151 (1890): 617–18.

25. Ibid., 618.

26. R. Swift, "Urban Policing in Early-Victorian England, 1835–1856: A Reappraisal," *History* 73 (1988): 211–37; D.J.V. Jones, *Crime, Protest, Community and Police in Nineteenth-Century Britain* (London: Routledge & Kegan Paul, 1982).

27. For details see Jones, *Crime, Protest*, chapter 4, 85–116, "The Conquering of China"; and Taylor, *Policing the Victorian Town*.

28. *The Times*, March 8, 1848, 5.

29. D. Grant, *The Thin Blue Line: The Story of the City of Glasgow Police* (London: Long, 1973), p. 34.

30. Ibid., pp. 30–35.

31. Smales, "Development," pp. 131ff.

32. *The Times*, November 14, 1887, 6.

33. *London Illustrated News*, November 19, 1887, 605; *Lloyd's Weekly Newspaper*, November 13, 1887, 1; and *Reynold's News*, "Warren's Ukase," November 13, 1887, 1.

34. *The Times*, August 14, 1911, 6 and 7, and August 15, 1911, 6.

35. Cited in B. Weinberger, *Keeping the Peace? Policing Strikes in Britain, 1906–1926* (Oxford: Berg, 1991), p. 92.

36. The transport strikes of 1911 did not all follow the Liverpool pattern. Despite serious divisions in the city, dating back to the early 1890s, the strike in Hull, for example, was managed in a way that defused rather than exacerbated tensions. See J. Morgan, *Conflict and Order: The Police and Labour Disputes in England and Wales, 1900–1939* (Oxford: Oxford University Press, 1987); R. Geary, *Policing Industrial Disputes, 1893–1985* (Cambridge: Cambridge University Press, 1985); and Weinberger, *Keeping the Peace?*

37. D. Evans, *Labour Strike in the South Wales Coalfield, 1910–1911* (Cardiff: Education Publishing, 1911), p. 10.

38. *The Times*, November 21, 1911, 6.

39. H. Mayhew, *London Labour and the London Poor*, ed. V Neuburg (London: Penguin, 1985), p. 23.

40. Ibid.

41. "Editorial," *Middlesbrough Weekly News*, June 19, 1868, 4. See also comments of Punch in *Middlesbrough Weekly News*, November 23, 1866, 4, denouncing "police bullies."

42. P.C. Wilkinson was set upon by a crowd of 500 when he tried to arrest Patrick Evans; Superintendent Saggerson was attacked by a drunk, *Middlesbrough Weekly News*, January 6, 1865, December 31, 1869, 2.

43. Gamon, *The London Police Court*, pp. 23–24.

44. Ibid., p. 38.

45. Ibid., p. 22.

46. Roberts, *Classic Slum*, p. 162.

47. Reynolds, Woolley, and Woolley, *Seems So!*, p. 68.

48. Ibid.

49. G. Doré and B. Jerrold, *London: A Pilgrimage* (1871; repr., New York: Dover, 1970), p. 165.

50. Gamon, *London Police Court*, p. 40.

51. Cited in Barrie, *Police in the Age of Improvement*, p. 215.

CHAPTER 9: THE DEATH PENALTY

1. *Daily Telegraph*, August 14, 1868, 4.

2. *The Complete Newgate Calendar*, http://www.law.utexas.edu/lpop/etextnewgate5/hunton.htm.

3. *The Times*, July 25, 1827, 2.

4. John Locke, *Two Treatises of Government*, Second Treatise, cited in Potter, *Hanging in Judgment*, p. 10.

5. William Paley, "Of Crimes and Punishment," in *The Principles of Moral and Political Philosophy* (London: R. Faulder, 1785), pp. 266–301 and esp. pp. 273–76.

6. See especially *A Treatise on the Police of the Metropolis*, first published in 1795 and reprinted on numerous occasions thereafter. Colquhoun's role as a "moral entrepreneur" is discussed by David Philips, "Three 'moral entrepreneurs' and the creation of a 'criminal class' in England, c. 1790s–1840s," *Crime, History and Society* 7 (2003): 79–107.

7. "Select Committee on Cause of Increase," 4. Peel was aware of this but did not allow the fact to prevent him for using claims of a real increase in crime as his justification for reforming the policing of London in 1829.

8. R.R. Follett, *Evangelicalism, Penal Theory and the Politics of Criminal Law Reform in England, 1808–1830* (Basingstoke: Palgrave, 2001), esp. chap. 6; R. McGowen, "A Powerful Sympathy: Terror, the Prison, and Humanitarian

Reform in Early Nineteenth-Century Britain," *Journal of British Studies* 25 (1986): 312–34.

9. "Report from the Select Committee on Criminal Laws," *Parliamentary Papers* 585 (1819): 4–7.

10. R. Peel, *The Speeches of Sir Robert Peel*, vol. 1 (London: Routledge, 1853), p. 456.

11. Cited in Potter, *Hanging in Judgment*, p. 40.

12. V.A.C. Gatrell, *The Hanging Tree* (Oxford: Oxford University Press, 1994), p. 581.

13. "2nd Report from the Commissioners on Criminal Law," *Parliamentary Papers* 343 (1836): 29–32.

14. The amendment was lost by 73 votes to 72 with Peel (unsurprisingly), Gladstone, and Russell voting against it.

15. Bentham's role has given rise to some debate. Follett, *Evangelicalism, Penal Theory*, pp. 8–9, refers to the "myth of Bentham's influence" and emphasizes the importance of Blackstone.

16. S. Moody, *The Impartial Justice of Divine Administration* (Chelmsford, UK: Buckland,1736), p. 7. See the important series of articles by R. McGowen, "He Beareth Not the Sword In Vain: Religion and the Criminal Law in Eighteenth-Century England," *Eighteenth Century Studies* 21 (1981): 192–211; "The Image of Justice and Reform of the Criminal Law in Early Nineteenth-Century England," *Buffalo Law Review* 32 (1983): 89–125; "The Body and Punishment in Eighteenth-Century England," *Journal of Modern History* 59 (1987): 651–79; and "The Changing Face of God's Justice: the Debate Over Divine and Human Punishment in Eighteenth-Century England," *Criminal Justice History* 9 (1988): 63–98.

17. "Bristol's Traumatic Last Hanging and the Gaol's Closure," *BBC Online*, September 20, 2001, http://www.bbc.co.uk/bristol/content/features/2001/09/20/new-gaol/new-gaol4.shtml.

18. There are various accounts of this execution. See, for example, Gatrell, *Hanging Tree*, p. 606, though he asserts that Calcraft merely pulled Bousefield's legs from below.

19. R. Whately, *Thoughts on Secondary Punishment*, (London: Fellowes, 1832), p. 30.

20. W. M. Thackeray, "Going to See a Man Hanged," *Fraser's Magazine* 22 (August 1840): 150–58 at 152.

21. See, for example, evidence of Joseph Conder, bookseller; Joseph Curtis, currier; Wendover Fry, type founder; and John Gaun, merchant and shoe manufacturer in "Report from the Select Committee on Criminal Laws," 89–93.

22. H. Martineau, *The History of England During the Thirty Years Peace, 1816–1846*, vol. II (London: Charles Knight, 1850), p. 420.

23. B. Henry, *Dublin Hanged: Crime, Law Enforcement and Punishment in Late Eighteenth-Century Dublin* (Dublin: Irish Academic Press, 1994), chap. 1.

24. Technically mutineers rather than pirates, 11 men of varying nationalities were arrested for mutiny and murder on the Singapore-bound *Flowery Land* in 1863. Seven were sentenced to death, but only five were executed. Unfortunately, the news of the reprieve of two men came too late for the makers of woodcuts who had produced images showing seven men on the gallows!

25. *Daily Telegraph*, July 14, 1856, 3. This was but a more spectacular example of what had been happening for several years. Execution crowds in Liverpool were greatly enhanced by visitors brought by train from Manchester and the various Lancashire Pennine towns from the 1830s onwards. See *Morning Herald*, April 12, 1836, cited in J. S. Cockburn, "Punishment and Brutalization in the English Enlightenment," *Law and History Review* 12 (1994): 174.

26. *Punch*, November 13, 1849. Leech drew the cartoon after watching.

27. *Daily News*, February 28, 1846, 6.

28. *The Times*, November 14, 1849, 5.

29. "Report of the Royal Commission on Capital Punishment," *Parliamentary Papers* 3590 (1866): 426–27. A minority of contemporary observers disagreed. It was pointed out that foul language was to be heard at state ceremonies as well as at executions; the reason being that many ordinary men and women habitually used foul language, irrespective of the occasion! For a more sympathetic and insightful historical discussion of crowd responses see Gatrell, *Hanging Tree*, esp. chap. 2, and R. McGowen, "Civilizing Punishment: The End of the Public Execution in England," *Journal of British Studies* 33 (1994): 257–82.

CHAPTER 10: THE DEATH PENALTY

1. Potter, *Hanging in Judgment*, chap. 3; D. D. Cooper, *Lesson of the Scaffold* (London: Allen Lane, 1974), chap. 2.

2. The Anti-Corn-Law League was a high profile extra-parliamentary pressure group that campaigned for the abolition of the Corn Laws on the grounds that bread prices were kept artificially high for the benefit of landowners only as the result of this tariff. Although the direct impact of the Anti-Corn-Law League has been exaggerated, it provided a model for pressure groups in the 19th century in terms of its organization and propaganda campaign. One of the best accounts remains, N. McCord, *The Anti Corn Law League* (London: Allen & Unwin, 1958).

3. A. H. Dymond, *The Law on Trial, or Personal Recollections of the Death Penalty and Its Opponents* (London: Society for the Abolition of Capital Punishment, 1865), p. 156.

4. *The Times*, March 14, 1878, 7.

5. Doubts had been growing since the mid-1850s. The publication of Mayhew and Binney's comprehensive study of London prisons highlighted the

failure to deal with the problem of recidivism. The emergence of Edmund Du Cane was a clear sign of the swing to deterrence rather than reform as the guiding principle in prison regimes.

6. Evidence of G. A. Cuxson, chaplain, Aylesbury Gaol, to Select Committee, cited in Potter, *Hanging in Judgment*, p. 83.

7. *Morning Herald*, February 23, 1864, 4. Not everyone agreed. At least one correspondent claimed the crowd had been well behaved. See *Manchester Times*, February 27, 1864, 6

8. See, for example, Anon, "Capital Punishments—The Royal Commission," *Law Magazine and Law Review* 17 (1864): 220–32; Anon, "Capital Punishment," *Bentley's Miscellany* 56 (1864): 171–75; J. F. Stephen, "Capital Punishment," *Fraser's Magazine* 69 (1864): 753–72; and Anon, "Capital Punishment," *Justice of the Peace*, March 28, 1868, 193–94.

9. Joseph Phillip Le Brun was executed in public in Jersey on August 11, 1875, for the murder of his sister and the attempted murder of her husband. The island of Jersey was not included in the current legislation.

10. Clauses 14 to 16 of the 1868 Act provided for attendance at executions, the requirement for a surgeon's certificate of death, and a coroner's inquest to follow each execution.

11. Radzinowicz and Hood, *The Emergence of Penal Policy*, p. 672, fn. 39. Iowa, Illinois, and Maine had de facto abandoned the death penalty. Portugal abolished the death penalty in 1864, as did Roumania, Holland in 1870, and Switzerland in 1874.

12. The most powerful argument against total abolition came from Mill in the parliamentary debate of April 21, 1868. *Parliamentary Debates* (Commons), 3rd series, vol. cxci, cols. 1047–55.

13. Introduction to the Criminal Statistics, 1905, Cmd. 3315, *Parliamentary Papers*, 1907, cited in Radzinowicz and Hood, *Emergence of Penal Policy*, p. 676. As the authors note, this argument could be turned round by retentionists to claim that the so-called criminal classes were deterred by the death penalty.

14. Mill made this point in 1868 but was repeating the claim to the same effect made by the Home Office since 1850.

15. For details see W. Ballantine, *Some Reminiscences of a Barrister's Life* (London: Richard Bentley, 1882).

16. Ibid., p. 679.

17. The point was made in certain legal journals but with limited impact. See Anon, 'Capital Punishments—The Royal Commission"; and Anon, "Capital Punishment," *Justice of the Peace*, March 28, 1868, 193–94.

18. The point was made by Mill and Stephen in the 1860s, but the same point had been made by Lord Macaulay in the 1840s. Stephen, "Capital Punishment" 770. Mill, *Parliamentary Debates*, April 21, 1868, cols. 1047–55

19. The political sensitivity of executions, especially if botched, was heightened by the fact that from 1877 the Prison Commissioners were responsible for local prisons and the executions that took place in them. This brought the Home Office and the Home Secretary more into the public gaze.

20. This and the following paragraph owe much to S. Fielding, *The Hangman's Record, 1868–1899* (Beckenham: Chancery House Press, 1994). The first private execution in Dublin, of a man called Andrew Carr in 1870, resulted in a decapitation, and according to the local press had it taken place in public it would have been the last execution, such was the horrendous sight. However, on at least two occasions, the execution of Laurence Smith at Cavan in 1873 and Joseph Poole in Dublin in 1883 the rope was so long that the victim's feet touched the floor after the drop had opened. In both cases the hangman had to pull up the rope by about two feet and allow the victims to die by strangulation.

21. Berry was involved in yet another botched execution at Oxford in 1888 when Robert Upton was all but decapitated.

22. John Lee, *The Man They Could Not Hang* (London: Arthur Pearson, n.d.); J. Berry, *My Experiences as an Executioner* (London: Percy Lund, 1892).

23. *Pall Mall Gazette*, February 24, 1885, 10; *The Times*, February, 24, 1885, 10, and February 25, 1885, 8.

24. *Truth*, August 27, 1891, cited in S. McConville, *English Local Prisons, 1860–1900: Next Only to Death* (London: Routledge, 1995), p. 427.

25. Marwood's expenses following his execution of David Wardlaw at Dumbarton in 1875 included a dozen bottles of beer, two bottles each of whiskey and brandy, and one each of sherry and port—half of which was allegedly consumed on the morning of the execution. However, he also sought to improve the techniques of killing, notably working with the Rev. Dr. Haughton, of Trinity College Dublin, in devising a scientific formula for the breaking of necks. He also improved the quality of the rope used for executions and modified the noose and its placement on the neck of the condemned. He was also critical of the use of raised gallows that required the condemned to mount several steps. Marwood's name also passed into popular culture, appearing in a number of ballads of the day. It was also the source of the music-hall joke: "If Pa killed Ma, who would kill Pa?" to which the answer was "Marwood"! Binns, by contrast, as well as being an incompetent executioner, was a petty criminal in his own right, appearing in court for taking the Dewsbury to Huddersfield train without paying his fare in January 1884 and later that year for stealing a watch from his mother-in-law.

26. It was not as if the City of London and Middlesex sheriffs were short of applicants. Binns was chosen from some 2,170 people who applied for the post of hangman.

27. *Liverpool Daily Post*, cited in S. P. Evans, *Executioner: The Chronicles of a Victorian Hangman* (Stroud: Sutton, 2004), p. 357. Evans provides a detailed

and sympathetic account of Berry's life and career as an executioner. Liverpool was not a happy city for Victorian executioners. Another hangman from the West Riding of Yorkshire, the Huddersfield-born Thomas Henry Scott, found himself the victim of robbery, having cruised the city in a taxi with a woman of "questionable virtue" before making it to the prison. The incident was insufficient to disconcert Scott who, with James Billington, executed Elijah Winstanley on December 17, 1895.

28. According to some advertisements of the 1890s, Berry's lectures were part of a campaign for the abolition of capital punishment. This might have been genuine; it might also be a part of a personal campaign to embarrass the authorities for the mistreatment he believed he had suffered at their hands.

29. Samuel George Emery, hanged at Newcastle in 1894, was James Billington's nominee for gamest man, while Henry Williams, who was dispatched at Pentonville in 1902, was Henry Pierrepoint's bravest man.

30. *The Times*, July 12, 1875, 10. The case aroused considerable interest at the time, not least because of concerns about increasing violence in the slum districts of Birmingham. Another of the accused claimed that Corkery had confessed to him, but as *The Times'* reports make clear, the evidence presented was very inconsistent. To confuse matters further *The Times* carried a report claiming that Corkery confessed at the last to a Catholic priest who had visited him on the eve of his execution. *The Times*, March, 31, 1875, 10; July10, 1875, 13; and July 28, 1875, 5.

31. For a general discussion of the subject see Pattenden, *English Criminal Appeals*.

32. See M. Drayton, "The Abolition of Capital Punishment," *Westminster Review* 155 (1901), which briefly touches on the subject, and C. Warren, "Is Capital Punishment Defensible?" *Westminster Review* 165 (1906): 515.

33. See for example Anon, "The Death Penalty," *Saturday Review*, July 22, 1899, 95.

34. Change was not universal. At Wandsworth, for example, even in the early 20th century, such was the walk that the executioner had to enter the condemned cell at three minutes to the appointed hour of execution.

35. Oscar Wilde, "The Ballad of Reading Gaol," 4 stanza 20. In *The Complete Works of Oscar Wilde* (Leicester, UK: Bookmark, 1990), 822–39.

CHAPTER 11: PRISON AND THE PROBLEM OF SECONDARY PUNISHMENT

1. Rev. John Clay, Annual Report, 1841, cited in W.L. Clay, *The Prison Chaplain: A Memoir of the Rev. John Clay* (London: Macmillan, 1861), p. 82.

2. A. Shaw, *Remarks on Prison Discipline and the Model Prison* (London: Shaw, 1841), p. 29.

3. Cited in M. Ignatieff, *A Just Measure of Pain: The Penitentiary in the Industrial Revolution* (New York: Columbia University Press, 1978), p. 22.

4. Mayhew and Binney, *The Criminal Prisons of London*, p. 104. There were 62 prisoners per 10,000 in Pentonville "attacked with insanity" compared with an average rate for all prisons of 5.8.

5. *The Satirist; or, the Censor of the Times*, "The Torture Prison Again," January 28, 1844, 31. Sir James Graham was referred to as "the Gaoler-General of England."

6. Bill Sykes [pseudonym], *Prison Life and Prison Poetry*, vol. 1 (London: Newman & Co., 1881), p. 170.

7. Hulks were to be found on the Thames at Woolwich and at Portsmouth and Plymouth but also later in Gibraltar and Bermuda. From the late 1790s prisoners awaiting transportation were held in the Hulks. Later those unfit for transportation were held in shipboard confinement. After 1824, one Hulk, initially *Bellepheron*, later *Euryalus*, was used exclusively for boy convicts. The Hulks were also used in emergencies, such as the clearing of Millbank because of disease in 1823. For a full account see C. Campbell, *The Intolerable Hulks: British Shipboard Confinement, 1776–1857* (Tucson, AZ: Fenestra Books, 2001).

8. Smith to Peel, 13 March 1826. C. S. Parker, ed., *Sir Robert Peel: From His Private Papers*, vol. 1 (London: John Murray, 1891), p. 400.

9. Ibid.

10. One of the most outspoken critics was the Archbishop of Dublin. See R. Whately, "Transportation," *London Review* 1 (1829): 112–39. See also Charles Grey, "Secondary Punishments—Transportation," *Edinburgh Review* 58 (1833–34): 336–62.

11. "Report of the Select Committee on Transportation," *Parliamentary Papers* 669 (1838): xxii and xxix ff.

12. Ibid., p. xli.

13. There is substantial literature on transportation. R. Hughes, *The Fatal Shore* (London: Pan, 1988) is a detailed and entertaining read, but see also A.G.L. Shaw, *Convicts and the Colonies* (London: Faber & Faber, 1966); C. Bateson, *The Convict Ships* (Glasgow: Brown, Son & Ferguson, 1985); J. Damousi, *Depraved and Disorderly: Female Convicts, Sexuality and Gender in Colonial Australia* (Cambridge: Cambridge University Press, 1997); S. Rees, *The Floating Brothel* (London: Hodder Headline, 2001); D. Kent and N. Townsend, *The Convicts of the Eleanor: Protest in Rural England, New Lives in Australia* (London: Merlin Press, 2002); N. Morris, *Maconochie's Gentlemen: The Story of Norfolk Island and the Roots of Modern Prison Reform* (Oxford: Oxford University Press, 2002); and A. Brook and D. Brandon, *Bound for Botany Bay* (Kew, Victoria: National Archives, 2005). Marcus Clarke, *His Natural Life* (1870; repr., London: Penguin, 1970), is the classic fictionalized account of the convict experience, but see also D. Kent and N. Townsend, *Joseph Mason: Assigned Convict, 1831–1837* (Melbourne:

Melbourne University Press, 1996) and D. Dunstan, ed., *Owen Suffolk's Days of Crime and Years of Suffering* (Kew, Victoria: Australian Scholarly Publishing, 2000).

14. Transportation was replaced by the new punishment of penal servitude. The first Penal Servitude Act was passed in 1853 and a second in 1864.

15. Penitentiary Act, 19 Geo. III, c. 74, section 5.

16. "Inspectors of Prison of Great Britain 1. Home District, 3rd Report," *Parliamentary Papers* 141 (1837–38): 2.

17. Ibid., p. 28.

18. Ibid.

19. The 1839 Act was a response to the practical failure of earlier legislation, notably the 1823 Gaol Act that was based on principles of classification, inspection, labor, and religious instruction but lacked sanctions and was largely a dead letter.

20. M. De Lacy, *Prison Reform in Lancashire, 1700–1850: A Study in Local Administration* (Manchester, UK: Manchester University Press, 1986); W. J. Forsythe, *A System of Discipline: Exeter Borough Prison, 1819–1863* (Exeter, UK: University of Exeter, 1983).

21. Robert Ferguson, "The Two Systems at Pentonville," *Quarterly Review* 92 (1852–53): 487–506.

22. "Select Committee on Prison Discipline," *Parliamentary Papers* 632 (1850): 1, v.

23. "Royal Commission appointed to enquire into the conditions and treatment of the prisoners confined in Birmingham Prison," *Parliamentary Papers* 1809 (1854): 1.

24. "Royal Commission on the Condition and Treatment of Prisoners Confined in Leicester County Gaol and House of Correction," *Parliamentary Papers* 1808 (1854): 197, viii.

25. The principle of "less eligibility" was particularly associated with the New Poor Law that had been passed in 1834. To discourage idleness, those poor relief had to be set at a level lower than the wages of an "industrious" laborer, that is, recipients of poor relief were less eligible. The same principle was applied to prison. Indeed, for Edwin Chadwick one of the scandals of the prison system in the 1840s was that prisoners were better fed (and came out weighing more) than law-abiding workers.

26. "Report on the Discipline and Management of the Convict Prisons," *Parliamentary Papers* 1846 (1854): 15.

27. The idea of conditional release was in itself widely accepted, but debate raged as to how this should be earned. Was it simply enough to be a well-behaved prisoner, observing the rules, or should something more positive be required?

28. For a detailed examination of the Chatham disturbance see A. Brown, *English Society and the Prison* (Woodbridge: Boydell, 2003), chap. 3.

29. Rev. S. Smith, *The Works of the Rev. Sydney Smith* (London: Longman, 1869), pp. 375–76.

30. Surveyor-General of Prisons quoted in Mayhew and Binney, *Criminal Prisons*, p. 100.

31. Ibid., p. 102.

32. Ibid., p. 107.

33. T. Carlyle, *Latter Day Pamphlets* (London: Chapman and Hall, 1858), p. 70.

34. For further details see T. Carey, *Mountjoy: The Story of a Prison* (Cork: Collins Press, 2000), chap. 4. On Maconochie, see Morris, *Maconochie's Gentlemen*.

35. Rev. W. L. Clay, *Our Convict Systems* (London: Macmillan 1862), p. 6.

36. Carey, *Mountjoy*, p. 74.

37. Ibid., p. 77.

38. Cited in Radzinowicz and Hood, *The Emergence of Penal Policy*, p. 516.

CHAPTER 12: PRISON AND THE PROBLEM OF SECONDARY PUNISHMENT

1. Contemporary anti-Jebb sentiments are well summed up in A. Griffiths, *Memorials of Millbank* (London: Cassell, 1875), chap. xxiii.

2. Caernarvon Committee, cited in L. Fox, *The English Prison and Borstal System* (London: Routledge, Kegan & Paul, 1952), p. 425.

3. Nonetheless, Du Cane still used the rhetoric of the progressive stage system in his account of the prison system during his period in office. See Sir Edmund Du Cane, *The Punishment and Prevention of Crime* (London: Macmillan, 1885).

4. McConville, *English Local Prisons*, pp. 317–19.

5. Of the prisoners sent from Millbank in 1868, 34 percent were sent to invalid prisons and a further 11 percent were certified fit for light work only. Brown, *English Society*, p. 91.

6. Ibid., p. 92.

7. Two more deaths linked to inadequate diet took place in 1880. For further details see McConville, *English Local Prisons*, pp. 471–80.

8. *The Times*, July 6, 1880, 12.

9. The crank comprised a box of sand or lead shot into which was inserted an arm on which there were three or four cups or scoops. The prisoner turned an exterior handle, and as he did so the cups scooped up and then deposited the sand or shot—a particularly pointless activity. According to Mayhew, 20 revolutions a minute was the normal speed, which meant that a task of 10,000 turns (the norm at Millbank) would take 8 hours and 20 minutes. See Mayhew and Binney, *Criminal Prisons*, p. 308. Equally pointless, but having the same effect of exhausting the prisoner, was shot-drill, which involved

carrying cannon balls taken from a pyramid at one end of the exercise yard to form another pyramid at the opposite end. The exercise was then reversed and repeated for the allotted 75-minute period.

10. Anon, "'Concerning Imprisonment' by One Who Has Suffered It," *Hibbert Journal* 8 (1910): 598.

11. W. Forsythe, "Loneliness and Cellular Confinement in English Prisons, 1878–1921," *British Journal of Criminology* 44 (2004): 764. Hence the importance attached by prisoners to kind words and even the presence of animals, even rats, in their cells.

12. The statistics are problematic. Allowing for changes in prison population, the incidence of punishment per 1,000 prisoners is largely unchanged, but this does not necessarily compare like with like. After nationalization the category "confinement in punishment cell" disappears, even though when prisoners were confined in their normal cells on bread and water this was no different to the experience of the punishment cells. For a more detailed discussion see McConville, *English Local Prisons*, pp. 241–48.

13. In theory, the 1865 Prison Act forbade the use of mechanical constraints such as irons and chains except in cases of "urgent necessity," but the evidence of prison visitors showed that this was ignored in several prisons.

14. The evidence presented to the commission contained several allegations of cruelty to prisoners and evasiveness on the part of prison authorities when challenged, but it appears that there was more sympathy for the difficulties and dangers faced by warders.

15. *Daily Chronicle*, March 24, 1898, 5.

16. "Report of the Commissioners appointed to inquire into the workings of the Penal Servitude Acts," *Parliamentary Papers* 2368 (1878–1979): 26.

17. *Punch* responded to this with the following piece of doggerel. January 26, 1895.

> Is it sadey ye're falin' an' pale, me bhoy,
> Loike a sprat that has swallered a whale, me bhoy?
> The best thing Oi know
> Is a sixer or so
> On skilly an' wather in jail, me bhoy.
> Ye're free from all koinds o' temptation, lad,
> Ye can't overate on thim rations, lad,
> There's so much a-head
> O' skilly an' bread
> Accordin' to jail regulation. Lad.
> They trate ye wid fatherly care, me bhoy
> They tell ye o' what to beware, me bhoy,
> They teach ye to be Teetotal, you see,
> For 'tis nothin' but wather is there, me bhoy.

So whin ye're beginnin' to fade, me lad,
That ye've dhrunk enough whiskey an' ale, me lad
The best of all ways
To lengthen your days
Is to spind a few wakes in the jail, me lad.

18. W. D. Morrison, "Are Our Prisons a Failure?" *Fortnightly Review* 64 (Old Series, 1894): 463.

19. For this and other problems in the method of work of the committee see McConville, *English Local Prisons*, chap. 15.

20. "Minutes of Evidence to the Departmental Committee on Prisons," *Parliamentary Papers* 7701–1 (1895): Q.11482.

21. "Report from the Departmental Committee on Prisons," *Parliamentary Papers* 56 (1895): 8.

22. Ibid, 14.

23. For the continuing faith in isolation Forsythe, "Loneliness and Cellular Confinement."

24. *Daily Chronicle*, July 28, 1898, 3.

25. Edward Carpenter, *Prisons, Police and Punishment* (London: Fifield, 1905), 94–05.

26. Labour Research Group, cited in Radzinowicz and Hood, *The Emergence of Penal Policy*, p. 587; and Parkhurst chaplain, 1912, cited in W. J. Forsythe, *Penal Discipline, Reformatory Projects and the English Prison Commission, 1895–1939* (Exeter, UK: University of Exeter, 1990), p. 70.

27. See chapter 2.

28. *Parliamentary Debates*, May 27, 1908, col. 1122.

29. *Parliamentary Debates*, November 24, 1908, col. 247.

CHAPTER 13: PRISON AND THE PROBLEM OF SECONDARY PUNISHMENT

1. The nursery was perhaps the most distinctive feature of female prisons, but the presence of mothers and children brought problems of its own.

2. Zedner, *Women, Crime and Custody*, p. 142.

3. Ibid., pp. 161–62. The situation was compounded by the fact that the social backgrounds of many prison warders were not that different from the prisoners in their charge.

4. "Report of the Departmental Committee on Prisons" [Gladstone Committee], *Parliamentary Papers* 7702 (1895), 1, Minutes of Evidence Q.5004.

5. Calculated from McConville, *English Local Prisons*, Table 8.1, p. 336.

6. The female convict prison system was later extended. In 1863–64 Parkhurst was used for Roman Catholic prisoners and was replaced by the

new prison at Woking in 1869. In the same year Brixton was closed as a female prison, and Fulham Refuge became an ordinary female convict prison.

7. The average for women was almost identical to that for men.

8. According to Mayhew and Binney the women of Brixton prison produced 20,000 shirts, 10,000 flannel drawers and waistcoats, 1,200 shifts, 3,500 petticoats, 5,700 sheets, 2,000 caps, 3,700 handkerchiefs, 2,800 aprons, 2,300 neckerchiefs, 1,200 jackets, and 3,400 towels to the value of £1,800 ($2,862) in 1854. Mayhew and Binney, *Criminal Prisons*, p. 194.

9. Figures for 1880 show that 53 percent of female prisoners had a previous conviction, compared with 33 percent of men, while 15 percent of females had 10 or more convictions compared with 3 percent of men.

10. Radzinowicz and Hood, *The Emergence of Penal Policy*, part 4, esp. chapter 9; Zedner, *Women, Crime and Custody*, chapter 6.

11. Holmes, *Pictures and Problems*, p. 123. Holmes, an experienced court missionary, devoted a chapter to Cakebread whom he presented in a sympathetic light.

12. Zedner, *Women, Crime and Custody*, chap. 7; and, more generally, Jackson, *The Borderland of Imbecility*.

13. E. Showalter, *The Female Malady: Women, Madness and English Culture, 1830–1980* (London: Virago, 1987).

14. Pearson, *Hooligan*; and J. Springhall, *Youth, Popular Culture and Moral Panics: Penny Gaffs to Gangsta-Rap, 1830–1996* (Basingstoke: Macmillan, 1998).

15. J. A. Stack, "Deviance and Reformation in Early Victorian social Policy: The Case of Parkhurst Prison, 1836–1864," *Historical Reflections* 6 (1979): 387–404.

16. Mary Carpenter, *Reformatory Schools for the Children of the Perishing and Dangerous Classes, and for Juvenile Offenders* (London: Gilpin, 1851); Carpenter, *Juvenile Delinquents*; Jo Manton, *Mary Carpenter and the Children of the Streets* (London: Heinemann, 1976).

17. Industrial School Act, 1866 29 & 30 Vict. c. 126.

18. Humphries, *Hooligans or Rebels?* Chapter 8 Reformatories is unambiguously subtitled "Resistance to Repression." J. Hurt, "Reformatory and Industrial Schools before 1933," *History of Education* 13 (1984): 45–58.

19. Sue Maidens, *The Linthorpe Industrial School. An Agency of Class Control?* Unpublished BA (Hons) Humanities History Dissertation, Teesside Polytechnic, Middlesbrough, UK, 1991.

20. T. Jeal, *Baden-Powell* (London: Pimlico, 1991); M. Rosenthal, *The Character Factory: Baden-Powell and the Origins of the Boy Scout Movement* (London: Collins, 1986); J Springhall, *Youth, Empire and Society* (London: Croom Helm, 1977); and J. Springhall, *Sure and Stedfast: A History of the Boys' Brigade, 1885–1983* (London: Collins, 1983).

21. Sir Evelyn Ruggles-Brise, *The English Prison System* (London: Macmillan, 1921), pp. 86 and 91.

22. Cited in Radzinowicz and Hood, *The Emergence of Penal Policy*, p. 385.

23. Ruggles-Brise, *English Prison System*, p. 94–95.

24. Forsythe, *Penal Discipline*, esp. pp. 50–55.

25. An alternative interpretation has been put forward by Garland, *Punishment & Welfare*, and Weiner, *Reconstructing the Criminal*, but as demonstrated in this chapter, the extent of change, both intellectual and practical, after 1895 was limited.

26. This paragraph owes much to the discussion of time in Brown, *English Society*.

27. Mayhew and Binney, *Criminal Prisons*, pp. 165–67.

28. Owen Suffolk, *Days of Crime and Years of Suffering* (Kew, Victoria: Australian Scholarly Publishing, 2000): 90–91.

29. M. Davitt, "Criminal and Prison Reform," *The Nineteenth Century* 36 (1894): 880.

30. M. Davitt, "The Punishment of Penal Servitude," *Contemporary Review* 44 (1883): 181.

31. A. Bidwell, *From Wall Street to Newgate* (1895; repr., London: Forum Press, 1996), 209. See also F. Brocklehurst, *I was in Prison* (London: Fisher Unwin, 1898); J. Balfour, *My Prison Life* (London: Chapman & Hall, 1901) and W.B.N. [Lord William Beauchamp Nevill], *Penal Servitude* (London: Heinemann, 1903).

32. W.B.N., *Penal Servitude*, p. 31.

BIBLIOGRAPHY

"1st Report of the Inspector of Constabulary, 1858–59," *Parliamentary Papers* 40 (1859).

"2nd Report from the Commissioners on Criminal Law," *Parliamentary Papers* 537 (1834).

"4th Report of the Inspector of Constabulary, 1861–62," *Parliamentary Papers* 310 (1862).

"7th Report of the Inspector of Constabulary, 1864–65," *Parliamentary Papers* 311 (1865).

Abel-Smith, B., & R. Stevens. *Lawyers and the Courts*. London: Heinemann, 1967.

Acton, W. *Prostitution Considered in its Moral, Social and Sanitary Aspects, in London and other Large Cities: With Proposals for the Mitigation and Prevention of its Attendant Evils*. First published 1856; 1870 edition. Reprint London: Cass, 1972.

Agar, N. E. *The Bedfordshire Farm Worker in the Nineteenth Century*. Bedford, UK: Bedfordshire Historical Record Society 1981.

Aisenberg, N., ed. *London Crimes*. Boston: Rowan Tree Press, 1982.

Alpert, M. *London 1849: A Victorian Murder Story*. London: Pearson, 2004.

Anderson, O. *Suicide in Victorian and Edwardian England*. Oxford: Oxford University Press, 1987.

Anderson, R. "Criminals and Crime." *Law Magazine Review* 33 (1908): 129–40, 257–64.

Anderson, R. *Criminals and Crime: Some Facts and Suggestions*. London: James Nesbit, 1907.

Anderson, R. "The Crusade Against Professional Criminals." *Nineteenth Century and After* 55 (1904): 811–21.

Anderson, R. "More about Professional Criminals." *Nineteenth Century and After* 52 (1902): 562–75.

Anderson, R. "Our Absurd System of Punishing Crime." *Nineteenth Century and After* 49 (1901): 268–84.

Anderson, R. "The Prevention of Crime Act." *Nineteenth Century and After* 65 (1909): 241–50.

Anderson, R. "The Punishment of Crime." *Nineteenth Century and After* 50 (1901): 77–92.

Andrews, D. T., and R. McGowen. *The Perreaus & Mrs. Rudd: Forgery and Betrayal in Eighteenth Century London.* Berkeley: University of California Press, 2001.

Annual Report of the Chief Constable of Middlesbrough, 1909, p. 16. Published in Minutes of Middlesbrough Borough Council, 1879–1914, Cleveland County Archive, CB/M/C, 1/70.

Anon. [W. R. Greg]. "Convicts and Transportation." *North British Review* 38 (1863): 1–35.

Anon. [S. Roe]. "A Convict's View of Penal Discipline." *Cornhill Magazine* 10 (1866): 489–512.

Anon. "Capital Punishment." *Bentley's Miscellany* 56 (1864): 171–75.

Anon. "Capital Punishments—The Royal Commission." *Law Magazine and Law Review* 17 (1864): 220–32.

Anon. "'Concerning Imprisonment' by One Who Has Suffered It." *Hibbert Journal* 8 (1910): 582–602.

Anon. "Criminal Statistics, 1910." *Law Magazine Review* 27 (1912): 308–25.

Archer, J. E. "A Fiendish Outrage? A Study of Animal Maiming in East Anglia." *Agricultural History Review* 33 (1985): 147–57.

Archer, J. E. *"By a Flash and a Scare": Arson, Animal Maiming and Poaching in East Anglia, 1815–1870.* Oxford: Oxford University Press, 1990.

Archer, J. E. "Men Behaving Badly? Masculinity and the Use of Violence, 1850–1900." In *Everyday Violence in Britain, 1850–1950*, ed. S. D'Cruze. London: Longman, 2000.

Archer, J. E. "Poachers Abroad." In *The Unquiet Countryside*, ed. G. E. Mingay. London: Routledge, 1989.

Archer, J. E. "The Violence We Have Lost? Body Counts, Historians and Interpersonal Violence in England." *Memoria y Civilización* 2 (1991): 171–90.

Arnot, M. L. "Understanding Women Committing Newborn Baby Murder in Victorian England." In *Everyday Violence in Britain, 1850–1950*, ed. S. D'Cruze. London: Longman, 2000.

Auden, G. A. "Feeblemindedness and Juvenile Crime." *The Medical Officer* 4 (1910): 375–78.

Bailey, P., ed. *Policing and Punishment in the Nineteenth Century.* London: Croom Helm, 1981.

Bailey, V. *Delinquency and Citizenship: Reclaiming the Young Offender, 1914–1948.* Oxford: Oxford University Press, 1987.

Bailey, V. "English Prisons, Penal Culture, and the Abatement of Imprisonment, 1895–1922." *Journal British Studies* 36 (1997): 285–324.

Bailey, V. *This Rash Act Suicide Across the Life Cycle in the Victorian City*. Stanford: Stanford University Press, 1998.

Balfour, J. *My Prison Life*. London: Chapman & Hall, 1901.

Ballantine, W. *Some Reminiscences of a Barrister's Life*. London: Richard Bentley, 1882.

Banks, O. *Faces of Feminism*. Oxford: Blackwell, 1986.

Barclay, H. "The Heredity of Crime." *British Medical Journal* 14 (1891): 251–59.

Barnes, Julian. *Arthur & George*. London: Jonathan Cape, 2005.

Barnett, M. *Young Delinquents*. London: Methuen, 1913.

Barrie, D. G. *Police in the Age of Improvement: Police Development and the Civic Tradition in Scotland, 1775–1865*. Cullompton, UK: Willan, 2008.

Bartley, P. *Prostitution: Prevention and Reform in England, 1860–1914*. London: Routledge, 2000.

Bateson, C. *The Convict Ships*. Glasgow, UK: Brown, Son & Ferguson, 1985.

Bauer, C., and L. Ritt. "'A Husband is a Beating Animal': Frances Power Cobbe confronts the wife-abuse problem in Victorian England." *International Journal of Women's Studies* 6 (1983): 99–118.

Bauer, C., and L. Ritt. "Wife-Abuse, Late-Victorian English feminists and the Legacy of Frances Power Cobbe." *International Journal of Women's Studies* 6 (1983): 195–207.

Bayley, D. H. ed. *Police and Society*. London: Sage, 1977.

Begg, P. *Jack the Ripper: The Definitive History*. Harlow, UK: Pearson, 2005.

Behlmer, G. K. *Child Abuse and Moral Reform in England, 1879–1908*. Stanford: Stanford University Press, 1982.

Bell, Lady. *At the Works: A Study of a Manufacturing Town*. 1907. Reprint, Newton Abbott: David & Charles, 1967.

Berridge, B. *Opium and the People: Opiate Use and Drug Control in Nineteenth and Early Twentieth Century England*. London: Free Association Books, 1999.

Berry, J. *My Experiences as an Executioner*. London: Percy Lund, 1892.

Bidwell, A. *From Wall Street to Newgate*. 1895. Reprint London: Forum Press, 1996.

Binns, J. *From Village to Town*. Batley, UK: Fearnsides & Sons, 1882.

Blackstone, William. "Of The Trial by Jury." In *Commentaries on the Laws of England*, Book 3, Chapter 23. http://www.lonang.com/exlibris/blackstone/bla-323.htm.

Booth, M. *Opium: A History*. London: Simon & Schuster, 1996.

Bottomly, K., and K. Pease. *Crime and Punishment: Interpreting the Data*. Milton Keynes, UK: Open University Press, 1986.

Boyle, T. *Black Swine in the Sewers of Hampstead*. New York: Viking, 1989.

Braber, B. "The Trial of Oscar Slater (1909) and Anti-Jewish Prejudice in Edwardian Glasgow." *History* 88 (2003): 262–79.

"Bristol's Traumatic Last Hanging and the Gaol's Closure." *BBC Online.* September 20, 2001. http://www.bbc.co.uk/bristol/content/features/2001/09/20/new-gaol/new-gaol4.shtml.

Bristow, E. J. *Vice and Vigilance: Purity Movements in Britain since 1700.* Dublin: Gill and Macmillan, 1977.

Brocklehurst, F. *I was in Prison.* London: Fisher Unwin, 1898.

Brogden, M. *The Police: Autonomy and Consent.* London: Academic Press, 1982.

Brook, A., and D. Brandon. *Bound for Botany Bay.* Kew, AU: National Archives, 2005.

Brown, A. *English Society and the Prison.* Woodbridge, UK: Boydell, 2003.

Brundage, A. "Ministers, Magistrates and Reform: The Genesis of the Rural Constabulary Act of 1839." *Parliamentary History* 5 (1986): 55–64.

Buchanan, W. *Remarks on the Causes and State of Juvenile Crime in the Metropolis.* London: Taylor, 1846.

Burt, C. *The Young Delinquent.* London: University of London Press, 1925.

Caine, B. *Victorian Feminists.* Oxford: Oxford University Press, 1992.

Cairns, D.J.A. *Advocacy and the Making of the Adversarial Criminal Trial, 1800–1865.* Oxford: Oxford University Press, 1998.

Campbell, C. *The Intolerable Hulks: British Shipboard Confinement, 1776–1857.* Tucson, AZ: Fenestra Books, 2001.

Carey, T. *Mountjoy: The Story of a Prison.* Cork, UK: Collins Press, 2000.

Carlyle, T. *Latter Day Pamphlets.* London: Chapman and Hall 1858.

Carpenter, Edward. *Prisons, Police and Punishment.* London: Fifield, 1905.

Carpenter, M. *Juvenile Delinquents: Their Condition and Treatment.* London: W. & F.G. Cash, 1853.

Carpenter, M. *Our Convicts.* London: Longman, Green, 1853.

Carpenter, Mary. *Reformatory Schools for the Children of the Perishing and Dangerous Classes, and for Juvenile Offenders.* London: Gilpin, 1851.

Chadwick, R. *Bureaucratic Mercy: The Home Office and the Treatment of Capital Cases in Victorian Britain.* London: Garland, 1992.

Clapson, M. *A Bit of a Flutter Popular Gambling and English Society, c. 1823–1961.* Manchester, UK: Manchester University Press, 1992.

Clark, A. "Domesticity and the Problem of Wife-Beating in Nineteenth-Century Britain: Working-Class Culture, Law and Politics." In *Everyday Violence in Britain, 1850–1950,* ed. S. D'Cruze. London: Longman, 2000.

Clark, A. *Women's Silence, Men's Violence: Sexual Assault in England, 1770–1845.* London: Pandora Press, 1987.

Clark, R. *Women and the Noose: A History of Female Execution.* Stroud, UK: Tempus, 2007.

Clarke, Marcus. *His Natural Life*. 1870. Reprint London: Penguin, 1970.

Clarkson, C. T. & J. Richardson. *Police!* London: Field & Tuer, Leadenhall Press, 1889.

Clay, J. *Maconochie's Experiment*. London: John Murray, 2001.

Clay, J. "On the Effects of Good and Bad Times on Committals to Prison." *Journal of the Statistical Society* 18 (1855): 74–79.

Clay, J. "On the Relation Between Crime, Popular Instruction, Attendance on Religious Worship and Beerhouses." *Journal of the Statistical Society* 20 (1857): 22–32.

Clay, Rev. W. L. *Our Convict Systems*. London: Macmillan, 1862.

Clay, W. L. *The Prison Chaplain: A Memoir of the Rev. John Clay*. London: Macmillan, 1861.

Cobbe, Frances Power. "Wife Torture in England." *Contemporary Review* 32 (1878): 55–87.

Cockburn, J. S. "Patterns of Violence in English Society: Homicide in Kent, 1560–1985." *Past & Present* 130 (1991): 70–106.

Cockburn, J. S. "Punishment and Brutalization in the English Enlightenment." *Law and History Review* 12 (1994): 155–79.

Cohen, E. *Talk on the Wilde Side*. London: Routledge, 1993.

Cohen, S., and A. Scull, eds. *Social Control and the State*. Oxford: Martin Robertson, 1983.

Conley, C. *The Unwritten Law: criminal Justice in Victorian Kent*. Oxford: Oxford University Press, 1991.

Cooper, D. D. *Lesson of the Scaffold*. London: Allen Lane, 1974.

Cornish, W. R. "Criminal Justice and Punishment." In *Crime and Law in Nineteenth Century Britain*, ed. W. R. Cornish and J. Hall. Dublin: Irish University Press, 1978.

Cornish, W. R., and Hall J., eds. *Crime and Law in Nineteenth Century Britain*. Dublin: Irish University Press, 1978.

Critchley, T. A. *A History of Police in England and Wales*. London: Constable, 1967.

Crown Office and Procurator Fiscal Service. "The Strange Case of Jessie McLachlan." http://www.procuratorfiscal.gov.uk/News/Historical/JessMach.

Curtis, L. Perry, Jr. *Jack the Ripper & the London Press*. New Haven, CT: Yale University Press, 2001.

Damousi, J. *Depraved and Disorderly: Female Convicts, Sexuality and Gender in Colonial Australia*. Cambridge: Cambridge University Press, 1997.

Davenport-Hines, R. *Sex, Death and Punishment: Attitudes to Sex and Sexuality in Britain Since the Renaissance*. London: Fontana, 1990.

Davenport-Hines, R. *The Pursuit of Oblivion: A Global History of Narcotics, 1500–2000*. London: Wiedenfeld & Nicholson, 2001.

Davey, B. J. *Lawless and Immoral: Policing a County Town, 1838–1857*. Leicester, UK: Leicester University Press, 1983.

Davidoff, L., and C. Hall. *Family Fortunes: Men and Women of the English Middle Class 1789–1850*. London: Hutchinson, 1987.

Davies, A. *The Gangs of Manchester*. Preston, UK: Milo Books, 2008.

Davies, A. "The Police and the People: Gambling in Salford, 1900–1939." *Historical Journal* 34 (1991): 87–115.

Davies, A. "'These Viragoes Are No Less Cruel Than the Lads': Young Women, Gangs and Violence in Late Victorian Manchester and Salford." *British Journal of Criminology* 39 (1999): 72–89.

Davies, A. "Youth Gangs and Violence, 1870–1900," in *Everyday Violence in Britain, 1850–1950*, ed. S. D'Cruze. London: Longman, 2000.

Davies, A. "Youth Gangs, Masculinity and Violence in Late Victorian Manchester and Salford." *Journal of Social History* 32 (1998): 349–69.

Davis, G. *The Irish in Britain, 1815–1914*. Dublin: Gill and Macmillan, 1991.

Davis, J. "From 'Rookeries' to 'Communities': Race, Poverty and Policing in London, 1850–1985." *History Workshop Journal* 27 (1989): 66–85.

Davis, J. *Law Breaking and Law Enforcement: The Creation of a Criminal Class in Mid-Victorian London*, Ph.D. dissertation, Boston College, 1984.

Davis, J. "The London Garrotting Panic of 1862: A Moral Panic and the Creation of a Criminal Class in mid-Victorian England. In *Crime and the Law: The Social History of Crime in Western Europe since 1500*, ed. V. Gatrell, B. Lenman, & G. Parker. London: Europa, 1980.

Davis, J. "A Poor Man's System of Justice: The London Police Courts in the Second Half of the Nineteenth Century." *Historical Journal* 27 (1984): 309–35.

Davis, J. "Prosecutions and Their Context: The Use of the Criminal Law in Later Nineteenth-Century London." In *Policing and Prosecution in Britain, 1750–1850*, ed. D. Hay and F. Snyder. Oxford: Oxford University Press, 1989.

Davitt, M. "Criminal and Prison Reform." *The Nineteenth Century* 36 (1894): 875–89.

Davitt, M. "The Punishment of Penal Servitude." *Contemporary Review* 44 (1883): 169–82.

Day, S. P. *Juvenile Crime: Its Causes, Character, and Cure*. London: Reeves, 1851.

D'Cruze, S., ed. *Everyday Violence in Britain, 1850–1950*. London: Longman, 2000.

D'Cruze, S. *Crimes of Outrage: Sex, Violence and Working-Class Women*. London: UCL Press, 1998.

De Lacey, M. "Grinding Men Good? Lancashire's Prisons at Mid-Century." In *Policing and Punishment in the Nineteenth Century*, ed. P. Bailey. London: Croom Helm, 1981.

De Lacy, M. *Prison Reform in Lancashire, 1700–1850: A Study in Local Administration.* Manchester, UK: Manchester University Press, 1986.

Dickens, C. *Bleak House.* 1853. Reprint London: Wordsworth, 1993.

Dickens, C. *Oliver Twist.* 1838. Reprint London: Collins, 1954.

Dickens, C. "On Duty with Inspector Fields." In *London Crimes,* ed. N Aisenberg. Boston: Rowan Tree Press, 1982.

Dixon, D. "'Class Law': The Street Betting Act of 1906." *International Journal of the Sociology of Law* 8 (1980): 101–28.

Dixon, D. *From Prohibition to Regulation: Book-making, Anti-Gambling and the Law.* Oxford: Oxford University Press, 1991.

Dobash, R. P., R. E. Dobash, and S. Gutteridge. *The Imprisonment of Women.* Oxford: Blackwell, 1986.

Dobson, C. R. *Masters and Journeymen: A Prehistory of Industrial Relations 1717–1800.* London: Croom Helm, 1980.

Doggett, M. E. *Marriage, Wife-Beating and the Law in Victorian England.* London: Weidenfeld & Nicholson, 1992.

Doré, G., and B. Jerrold. *London: A Pilgrimage.* 1871. Reprint New York: Dover, 1970.

Drayton, M. "The Abolition of Capital Punishment." *Westminster Review* 155 (1901): 424–31.

Du Cane, Sir Edmund. *The Punishment and Prevention of Crime.* London: Macmillan, 1885.

Duckworth, J. *Fagin's Children: Criminal Children in Victorian England.* London: Hambledon, 2002.

Dunbabin, J.P.D. *Rural Discontent in Nineteenth-Century Britain.* London: Faber & Faber, 1974.

Dunning, E., P. Murphy, P., and J. Williams. *The Roots of Football Hooliganism: An Historical and Sociological Study.* London: Routledge, 1988.

Dunstan, D., ed. *Owen Suffolk's Days of Crime and Years of Suffering.* Kew, AU: Australian Scholarly Publishing, 2000.

Dymond, A. H. *The Law on Trial, or Personal Recollections of the Death Penalty and Its Opponents.* London: Society for the Abolition of Capital Punishment, 1865.

Eigen, J. P. *Witnessing Insanity: Madness and Mad-Doctors in the English Court.* New Haven, CT: Yale University Press, 1995.

Ellis, H. *The Criminal.* London: Walter Scott, 1890.

Ellis, H. *Man and Woman.* London: Walter Scott, 1904.

Emsley, C. *Crime and Society in England,* 3rd ed. London: Longman, 2004.

Emsley, C. "Detection and Prevention: The Old English Police and the New." *Historical Social Research* 37 (1986): 69–68.

Emsley, C. *The English Police: A Social and Political History,* 2nd ed. Hemel Hempstead, UK: Longman, 1996.

Emsley, C. *Policing and Its Context*. Basingstoke, UK: Macmillan,1983.

Emsley, C. "The Thump of Wood on a Swede Turnip: Police Violence in Nine-teenth-Century England." *Criminal Justice History* 6 (1985): 125–49.

Emsley, C., and M. Clapson. "Recruiting the English Policeman, c. 1840–1940." *Policing and Society* 3 (1994):269–86.

Emsley, C. *Hard Men: Violence in England Since 1750*. London: Hambledon, 2005.

Engels, F. *Condition of the Working Class in England in 1844*. Translated by W. O. Henderson and W. H. Chaloner. London: Macmillan, 1973.

Evans, D. *Labour Strike in the South Wales Coalfield, 1910–1911*. Cardiff, UK: Education Publishing, 1911.

Evans, S. P. *Executioner: The Chronicles of a Victorian Hangman*. Stroud, UK: Sutton, 2004.

Farmer, L. *Criminal Law, Tradition and Legal Order: Crime and the Genius of Scots Law from 1747 to the Present*. Cambridge: Cambridge University Press, 2005.

Feeley, M., and D. Little. "The Vanishing Female: The Decline of Women in the Criminal Process, 1687–1912." *Law & Society Review* 25 (1991): 719–57.

Ferguson, Robert. "The Two Systems at Pentonville." *Quarterly Review* 92 (1852–1853). 487–506.

Fielding, S. *The Hangman's Record, Vol. 1 1868–1899 and Vol. 2 1900–1929*. Beckenham, UK: Chancery House Press, 1994 and 1995.

Finnegan, F. *Poverty and Prejudice: A Study of Irish immigrants in York, 1840–1875*. Cork, UK: Cork University Press, 1982.

Finnegan, F. *Poverty and Prostitution: A Study of Victorian Prostitution in York*. Cambridge: Cambridge University Press, 1979.

Fisher, T. *Prostitution and the Victorians*. Stroud, UK: Sutton, 1997.

Fishman, W. J. *East End 1888*. London: Duckworth, 1988.

Foard, I. "The Criminal: Is He Produced by Environment or Atavism?" *Westminster Review* 150 (1898): 90–103.

Foard, I. "The Power of Heredity." *Westminster Review* 152 (1899): 538–53.

Follett, R. R. *Evangelicalism, Penal Theory and the Politics of Criminal Law Reform in England, 1808–1830*. Basingstoke, UK: Palgrave, 2001.

Forster, M. *Significant Sisters: The Grassroots of Active Feminism, 1839–1939*. London: Penguin, 1984.

Forsythe, W. "Loneliness and Cellular Confinement in English Prisons, 1878–1921." *British Journal of Criminology* 44 (2004): 759–70.

Forsythe, W. J. *Penal Discipline, Reformatory Projects and the English Prison Commission, 1895–1939*. Exeter, UK: University of Exeter, 1990.

Forsythe, W. J. *The Reform of Prisoners, 1830–1900*. London: Croom Helm, 1987.

Forsythe, W. J. *A System of Discipline: Exeter Borough Prison, 1819–1863*. Exeter, UK: University of Exeter, 1983.

Foucault, M. *Discipline and Punish: The Birth of the Prison*. London: Penguin, 1991.

Fox, L. *The English Prison and Borstal System*. London: Routledge, Kegan & Paul, 1952.

Foxcroft, L. *The Making of Addiction: The "Use and Abuse" of Opium in Nineteenth Century Britain*. Aldershot, UK: Ashgate, 2007.

Gamon, H.R.P. *The London Police Court, Today and Tomorrow*. London: Dent, 1907.

Gamon, H.R.P. "The Punishment of Crime and the Indeterminate Sentence." *Law Magazine and Review* 35 (1910): 191–203.

Garland, D. *Punishment and Modern Society*. Oxford: Oxford University Press, 1994.

Garland, D. *Punishment and Welfare: A History of Penal Strategies*. Aldershot, UK: Gower, 1985.

Gatrell, V.A.C. "Crime, Authority and the Policeman State. In *The Cambridge Social History of Britain*, vol. III, ed. F.M.L. Thompson. Cambridge: Cambridge University Press, 1993.

Gatrell, V.A.C. "The Decline of Theft and Violence in Victorian and Edwardian England." In *Crime and the Law: A Social History of Crime in Western Europe since 1500*, ed. V.A.C. Gatrell, B. Lenman, and G. Parker. London: Europa, 1980.

Gatrell, V.A.C. *The Hanging Tree*. Oxford: Oxford University Press, 1994.

Gatrell, V.A.C., and T. B. Hadden. "Criminal Statistics and Their Interpretation." In *Nineteenth-Century Society: Essays in the Use of Quantitative Methods for the Study of Social Data*, ed. E. A. Wrigley. Cambridge: Cambridge University Press, 1972.

Geary, R. *Policing Industrial Disputes, 1893–1985*. Cambridge: Cambridge University Press, 1985.

Gillis, J. R. "The Evolution of Juvenile Delinquency in England, 1890–1914." *Past & Present* 67 (1975): 96–126.

Godfrey, B. "Changing Prosecution Practices and Their Impact on Crime Figures, 1857–1940." *British Journal of Criminology* 48 (2008): 171–89.

Godfrey, B. "Judicial Impartiality and the Use of the Criminal Law Against Labour: The Sentencing of Workplace Appropriators in Northern England 1840–1880." *Crime, Histoire & Sociétés/Crime, History & Societies* 3 (1999): 57–72.

Godfrey, B. "Law, Factory Discipline and Theft." *British Journal of Criminology* 39 (1999): 56–71.

Godfrey, B. "'Policing the Factory': The Worsted Committee 1840–1880." *Criminal Justice History* 14 (1996): 87–107.

Godfrey, B. S., S. Farrall, and S. Karstedt. "Explaining Gendered Sentencing Patterns for Violent Men and Women in the Late-Victorian and Edwardian Period." *British Journal of Criminology* 45 (2005): 696–720.

Goring, C. *The English Convict: A Statistical Study.* London: HMSO, 1913.

Grant, D. *The Thin Blue Line: The Story of the City of Glasgow Police.* London: Long, 1973.

Grant, J. *Sketches in London.* London: Tegg, 1838.

Grant, J., and G. Serle. *The Melbourne Scene, 1803–1956.* Melbourne, AU: Melbourne University Press, 1957.

Greenwood, James. *The Prisoner in the Dock.* London: Chatto & Windus, 1902.

Greenwood, J. *The Seven Curses of London: Scenes from the Victorian Underworld.* 1869. Reprint Oxford: Oxford University Press, 1981.

Grey, Charles. "Secondary Punishments—Transportation." *Edinburgh Review* 58 (1833–1834). 336–62.

Griffiths, A. *Fifty Years of Public Service.* London: Cassell, 1905.

Griffiths, A. *Memorials of Millbank.* London: Cassell, 1875.

Guy, J. A., and H. G. Beale, eds. *Law and Social Change in British History.* London: Royal Historical Society, 1984.

Haggard, L. Rider, ed. *I Walked by Night: Being the Life & History of the King of the Norfolk Poachers written by HIMSELF.* 1935. Reprint, Oxford: Oxford University Press, 1982.

Hammerton, A. J. *Cruelty and Companionship: Conflict in Nineteenth-Century Married Life.* London: Routledge, 1992.

Harding, C. "The Dream of a Benevolent Mind: The Late-Victorian Response to the Problem of Inebriety." *Criminal Justice History* 9 (1988): 189–207.

Harding, C. "The Inevitable End of a Discredited System? The Origins of the Gladstone Committee Report on Prisons, 1895." *Historical Journal* 31 (1988): 591–608.

Harding, C., Hines, B., Ireland, R., and Rawlings, P. *Imprisonment in England and Wales.* London: Croom Helm, 1985.

Harrison, B. *Drink and the Victorians: The Temperance Question in England, 1815–1872.* Keele, UK: Keele University Press, 1994.

Hartman, M. S. *Victorian Murderesses.* London: Robson, 1985.

Hawker, J. *A Victorian Poacher.* n.d., ca. 1930. Reprint, Oxford: Oxford University Press, 1961.

Hay, D. "Poaching and the Game Laws on Cannock Chase." In *Albion's Fatal Tree: Crime and Society in Eighteenth-Century England,* edited by D. Hay, P. Linebaugh, J. G. Rule, E. P. Thompson, and C. Winslow. London: Penguin, 1977.

Hay, D. "Property, authority and the Criminal Law." In *Albion's Fatal Tree: Crime and Society in Eighteenth-Century England*, edited by D. Hay, P. Linebaugh, J. G. Rule, E. P. Thompson, and C. Winslow. London: Penguin, 1977.

Hay, D. "War, Dearth and Theft in the Eighteenth Century: The Record of the English courts." *Past & Present* 95 (1982): 117–60.

Hay, D., and F. Synder. *Policing and Prosecution in Britain, 1750–1850*. Oxford: Oxford University Press, 1989.

Hay, D., Linebaugh, P., Rule, J. G., Thompson, E. P., and Winslow, C. *Albion's Fatal Tree: Crime and Society in Eighteenth-Century England*. London: Penguin, 1977.

Hellerstein, E. O., L. P. Hume & K. M. Offen, eds. *Victorian Women*. Palo Alto, CA: Stanford University Press, 1981.

Henry, B. *Dublin Hanged: Crime, Law Enforcement and Punishment in Late Eighteenth-Century Dublin*. Dublin: Irish Academic Press, 1994.

Hergenham, L. T., ed. *A Colonial City: High and Low Life, Selected Journalism of MARCUS CLARKE*. St. Lucia, AU: University of Queensland Press, 1972.

HMSO. *Select Committee on Capital Punishment*. London: HMSO, 1931.

HMSO. *The Strange Story of Adolph Beck*. London: HMSO, 1999.

HMSO. *The Trials of Oscar Wilde, 1895*. London: HMSO, 2001.

Hoare, P. *Wilde's Last Stand: Decadence, Conspiracy & the First World War*. London: Duckworth, 1997.

Hollingshead, J. *Ragged London in 1861*. Reprint London: Dent, 1986.

Holloway, H. *An Echo from Prison*. Manchester, UK: J. Heywood, 1887.

Holloway, H. *A Voice from the Convict Cell*. Manchester, UK: J. Heywood, 1887.

Holmes, T. *Known to the Police*. London: Arnold, 1908.

Holmes, T. *Pictures and Problems from London Police Courts*. London: Arnold, 1908.

Hopkins, H. *The Long Affray: The Poaching Wars in Britain*. London: Macmillan, 1986.

Hoyle, W. *Crime in England and Wales in the Nineteenth Century: An Historical and Critical Retrospect*. London: Effingham Wilson & Co., 1876.

Hughes, R. *The Fatal Shore*. London: Pan, 1988.

Humphries, S. *Hooligans or Rebels? An Oral History of Working-Class Children and Youth, 1889–1939*. Oxford: Blackwell, 1983.

Hurt, J. "Reformatory and Industrial Schools Before 1933." *History of Education* 13 (1984): 45–58.

Hyde, H. M. *The Trials of Oscar Wilde*. New York: Dover, 1982.

Ignatieff, M. *A Just Measure of Pain: The Penitentiary in the Industrial Revolution*. New York: Columbia University Press, 1978.

Ignatieff, M. "State, Civil Society and Total Institutions: A Critique of Recent Social Histories of Punishment." In *Social Control and the State*, ed. S. Cohen and A. Scull. Oxford: Martin Robertson, 1983.

"Inspectors of Prison of Great Britain 1. Home District, 3rd Report." *Parliamentary Papers* 141 (1837–38).

"Introduction to the Judicial Statistics for 1893." *Parliamentary Papers*, 7725 (1895): 7.

Irving, H. B. *The Trial of Mrs Maybrick*. London: Hodge, 1912.

Jackson, L. A. *Child Sexual Abuse in Victorian England*. London: Routledge, 2000.

Jackson, M. *The Borderland of Imbecility: Medicine, Society and the Fabrication of the Feeble Mind in Late Victorian and Edwardian England*. Manchester, UK: Manchester University Press, 2000.

Jay, M. *Emperors of Dreams*. Sawtrey, UK: Dedalus, 2000.

Jay, O. "The East End and Crime." *New Review* 11 (1894): 401–8.

Jay, O. *Life in Darkest London*. London: Webster, 1891.

Jeal, T. *Baden-Powell*. London: Pimlico, 1991.

Jefferson, T., and R. Grimshaw. *Controlling the Constable: Police Accountability in England and Wales*. London: Frederick Muller, 1982.

Jervis, R. *Chronicles of a Victorian Detective*. 1907. Reprinted Runcorn, UK: P & D Riley, 1995.

Jones, D.J.V. *Crime in Nineteenth Century Wales*. Cardiff, UK: University of Wales Press, 1992.

Jones, D.J.V. *Crime, Protest, Community and Police in Nineteenth-Century Britain*. London: Routledge & Kegan Paul, 1982.

Jones, D.J.V. "The New Police, Crime and People in England and Wales, 1829–1888." *Transactions of the Royal Historical Society* 33 (1983): 5–43.

Jones, D.J.V. "Thomas Campbell Foster and the Rural Labourer: Incendiarism in East Anglia in the 1840s." *Social History* 1 (1976): 5–43.

Jones, G. S. *Outcast London: A Study in the Relationship Between Classes in Victorian Society*. London: Penguin, 1976.

Jones, J. "'She Resisted With All Her Might': Sexual Violence Against Women in Late-Nineteenth Century Manchester and the Local Press." In *Everyday Violence in Britain, 1850–1950*, ed. S. D'Cruze. London: Longman, 2000.

Jordan, J. *Josephine Butler*. London: Murray, 2001.

"Judicial Statistics for England & Wales for the Year 1900." *Parliamentary Papers* 953 (1902): 14.

"Judicial Statistics for Scotland for the Year 1899." *Parliamentary Papers* 107 (1900): 11.

Kent, D., and N. Townsend. *The Convicts of the Eleanor: Protest in Rural England, New Lives in Australia*. London: Merlin Press, 2002.

Kent, D., and N. Townsend. *Joseph Mason: Assigned Convict, 1831–1837*. Melbourne, AU: Melbourne University Press, 1996.

King, J. E. "'We Could Eat the Police': Popular Violence in the North Lancashire Cotton Strike of 1875." *Victorian Studies* 28 (1985): 439–71.

King, P. *Crime, Justice and Discretion in England, 1740–1820.* Oxford: Oxford University Press, 2000.

King, P. "Gleaners, Farmers and the Failure of Legal Sanctions in England, 1750–1850." *Past & Present* 125 (1989): 116–50.

King, P., and J. Noel. "The Origins of 'the Problem of Juvenile Delinquency': The Growth of Juvenile Prosecutions in London in the Late Eighteenth and Early Nineteenth Centuries." *Criminal Justice History* 14 (1993): 17–41.

Knelman, J. *Twisting in the Wind: The Murderess and the English Press.* Toronto: University of Toronto, 1998.

Knepper, P. "British Jews and the Racialisation of Crime in the Age of Empire." *British Journal of Criminology* 47 (2007): 61–79.

Kohn, M. *Dope Girls: The Birth of the British Drug Underground.* London: Granta, 2001.

Langbein, J. H. *The Origins of the Adversarial Criminal Trial.* Oxford: Oxford University Press, 2003.

Lee, John. *The Man They Could Not Hang.* London: Arthur Pearson, n.d.

Lee, W.L.M. *A History of the Police in England.* London: Methuen, 1901.

Lewis, F. D. "The Cost of Convict Transportation from Britain to Australia, 1796–1810." *Economic History Review* 41 (1988, 2nd ser.): 507–24.

Lewis, J. R. *The Victorian Bar.* London: Robert Hale, 1982.

Lombroso, C. *On Criminal Man.* Reprint Montclair, NJ: Patterson Smith, 1972.

Lombroso, C., and E. Ferrero. *The Female Offender.* 1895. Reprint New York: Philosophical Library, 1958.

MacIlwee, M. *The Gangs of Liverpool.* Preston, UK: Milo Books, 2007.

Maconochie, A. *Norfolk Island.* London: Hatchard, 1847.

Madge, T. *White Mischief: A Cultural History of Cocaine.* Edinburgh, UK: Mainstream Publishing, 2001.

Magarey, S. "'The Invention of Juvenile Delinquency in early-Nineteenth Century England." *Labour History* 43 (1978): 11–27.

Mahood, L. *The Magdalenes: Prostitution in the Nineteenth Century.* London: Routledge, 1990.

Maidens, S. *The Linthorpe Industrial School: An Agency of Class Control?* Unpublished BA (Hons) Humanities History Dissertation. Teesside Polytechnic, Middlesbrough, UK, 1991.

Manchester, A. H. *Modern Legal History.* London: Butterworth, 1980.

Mangan, J. A., & J. Walvin, eds. *Manliness and Morality: Middle-Class Masculinity in Britain and America, 1800–1940.* Manchester, UK: Manchester University Press, 1987.

Manson-Smith, D. *The Legal System of Scotland.* Edinburgh, UK: HMSO, 1995.

Manton, Jo. *Mary Carpenter and the Children of the Streets.* London: Heinemann, 1976.

Marriot, T. *A Constable's Duty and How To Do It.* 2nd ed. London: Reeves & Turner, 1894.

Martin, J. P., and G. Wilson. *The Police: A Study in Manpower. The Evolution of the Service in England and Wales, 1829–1965.* London: Heinemann, 1969.

Martineau, H. *The History of England During the Thirty Years Peace, 1816–1846.* London: Charles Knight, 1850.

Maudsley, H. *Body and Mind.* London: Macmillan, 1870.

Maudsley, H. "Remarks on Crime and Criminality." *Journal of Mental Science* 34 (1888): 159–67.

May, A. N. *The Bar & the Old Bailey, 1750–1850.* Chapel Hill: University of North Carolina, 2003.

May, M. "Innocence and Experience: The Evolution of the Concept of Juvenile Delinquency in the Mid-Nineteenth Century." *Victorian Studies* 17 (1973): 7–29.

Mayhew, H. *London Labour and the London Poor,* ed. V Neuburg. London: Penguin, 1985.

Mayhew, H., and J. Binney. *The Criminal Prisons of London.* 1862. Reprint London: Cass, 1968.

McConville, S. *English Local Prisons, 1860–1900: Next Only to Death.* London: Routledge, 1995.

McConville, S. *A History of English Prison Administration, vol. 1, 1750–1877.* London: Routledge & Kegan Paul, 1981.

McCord, N. *The Anti Corn Law League.* London: Allen & Unwin, 1958.

McGowen, R. "He Beareth Not the Sword In Vain: Religion and the Criminal Law in Eighteenth-Century England." *Eighteenth Century Studies* 21 (1981): 192–211.

McGowen, R. "The Body and Punishment in Eighteenth-Century England." *Journal of Modern History* 59 (1987): 651–79.

McGowen, R. "The Changing Face of God's Justice." *Criminal Justice History* 9 (1988): 63–98.

McGowen, R. "Civilizing Punishment: The End of the Public Execution in England." *Journal of British Studies* 33 (1994): 257–82.

McGowen, R. "The Image of Justice and Reform of the Criminal Law in Early Nineteenth-Century England." *Buffalo Law Review* 32 (1983): 89–125.

McGowen, R. "A Powerful Sympathy: Terror, the Prison, and Humanitarian Reform in Early Nineteenth-Century Britain." *Journal of British Studies* 25 (1986): 312–34.

McHugh, P. *Prostitution and Victorian Social Reform.* London: Croom Helm, 1980.

McKibbin, R. "Working-Class Gambling in Britain, 1880–1939." *Past and Present* 82 (1979): 147–78.

McWilliams, W. "The Mission to the English Police Courts, 1876–1936." *The Howard Journal* 22 (1983): 129–47.

Mearns, A. *The Bitter Cry of Outcast London*. 1883. Reprint London: Frank Cass, 1970.

Merrick, Rev. G. P. *Life Among the Fallen as Seen in the Prison Cell*. London: Ward Lock, 1891.

Miller, W. R. *Cops and Bobbies: Police Authority in New York and London, 1830–1870*. Columbus: University of Ohio Press, 1999.

Miller, W. R. "Never on Sunday: Moralistic Reformers and the Police in London and New York." In *Police and Society*, ed. D. Bayley. London: Sage, 1977.

Mills, J. H. *Cannabis Britannica: Empire Trade and Prohibition*. Oxford: Oxford University Press, 2003.

Mingay, G. E., ed. *The Unquiet Countryside*. London: Routledge, 1989.

"Minutes of Evidence to the Departmental Committee on Prisons." *Parliamentary Papers* 7701–1 (1895).

Monro, J. "The London Police," *North American Review* 151 (1890): 617–18.

Moody, S. *The Impartial Justice of Divine Administration*. Chelmsford, UK: Buckland, 1736.

Morgan, J. *Conflict and Order: The Police and Labour Disputes in England and Wales, 1900–1939*. Oxford: Oxford University Press, 1987.

Morris, N. *Maconochie's Gentlemen: The Story of Norfolk Island and the Roots of Modern Prison Reform*. Oxford: Oxford University Press, 2002.

Morris, R. M. "Lies, damned lies and Criminal Statistics: Reinterpreting the criminal statistics in England and Wale", *Crime, History & Societies*, 5 (2001): 111–27.

Morrison, W. D. "Are Our Prisons a Failure?" *Fortnightly Review* 64 (Old Series, 1894): 459–69.

Morrison, W. D. *Crime and Its Causes*. London: Swan Sonnenschein, 1891.

Mort, F. *Dangerous Sexualities: Medico-Moral Politics in England since 1830*. London: Routledge & Kegan Paul, 1987.

Munsche, P. B. *Gentleman and Poachers*. Cambridge: Cambridge University Press, 1981.

Murphy, P., J. Williams, and E. Dunning. *Football on Trial*. London: Routledge, 1990.

Muskett, P. "The Suffolk Incendiaries, 1843–45." *Journal of Regional and Local Studies* 7 (1987): 33–44.

Ogborn, M. "Ordering the City: Surveillance, Public Space and the Reform of Urban Policing in England, 1835–56." *Political Geography* 12 (1993): 505–21.

O'Neill, J. *Crime City: Manchester's Victorian Underworld*, Wrea Green, Lancashire: Milo, 2008.

Owen, M. E. "Criminal Women." *Cornhill Magazine* 14 (1866): 152–60.

Paley, W. Chapter IX "Of Crimes and Punishment." In *The Principles of Moral and Political Philosophy*. London: R. Faulder, 1785.

Palk, D. *Gender, Crime and Judicial Discretion, 1780–1830*. London: Boydell, 2006.

Palmer, A. *The East End: Four Centuries of London Life*. London: John Murray, 2000.

Palmer, S. H. *Police and Protest in England and Ireland, 1780–1850*. Cambridge: Cambridge University Press, 1988.

Parker, C. S. ed. *Sir Robert Peel: From His Private Papers*, vol. 1. London: John Murray, 1891.

Parker, G. "The Prisoner in the Box—The Making of the Criminal Evidence Act, 1898."In *Law and Social Change in British History*, ed. J. A. Guy and H. G. Beale. London: Royal Historical Society, 1984.

Parliamentary Debates (Commons), 3rd series, vol. cxci, cols. 1047–55.

Pattenden, R. *English Criminal Appeals, 1884–1994*. Oxford: Oxford University Press, 1996.

Pearson, G. *Hooligan: A History of Respectable Fears*. London: Macmillan, 1983.

Peel, R. *The Speeches of Sir Robert Peel*, vol. 1 London: Routledge, 1853.

Perkin, H. *The Origins of Modern British Society, 1780–1880*. London: Routledge & Kegan Paul, 1969.

Petrow, S. *Policing Morals: The Metropolitan Police and the Home Office, 1870–1914*. Oxford: Oxford University Press, 1994.

Philips, D. "The Black Country Magistracy 1835–60: A Changing Elite and the Exercise of Its Power." *Midland History* 3 (1976): 161–90.

Philips, D. *Crime and Authority in Victorian England, 1835–1860*. London: Croom Helm, 1977.

Philips, D. "Three 'moral entrepreneurs' and the creation of a 'criminal class' in England, c. 1790s–1840s." *Crime, History and Society* 7 (2003): 79–107.

Philips, D., and R. D. Storch. *Policing Provincial England, 1829–1856: The Politics of Reform*. Leicester, UK: Leicester University Press, 1999.

Plint, T. *Crime in England: Its Relation, Character and Extent as Developed From 1801 to 1848*. London: Gilpin, 1851.

Potter, H. *Hanging in Judgment: Religion and the Death Penalty in England*. London: SCM Press, 1993.

Priestley, P. *Victorian Prison Lives*. London: Methuen, 1985.

Quennell, P., ed. *London's Underworld*. 1862. Reprint London: Hamlyn, 1969.

Quinton, R. F. *Crime and Criminals, 1876–1910*. London: Longman, 1910.

Quinton, R. F. "The Need for Preventive Detention." *Edinburgh Review* 220 (1914): 167–79.

Radzinowicz, L., and Roger Hood. *The Emergence of Penal Policy in Victorian and Edwardian England*. Oxford: Oxford University Press, 1990.

Rees, S. *The Floating Brothel*. London: Hodder Headline, 2001.

Reiner, R. *The Politics of the Police*. Hemel Hempstead: Harvester Wheatsheaf, 1992.

Rentoul, R. R. *The Proposed Sterilisation of Certain Mental and Physical Degenerates*. London: Walter Scott Publishing, 1903.

"Report from the Select Committee on Criminal Laws." *Parliamentary Papers* 585 (1819): 7.

"Report of Select Committee on the State of Municipal Corporations in England and Wales." *Parliamentary Papers* 344 (1833).

"Report of the Commissioners appointed to inquire into the operation of the Acts relating to Transportation and Penal Servitude." *Parliamentary Papers* 6457 (1863). (Cited in Abel-Smith, B., and R. Stevens. *Lawyers and the Courts*. London: Heinemann, 1967, p. 31.)

"Report of the Commissioners appointed to inquire into the workings of the Penal Servitude Acts." *Parliamentary Papers* 2368 (1878–1979).

"Report of the Departmental Committee on Prisons" [Gladstone Committee]. *Parliamentary Papers* 7702 (1895).

"Report of the Select Committee on Transportation." *Parliamentary Papers* 669 (1838).

"Report of the Penal Servitude Acts Commissioner." *Parliamentary Papers* 31 (1863).

"Report of the Royal Commission on Capital Punishment." *Parliamentary Papers* 3590 (1866).

"Return of Description of Buildings in which Justices of Petty Sessions Districts in England and Wales Hold Usual Sittings." *Parliamentary Papers* 606 (1845).

"Report on the Discipline and Management of the Convict Prisons." *Parliamentary Papers* 1846 (1854).

Reynolds, S., B. Woolley, and T. Woolley. *Seems So! A Working-Class View of Politics*. London: Macmillan, 1911.

Richter, D. *Riotous Victorians*. Columbus: Ohio University Press, 1981.

Robb, G. *White-Collar Crime in Modern England, 1845–1929*. Cambridge: Cambridge University Press, 1992.

Roberts, D. "The Scandal of Birmingham Borough Gaol, 1853: A Case for Penal Reform." *Journal of Legal History* 7 (1986): 315–40.

Roberts, R. *The Classic Slum*. London: Penguin, 1973.

Rook, C. *The Hooligan Nights*. 1899. Reprint Oxford: Oxford University Press, 1979.

Rose, L. *Massacre of the Innocents: Infanticide in Great Britain, 1800–1939*. London: Routledge & Kegan Paul, 1986.

Rose, L. *"Rogues and Vagabonds": The Vagrant Underworld in Britain, 1815–1985*. London: Routledge, 1988.

Rosenthal, M. *The Character Factory: Baden-Powell and the Origins of the Boy Scout Movement.* London: Collins, 1986.

Ross, E. "'Fierce Questions and Taunts': Married Life in Working-Class London, 1870–1914." *Feminist Studies* 8 (1983): 575–602.

Ross, E. *Love and Toil.* Oxford: Oxford University Press, 1993.

Rowbotham, J. "'Only When Drunk': The Stereotyping of Violence in England, c. 1850–1900." In *Everyday Violence in Britain, 1850–1950,* ed. S. D'Cruze. London: Longman, 2000.

"Royal Commission appointed to enquire into the conditions and treatment of the prisoners confined in Birmingham Prison." *Parliamentary Papers* 1809 (1854).

"Royal Commission on the Condition and Treatment of Prisoners Confined in Leicester County Gaol and House of Correction." *Parliamentary Papers* 1808 (1854).

Rudé, G. *Criminal and Victim: Crime and Society in Early Nineteenth-Century.* Oxford: Oxford University Press, 1985.

Rudé, G. *Protest and Punishment.* Oxford: Oxford University Press, 1978.

Ruggles-Brise, Sir Evelyn. *The English Prison System.* London: Macmillan, 1921.

Rule, J. *The Experience of Labour in Eighteenth-Century Industry.* London: Croom Helm, 1981.

Ryan, M. *Prostitution in London with a Comparative View of That of Paris and New York.* London: Bailliere, 1839.

Ryland, G. *Crime: Its Causes and Remedy.* London: Fisher Unwin, 1889.

Safford, A. Herbert. "What Are the Best Means of Preventing Infanticide?" *Transactions of the National Society for the Promotion of Social Science* (1867): 220–28.

Said, E. *Orientalism: Western Conceptions of the Orient.* London: Routledge & Kegan Paul, 1978.

Samuel, R. ed. *East End Underworld: Chapters in the Life of Arthur Harding.* London: Routledge & Kegan Paul, 1981.

Searle, G.R. *The Quest for National Efficiency: A Study in British Politics and Political Thought, 1899–1914.* Oxford: Oxford University Press, 1971.

"Select Committee on Cause of Increase in Number of Criminal Commitments and Convictions in England and Wales." *Parliamentary Papers* 545 (1828).

"Select Committee on Criminal and Destitute Juveniles." *Parliamentary Papers* 23 (1852–53).

"Select Committee on Prison Discipline." *Parliamentary Papers* 632 (1850).

"Select Committee on the Game Laws." *Parliamentary Papers* 13 (1872).

Selleck, R.W.J. "Mary Carpenter: A Confident and Contradictory Reformer." *History of Education* 14 (1985): 101–15.

Sharpe, J. *Dick Turpin: The Myth of the English Highwayman*. London: Profile Books, 2004.

Shaw, A. *Remarks on Prison Discipline and the Model Prison*. London: Shaw, 1841.

Shaw, A.G.L. *Convicts and the Colonies*. London: Faber & Faber, 1966.

Shoemaker, R. B. *Gender in English Society, 1650–1850*. London: Longman, 1998.

Shore, H. *Artful Dodgers Youth and Crime in early Nineteenth-Century London*. London: Boydell, 1999.

Showalter, E. *The Female Malady: Women, Madness and English Culture, 1830–1980*. London: Virago, 1987.

Sindall, R. S. "The London Garotting Panics of 1856 and 1862." *Social History* 12 (1987): 351–59.

Sindall, R. S. "Middle-Class Crime in Nineteenth Century England." *Criminal Justice History* 4 (1983): 23–40.

Sindall, R. S. *Street Violence in the Nineteenth Century*. Leicester, UK: Leicester University Press, 1990.

Sims, G. R. *How the Poor Live*. London: Chatto & Windus, 1889.

Smales, D. *The Development of the New Police in the Scottish Borders, c. 1840–1890*. Unpublished Ph.D. dissertation. Open University, Milton Keynes, UK, 2008.

Smith, D. "The Demise of Transportation in Mid-Victorian Penal Policy." *Criminal Justice History* 3 (1982): 22–45.

Smith, P. T. *Policing Victorian London*. Westport, CT: Greenwood Press, 1985.

Smith, R. *Trial by Medicine*. Edinburgh, UK: Edinburgh University Press, 1981.

Smith, Rev. S. *The Works of the Rev. Sydney Smith*. London: Longman, 1869.

Spraggs, G. *Outlaws & Highwaymen: The Cult of the Robber in England from the Middle Ages to the Nineteenth Century*. London: Pimlico, 2001.

Springhall, J. *Sure and Stedfast: A History of the Boys' Brigade, 1885–1983*. London: Collins, 1983.

Springhall, J. *Youth, Empire and Society*. London: Croom Helm, 1977.

Springhall, J. *Youth, Popular Culture and Moral Panics: Penny Gaffs to Gangsta-Rap, 1830–1996*. Basingstoke, UK: Macmillan, 1998.

Stack, J. A. "Deviance and Reformation in Early Victorian Social Policy: The Case of Parkhurst Prison, 1836–1864." *Historical Reflections* 6 (1979): 387–404.

Stanford, T. G. *The Metropolitan Police, 1850–1914: Targeting, Harassment and the Creation of a Criminal Class*. Unpublished Ph.D. dissertation. University of Huddersfield, Huddersfield, UK, 2008.

Steedman, C. *Policing the Victorian Community: The Formation of the English Provincial Police from 1856 to 1880*. London: Routledge & Kegan Paul, 1984.

Stephen, J. F. "Capital Punishment." *Fraser's Magazine* 69 (1864): 753–72.

Stephen, J. F. *A General View of the Criminal Law*, 2nd ed. London, 1890.

Stephen, J. F. *History of the Criminal Law*, vol. 1. London: Macmillan, 1883.

Stevenson, J. *Popular Disturbances in England*. London: Longmans, 1992.

Stevenson, J., and R. Quinault, eds. *Popular Protest and Public Order*. London: Allen & Unwin, 1974.

Stevenson, S. "The 'Habitual Criminal' in Nineteenth-Century England: Some Observations on the Figures." *Urban History Yearbook* 14 (1986): 37–60.

Stockdale, E. "A Short History of Prison Inspection in England." *British Journal of Criminology* 23 (1983): 209–28.

Storch, R. D. "The Plague of Blue Locusts: Police Reform and Popular Resistance in Northern England, 1840–57." *International Review of Social History* 20 (1975): 61–90.

Storch, R. D. "Police Control of Street Prostitution in Victorian London." In *Police and Society*, ed. D. Bayley. London: Sage, 1977.

Storch, R. D. "The Policeman as Domestic Missionary." *Journal of Social History* 9 (1976): 481–509.

Storch, R. D. "Policing Rural Southern England Before the Police: Opinions and Practice, 1830–1856." In *Policing and Prosecution in Britain, 1750–1850*, ed. D. Hay and F. Synder. Oxford: Oxford University Press, 1989.

Storch, R. D. ed. *Popular Culture and Custom in Nineteenth-Century England*. London: Croom Helm, 1980.

Strahan, S.A.K. "What to Do With Our Habitual Criminals." *Westminster Review* 143 (1895): 660–66.

Streatfield, D. *Cocaine*. London: Virgin, 2001.

Suffolk, Owen. *Days of Crime and Years of Suffering*. Kew, AU: Australian Scholarly Publishing, 2000.

Sugden, P. *The Complete History of Jack the Ripper*. New York: Caroll & Graf, 1995.

Sullivan, Dr. W. C. "Eugenics and Crime." *Eugenics Review* 1 (1909): 112–20.

Summerscale, K. *The Suspicions of Mr. Whicher*. London: Bloomsbury, 2008.

Swift, R. "Another Stafford Street Row." *Immigrants and Minorities* 3 (1984): 5–29.

Swift, R. "The English Urban Magistracy and the Administration of Justice During the Early-Nineteenth Century: Wolverhampton 1815–60." *Midland History* 17 (1992): 75–92.

Swift, R. "Heroes or Villains? The Irish, Crime and Disorder in Victorian England." *Albion* 29 (1997): 399–421.

Swift, R. "Urban Policing in Early-Victorian England, 1835–1856: A Reappraisal." *History* 73 (1988): 211–37.

Swift, R., and S. Gilley, eds. *The Irish in Britain, 1815–1939*. London: Pinter, 1989.

Sykes, Bill [pseudonym]. *Prison Life and Prison Poetry*, vol. 1. London: Newman & Co., 1881.

Symons, J. "Crime and Criminals." *The Law Magazine* 10 (1849): 204–82.

Tait, W. *Maddalenism. An Inquiry into the Extent, Causes and Consequences of Prostitution in Edinburgh*. Edinburgh: Rickard, 1852.

Tallack, W. *Some General Observations on the Penalty of Death*. London: Howard Association, 1890.

Taylor, D. "The Antipodean Arrest: Or How to Be a Successful Policeman in Nineteenth-Century Middlesbrough." *Bulletin of the Cleveland and Teesside Local History Society* 58 (1990): 26–30.

Taylor, D. "Crime and Policing in Early Victorian Middlesbrough, 1835–55." *Journal of Regional and Local Studies* 11 (1991): 48–66.

Taylor, D. *Crime, Policing and Punishment in England, 1750–1914*. Basingstoke, UK: Macmillan 1998.

Taylor, D. *The New Police in Nineteenth-Century England*. Manchester, UK: Manchester University Press, 1997.

Taylor, D. "Policing and the Community: Late-Twentieth Century Myths and Late-Nineteenth Century Realities." In *Social Conditions, Status and Community*, ed. K Laybourn. Stroud, UK: Sutton, 1997.

Taylor, D. *Policing the Victorian Town: The Development of the Police in Middlesbrough, c. 1840–1914*. Basingstoke, UK: Palgrave Macmillan, 2002.

Taylor, D. "The Standard of Living of Career Policemen in Victorian England: The Evidence of a Provincial Borough Force." *Criminal Justice History* 12 (1991): 107–31.

Taylor, D. *"A Well-Chosen, Effective Body of Men": The Middlesbrough Police Force c. 1841–1914*. Middlesbrough, UK: University of Teesside, 1995.

Taylor, H. "Rationing Crime: The Political Economy of Criminal Statistics Since the 1850s." *Economic History Review* 51 (1998): 569–90.

Thackeray, W. "Going to See a Man Hanged." *Fraser's Magazine* 22 (1840): 150–58.

Thomas, H. "Poverty and Crime." *Westminster Review* 145 (1896): 75–77.

Thompson, E. P. *Customs in Common*. London: Penguin, 1993.

Tobias, J. J. *Crime and Industrial Society in the Nineteenth Century*. London: Penguin, 1972.

Tomes, N. "A 'Torrent of Abuse': Crimes of Violence Between Working-Class Men and Women in London." *Journal of Social History* 11 (1978): 328–45.

Tomlinson, M. H. "'Not an Instrument of Punishment': Prison Diet in the Mid-Nineteenth Century." *Journal of Consumer Studies and Home Economics* 2 (1978): 15–26.

Tosh, J. *A Man's Place: Masculinity and the Middle-Class Home in Victorian England*. New Haven, CT: Yale University Press, 1999.

Tredgold, A. F. "The Feeble Minded—A Social Danger." *Eugenics Review* 1 (1909): 717–27.

Vicars, G. Rayleigh. "Ought Capital Punishment to be Abolished?" *Westminster Review* 143 (1895): 561–66.

Vogler, R. *Reading the Riot Act*. Milton Keynes, UK: Open University Press, 1991.

Waddy, H. T. *The Police Court and Its Works*. London: Butterworth, 1925.

Walkowitz, J. R. *City of Dreadful Delight: Narratives of Sexual Danger in Late-Victorian London*. London: Virago, 1992.

Walkowitz, J. R. *Prostitution and Victorian Society: Women, Class and the State*. Cambridge: Cambridge University Press, 1980.

Warren, C. "Is Capital Punishment Defensible?" *Westminster Review* 165 (1906): 512–16.

W.B.N. [Lord William Beauchamp Nevill]. *Penal Servitude*. London: Heinemann, 1903.

Weeks, J. *Coming Out: Homosexual Politics in Britain from the Nineteenth Century to the Present*. London: Quartet Books, 1977.

Weeks, J. *Sex, Politics and Society: The Regulation of Sexuality Since 1800*. London: Longman, 1989.

Weinberger, B. *Keeping the Peace? Policing Strikes in Britain, 1906–1926*. Oxford: Berg, 1991.

Weiner, M. J. "Judges v Jurors: Courtroom Tensions in Murder Trials and the Law of Criminal Responsibility in Nineteenth-Century England," *Law and History Review* 17 (1999): 467–506.

Weiner, M. J. *Men of Blood: Violence, Manliness and Criminal Justice in Victorian England*. Cambridge: Cambridge University Press, 2004.

Weiner, M. J. *Reconstructing the Criminal: Culture, Law and Policy in England, 1830–1914*. Cambridge: Cambridge University Press, 1990.

Weiner, M. J. "The Sad Story of George Hall: Adultery, Murder and the Politics of Mercy in Mid-Victorian England." *Social History* 14 (1999): 174–95.

Wells, R. "Sheep Rustling in Yorkshire in the Age of the Industrial and Agrarian Revolutions. *Northern History* 20 (1981): 127–45.

Whately, R. *Thoughts on Secondary Punishment*. London: Fellowes, 1832.

Whately, R. "Transportation." *London Review* 1 (1829): 112–39.

White, J. *London in the 19th Century*. London: Vintage, 2008.

Wilde, Oscar. " The Ballad of Reading Gaol." In *The Complete Works of Oscar Wilde* (pp. 822–39). Leicester, UK: Bookmark, 1990.

Williams, C. A. "Counting Crimes or Counting People: Some Implications of Mid-Nineteenth Century British Police Returns." *Crime, Histoire & Société/ Crime, History & Societies* 4 (2000): 77–93.

Wills, A. "Criminals and Crime." *The Nineteenth Century and After* 62 (1907): 879–94.

Wilson, D. *The Beat: Policing a Victorian City.* Beaconsfield, AU: Melbourne Publishing, 2006.

Wise, S. *The Blackest Streets: The Life and Death of a Victorian Slum.* London: Vintage, 2009.

Wise, S. *The Italian Boy: Murder and Grave-Robbery in 1830s London.* London: Jonathan Cape, 2004.

Wood, J.C. "Criminal Violence in Modern Britain." *History Compass* 4 (2006): 77–90.

Wood, J.C. "'A Useful Savagery': The Invention of Violence in Nineteenth-Century England. *Journal of Victorian Culture* 9 (2004): 22–42.

Wood, J.C. *Violence and Crime in Nineteenth Century England: The Shadow of Our Refinement.* London: Routledge, 2004.

Woods, D.C. "The Operation of the Master and Servants Act in the Black Country, 1858–1875." *Midland History* 7 (1982): 93–115.

Wrigley, E.A., ed. *Nineteenth-Century Society: Essays in the Use of Quantitative Methods for the Study of Social Data.* Cambridge: Cambridge University Press, 1972.

Zedner, L. *Women, Crime, and Custody in Victorian England.* Oxford: Oxford University Press, 1994.

WEB SITES

http://www.procuratorfiscal.gov.uk/News/Historical/HistDevPF

http://www.procuratorfiscal.gov.uk/News/Historical/OffLordAdv

http://www.procuratorfiscal.gov.uk/News/Historical/JessMach

The Complete Newgate Calendar, http://www.law.utexas.edu/lpop/etextnewgate5/hunton.htm

INDEX

ABOUT THE AUTHOR

David Taylor won a scholarship to Wadham College, Oxford, where he read modern history as an undergraduate and then completed his doctorate. He is now an emeritus professor of history at Huddersfield University where he was head of history before becoming Dean of the School of Music, Humanities & Media. He is the author of *The New Police in Nineteenth Century England: Crime, Policing and Punishment in England, 1750–1914; Policing the Victorian Town;* and several articles on crime and policing in the 19th and 20th centuries.

ABOUT THE SERIES EDITOR

Professor Barry Godfrey is Director of the Research Institute for Law, Politics and Justice at Keele University. Recent publications include the cowritten and edited books *Criminal Lives: Family Life, Employment, and Offending; History and Crime; Crime and Empire; Crime and Justice 1750–1950;* and *Comparative Histories of Crime.*

Lightning Source UK Ltd.
Milton Keynes UK
UKOW06n1925140916

283011UK00016B/186/P